AN ECONOMIC HISTORY
OF WOMEN IN AMERICA

AN ECONOMIC HISTORY OF WOMEN IN AMERICA

Women's Work, the Sexual Division of Labor, and the Development of Capitalism

JULIE A. MATTHAEI

SCHOCKEN BOOKS · NEW YORK

THE HARVESTER PRESS · BRIGHTON

First American edition published by Schocken Books 1982

First published in Great Britain in 1982 by
The Harvester Press Limited; Publisher: John Spiers
16 Ship Street, Brighton, Sussex

10 9 8 7 6 5 4 3 2   83 84 85
Copyright © 1982 by Julie A. Matthaei

Library of Congress Cataloging in Publication Data
Matthaei, Julie.
    An economic history of women in America.
    Includes index.
    1. Women—United States—Economic conditions.
2. United States—Economic conditions—1971–
3. Division of labor—History.   I. Title.
HQ1410.M37   305.4′3   81-84111   AACR2

Manufactured in the United States of America
Designed by Ed Kaplin

ISBN 0-8052-3804-2 hardback (Schocken Books)
      0-8052-0744-9 paperback

ISBN 0-7108-0474-1 (Harvester Press)

To my foremothers, especially Betty, Mary, and Mimi, whose livings out of the contradictions of womanhood have allowed me to free myself from its restrictions and to reach toward a more human future

Contents

Tables

Acknowledgments

Although it is presently the mode among social scientists to portray their research as impersonal and apolitical, I freely admit to undertaking this study as part of a personal and political quest, a quest for which an understanding of women's economic past was essential. My participation in the "second wave" of feminism began my education in this area by exposing me to "consciousness raising" and to the literature of feminism and women's studies, inspiring me to choose this subject for my dissertation and giving me the self-confidence to follow the project through. The writing of this book has indeed contributed importantly to my personal development; I hope that, as a contribution to women's studies and to social scientific literature in general, it will inform the personal development of others, and aid us in our quest for a better, more humane, society.

Many colleagues have contributed to the development of these ideas. David Levine, Lynn Levine, William Parker, and Anna Yeatman read extensive portions of the manuscript, discussed it with me in depth, and were important influences on its writing. Teresa Amott, Locke Anderson, Carolyn Shaw Bell, Maureen Brodoff, Nancy Cott, Ellen Fitzpatrick, Eugene Genovese, Donald Harris, Jacqueline Jones, Nai Pew Ong, Elizabeth Pleck, Tirsa Quinones, Elyce Rotella, Nina Shapiro, and Rona Wilensky provided me with valuable insight through discussions and/or the reading and criticism of chapters. The forums provided by meetings of the Union for Radical Political Economics, the Northeast Feminist Scholars Conference (MF I), the Social Science History Association, the *Social Concept* History Study Group, the Wellesley Mellon Seminar, as well as by other academic gatherings, have been extremely helpful. My editor, John Simon, and the readers of my manuscript provided constructive criticism as well as encouragement. And, of course, my work is indebted to many,

many individuals whom I have never met except through the printed page, whom I acknowledge in the notes.

My students have also made major contributions to this project. Presented with the book at different stages of its development in classes at Yale University, the New Haven Women's Liberation Center, and Wellesley College, they asked penetrating questions, challenged inconsistencies, pointed out blind spots, and contributed their own experiences with generosity and enthusiasm. Some also provided expert and dedicated research assistance. Both Emine Kiray and Nina Lipton made major contributions by compiling tables, literature searching, and criticizing drafts of the manuscript. Ardith Eicher, Priscilla Hayes, June Hsiao, Lorie Jackson, Anhar Mulla, Beth Snell, and Barbara Swartz all helped with research and/or typing the manuscript into the Wellesley computer.

During its dissertation stage, this project was financially supported by my parents, Betty and Fred Matthaei, by a teaching fellowship from Yale University, and by a fellowship from the Danforth Foundation. Since then, Wellesley College has provided generous financial assistance including stipends for research assistance and computer facilities and consultation.

Finally, this book could not have been completed without the love, encouragement, patience, advice, and understanding of my family and friends, especially Betty, Fred, David, Lynn, Maureen, Teresa, Anna, and, above all, Tirsa.

AN ECONOMIC HISTORY
OF WOMEN IN AMERICA

Introduction

Today's women—and men—are living in an exciting and perplexing time in history. Women's lives are being revolutionized, changing so rapidly that daughters no longer replicate the life patterns of their mothers, and women decide at mid-life to transform their work lives and marriages. Women, particularly married women, are entering the labor force in ever-increasing numbers. Some of them are entering into jobs that have always been monopolized by men. There is no longer one clear conception of woman's work, or of what true womanhood means. The questions raised by the transformation of womanhood are now being extended to family life; what indeed constitutes ethical family life is now unclear.

These transformations in womanhood and the family, now espoused openly by the feminist movement, have raised deep and difficult ethical questions about the sexes and about family life. These questions have never really been asked before, for family life and the sexual difference that stands at its core have been taken as givens by our society. Rather than be subjected to rational choice and public policy making, they have been inherited from the past as nature-and/or God-given. As they become the object of social concern, social scientists have begun to study them, and a new interdisciplinary field, "women's studies," has sprung up.[1] This book is a part of this process, built on the burgeoning literature addressing the problem of women's work.

The key to understanding woman's present and future economic position in the capitalist world lies in history. For history is not simply the compilation of facts, but, at its best, the discovery of the general principles and process that have given rise to these concrete experiences; not simply the study of the past, but the study of the creation of the present and future. The development of capitalism has had profound effects upon womanhood and the sexual division of labor; it is the object of this book to uncover and understand these effects. Hence we will undertake an analysis of the manner in which capitalist development transforms womanhood and the sexual division of labor through the study of one concrete history of capitalist development—the history of the United States from colonial times through the present.[2] While this analysis is specific to the United States, it sheds light on the larger question of the relationship of capitalist development to womanhood and the sexual division of labor.[3]

Before we begin our analysis of history, we must develop the concept of the sexual division of labor, for the existence of woman's work is only one side of this larger phenomenon, the division of social activities between the sexes. "Women's work" means activities done by women or females from which men or males are excluded; "men's work" likewise delineates those activities done by men or males, activities from which women or females are excluded. Women's work can not be properly understood without studying the other side of the sexual division of labor, men's work, nor, indeed, without studying the sexual division of labor itself. To conceptualize the sexual division of labor, we must move beyond economic analysis to an analysis of family relationships. Furthermore, we must examine carefully the place of ideas in social life and, in particular, society's conception of "nature" as the source of the sexual division of labor.

The relationship between natural sexual differences and the sexual division of labor is a complicated one. The sexual division of labor is no more the immediate product of natural differences than society is. Certainly, our biological constitution sets certain limits on social life. Our bodies require a certain range of temperatures, and a range of caloric intakes, to survive. Yet these limits hardly suffice to determine social life. Similarly, males are biologically incapable of bearing and nursing children and have greater ability to acquire muscle mass than females. These differences, however, do not even come close to necessitating a sexual division of activities: they do not make females unable to participate in "men's work," nor males unable to do "women's work," if bearing and nursing children are excluded.

Neither does biology determine social life through instincts. Within society, individuals do not act instinctually, do not immediately express naturally held drives. Rather, individuals are "socialized" from their earliest years to rule their actions by society's conceptions of appropriate social behavior. This socialization is not merely an external constraint upon human freedom, but indeed that which raises humans from the level of animals to that of individuals capable of freedom.[4]

An individual who acts according to instinct in society is not considered human. Even activities we consider to be biologically based such as eating or sexual intercourse are ruled by ideas rather than instinct. We eat according to our ideas as to which foods are proper— ideas that may or may not include a correct knowledge of our bodies' nutritional requirements—and according to a complex etiquette as to when, how, and with whom we can eat, as well as how we can acquire our food. Sexual interaction within society is not ruled by biological sex drives, but rather by conceptions of morality and marriage. It is because society has its own laws, separate from those of nature and human biology, that social science exists; it is because the sexual division of labor is in fact a social phenomenon that its study properly falls within the realm of social science.[5] Because ideas constitute the essential fabric of social life, social science involves the study of these conceptions.

While the sexual division of labor is not, then, the immediate product of natural differences between the sexes, neither is it divorced from these natural sexual differences. For the sexual division of labor not only divides social activities into two sets, men's work and women's work, but also assigns individuals to one or the other according to his or her biological sex. However, individuals do not automatically and instinctually fall into a sexual division of labor; rather, they participate in it because of ideas they hold as to the proper behavior of their biological sex. Biological females believe that they must do women's work, and shun men's work; biological males believe that they must do men's work, and shun women's work.

Society has believed, with great unanimity through the ages, that one must determine one's activities according to one's biological sex. Society has understood the biological sexual difference to necessitate the sexual division of labor. It has therefore taught its males and females to undertake work "proper to their sex," and to shun that of the opposite sex. Preparation for and exercise of either man's work or woman's work according to one's physical sex, however, requires and sustains a difference of personality, of self, between the sexes. In this way, society turns the natural biological difference into a social difference. The sexual division of labor turns males and females, differentiated by biology, into men and women, masculine and feminine social beings, differentiated by their social activities.[6] In other words, woman(hood) and man(hood) are first and foremost ideas, conceptions which females and males strive to realize in their actions.[7] The social differentiation of the sexes includes the development in the sexes of distinct and different psychic structures, psyches that indeed make undertaking the activities of the opposite sex difficult or impossible. The social differentiation of the sexes is so great as to virtually construct distinct male and female worlds.[8]

Societies up through the present have been unaware of their part in creating a social difference between the sexes. They have rather tended to attribute the social differences between men and women directly to their "human natures," and/or to God as the creator of the "natural" order of things. For this reason, language does not distinguish between male and man, female and woman; biological sex is automatically equated with social sex. Similarly, individuals in society are unconscious of the manner in which they transform themselves from male or female into man or woman, respectively; they see their masculinity and manhood (or femininity and womanhood) as parts of their human natures.[9]

Individuals do not, in other words, make choices between being a woman (doing women's work), being a man (doing men's work), or combining the two.[10] Neither do men and women fight openly over who shall serve the other.[11] Rather, males (females) automatically undertake men's work (women's work), shun women's work (men's work), and constitute themselves as men, as masculine beings (women, or feminine beings). They accept this restriction without question for they do not see it as such; they believe themselves to be inherently unable to do or unsuited for the work of the opposite sex. Hence, the sexual division of labor turns the sexes into differentiated social beings who are, indeed, better suited for the work of their sex, "proving" the "natural" basis of the sexual division of labor.

For example, society in the seventeenth and eighteenth centuries believed that women's brains were smaller than men's and hence less capable of study and learning. On the basis of this understanding, women were not admitted to the first colleges. And given that women were less educated than men, it indeed seemed that women had less intellectual capacity than men. (Similarily black women and men, forbidden as slaves to learn to read or write due to their "inferior" natural race, indeed appeared incapable of reading.) When nineteenth-century reformers began to demand higher education for women, as training for enlightened mothering, society carefully scrutinized the physical condition of these first college women, convinced that studying would overtax their brains, resulting in physical damage, even sterility.[12]

While society has understood the sexual division of labor to be a product of nature, the social basis of this division has been expressed in the strength of the taboo against participation in the work of the opposite sex. Indeed, because womanhood and manhood, femininity and masculinity, are social states, they must be proven through social actions, in particular through doing woman's work or man's work, respectively. Yet, given the equation in society of natural and social sex—of male and man, female and woman—the failure of an individual to achieve the appropriate sexual differentiation leads to a questioning not of the rationale of the sexual division of labor, but rather of one's biological sex. The individual, rather than the sexual division of labor, is seen as "unnatural."

While society locates the rationale for the sexual division of labor in nature or God, this division fulfills a critical social function—unifying the sexes in marriage.[13] Along with the incest taboo, it has insured the reproduction of society as a system of families; these two "rules" have been present in all known societies. First, the sexual division of labor underlies the marriage relationship. Its exclusion of man from women's work makes him need a woman to procure for himself the products of women's work; its exclusion of woman from men's work makes her dependent upon a man to provide her with the products of man's work. The sexual division of labor, then, creates an interdependence between man and woman—to live out their lives as members of society, they must be united with the opposite sex in a recognized, sharing entity: they must marry the opposite sex. The sexual division of labor underlies the marriage relationship as a unity of different social beings. It hence creates a social relationship between males and females who are biologically capable of producing offspring together, and sustains the reproduction of society generationally. The child is born into a social institution, the family, where the sexual division of labor is lived out, in particular, as the monopolization of primary child-care by women. This experience builds into the child's personality an unconscious awareness of the centrality of the difference between the sexes. As children grow up and are taught to identify with the appropriately sexed parent, they are driven into marriage with the opposite sex, continuing the cycle. The incest taboo, by forcing them to marry outside of their immediate families, makes social life into a relationship between families. Given the incest taboo, families need each other to provide spouses for their children. Marriage becomes then not only a social relationship between a man and a woman, but also a social relationship between the families of this man and this woman.

The construction of the family as a unity of differentiated sexes and the concomitant division of activities and personality between the sexes have had specific implications for the content of social life. First, family life is not understood as a set of relationships (spouse and parent–child) which constructs and sustains particular personalities. Rather, it is viewed as natural processes—sexual intercourse between a naturally different man and woman, childbirth, and the physical nurturing of a naturally determined being. Second, the perception of family life and parenting as natural has tied it to the female, the biological creator of the children, leaving for men activities within the public, interfamilial sphere. Hence woman has been constructed as a private, intrafamilial, and natural being, and man as the more public person, engaged in interfamilial or tribal activities such as collective hunting, war, or exchange between tribes.[14]

Given that women's work has been centered in the intrafamilial or private family sphere and men's work in the interfamilial or public sphere, it follows that men have been placed above women in the social hierarchy, in a relationship of domination with women. In the marriage unity of man and woman, man represents the world of families, society as a whole and its laws, which must determine and prescribe the activities of the individual family unit if society is to continue to exist as a system of families. This places the husband in a position of domination and determination of the private, family-centered activities of his wife. Hence the seemingly universal subordination of woman derives from the content of feminine activities themselves; as intrafamilial, private, parent–child activities, they must be under the determination of the masculine or interfamilial sphere. This hierarchy created between the sexes can also be understood as making woman more "natural" than man, or inversely, making man more "social" than woman, and hence necessitating man's domination of woman.[15]

The sexual division of labor, the incest taboo, and the concentration of man and woman in public and private spheres have characterized all known societies up through the present. However, the concrete activities of men and women have varied cross-culturally and, most importantly, through history. This book will examine one of these histories.

As a Marxist, I view history as the process of the development of society; a process which has its own laws, and which is progressive. In its historical development, society becomes more self-conscious and hence in control of its own laws and allows more freedom and equality for its members. Capitalism constitutes a high stage of social development: one that differentiates society from nature and scientifically studies both; one that embraces the principle of equality; one that allows for a high degree of individual freedom within exchange. However, capitalist society is not the endpoint of social development. Its economy is dominated by the accumulation of capital, a process which developed unplanned and which does not allow for either full democracy or full equality. Furthermore, it has inherited and incorporated into itself the sexual division of labor, not as a consciously chosen rule, but as a fact of nature.

Since this book conceives of history as a process of development, it will not present a chronological arrangement of empirical events. Indeed, since development is uneven, and happens *through* time, rather than *at* particular times, the book's arguments are constructed in logical rather than chronological time and situate developments in decades and centuries, rather than days or years. Only through such abstraction can one distill the history of womanhood and capitalism from the plethora of concrete events filling four centuries of time. Furthermore, this study will leave aside, for the most part, the political sphere in order to focus on the family, the economy, and their interface; I believe that these arenas hold the key to our subject.

Given the extent of social transformation within history, and even in the last three centuries of American history, it is difficult to use the concepts family, work, and labor with precision. First, the "sexual division of labor" is not a division of *labor* properly speaking, where labor refers to the wage labor process of capitalism; rather, it is a division of social activities including elements of family, economic, and political life. Therefore, the concept of "women's work" does not refer to purely economic activity. At the same time, the merging of family and economic life which characterized the colonial economy and which persist today—for example, in the phenomenon of "housework"—means that women's activities are, in some sense, economic. A large part of our task in this "work" is to conceptualize clearly what exactly it is that women have been doing, and how this has been qualitatively differentiated from men's "work." Second, we must be careful with our use of the word *family*. In society, family life has heretofore been conceptualized predominantly as a naturally determined and hence fixed activity. Thus conservatives grasp modern developments as the "breakdown of *the* family," while feminists criticize "*the* family" as the source of women's oppression. However, family life is a *social* construct, a set of social relationships through which individual personalities are constituted and sustained; its content has changed through history, as we shall see, and is no more limited by its present form than the content of economic life is restricted to its capitalist forms. It is not even necessary that family life be built on the physical sexual difference: indeed, the full development of society will bring a clear understanding of the inherent differences between the biological sexes and a conscious decision by society whether or not to differentially constitute individuals according to their physical sex.

Now we will begin our journey through American economic history. We are focusing on a particularly important time for women's work and the sexual division of labor, for the configuration of the sexual division of labor changed dramatically with the development of capitalism. In the family economy of colonial times, our starting point, economic and family life were merged: the household was a commodity production unit. During the period which we will examine, economic and familial activity grew increasingly separate and distinct. Economic life became more and more impersonal, organized by relationship of exchange between property-owning individuals and firms. Family life began to acquire a content of its own: in particular, woman's work of child-rearing, as the center of family life, gained a distinctly social content, as "socialization" of the child. Woman's sphere of the family became clearly distinct from man's new sphere, the economy. At the same time, contradictions in this new articulation of the sexual division of labor, and, in particular, in womanhood, began to draw women out of their "proper sphere," into the labor force and even into men's jobs. In this way, the sexual division of labor has begun to undermine itself.

These developments are the subject of this study, which is divided into three parts. Part I will examine women's work in the family economy, corresponding roughly to the colonial period of American history. Part II will examine women's work under the cult of domesticity of the nineteenth century, during which home and economy emerged as separate spheres, family life was elevated as a vocation for woman, and the ideal woman was separated from economic life. The cult of domesticity conception of woman as a vocational homemaker has persisted into the twentieth century and into the present: however, recently, the separation of spheres which stands at its core has been disintegrating, bringing into question the idea of womanhood and of family life. Part III will examine these twentieth-century transformations and speculate on woman's future economic role.

Let us begin.

Part I

WOMEN'S WORK IN THE COLONIAL FAMILY ECONOMY

1

The Family Economy

Our study commences with the colonial economy. As the sexual division of labor and women's work were built into the fabric of the colonial economy and society, we will begin by examining the content and dynamic of this economy. Then we will study the sexual division of labor as lived out in colonial times and see how it determined the concrete content of womanhood and woman's work.

The early American economy was a colony of Britain, and as such bore the imprint of her colonizer. Furthermore, since the colonists were unable to exploit the indigenous population to their ends, the American colonial society was, effectively, a transplantation of British society onto North American soil. For this reason, our study of the colonial economy must begin with a brief examination of the British economy in the seventeenth and eighteenth centuries.

The Development of the Family Economy in Britain

At the time of the British settlement of North America, feudal institutions were breaking down in the face of a developing commercial economy. Feudalism had developed in England and Western Europe after the disintegration of the Roman Empire. The feudal order was a stable and static one, changing little in almost one thousand years. Individual lives were externally determined by a social order seen as God-given, its laws articulated through God's representatives on earth, the Catholic Church and the King. To challenge this order or to lack "faith" was heresy, a crime punishable by death. Self-seeking—the individual's expression of and advancement of self—was absent from feudalism. The individual was taught to function, in the words of Paul, as one part of the "body" of society—not

15

for his own sake, but for the sake of society as a whole, and under the direction of the "head."[1]

The individual's life was organized by two kinds of relationships. First, relationships of subordination and dependence determined the actions of king and vassal, lord and serf. Fiefdoms were granted to vassals by the King in exchange for loyal service, particularly in the military. The vassal then granted the use of his land and his protection to serfs who were, in turn, obliged to repay him with part of their product and with labor services in his field, the desmesne or domain. There was a clear hierarchy: the lords were under the King's "law," while the serfs lived under the law of their lord. While many of these relationships originated as voluntary contracts, they became compulsory as they were passed on through generations; children inherited their station in life as serfs, tied to the family plot, or as nobility, responsible to their King and serfs.[2] One's place in the hierarchy was thus inherited or ascribed, rather than achieved through one's own actions. Second, the extended kin group and community determined the lives of its members. At all social ranks, children were born into a family and community which regulated their actions through adulthood, including their rank, occupation, and choice of spouse. The individual's immersion in his kin group was exemplified in the practices of collective punishment and feuds between families.[3] The combination of kinship, community, and lordly control determined the individual peasant's life to a degree that is today difficult to imagine. For example, the manorial court in Northumberland regulated almost all aspects of economic and personal life. Steeping flax or hemp in water where horses drink or in running water, letting scabbed or infected cattle on the common lands, not adhering to the prescribed weights and measures, stopping up the public ways or footpaths, taking in lodgers, erecting cottages, shooting with guns or cross-bows, not ringing pigs, failing to repair hedges, scolding, chiding, brawling, singing scandalous songs, and offenses against the economic monopolies of the lord were all offenses punishable by fines.[4]

Feudal economic life was immersed in this web of customary relationships. The basic economic unit was the lord's manor, all or part of his fiefdom of land, settled by from 30 to 150 households. The energies of the laboring population were dedicated almost entirely to the provision of agricultural goods, although some worked full- or part-time in direct service of the lord. Agricultural production on the manor was organized collectively in an "open field system." "Common lands" were used by serfs for the grazing of their livestock and for firewood. Crops were farmed by families on strips of land allotted by the community, which also controlled plowing, sowing, reaping, and grazing. Serfs used a simple plow and crop rotation, leaving fields fallow every two to three years. This technology was fixed by custom and changed little during the feudal period; the major innovations were the improvement of the plow, more efficient crop rotation, and the introduction of the potato.[5]

The rise of long-distance trade in the eleventh century and the merchant capital that it inspired created the growth of towns on the edges of feudal society. The towns received charters from the Crown, and their people enjoyed limited rights to self-government as well as the privilege of substituting money payments for feudal service. The towns housed the merchants, organized into guilds, and were the seat of their trading activities. Craft production grew up in the towns to provision the needs of the burghers; it was regulated by guilds, who fixed both the technique of production and minimum prices, controlled quality, and limited access by controlling apprenticeships. While the towns' economies resembled the manors' in their fixity of technique, they were based on production for sale or commodity production, and hence involved private property and contract, absent from the manorial economy.[6]

The presence of towns and commodity exchange exacerbated contradictions inherent in feudal society, resulting in the gradual transformation of feudal relations into exchange relations.[7] Serfs could escape from the service of the lord to the towns and become free after one year's residence; furthermore, serf labor became scarce in the fourteenth century when the Black Death halved the rural population. Faced with labor shortages and peasant revolts, the lords were forced to reduce their demands on their serfs, transforming their labor dues into rents in kind and, eventually, into fixed money rents. Moreover, by the sixteenth century the temptations of merchants, who offered for sale exotic commodities from the world market, had begun to draw the lords into production for the market, in particular into wool production for the growing cloth industry. Enterprising lords evicted tenants with a wave of "enclosures," turning their lands to sheep-raising for profit and creating a landless underclass. Meanwhile, with the dissolution of the monasteries by the Crown during the Reformation, the extensive church lands were transformed into private property and farmed for the market. Futhermore, the market economy began to penetrate into the countryside with the growth of cottage or putting-out industry. Merchants seeking involvement in cloth production avoided the craft guilds' restrictions by initiating production in rural areas. They provided peasants with wool or yarn, which the latter spun or wove in their cottages in exchange for a money payment. The putting-out system allowed for the dividing up of the production process between families. This greater division of labor made putting-out more efficient than craft or self-sufficient production; in the latter two, the worker, or family, made the entire product.

Hence, by the time of the colonization of North America in the seventeenth century, the development of the market had radically transformed British society. Feudal manors had been broken up into property-owning households. Agricultural laborers had been freed from their dependence on and determination by the lords, and vice versa. Peasant men who acquired land—yeoman farmers—undertook production for profit along with the nobility: they were able to support wives and children, and maintain households of their own. Those with insufficient land for household support worked for merchants as cottagers or for farmers as day laborers, or became dependent members of the wealthier households. The household owned its means of production—its land and/or tools—and its product, in entirety; all of these, as private property, were alienable. In addition, the establishment of private property in land also began to free the household from the control of extended kin and community. Production decisions could now be made by the individual household, with a view, not to mere subsistence, but to the accumulation of wealth. This growing economic freedom was accompanied by the Protestant Reformation's challenge to the Papacy and its replacement of the clerical monopoly on religious interpretation with the "priesthood of the believers," the household heads.[8]

This economic system that emerged from the breakdown of feudalism and the rise of exchange had as its basic unit the property-owning family and its household: for this reason, we will refer to it as the "family economy."[9] The family economy was radically different from feudalism. The family's position in the social hierarchy was no longer simply ascribed through inheritance; it depended, instead, on the family's ability to earn wealth, as well as on the previous economic successes of its parent families. The family was not guaranteed sufficient wealth to maintain a household of its own; to properly marry and have children, a couple needed property in at least a home, and in a means of production, yet membership in a community no longer guaranteed the family land to farm and use of the commons. At the same time, the family had the opportunity, through its efforts, to accumulate wealth and better its position. Its economic initiative or lack of it, along with that of its parent families, was responsible for its existence as an intact family, its economic and social position, and the economic legacy of its children. The threat of losing its independence as a family, combined with the possibility for bettering it, both whipped and enticed families to struggle to protect and expand their wealth by harnessing themselves to production for the market.

The development of private property, by breaking up feudal communal restrictions and protections, allowed for the individuation of the family as more or less wealthy, producing this or that commodity, working as day laborers or putting-out workers, or living as dependent servants of other, wealthier families. And as their feudal interrelationships were broken, families began to live in seeming isolation from each other. Nevertheless, in its individuation and isolation, the family was integrally tied to others; in order to survive and earn wealth, the family had to submit itself to the strict discipline of the market, that is, to provide the market with a commodity needed by others. There grew up, therefore, a division of labor between families, each specializing in the production of one or more commodities for the use of the others, a specialization mediated by the market. For this reason, as familial striving after wealth developed, it brought, not pandemonium, but an increasingly wealthy society.[10]

A wealthy family could maintain a household of its own, using its income both to fill family needs through the purchase of consumer goods, services, and/or the maintenance of domestic servants, and to purchase the means to expanded commodity production. Likewise, if the household's property and income were limited, it became unable to accumulate wealth or to fill the family's commodity needs; it was forced to seek extra cash in day labor or putting-out work, to obtain essential goods through home production and barter, and/or to put out its children as apprentices. Individuals who did not inherit sufficient property or skills from their parents, or families who lost theirs, were forced to retreat into crude self-sufficiency, attach themselves to prosperous households, or go on poor relief.

The members of the property-owning, commodity-producing household specialized in different parts of the household's production and were rewarded with part of their joint product, as determined by the head of the household. A division of labor within the household unit organized the production of commodities for the market as well as that of goods for home consumption. The role of the family as producer caused it to take on or send off members according to its need for labor. Hence, the household was not necessarily coterminous with the nuclear family; as an Italian described England in the late fifteenth century:

> The want of affection in the English is strongly manifested towards their children; for after having kept them at home till they arrive at the age of seven or nine years at the utmost, they put them out, both males and females, to hard service in the houses of other people, binding them generally for another seven or nine years. And these are called apprentices, and during that time they perform all the most menial offices; and few are born who are exempted from this fate, for everyone, however rich he may be, sends his children into the houses of others, whilst he, in return receives those of strangers into his own.[11]

The practice of "exchanging children" varied across classes. Poor families, eking out a living as day laborers and putting-out workers, were often unable to employ and support their children; they bound them out, as apprentices or servants, to more prosperous families. The latter were able to expand their households with children from other families, although the wealthiest households often sent their babies out to live with wet-nurses and their older children to boarding school.[12]

The development of the market and commodity production brought the development of economic freedom. But this freedom was greatly circumscribed. It was largely restricted to the household head, the husband/father/master, who dictated the activity of the members of his household and whose actions had, likewise, been dictated by his father.[13] He was the household's moral authority, charged by Protestantism to "indoctrinate his household in piety and morality through daily family prayers and Bible reading."[14] He acted as both employer and parent in his household, which was both family and enterprise. He had the power to apprentice out his children or keep them in the household and to determine their future occupations. The father also determined his children's marriages. Since to exist intact, a family had to act as an enterprise, the formation of a new family in marriage was determined by clearly economic motives. In order to marry properly, the couple had to own property; indeed, in old English, the word "husbond" meant a bond-tenant sufficiently wealthy to maintain a full house.[15] Marriage contracts (between the parents of the bride and groom) often included clear specifications of the gifts each family would provide. Children, particularly sons, could not properly marry until they received their inheritance; the father, as household head, had to occupy himself with assuring their futures, as well as that of the family enterprise. In England, inheritance according to primogeniture kept the family enterprise intact but discriminated against the younger siblings.

In the family economy, economic and family relationships were merged; hence neither one had developed a specificity of its own. Family life had an economic character; family members were co-workers. Marriages among the propertied were arranged according to family economic motives, and a large percentage of the population owned some property. Propertyless children were freed from these concerns, as they grew up in the households of strangers, but their marriages were economic partnerships since the sexes engaged in different and complementary work. Parenting, a distinctive personal and familial activity in the twentieth century, was not so in the household economy. Rather, parenting meant, first, the physical nurturing of the infant, and then, its training for its future occupation, as determined by the household head, through apprenticeship to and working with an adult: "transmission from one generation to the next was ensured by the everyday participation of children in adult life."[16] Hence families unable to provide their children with the proper training freely bound them out to the families of strangers, who could better perform the activity of "parenting" or training them.

If family members related to each other as co-workers, workers—those who worked for others—were also treated as family members. If a family did not own or lease sufficient land to support itself (or craft tools and skills, in the city)—and many did not in England—its members were forced to, in a sense, become part of another family as live-in apprentices or servants. A borderline family that had some land could retain its home with some supplementary wage income from day laboring during the harvest. Often, though, such a family was unable to keep its children and, hence, was unable to be a real family. Since they could not provide work and subsistence for their children, these parents would "put them out" as servants or apprentices. These children would become second-class members of their master's family, and in a sense were his children. The landless could not maintain an independent home and family solely on wage income, which was in those times at less than subsistence level. These people became part of other families as live-in servants, or entered the growing class of paupers, maintained at the expense of the parish.[17]

Hence, in the family economy, children were treated as little workers, and workers were treated as children. Adulthood meant living in one's own household, as husband or wife, and working for oneself, as a farmer, craftsman, or putting-out worker. Childhood was preparation for an adulthood determined by one's parents, acquired through actual practice of the chosen trade. Hence domestic service and apprenticeship were forms of childhood training. So complete was the mixing of the dependent relationships of parent–child and master–servant that language did not distinguish between them: in England, servants were taught proper manners in poem books called "babees books," and the word "valet" meant a young boy. As Aries wrote in *Centuries of Childhood*, "the servant was child, a big child, whether he was occupying his position for a limited period in order to share in the family's life and thus initiate himself into adult life, or whether he had no hope of ever becoming a master."[18]

If the specificity of family and economic relationships was undeveloped in the family economy, the economy was also at a low level of development when compared to its successor, industrial capitalism. The market was still undeveloped and unstable as a source of demand for the commodity-producing households. Furthermore, the subjective, familial nature of commodity production limited the quantity and stability of supply to the market. This instability often forced families to retreat into self-sufficient production and barter.

The Establishment of the Colonial Family Economy

This system of property-owning family production units engaging in production for exchange characterized the British economy in the sixteenth and seventeenth centuries. It was this society that spawned American colonial society. It is estimated that about 750,000 people journeyed to the North American colonies between 1600 and 1770, the majority of them from Britain. The colonists were from all orders: from the landed gentry to the yeoman farmers to the landless peasants. By 1733, they had established thirteen colonies along the eastern seaboard. These immigrants brought with them the essence of British society on the eve of industrialization: "All the factors of previous living—home, church, military organization, political representation—were enfolded in the families and the persons of these English men and women."[19] It is crucial to understand how the colonizing families transplanted British society and its incipient industrial development to America.[20]

The families that established the North American colonies brought with them not only the remnants of feudal institutions but also the principles that were breaking these down. Many sought religious freedom and escape from the inequities of aristocratic privilege. Most possessed a desire for private property of their own and planned to accumulate wealth; most brought with them needs for the civilized commodity products of their proto-industrial homeland. Although they often lived in primitive self-sufficiency and geographical isolation, colonial households were not fleeing European civilization and its developing exchange system to revert to the state of nature. Families were willing to venture out into small, isolated communities, even to live on isolated land holdings, because they anticipated tying themselves to a developing market. However, in the words of one eighteenth-century historian, "They exchanged a pleasant land for a howling wilderness."[21]

The motive behind the colonization of North America was revealed in the colonists' treatment of the indigenous populations. North America was inhabited by tribal, "Indian" societies that had no conception of either private property or servile or slave relationships. Indeed the Iroquois society has been described as "primitive communism," due to its egalitarian and collective character.[22] Colonists did not seek to join these indigenous societies, but rather to use their people and resources as a means to accumulate wealth. The Indian peoples on the whole refused to cooperate with the settlers, neither submitting to bondage as slaves or servants, nor giving up their lands. Hence, they became enemy "savages" in the eyes of the colonists, to be displaced or destroyed, and the continent became a hostile wilderness to be conquered and tamed.

In order to retain their civilization and wealth, the colonists attempted to establish trade with Britain. From the beginning they sought to produce salable commodities that would procure them access to British wealth.[23] Companies, individuals, and later families came to North America with the goal of producing commodities valuable to the mother country or to her colonial system. They actively strove to link their activities to the needs of the British economy. While the Navigation Acts enforced this division of labor by prohibiting the export of most manufactures from the colonies, Britain did not force her colonies into exchange. Colonists were not enslaved to produce for England; they chose to. They were tied to their mother country by their civilized needs, which could be filled only by her products. They were further tied by their needs to advance themselves and accumulate wealth—which they could do only by hooking themselves up to the developing market. Developing an export crop was not always easy, and the colonists were often isolated from this exchange by crop failure or market fluctuations. This forced them to subsist on their own family product and gave a subsistence character to their production. Yet this did not brand them as primitive. Their system of private property, and the struggle for wealth that underlay it, placed them on the road to capitalism. The primitive quality of colonial existence was the price early colonizers paid for their desires for wealth, freedom, and private property. In this contradiction lies the secret to the dynamism of the early American economy.

America's colonial relationship with the most advanced manufacturing country caused its early economic development to be the reverse of the British trend. In Britain, manufactures in the form of handicrafts and putting-out were the dynamic "sector." Britain sought a market for her manufactures, particularly wool products, in her colonies. Her colonial policy encouraged the production and export of agricultural staple crops and raw materials, in exchange for British manufactures. This policy was enforced through the Navigation Acts, price incentives, and the practices of mercantile houses. Hence, the development of manufacturing, which characterized the British economy, was markedly absent from her American colonies. But this did not mean that the colonies simply reverted to a more primitive stage of economic development, with self-sufficient agriculture and home manufacture. The colonies specialized in primary product production for exchange. They sold raw materials—fur, fish, timber, agricultural products—and ships and shipping services to the British and provided a market for British manufactures. To the extent that they were successful at finding a cash crop and a way to transport it, they were able to import all of their "necessities and luxuries."

The southern colonies produced and exported crops of rice, indigo, tobacco, and later cotton; this allowed them to specialize in these crops, import slaves and British goods, and develop a class that could live in wealth and luxury. Robert Beverly described and condemned this extreme dependence on imports in his *History and Present State of Virginia* of 1705:

> They have their Cloathing of all sorts from England, as Linnen, Woollen, Silk, Hats, and Leather. Yet Flax, and Hemp grow no where in the World, better than there; their Sheep yield a mighty Increase, and bear good Fleeces, but they shear them only to cool them. The Mulberry-Tree, whose Leaf is the proper Food of the Silk-Worm, grows there like a Weed, and Silk-Worms have been observ'd to thrive extremely, and without any hazard. The very Furrs that their Hatts are made of, perhaps go first from thence; and most of their Hides lie and rot, or are made use of, only for covering dry Goods, in a leaky House. Indeed some few Hides with much adoe are tann'd, and made into Servants Shoes; but at so careless a rate, that the Planters don't care to buy them, if they can get others; and sometimes perhaps a better manager than ordinary, will vouchsafe to make a pair of Breeches of a Deer-Skin. Nay, they are such abominable Ill-Husbands, that tho' their Country be over-run with Wood, yet they have all their Wooden Ware from England; their Cabinets, Chairs, Tables, Stools, Chests, Boxes, Cart-Wheels, and all other things, even so much as their Bowls, and Birchen Brooms to the Eternal Reproach of their Laziness.[24]

The northern colonies had more difficulty finding ways to get rich. They lacked good agricultural lands; furthermore, what foodstuffs they could produce—grain, corn, flour, and meat—were not needed by the British. The lack of markets was aggravated by poor transportation. These economic problems were exacerbated by the family nature of production. Many of the northern colonies did not practice primogeniture; divided more or less equally among the children, family estates dwindled through the generations until they were barely able to support a family. In order to gain sufficient land, some children pushed westward, only to isolate themselves further from the market.[25]

Although the developing northern economy could support some profitable businesses, particularly in the towns, the farmers who made up the bulk of the population were not unilaterally successful; indeed, quite the opposite result characterized northern commerical agriculture in colonial times. For example, one historian estimates

that only one-third of the farms in late eighteenth-century Kent produced at least a small salable surplus.[26] What did families do when
they were unable to produce marketable commodities? Let's look at
the example of early New England. These colonists first found a
market in the flood of arriving settlers who needed cattle and corn to
set up farms of their own; by specializing in the production of cattle
and corn for these immigrants, they were able to purchase the British
manufactures that usually accompanied the arriving ships. But in the
1640s, civil war in England brought religious and social reform, which
dampened desires to emigrate, and the New Englanders' market
dried up. As Winthrop, one of the early colonists, described:

> The [reform begun by Parliament in 1641] caused men to stay in England
> in expectation of a new world, so as few coming to us, all foreign com-
> modities grew scarce, and our own of no price. . . . These straits set out
> people on work to provide fish, clapboards, planks, etc., and to sow hemp
> and flax (which prospered very well), and to look out to the West Indies
> for a trade in cotton.[27]

This failure in export commodity production forced the New Englanders to search for other markets and, meanwhile, to "import
substitute," to begin to fabricate themselves the products they had
hitherto been purchasing from England. The same introduction of
home production occurred in Maryland in 1680: stagnation in the
tobacco market brought home textile production to wealthy households that had previously purchased imported cloth.[28] By the end of
the seventeenth century, both the import of machinery from Britain
and the sale of domestic manufactures were forbidden by law, forcing
the colonies' import substitution to continue as household production.
Colonial governments encouraged the home production of textiles,
the most popular import good, with bounties on hemp and flax production and manufacture, the establishment of spinning schools, and
the holding of contests.[29]

The prevalence of self-sufficient production on northern farms had
brought uncertainty about whether or not these farmers possessed
the "entrepreneurial spirit."[30] There was truth on both sides of the
debate. First, their self-sufficiency was not inconsistent with entrepreneurship. The goal of economic advancement combined with the
weakness and instability of the market led many northern farmers to
work toward self-sufficiency as a strategy not for simple survival but

for accumulation: by minimizing their purchases of consumer goods, they could use all their money earned for capital improvements.[31] If they succeeded, they could eventually supply more of their needs through the market. Some of those who continually failed to market their produce gave up and lived on in self-sufficiency outside out of the mainstream of civilization. Such families failed to retain their "entrepreneurial spirit"; as a migrant wrote in 1810, "We know that people who live far from markets and cannot sell their produce, naturally become indolent and vicious."[32] The fact that uneven and unsuccessful economic development could not sustain commodity production and growth for all the colonists does not obliterate the fact that the colonies embodied the principle of private property, and the accompanying principle of the individual family's freedom and responsibility for its economic fate. The successes in the struggle for increased property shaped the future of the continent; the losers dropped out, only to be eventually reincorporated into the market as wage laborers. The existence of competition for economic self-advancement is verified by the rapid concentration of property holdings in the hands of the winners.[33]

Self-sufficient production represented the response of the property-owning entrepreneurial family to an insufficient market (as well as a result of the prohibition of domestic manufactures). The degree of self-sufficiency of families varied between more and less successful families, as well as between more and less developed regions. While northern farmers were pushed into entrepreneurial self-sufficiency, their southern counterparts were able to maintain sophisticated standards of livings with European imports, due to their successful cash crop production. Families moving to the frontier were forced to undergo a period of almost complete self-sufficiency; as areas became more settled, links to the market and the development of indigenous crafts allowed them to increase their specialization in commodity production.

During and after the Revolutionary War, such household manufacture and the economic independence from Britain that it brought was a necessary part of the establishment of the political independence of the colonies, both in the North and in the South; the production and wearing of homespun became a patriotic act. The campaign to institute home production allowed the complete cessation of textile imports from England to be withstood during the Revolutionary Period. As Macy described in his *History of Nantucket:*

The suffering for clothing was inconsiderable throughout the war. For immediately, on being cut off from the use of English manufactures, the women engaged within their own families in manufacturing of various kinds of cloth for domestic use. They thus kept their household decently clad, and the surplus of their labors they sold to such as chose to buy rather than make for themselves. In this way the female part of the families, by their industry and strict economy, frequently supported the whole domestic circle; evincing the strength of their attachment and the value of their service to those on whom they themselves were wont to depend for protection and support.[34]

Throughout the colonial period and into the nineteenth century, the development of frontier outposts, separated from the market and supplied by poor transportation, continually introduced self-sufficiency into the development of the American economy.

The Sexual Division of Labor in the Colonial Family Economy

Now we will use our understanding of the family economy to analyze the sexual division of labor in colonial times, as well as the concrete work experiences of women. This is not an easy task, for the uneven development of the colonial economy manifested itself in a tremendous variation in the economic activities of the family and of individual men and women. Indeed, the institution of slavery in the southern colonies created a life for black families so different from that of free whites that it will be the subject of a separate chapter, Chapter 4. But we will find that, in both instances, family relationships differentiated husband and wife, man and woman, and created a sexual division of labor within the family.

The sexual division of labor in the colonial family economy was a complicated one, without any clear rationale. While, for the most part, men centered in production for sale and women in production for the household, this division was by no means absolute. And while concrete work activities were clearly understood to be either men's or women's work, it was not uncommon for women to engage in men's work. For these reasons, historians have had difficulty analyzing women's work and the sexual division of labor in the colonial economy.

One set of writers, following the lead of Clark, Dexter, and Earle, note and stress the presence of women in many traditionally "masculine" vocations—as skilled crafts "men," merchants, shopkeepers, teachers, and farmers.[35] From this evidence they conclude that the colonial times represented a period during which women were emancipated from the confines of the sexual division of labor. A second group of historians holds an opposite conception: they claim that the colonial times were characterized by a strict and simple division of labor between men and women which assigned them to fields and house, or to the public and private spheres, respectively.[36] This latter group dismisses the examples of women and men doing the same work as exceptions to a rule which excluded women from any common activities with men. They are then able to explain the sexual division of labor as the product of natural, physical differences in ability between men and women. As both groups base their arguments on concrete analysis of work activities, their disagreement seeks empirical resolution: was the phenomenon of women and men doing common work in colonial times prevalent enought to be "significant"? Yet they have no theoretical basis upon which to make such a judgment.

The inability to resolve this dilemma has encouraged a third interpretation—one which ignores the issue of whether or not a sexual division of labor existed. These scholars emphasize instead the fact that women worked as hard as men, making the wife's efforts essential to the economic survival of the family. They claim that the participation of both sexes in work brought a relationship of equal partnership to colonial couples—an equality which was lost when nineteenth century developments excluded women from "work."[37] But the impact of work on the social position of the worker has never been determined by the importance of that work to the economy; rather, work's social meaning is determined by the constellation of social relationships within which the work takes place. Just as the fact that the slave worked harder than the master did not place the former above the latter, neither did the fact that husband and wife often worked equally hard create, between them, a relationship of equality.

To correctly analyze women's work in the family economy, we must focus on the social relationships surrounding this work, rather than upon its particular physical content. We can understand the diversity of women's work experiences if we see them as the product of the sexual division of labor in the family. To analyze this, we must begin with the marriage relationship.

The husband was the property-owner and head of household. He established himself as such by acquiring property—land, means of production, or craft skills—and striving to increase this property through production for the market. He competed with other property-owning household heads for wealth. To earn wealth, a man had to orient his life and sensibility toward the market; he had to produce goods and/or services for sale, or engage in craft labor. As head of household, the husband was responsible for the well-being of his wife and children, responsibilities that fueled his struggle for economic survival and advancement. Therefore, if a man did not own property sufficient to support a household of his own, he could not properly marry; this meant waiting for an inheritance or saving money from work as a day laborer. If he awaited an inheritance, a son was at the mercy of his father; fathers in need of laborers to farm their land could simply delay the promised inheritance to keep their sons on the land. This conflict was handled in various manners. Some parents let their sons marry but live on with them, working their lands; in other families, the father transferred his land to his sons before death, with the understanding that the latter would care for their parents in their old age. While under the roof of his father, a man remained a son, and under the authority of his father whether or not he was married; it was not until he moved away, or his father died, that he could become a household head and a real man.[38]

When he acquired a household of his own, a man was its unquestioned head; he represented society at large within the family and exercised society's authority over its members. He had the ultimate say over the work of his wife. "In every lawful thing she submits her Will and Sense to his, where she cannot convince him of Inexpediencies . . . she acts as if there were but one Mind in two Bodies" wrote Cotton Mather, in his widely read treatise on womanhood, *Ornaments to the Daughters of Zion;* his view of patriarchal power was shared by families in England as well as in the colonies.[39] As society's representative in the family, the man was, as father, responsible for imbuing his children with understanding of their place in society.

The wife's existence was constructed differently. A woman's marriage was arranged by her parents; if they did not pick her husband, she at least needed their approval. Upon marriage, a woman moved from the household of her father to that of her husband. Her dowry, if any, was arranged between these two men; as a married woman, she had no property rights in it, nor over the use of their jointly earned property. (She also was without political rights.) Unlike her husband, a wife did not exist as an individual in the public sphere; rather, she defined herself in relation to the members of her family, as the wife of her husband and the mother of her children. Her work was to fill their needs; her life and work were, hence, defined by these needs. Since the needs of the family varied according to its relationship to the market, her work varied according to the particular work and success of her husband, complementing his. Her husband's income, class position, and particular work determined the concrete content of her homemaking work. In this way, she normally passed her life constrained to the private, familial sphere; she was viewed and referred to by society at large in relation to her husband, as Mrs. Jones, in keeping with the dependence of her existence upon his.[40] In colonial times, women were "People who make no Noise in all the World, People hardly known to be in the World," that is, the public and masculine world.[41]

In general, husbands took up commodity production, while wives centered in self-sufficient production, given that the former was production of wealth, oriented toward the market, while the latter was production to directly fill the needs of the family. And because a woman defined her work in relation to her husband's, man's work of commodity production and woman's work of self-sufficient production were inversely linked through the marital relationship. In cash-poor or frontier families, as the husband struggled to succeed in production for the market, building up capital goods and saving up cash income for future investment, his wife worked to reduce family expenditures by providing for most of the family's basic subsistence needs. Her work could include the home production of food, clothing, candles, soap, household furnishings, and drink. If her husband were wealthy, with more than adequate cash for investment, cash purchases of commodities and/or the hiring of servants eliminated self-sufficient production from the homemaker's work; homemaking in these families became overseeing the servants or the household slaves, purchasing commodities, and playing a social, entertaining, and decorative role. The link between the pampered lady and the farm wife is not apparent; however, it was actually lived out in the lives of homemakers who moved with their husbands from Britain to the early colonies, or from settled areas to the frontier. Women were transformed from ladies to overworked farm wives by their families' isolation from the market. Little wonder that some husbands had difficulty persuading their wives to make the journey into the wilderness.[42]

If it was needed by the family, wives moved into production for exchange, but never on an equal footing with their husbands. The energies of farm wives often extended themselves into selling or bartering their extra product in order to obtain consumer goods essential for the household, so as to leave the husband's earnings for capital accumulation.[43] A shortage of labor at planting or harvest time could draw the homemaker and her children into the production of a cash crop.[44] If her husband was a petty producer or retailer, a homemaker's energies, along with those of her children, could be enlisted to help in the family business—for example, by working in the family store or aiding in the production of a craft good. In these ways, wives were directly or indirectly involved in the production of commodities. But a wife's involvement was qualitatively different from that of her husband. He worked as a property owner and family head, to establish his identity as a man; she worked as a homemaker, in order to aid her family. Seen from this vantage point, his work was to earn wealth, while her provision of income was seen as saving money, reducing the family's demands on his capital. As Cotton Mather wrote in his *Ornaments to the Daughters of Zion*, "Her husband's gains are so managed by her Housewifry and Providence, that he finds it to his advantage to let her keep the keys of all . . . the Pennies she saves do add unto the Heap of the Pounds got by him."[45] Another eighteenth-century writer described the difference as follows: "As the Man's Part is to provide industriously, so the Woman's is to preserve discreetly. . . . The Man must be seeking with Diligence; the Woman must be saving with Providence."[46]

Likewise, men occasionally engaged in production that was not directed toward the market. His home production of consumer goods for the family—through staple crop farming, hunting, whittling—could save the cash-poor family's earnings for purchases of needed capital goods. Production of his own means of production both saved the family's income for those capital goods that could be acquired only through purchase and built up the value of his enterprise. Hence much of a man's self-sufficient production was, in fact, capital formation. Such work was an integral part of pioneer living: "His entire stock of capital which he took to his new home consisted of an axe, a gun, a few tools, perhaps a plough, some flour, and a few head of livestock . . . in his first years the pioneer was chiefly engaged in producing capital goods . . . the clearing of land, erection of build-ings, and the building of roads."[47] Done within the context of his larger struggle to accumulate wealth, and concretely different from the work of his wife, such self-sufficient production was part of man-hood: however, a man whose life work never involved production for income and the building up of his property was a failed man.

The sexual division of labor did not disappear even when the house-holds entered into the totally novel activity of journeying to the fron-tier in covered wagons. John Faragher's study of *Women and Men on the Overland Trail* describes the strict division of labor established between the sexes, a division that mimicked that of settled society. Men were the leaders, women the followers. On the trail, men took over the work of leading the expedition, caring for and driving the wagons and stock, hunting for game, and guarding and protecting their families. Women's work was homemaking, tending to the needs of the family: collecting fuel and caring for the fire, preparing and cooking the meals on the open fire, sewing, washing, and otherwise caring for the clothes, milking the cows, packing and unpacking, and watching the small children. Men drove the wagons and stock; women rode. As in the normal family economy, "women's trail work was structured around the men's."[48]

Hence the marriage relationship created a sexual division of labor which was clear, if fluid; this difference of activities sustained men and women as clearly differentiated social beings. The difference in the worlds of colonial men and women is illustrated in a recent study of claims of loyalists upon the British government for property confis-cated during the Revolution. Women making claims described in detail the household contents, but were unable to specify the value of the household's property and assets, often referring the commission to male relatives; men, on the other hand, were quick to assess the value of the household assets, but described household contents vaguely.[49]

Since the family economy was a transitional stage, during which the work of provisioning needs was moving unevenly into the sphere of the market and of commodity production, we can find examples of women and men working at technically similar activities that were in the process of moving from woman's sphere into man's sphere. These illustrate the point that the division between man's and woman's work was not a physical one, even while the sexual division of labor was seen by society as a fixed and naturally based phenomenon. It also illustrates the fact that "work" cannot be understood as a technical, physical activity, but must be grasped as a social activity involving a set of social relationships that not only produces a social product but also constitutes the "worker" as a particular social being. The technically similar activities of agriculture and gardening were men's and women's work, respectively, because agriculture was production for the market while gardening was production for the family table. Similarly, weaving and sewing were done by both men and women; however, men wove or sewed for money as craftsmen, fine weavers, or fancy tailors, whereas women wove and sewed at home, for their families. With the increasing wealth of the family, and with the historical development of commodity production, woman's self-sufficient production was replaced by commodity production, which better and more efficiently filled family needs. This process branded woman's home work as primitive, reinforcing the prevailing conception of woman's private work in the household as "natural," opposed to man's public and "social" work, and justified man's domination over women in the household, and his monopoly on the political sphere.

Since the sexual division of labor was based in marriage, it was disrupted by the failure, illness, disappearance, or death of one of the spouses. The easiest solution to this disruption was, of course, the substitution of a new partner through separation (or divorce where legal) and remarriage. Nancy Cott's study of divorce records in the eighteenth century reveals that a main reason for divorce cited in petitions was the economic default of the spouse—nonsupport by the husband, desertion or mismanagement of the household by the wife.[50] When a woman lost her husband/provider, she sought a new husband or the help of a male relative. If this failed, and she was without a substantial inheritance, her responsibilities to her family as homemaker drew her into the masculine sphere of exchange to seek income to support her family. This could mean taking her husband's place in the family business; if no business existed, these circumstances forced her to find other ways of earning cash income for the family. When a man lost his wife/homemaker, it was less common and less necessary for him to actually take on women's work; if he could not find a relative or new wife, he could hire one in the form of a domestic.

Finally, the sexual division of labor was perpetuated generationally through the actual apprenticeship of the children to the work proper to their sex, in their parents' families or, if that was not possible, the households of strangers. In the colonial economy, children were seen as little workers, prepared through working at home to continue their parents' jobs of carrying on the family traditions and sustaining, if not bettering, its social position. Young children stayed in the household and, hence, helped their mother (or the master's wife) with her woman's work; however, once the boys were able, they left women's work and helped their father, while their sisters remained under the purview of their mothers. "Barbed male jokes about boys doing 'women's work'—milking, churning, or feeding the hens—were like spurs urging sons to their fathers' sides in the fields. . . . The same process occurred on the trail, where circumstances demanded that boys make the leap to manhood under the added compulsion of necessity."[51] Children learned, from birth, to construct themselves as little men or little women and to spurn the activities of the opposite sex. Hence they "naturally" grew up to seek their sexual complement in marriage, and construct a sexual division of labor within their households.

2

Homemaking: The Work of the Married Woman

It was upon marriage that a woman became an adult, for it was at this time that she acquired a family of her own and took up woman's work of homemaking. She trained for her future work of homemaking as a girl by serving her parents in a similar manner. If she remained unmarried, which few women did in colonial times, she was unable to take up women's work; she remained a dependent girl, living in the household of a different couple as a relative or servant; she was not fully a woman, and was stigmatized by society as a failure. So while homemaking was not literally the work of all women, i.e., all adult females, it was indeed the work by which a female constituted herself as a real woman.

Homemaking entailed filling the needs of her family. The needs that a married woman might perceive and attempt to fill were diverse and endless. Homemaking could involve a woman simultaneously in the work of gardener, livestock tender, cook, cleaner, laundress, spinner, weaver, seamstress, doctor, nurse, mother, overseer, and teacher. One colonial man described the work of his wife in his diary as follows:

> (January 1778) As I have, in this Memorandum, taken scarcely any notice of my wife's employment, it might appear as if her engagements were very trifling, the which is not the case but the reverse, and to do her that justice which her services deserve by entering them minutely would take up most of my time, for this genuine reason how that, from early in the morning till late at night, *she is constantly employed in the affairs of the family [emphasis added]*.[1]

Marshall shared a household with his wife, yet her work as a family-oriented activity was outside of her husband's sphere of interests and hence was not described in his diary. Furthermore, it was so limitless and varied that its content was almost indescribable. He continued:

> [She is constantly employed in the affairs of the family,] which for some months has been very large, for besides the addition to our family in the house [is] a constant attendance not only to provide, but also to attend at getting prepared in the kitchen, baking our own bread and pies, meat, and c., but also on the table. Her cleanliness about the house, her attendance in the orchard, cutting and drying apples, of which several bushels have been procured, add to which her making of cider without tools, for the constant drink of the family, her seeing all our washing done, and her fine clothes and my shirts which are all smoothed by her, add to this her making of twenty large cheeses, and that from one cow, and daily using milk and cream, besides her sewing, knitting, and c. . . . . Thus she looketh well to the ways of her household, and eateth not the bread of idleness.[2]

Marshall ended the entry by mentioning that, due to her busy state, his wife had only visited his neighbor four times since living there. She was a true housewife and homemaker.

Homemaking was not only extremely broad; there was also great variation in the work of homemaking, due to its particular and self-sufficient character. Woman's work in the home had a personal and unique quality, due to the fact that it was work done by a particular woman for her particular family. Needs varied widely between families according to the origins of their colony, the climate and natural resources of their region, and other particularities of the family—its size, tastes, history, family traditions. Furthermore, there remained latitude for the homemaker in the concrete determination of these needs. While fixed by her femaleness in the activity of homemaking, a woman was not fixed in the particular way she did so. Her choice to produce or acquire certain goods for her family expressed a woman's sensitivity to the particular personalities of the members of her family. Since homemaking often involved a good deal of self-sufficient production, it gave the homemaker a means to express her own personality, skills, and even creativity in her work: the actual quality of goods used and consumed depended upon her abilities and personality.

We cannot, in this chapter, discuss all of the different concrete tasks that constituted the homemaker's possible work. Furthermore, we cannot discuss all of the differences in homemaking due to the particular characteristics of a homemaker's family. We will instead focus on four main aspects of homemaking—mothering, meal provision, clothing provision, and nursing—and discuss the manner in which they varied according to the household's relationship to the market.

The Core of Homemaking: The Homemaker as Mother

Mothering was the core of homemaking in the family economy, as it has been in previous societies. The female's distinctive difference from males is her ability to bear children, and woman's homemaking work was structured around mothering. Yet mothering in the family economy had a very evasive content, which we will pursue in this section.

The primary aspect of mothering in colonial times was the physical process of carrying and bearing the child. Pregnancy and childbirth occupied many of a woman's adult years. The average woman bore eight children, both because large families were desired then to help with the family business, and because infant mortality was so high (roughly one child in three did not reach his or her twentieth birthday).[3] Child-bearing was dangerous "work," given the lack of development of medicine: in seventeenth-century Plymouth, every fifth woman died from causes associated with childbirth.[4] But the physical bearing of children was essential to homemaking. When the homemaker as wife bore the children of her husband, the family was perpetuated according to the rules of kinship; children were born who in fact shared the "blood" of both parent families. There was no failure greater for a homemaker than to be unable to bear children.

The care of infants, both their physical nursing and their supervision, was part of women's work, again for "natural" reasons, since bottle-feeding was rare. The mothering of infants was an activity which took place in the home, for they needed to be watched over and cared for. Since a woman was seen as naturally tied to the care of infants, in particular to breast-feeding them, her place was in the home with them. Woman's definition as mother worked to restrict her permanently to the home's protected environment.

However, the fact that the care of infants was seen as a natural process had a curious result: while this work was necessarily women's work, it was not necessarily the work of the biological mother. Infant care, even "wet-nursing," could be done by strangers to the infant's family and in a strange home. In colonial times, wealthy families often sent their infants out to wet-nurses for their first two years of life. In England, wet-nursing did not go out of fashion until the late eighteenth century, in spite of moralists' and doctors' warnings against it.[5] There is evidence that wet-nursing was also practiced in the colonies. In 1782, a Pennsylvania woman advertised without shame "a good breast of milk," offering to take a child into her home.[6] In his *Ornaments*, Cotton Mather described the virtuous mother as one who nursed her own children, implying that this was not yet universal practice.[7] Infants were also cared for in the mother's home by hired women servants. In the South, the children of the wealthy were suckled by slaves, shocking one visitor from the North who wrote in his diary, "I find it is common here for people of Fortune to have their young Children suckled by the Negroes!"[8] Thus, the suckling and care of infants was not necessarily the work of the homemaker.

While the care of infants was treated as a physical, impersonal, and natural process, the raising of children was virtually reduced to an economic one. The apprenticeship of children, as we have seen in Chapter 1, was considered proper parenting in the family economy. Once children possessed the ability to follow directions, they were dressed as "little adults" and put to work for the household in work appropriate to their sex.[9] Active parenting, then, was not women's work exclusively, but was shared by the sexes. Furthermore, since parenting children essentially meant putting them to work at their future work, children could be parented by non-family members; by servants of their biological parents in the latters' household, or by adults in a different household.[10] Hence while homemaking could involve the active parenting of daughters, it did not necessarily do so. In a poor household that could not support its daughters, they were sent out and mothered by other women; in wealthier households, the homemaker could be called upon to parent the daughters of strangers, or she might give over her mothering to domestic servants. A final and essential part of parenting was "breaking the will of the child," and teaching him or her basic religious principles. This was predominantly men's work, as was determining the child's future life course.[11]

In summary, the physical bearing of children was the only part of parenting essential to homemaking; given the family economy's conception of childhood, none of the other parenting activities were necessarily part of homemaking. Indeed, in wealthy or very poor families, the homemaker was unlikely to be raising her children. Hence the essence of women's mothering work in colonial times was the physical process of conceiving, carrying in pregnancy, and bearing a child. Reduced to this physical process, mothering branded woman as natural, almost animal. Woman's natural role of child-bearing was clearly distinguished from, and inferior to, her husband's social role of catechizing the children and determining their inheritance, future occupation, and spouse.

The Provision of Meals

As homemakers, women were responsible for providing the family and the household with meals. Due to the absence of privacy and intimacy in the family economy, meals were spent in eating, not in familial intercourse, except perhaps among the very wealthy. Nonfamily members—apprentices and servants who lived in the household—most often ate with the family. A meal was a hurried affair, with little talking or lingering afterwards.[12] A book of etiquette widely circulated in colonial times contains the following description of table behavior for children:

> Never sit down at the table till asked, and after the blessing. Ask for nothing; tarry till it be offered thee. Speak not. Bite not thy bread but break it. Take salt only with a clean knife. Dip not the meat in the same. Hold not thy knife upright but sloping, and lay it down at right hand of plate with blade on plate. Look not earnestly at any other that is eating. When moderately satisfied leave the table. Sing not, hum not, wriggle not. Spit nowhere in the room but in the corner. . . . When any speak to thee, stand up. Say not I have heard it before. Never endeavor to help him out if he tell it not right. Snigger not; never question the truth of it.[13]

Studies of household inventories have confirmed the impersonality of meals: the furniture necessary for such experiences was absent from most households; the dining table was often nothing more than a couple of planks on trestles; household members sat on benches, and ate with few utensils.[14]

The homemaker's decision as to the content of the meal was based upon her perception of the tastes and needs of the members of her family, and the available supply of food from the family larder or, given the cash available, from the market. In this choice of meals, the woman expressed her understanding of, concern for, and dedication to the needs of her family. It was not necessary that she totally produce the product; the only requirement of good homemaking was that her family was well fed, or as well fed as family resources allowed. A well-to-do woman might have a domestic or cook (the cook might even be a male) who purchased the food at the market and prepared it, but as a good wife and mother, she planned meals that would best please the family, oversaw her servant's preparation and service of such meals, and participated in the meals as a hostess. In such instances, she was relieved of much of the impersonal work and able to concentrate on making the meal a pleasing family experience. Most women could not afford cooks: for these women, the provision of meals necessarily involved them in the preparation of food and the cooking of the meals.

Food processing in those days involved not simply mixing and baking foods but also preserving them, dressing meats, and making cheeses. This work demanded knowledge both of general food preparation processes and of particular foods and recipes. (It also involved the knowledge and cultivation of the tastes of her family.) Most such knowledge was acquired informally, in the girl's apprenticeship to her mother or to another homemaker. Early settler-women also learned about the preparation of native American foods such as corn and squash from the Indians.

For those who could read—about 40 to 80% of women[15]—there were recipe books, private ones passed down from mothers as well as published works. These give us an idea of the content and scope of the homemaker's cooking work. One popular British cookbook, reprinted and edited for colonial use, bears the complete and informative title:

> The Frugal Housewife or Complete Woman Cook wherein the Art of Dressing all Sorts of Viands, with Cleanliness, Decency, and Elegance, is explained in Five Hundred approved *Receipts*, in Roasting, Boiling, Frying, Gravies, Sauces, Stews, Hashes, Soups, Fricassees, Ragoos, Pastries, Pies, Tarts, Cakes, Puddings, Syllabubs, Creams, Flummery, Jellies, Giams, and Custards, together with the Best Methods of Potting, Collaring, Preserving, Drying, Candying, Pickling, and making of English Wines. To which are prefixed various Bills of Fare for Dinners and Suppers in every month of the Year; and a copious Index to the whole.[16]

Recipes in cookbooks were inexact, often advising the cook to season "to taste," add "a little," or choose between ingredients according to the tastes of her family or the available ingredients. For example, the following recipe appeared in Mrs. Washington's cookbook, which contained over 550 recipes passed down from "Eleanor Parke Custis's great grandmother":

To Make a Frykecy

Take 2 chicken, or a hare, and kill and flaw them hot, take out theyr intrills and wipe them within, cut then in pieces and break theyr bones with a pestle, yn put halfe a pound of butter into ye frying pan, and fry it till it be browned, yn put in ye chickin and give it a walme or two, yn put in halfe a pinte of faire water well seasoned with pepper and salt and a little [??] put in a handfull of parsley, and time, and onion, shread all small fry all these together till they be enough, and when it is ready to be dished up put into ye pan ye youlks of 5 or 6 eggs, well beaten and mixed wth a little wine vinegar or juice of leamons, stir them well together least it curdle yn dish it up without any more frying.[17]

The use of recipes and recipe books reveals the special qualities of woman's cooking work. Homemaking involved acquiring a cooking repertoire, the skills necessary to process food in various ways to please the family. A good meal provided the family not only with physical nourishment and the collective experience of a meal, but also with culinary pleasure and even variety.[18]

Those who suspect that the content of woman's work is determined by her "weakness and delicacy" relative to men will be surprised by the physical demands of cooking in colonial days. Cooking was a crude process, done over a hearth or in a brick oven with clumsy utensils, and without running water, electricity, or refrigeration. Women cooked with brass or copper kettles often holding fifteen gallons of liquid, and the huge iron pots they used weighed alone up to forty pounds each.[19] Cooking was not a physically easy job, nor was it a delicate one. Women slaughtered animals and dressed the meat. Here is an eighteenth-century recipe for dressing a pig from *The Compleat Housewife: Or Accomplished Gentlewoman's Companion*, a popular treatise on housewifery written in England and republished in the colonies: "Cut off the Head of your Pig; then cut the Body asunder; bone it, and cut two Collars of each side; then lay it in Water to take out the Blood. . . ."[20] Cooking was not, then, woman's work because of its delicacy or physical ease. Rather, it was woman's work because it was part of the immediate sustenance of the family.

The "feeding" job of women often extended back into food processing and, in many instances, into food production itself. Since all of these operations were done in the home for the family by the homemaker, it is difficult to divide them into discrete processes—the woman made and served *meals*. A woman's preparation of meals could include growing vegetables in her kitchen garden, harvesting wild fruits and vegetables, and caring for livestock and poultry. In these cases she was involved in the entire food production process—purchasing or saving seeds, planting, cultivating, weeding, harvesting, milking, processing (drying, salting, pickling, dressing, cheese- and cider-making), cooking, and serving. From its inception, such work was aimed at filling the particular needs of the family.

However, woman's work of feeding the family did not necessarily include all of these. A family forced to rely upon its own food production found its diet reduced to the limited and crude food available on the family farm. Most colonial families had already developed dietary needs that exceeded the household's own product. A large number of the basic cooking ingredients used by women were not produced in the colonies at all and were imported. Capers, walnuts, anchovies, nutmegs, pepper, mace, cloves, cinnamon, ginger, olives, salad oil, almonds, raisins, dried currants, coffee, tea, and cocoa beans were imported from England; lemons, molasses, sugar, sweetmeats, tamarins, citrons, and limes were imported from the Mediterranean and the West Indies.[21] The housewife purchased or bartered for them from the local merchant.

Hence, the particular amount and type of work that a woman did to provide the family with meals varied greatly according to the degree of self-sufficiency forced upon the household. Woman's goal was the filling of family needs, the serving of meals to the family which pleased them. This goal did not necessitate any particular work content. If a woman had to produce the food herself because it was either unavailable or unaffordable, she would. In those times, the lack of development of transportation, of exchange, and of production of food for the market made some degree of home production a necessity for most households, and it was woman's work to undertake or at least supervise this work. However, if both cash and food commodities were available, she often preferred to purchase much of the family's food and employ a trained cook in order to serve more sophisticated and exotic meals.

A homemaker's food production and preparation were not motivated by a desire for income and wealth, but by a desire to help the family save money for capital accumulation—or prevent the family from falling into debt due to household needs. We have looked at the ways in which she provided needed meals to her family, with, if necessary, a minimum of cash expenditure. In some farm households, the homemaker's duties were expanded to include cooking and cleaning for hired hands, who were usually single men without wives to provide for them.[22] Furthermore, homemakers sometimes bartered or sold their surplus product in order to fill family needs. The most common source of such funds were butter and eggs; rural women also developed truck farming, selling the extra produce of their kitchen garden.[23] However, these efforts of homemakers remained subsumed into their overall work of homemaking. Successful marketing of her produce, therefore, did not lead a homemaker to specialize in such activity and invest her earnings in expanded production, as was her husband's way.

The historical development of the division of labor and exchange worked to eliminate productive activity from the homemaker's job of providing the family with meals. The disengagement of the wealthy woman from food production, with the substitution of commodities and servants, foreshadowed this eventual separation of food production from homemaking and its movement into the impersonal sphere of commodity production.

Clothing the Family

A second basic need of the family which homemakers were responsible for seeing filled was the need for clothing and other textile products such as sheets, curtains, and rugs. As with meal preparation, there was great variation in the amount of cloth and clothing production undertaken by homemakers, according to the family's relationship to the market.

The making of clothing, when carried on in and for the home, was women's work. Making clothing from "scratch" was a complex and time-consuming process. Women started with flax, wool, and/or cotton that was homegrown or purchased; when even these were not available, wild nettles, buffalo wool, cattle hair, or animal skins were substituted. Linen thread production involved both men and women. Pulling the flax, rotting it, and braking or swingling it to remove the woody portion were predominantly the work of men and boys. Hatcheling or combing it and spinning it were done by women and girls. Wool yarn production involved women in the following steps: separating and cleaning the fleeces, greasing them thoroughly with rape oil or melted swine grease, carding or combing the wool, rolling it, and finally spinning it—once for knitting, twice for weaving. Cotton yarn production paralleled that of wool except that there was no greasing. After the yarn was spun, it was knit into clothing or woven into cloth. Usually at some point in the process, the material was dyed with homemade or purchased dyes or was bleached in the sun. Wool cloth had to be fulled. Finally, cloth was sewed into clothing for the family.[24]

Such totally self-sufficient production of clothing was much rarer than many romanticized accounts of colonial life suggest. By colonial times, textile production had already begun to be industrialized. In Britain the textile industry was one of the first to begin to leave the self-sufficient stage and become the production of commodities for long-distance trade. Spinning and knitting were done by women in their homes both for income as part of a putting-out system and for the direct use of the family. Weaving in sixteenth- and seventeenth-century Britain was a male craft as well as a home activity through which women filled family needs. Sewing was both a male craft—tailoring—and the home work of most women. In the Britain that spawned the North American colonies, self-sufficient textile production coexisted with these more advanced craft and putting-out forms. Hence, the textile industry transplanted to the colonies was in a transitional stage which included self-sufficient, craft, and putting-out forms of production. The British encouraged the colonial market for cloth by favorable pricing as well as penalties for domestic production for exchange. These policies discouraged the development of a domestic division of labor in cloth production; most cloth marketed in the colonies before the Revolution was imported from Britain. In fact, by 1750, the North American colonies were the leading market for British textiles, especially woolens.

Families had the option of obtaining their clothing through home production or through purchase of the labor of others, either in the form of a finished product such as yarn or cloth (ready-made clothing did not exist then), as custom labor in weaving, dyeing, or tailoring to their particular needs or as part of the home work of a servant or slave. Such labors were not directly substitutable. The home-produced version of cloth, homespun, was crude compared to imported cloth, and home-designed and -sewn clothes could not match the work of a skilled tailor or mantua-maker (dressmaker). Clothing production itself was not a necessary part of women's homemaking work. Not only was the home production of clothing extremely labor intensive, its product was considered inferior to the craft and put-out forms.

Therefore, home textile production was undertaken only when the family was unable to purchase cloth and have it made up. Families with wealth purchased their cloth and had it professionally tailored. Successful southern planter families eschewed home production altogether, as we have seen. However, if cash was scarce or supplies were cut off, homemakers took up home production. Servants or slaves were put to home clothing production, or, in a servantless family, the homemaker stepped in to fill the family's need for clothing with her crude but functional substitute. Some homemakers made extra product for barter or sale.[25] The extent of household textile production varied greatly between families, home sewing and knitting being the most common. But no aspect of clothing production was essential to homemaking.[26]

By colonial times, women's homemade, family-oriented work had already shown itself to be dépassé, important during household or national emergencies but forsaken as soon as possible by family and country. Most colonial households were not self-sufficient in textiles and certainly did not desire to be so. The existence of this household market explains the rapid expansion of the domestic textile industry experienced in North America during Revolutionary and post-Revolutionary times when textile imports were no longer available. This expansion first took the putting-out form, based in home-production by women. But, as production for income, such work was monopolized by husbandless women; it will be discussed in the next chapter.

While wealthy homemakers in the family economy did not produce their own cloth nor sew their families' clothing, they did engage in needlework of another sort. Such women spent hours in fancy and decorative needlework, as well as other decorative arts.[27] How did such "work" fit into homemaking in their case? Among the wealthy, the family's needs for clothing and other objects could be better and more fully filled by the purchase of commodities and of the services of skilled craftsmen and domestics. Yet the wealthy woman, just like all other women, needed to homemake to be a woman; her family needed her to be dedicated to their service. Needlework filled the need of the wealthy woman to fill her time with homemaking, to occupy herself in the service of her family. While an intricate piece of needlework exhibited in a home did not fill a need for clothing, it did decorate the home in a special way, for it expressed the existence, dedication to the family, and special family-centered abilities of the homemaker. As such, it was an artistic, creative outlet appropriate to women as homemakers.

Nursing the Family

In colonial times, medical care was also in the process of being commoditized or professionalized. Medical science was undeveloped, a conglomeration of different "theories" merged with religion and superstition. Prevalent were the conceptions that health was a balance of the four humors; that gold, bezoan (a concretion taken from the intestines of wild goats and other animals), and viper's flesh were universal remedies; that blood-letting was good for the health; that God had placed a metaphorical "signature" on each substance indicating its curative powers; and that witches could use their pacts with the devil to cause illness, death, and sterility. Medical practitioners ranged from university-trained doctors to barbers, bone-setters, midwives and good-wives, and ministers and their wives, who learned through formal or informal apprenticeships, books, and practice.[28]

Homemaking meant keeping the family healthy. While specialized medical practitioners were sought for severe illness or childbirth, homemakers also diagnosed family illnesses and treated them with homemade or store-bought remedies; they also often took responsibility for the health of non-family members of the household, including slaves. Furthermore, in emergencies when a specialist was not available, the homemaker remained responsible for tending the ill. This was part of her care of the physical health of her family and household, similar to her responsibility for the provision of meals.

Woman's healing art was learned as a child in her apprenticeship to her mother or to the household mistress. However, like cooking recipes, home medicines were also written in manuals of housewifery, published and unpublished. *The Compleat Housewife or Accomplished Gentlewoman's Companion*, a popular treatise on housewifery written in England and republished in the colonies, contained, along with "several Hundred of the most approved Receipts in Cookery, Pastry, Confectionary, Preserving, Pickles, Cakes, Creams, Jellies, Made Wines, Cordials":

> a collection of near Two Hundred Family Receipts of Medicines; vis. Drinks, Syrups, Salves, Ointments, and many other Things of sovereign and approved Efficacy in most Distempers, Pains, Aches, Wounds, Sores, & c. *never before made publick in these parts;* fit either for private Families, or such publick-spirited Gentlewomen as would be beneficient to their poor Neighbors [emphasis added].[29]

These recipes were from the homes of women. They were private, "never before made Publick," part of woman's "natural" craft of healing.

Home healing was a blend of medical "knowledge," custom, superstitution, and common sense—just like that practiced by male and female specialists. The superstitious quality of such healing is evident in the following medicines from Smith's book:

> For the Falling-Sickness: Take the After-birth of a Woman, and dry it to Powder, and drink half an Ounce thereof in a glass of White-wine for six mornings together. If the Patient be a Man, it must be the Afterbirth of a Female Child; if a Woman, the contrary.

> For the Cramp: Take of Rosemary leaves and chop them very small, and sew them in fine Linen, and make them into Garters, and wear them Night and Day; lay a Down-pillow on your Legs in the Night.[30]

Mrs. Washington's cookbook, referred to earlier, contains some equally exotic medicines:

> *To make Dr. Smith's Cordiall Powder* Take crabbs claws soe far as they are black in fine powder 3 ounces seed pearle one ounce red corral in fine powder crabbs eyes white amber, hartshorne calcin'd of each an ounce, gallingall angelico roots ye scull of a dead man calcin'd of each halfe an ounce, chocheneale 2 drams, powder all these finely, & make a Jelly of 3 ounces of hartshorne and 2 cast snakes skines, in which make yr powder into balls, & put in, in ye makeing up, of muske 3 grayns ambergreece 6 graynes & saffron halfe a dram, of this powder give 10 or 12 grayns to a man or woman, & 5 to a child.[31]

Many of the recipes included strong doses of alcohol and sugar. Mrs. Washington's "cock water," "excellently good for a consumption," was made from a blooded red cock, set raw in a still with a "pottle of sack" and ground sugar candy, along with assorted herbs, dates, currants, and leaf gold.[32]

The Ultimate Content of Homemaking in the Family Economy

What emerges most forcibly in our study of woman's homemaking work in the family economy is the variety in its concrete content. Due to the prevailing conception of child-rearing, even mothering failed to give much of a core to homemaking. Determined by the positions of their husbands in the economy, the contents of women's homemaking work varied as greatly as that of their husbands' work, and as a function of the latter. Colonial homemakers' lives shared two basic elements. First, they were controlled by the homemakers' husbands—not only lived under their formal authority, but also actually determined by their lives and work choices. So although homemakers exercised initiative and judgment in their work, this individuality was dependent upon that of their husbands. Second, homemakers' lives were lived outside of the public sphere, within the privacy of the home; the home was women's place. As Cotton Mather explained in his popular *Ornaments to the Daughters of Zion:*

> She will not therefore be too much from Home, upon Concerns, that perhaps are to him unaccountable; But if the Angels do enquire, where she is, her husband may reply as once Abraham did, my Wife is in the Tent. . . . She is willing to be painted as the wife of the Ancients were, with a Snail under her Feet. . . . She affects to be an Esther, that is, an hidden one.[33]

The snail metaphor was a popular one for womanhood. William Secker, another colonial minister, expanded upon it in his "Wedding Ring" sermon: "One of the Ancients speaks excellently; She must not be a Field-Wife, like Dinah; nor a Street-Wife, like Thamar; nor a Window-Wife, like Jezebel . . ." He continued: "Phideas when he drew a Woman, painted her fitting under a snail-shell, that she might imitate that little Creature, that goes no further than it can carry its House upon its Head."[34]

The character of woman's homemaking work in colonial times gave to her a clearly secondary status. Not only was her work determined by her husband, it was often simply a crude, home-produced version of men's commodity products. The one part of her work which was clearly unique—childbearing—was reduced to a biological activity. Therefore, despite its centrality to the health of the family economy, it only branded woman as a natural, animal-like being, further justifying her exclusion from the public, masculine spheres and her clear subordination to her husband and to the world of men.

3

Husbandless Women in the Colonial Economy: Women Working for Income

The Problem of the Husbandless Woman

Under the sexual division of labor in the family economy, true womanhood was dependent upon the presence of a husband-provider, for only if she possessed a husband could a woman specialize in private homemaking. Without a husband, a woman could not really be a woman. Yet all women did not have husbands. In spite of the relative lack of women in the colonies, some women were unable to find acceptable husbands and remained single. And all homemakers faced the threat of widowhood or desertion. As Cotton Mather wrote in *Ornaments to the Daughters of Zion:* "The vast number of poor Widows in every Neighborhood, make it very suspicious that our virtuous Mother may at some Time or other taste the sad, sour, tearful Cup of Widowhood."[1]

Such women did not automatically move into the masculine world of exchange but, if possible, tried to stay in the feminine domestic sphere. The family economy was able to absorb many of them in private familial activity. Many single women were able to live with the families of their relatives, acting as "assistant homemakers" for female family members, or homemakers for unmarried male family members, while they waited to be married.

Widowhood forced the homemaker to fend for herself and her children, to take her husband's place as head of the family:

She reckens that she must now be Father as well as Mother to the Orphans with whom she is left entrusted; . . . while her Husband was alive she still acted as a deputy Husband for maintaining all the good works of

> Orders in the House, when he was out of the Way. And now her Husband
> is deceas'd, she thinks that upon the Setting of the Sun, the Moon is to
> govern.[2]

Although colonial law usually specified that a widow receive at least
one-third of her husband's property, her inheritance was rarely sizable and liquid enough to allow her to continue her life as before. In
most cases the widow was forced to seek a source of income. The
most "natural" way to do so was to simply replace the lost husband
through remarriage. Widows made attractive wives, for they often
had more property than single women, as well as children. Anticipating such remarriages, husbands often restricted their wives' inheritance to the period during which they remained widows. It was not
uncommon for a colonial woman to have more than one husband in
her lifetime. A widow could also live in the households of her extended family; many were supported by the earnings of their older
sons, who were often charged by their fathers' wills to support their
mothers.[3]

While the family economy was able to absorb many husbandless
women as new wives or as family-member domestic helpers, there
were still a considerable number of husbandless women forced to
fend for themselves. Some families were unable to continue supporting their single daughters and sent them out on their own. Some
widows could not find husbands or an extended family to live with.[4]
These women were forced to turn their energies toward earning income: they were, as Mather put it, "put upon doing the Works of
Men; may their God help them."[5]

The experiences of these husbandless women in the family economy are the subject of the remainder of this chapter; they fall into
two categories. Most entered their "independent state" with little:
debts, a house, limited cash. These husbandless women had a choice
between two options: to work to retain the independence of their
households through production for income, or to become dependent
members of other households, as domestics. Their strategy was to
turn their homemaking skills toward the earning of income; if they
failed, they were supported by their parishes, or congregated in
towns as paupers. A few women inherited viable family businesses
from their husbands, fathers, or siblings; in this case, their duty of
homemaking, or serving the family, meant taking on the work of

men. We will examine the experiences of these two groups in the next two sections.

When women were forced into the earning of income for themselves and their families, they left the private hidden existence of the home and entered public life. While the ideal woman, the homemaker, was hidden from public record and from history, the woman working for income most often left some public trace of her work. It is hence not an accident that in the following sections we move from the world of journals and personal accounts into the public record and, in particular, into the newspaper advertisements of businesses.

Homemaking for Income

Women forced into independence did not become men. They sought income in a feminine way, and sought feminine ways to earn income. They were not interested in or qualified for man's work. Rather, they tried to find work similar to woman's lifework of homemaking: they undertook homemaking for income, homemaking work for other families. As we have seen, wealthy homemakers used their husbands' wealth to enlist the energies of other women in their homemaking work (as well as to purchase commodities); in other words, husbandless homemakers and poor, unmarried women were put to doing women's work of homemaking for affluent women in exchange for the income or subsistence they needed. Most often this took the form of domestic work, homemaking in the home of the employer. A few enterprising women were able to specialize in the production of particular commodities to sell to homemakers and hence could retain their independent family lives as petty commodity producers. Still another group of women, comprised predominantly of homemakers with young children, remained in their homes and exercised their homemaking skills for a merchant as part of the putting-out system. We will examine these ways in which women earned income in the following sections, understanding them as different ways in which impoverished women sought to turn their homemaking training toward the earning of income. This will show us why domestic work, tavern-keeping, teaching, cooking, nursing, midwifery, textile production, cleaning, and putting-out were, in the family economy, all instances of women's work.

LIVE-IN DOMESTIC SERVICE

Through the end of the nineteenth century, domestic work was the most common way in which women worked for income. Domestic work was work in and for the home, done by a woman who was not a family member. Hence, it was at the same time both woman's ultimate work—work of filling the needs of others, of a family—and the polar opposite of woman's work—being work not for a woman's own family but for strangers, work which most often denied a woman a family of her own and a life as a homemaker.

The content of domestic work directly reflected that of women's work of homemaking. In the family economy, domestic work was a general type of employment; the domestic helped a homemaker with her homemaking work, including child-rearing as well as production. Occasionally, she actually acted as a substitute wife/mother for a bachelor or widower; here is an advertisement for such a substitute wife/mother, placed in 1780 in the *Pennsylvania Packet:*

> Wanted at a Seat about half a day's journey from Philadelphia on which are good improvements and domestics, A single Woman of unsullied Reputation, an affable, cheerful, active and amiable Disposition; cleanly, industrious, perfectly qualified to direct and manage female concerns of country business, as raising small stock, dairying, marketing, combing, carding, spinning, knitting, sewing, pickling, preserving, etc., and occasionally to instruct two young Ladies in those Branches of Oeconomy, who, with their father, compose the Family. Such a person will be treated with respect and esteem, and meet with every encouragement due to such a character.[6]

Domestic work fit into many colonial women's lives as a training ground for or apprenticeship to housewifery. As we have discussed, it was common in colonial times for children and adolescents to learn their trades as apprentices bound to skilled adults from other families, living in the households of their masters. The boy's apprenticeship took the form of a specific trade, which he would learn in a seven-year period and then practice on his own as an adult. A girl's apprenticeship also prepared her for adulthood, but her future as a homemaker made her training the broad unspecialized practice of housewifery. In a good apprenticeship, she would learn cooking. cleaning, knitting, spinning, sewing, child-care, "healing arts," and perhaps how to read. One such contract, signed in 1702, apprenticed a daughter for seven years, specifying tht she "shall be taught to read English with Such Other Needle

worke and Other matters fitting for a good housewife of her ability."[7]
Hence, domestic work fit logically into girlhood as training for the
future calling of wife, mother, and homemaker. Of course, a girl
could learn housewifery in her own home from her mother without
such an apprenticeship. Apparently, however, domestic apprenticeships were not restricted to the children of poor families who could
not afford to keep them; even the famous Sewall family bound out
one of its girls.[8]

In colonial times, much of domestic work was performed by women
as indentured servants who were bound out to families, like male
apprentices, for a limited period of time. Indenture was a common
form of laboring in the family economy, where, most often, one labored for another as a servant, as a subordinate and second-class family
member, rather than as a wage-earner and property-owner with one's
own family life. Generally the laborer sold him- or herself for a period
of years in exchange for passage to the colonies, or for a debt, or in
punishment for a criminal sentence in Britain. A few such servants
were kidnapped against their will. At the end of the period of indenture, or upon successful escape, the servant became free to follow his
or her own trade—the woman to marry, the man to sell his labor for a
wage, practice a craft, or farm his own land. The slave, on the other
hand, was never freed and was hence in an entirely different category; for this reason, we will put off the study of women's domestic
work under slavery until Chapter 4.

Female indentured servants were purchased to do women's work,
and women's work in those times was "housewifery." John Hammond
described the work of indentured white women in the South in "Leah
and Rachel":

> The Women are not [as is reported] put into the ground to worke, but
> occupie such domestique imployments and housewifery as in England,
> that is dressing victuals, righting up the house, milking, imployed about
> dayries, washing, sowing, etc. and both men and women have times of
> recreation, as much or more than in any part of the world besides; yet som
> wenches that are nasty, beastly and not fit to be so imployed are put into
> the ground, for reason tells us, they must not at charge be transported,
> and then maintained for nothing, but those that prove so awkward are
> rather burthensome then servants desirable or usefull.[9]

Indentured service was certainly hard and thankless work for both
sexes. As William Eddis wrote in one of his letters, "there are doubt-

less many exceptions to this observation, yet, generally speaking, they groan beneath a worse than Egyptian bondage."[10] Because of bad working conditions, many indentured servants tried to escape, as evidenced by the many advertisements in newspapers offering rewards for runaways. Yet most indentured servants chose their fates, seeing indenture as a means to bettering their lives. Evidence is hard to come by as to the origins and motives of such free-willers, but we do know that many of them ended up as upstanding and successful citizens or wives. For men, there were high wages and access to land when they finished their service; for women, a good chance of upward mobility through the "marriage market." Domestic work was, in this case as in that of an apprenticeship, a training ground and road to success as a wife. In 1666, Carolina advertised the potential of the colonies for women in the following way: "If any maid or single woman have a desire to go over, they will think themselves in the golden age, when men paid a dowry for their wives; for if they be but civil, and under fifty years of age, some honest man or other will purchase them for their wives."[11] Bullock mentioned that "no maid whom he had brought over failed to find a husband in the course of the first three months after she had entered into his service."[12] The success of one such indentured women was described in "The Sot-Weed Factor" by a jealous peer:

> D-m you says one, tho' now so brave,
> I knew you late a Four-Years Slave;
> What if for a Planter's Wife you go
> Nature designed you for the Hoe.[13]

Thus the familial qualities of domestic work occasionally led the domestic to marry into the family of her employer.

Some women apparently came over to escape unhappy family situations in Britain. In "The Sot-Weed Factor" one such lady, working as a chambermaid in Maryland, describes her past:

> In better Times, e'er to this Land,
> I was unhappily Trappann'd;
> Perchance as well I did appear,
> As any Lord or Lady here . . .
> Kidnap'd and Fool'd, I hither fled,
> To shun a hated Nuptial Bed.[14]

Here the author put the following footnote: "These are the general Excuses made by English Women, which are sold, or sell themselves to Mary-land." The niece of Daniel Defoe ran away from England at the age of eighteen to escape an unhappy marriage, selling herself as a redemptioner. She was purchased by a family in Maryland and ended up marrying her employer's son.[15]

While live-in domestic work was acceptable and even desirable work for a young unmarried woman, as a permanent occupation it denied a woman her major goal in life, homemaking for a family of her own. Positions for married couples in domestic service were rare, as were positions where children were accepted. The domestic's twenty-four-hour-a-day job made her part of another's family, leaving no space for her own family life. Yet having her own family and caring for them were the essence of womanhood. An adult woman who worked as a domestic was a failed woman—a woman who had been unable to find a suitable husband, a married woman who had lost her husband and was childless, or a widow whose children were grown or farmed out to other families. Domestic work offered such women a feminine means to stay alive—room and board and perhaps a pittance of a wage—but at the same time prevented them from experiencing true womanhood in families of their own.

If domestic work was a respectable training ground for young women, it was not the only way a woman could earn income. Furthermore, it was not an option for the husbandless homemaker who wished to keep her children and retain her own family life. Colonial women found other ways to use their homemaking experience to eke out livings for themselves and their families.

SELF-EMPLOYED WOMEN

Widows whose husbands' deaths had left them with houses often turned their homes and homemaking into self-supporting businesses by opening them up to the temporarily homeless in exchange for money. These taverns were used primarily to house travelers, mostly men in those times, but they also became centers for public meetings, auctions, and business transactions. Some inn-keepers established more community-oriented businesses such as restaurants and coffee houses. Here is an advertisement run in the *Providence Gazette* by one enterprising woman:

> For the Convenient Reception and Entertainment of Gentlemen and Ladies, whenever they are disposed to recreate themselves by an Excursion into the Country, whether at Morning or Evening; on Monday next will be open'd by Abigail Williams, At the Sign of the White Horse, (the House of Jeremiah Williams, Cranston) *The Rural Tea and Coffee House* Very pleasantly situated about three miles from the Town of Providence, on one of the most delightful Roads in New England.
>
> Those who are pleased to favour her with their Company may depend on the best of Entertainment, and the civilest Usage, as it will be her Constant Endeavour to deserve a continuance of their Favour.
>
> N.B. Travellers may be genteely accommodated at the same Place.[16]

Tavern-keeping allowed a widow to keep her children and to use the house she inherited to earn income by homemaking for strangers.

A related money-making venture for women was boarding children or holding a "dame school" in her home. Here a widow or spinster was able to receive money for her traditional work of child-rearing and early child education. A woman's motherly/wifely virtues disposed her to paid work as an educator of the young. Widowed or single women were often the teachers at the elementary level for both sexes in both rural and town schools. Often their homes doubled as the school. At more advanced levels, they taught young women reading, writing, and housewifery in their homes, both as boarding and day students. Early American newspapers are full of advertisements offering such services. Here is one example from *The New York Gazette*, June 22, 1747:

> *Sarah Hay* takes this method to inform the public that she proposes to open a Boarding School, the first of May next, in the house where she formerly lived, in Smith Street. She undertakes to teach young Ladies reading English with the greatest correctness and propriety, both prose and verse; plain work, Dresden, catgut and all kinds of collar'd work, on canvas and camllet; all in the neatest manner and newest taste. She instructs them in the strictest principles of religion and morality and in the most polite behaviour, and takes the utmost care to instruct them in a perfect knowledge of the subjects they read, (as far as their capacity can take) and provides the principle part of the books proper for their improvements at her own expense. She also takes day scholars, which will have the same improvement as the boarders. If any that board their children chuse they should learn the French language, she will have a master attend at her house.[17]

Sarah Hay had special skills; most colonial women did not know how to read and write well enough to teach it. In that case, they had little to offer that could distinguish their "boarding school" from an apprenticeship as a domestic, for which a girl's parents did not have to pay. However, women with special decorative and needlework skills could find a market for them among the rich town women and their daughters:

> This may inform young Gentlewomen in Town and Country, that early in the Spring Mrs. Hiller designs to open a Boarding School at the house where she lives, in Fish-Street, at the North End of Boston, next Door to Dr. Clark's, where they may be taught Wax-Work, Transparent and Filligree Painting upon Glass, Japanning, Quill Work, Feather-Work and Embroidering with Gold and Silver, and several other sorts of Work not here enumerated, and may be supplied with Patterns and all sorts of Drawing, and Materials for their Work.[18]

Women faced with the necessity of earning income to support themselves and their families found other ways of turning their home-making skills into money income. We have discussed woman's work as food producer, processor, and cook for her family; a perusal of colonial advertisements reveals examples of women who used these skills to earn income. One woman, "Sarah Sell, Muffin-Maker," sold hot muffins from her home, which she advertised in the town newspaper.[19] Another advertised a broad range of homemade dishes:

> Jane Moorland, from London, . . . begs Leave to inform the Public, that she prepares and sells Sausages, Black and White Puddings, Tripes and Cowheels, likewise pickled Sheeps Tongues; which she sells ready boiled, or green, out of the Pickle. Whoever is pleased to favour her with their custom may depend on all the above Articles being done from the best Recepes, and in the nicest Manner.[20]

The above women probably lived, worked, and sold in their shops, something restricted to town women. Women without such easy access to a market, especially rural women, sold their products to merchants. One such enterprising woman advertised her product of pickled sturgeon as "different to any that has been put up in these parts," listing the shops of the merchants where it could be purchased.[21] Such professional cooking was a likely craft for women; it was an extension of their traditional training, it did not demand a large capital outlay, and it could be practiced within the confines of their homes. Nevertheless, since they involved commodity production, the great majority of such food-processing enterprises were run by men.

Another type of homemaking for income open to needy and enterprising women was nursing and midwifery. As we have said, nursing was an integral part of the homemaker's caring duties. Women were seen then as having magical natural powers; they also inherited from their mothers a folk knowledge of curative herbs and other medicines. Some women turned this talent into a business. One of the most advertised remedies in colonial papers was "Mary Bannister's Drops of Spirit of Venice."[22] Another woman's advertisement promised to cure the "itch" with a smell:

> Hanna Chapman makes and Sells a Smell in Mixture, that will cure the Itch or any other breaking out, by the smell of it. Enquire for me at the Sign of the Stayes at the Head of Seven-Star Lane.[23]

Nurse Tucker advertised an ointment promising to cure:

> . . . the Piles, Rheumatism, strains, all kinds of Pains, Ring-worm, Moths, Carbuncles, Sun-burning, Freckles, and chopping of the Skin; and Women that are likely to have sore Breasts, if they apply in Time, it will certainly be of great Service to them.[24]

Such cure-alls, popular in those days, were commonly produced and sold by women. We also detect, in other women's advertisements for beauty potions, the beginnings of the cosmetic industry. Mrs. Edwards made and sold, at home, a wonder "Beautifying Wash" which she advertised as follows:

> . . . it makes the Skin soft, smooth and plump, it likewise takes away Redness, Freckles, Sun-burnings, or Pimples, and cures Postures, Itchings, Ring-Worms, Tetters, Scurf, Morphew, and other like Deformities of the Face and Skin, (Intirely free from any Corroding Qualities) and brings to an exquisite Beauty. . . . [25]

A woman who needed to make a living could also turn her experience of childbirth into a midwife profession. Few midwives had had any formal training. Some women developed general medical practices.[26] They followed in the European tradition of women healers, often pagan, whose empirical healing methods were often more successful than those of the trained male doctors who used Christian methods. Women healers had been persecuted as witches in Europe from the fourteenth through the seventeenth centuries—their success being attributed to a pact with the devil. Such persecution continued, at a much reduced level, in the colonies.[27] Since the practice of medicine required special skills, considerable bravery, and a willingness to travel, it was suitable for only a few exceptional women. We find mention of one such woman in the church records of Dorcester, Massachusetts:

> 1705, Feb. 6th. Old widow Wiat died, having arrived at the great age of 94 years. She had assisted as midwife at the birth of upwards of one thousand and one hundred children.[28]

Given that women had engaged in self-sufficient textile production in the home, it is not surprising that they attempted textile production for the market when they were forced to replace their husbands. Needlework, dressmaking, and hat-making were done by colonial women as custom crafts. In rural areas, many women seamstresses worked as domestics in the homes of their employers, and some women were itinerant seamstresses. Rural mothers who wished to keep their children at home had no such option, however, so most of them turned to putting-out, which we will describe below. In the towns, some women had their own businesses, often combining custom needlework and dressmaking with the teaching of these skills. One woman's diversified home business even included the teaching of hair-cutting:

> Lately come from London, Mrs. E. Atkinson, who designs the making of Mantos and Riding dresses after the newest fashion, the taking in of all sorts of Millinary Work, teaching Young Ladies all sorts of Works, and dressing of Heads and cutting of Hair. Now living with Mrs. Edward Oakes's in Cornhill Street, Boston, near the Brick Meeting House.[29]

It is interesting that most of the needleworkers and dressmakers who advertised in town papers claimed to be "from London"; in those times, fashions were copied from the mother country, and British craftspersons were the most popular.

Women in cities without special fashion skills offered to do washing, mending, and reknitting—at extremely low prices. They were really domestic workers who were able (or forced) to retain homes of their own. The following advertisement from *The New York Journal and Weekly Register*, 1786, paints the plight of a widow with children offering to sell her homemaking energies:

> Washing done in the best Manner, Also Mending, and all kinds of Sewing Work, by the Widow, Keziah Parker. Mrs. Parker has particular Recommendations, from Persons of Character, as an honest, industrious woman, and as she has no other means of getting an honest livelihood for herself and family, begs Employment in this Line from such Ladies & Gentlemen as wish to have their work done reasonably and expeditiously, by the dozen or single piece.[30]

PUTTING-OUT WORK

The chances for a single, widowed, or deserted woman to successfully start up her own business as a petty commodity producer were slight. Few women had specialized skills that could differentiate them from domestics and bring them an independent craft status. A woman forced into supporting herself most commonly lived in another's home as a domestic, governess, seamstress, nurse (or new wife). If not, she probably worked in her own home, not as a craft producer with her own clientele, but as a piece worker for a merchant. As we saw in Chapters 1 and 2, the putting-out manufactory system developed alongside of and intertwined with the craft/petty producer system, as a higher stage of the division of labor. Its development, as well as that of most domestic crafts, had been limited in the North American colonies by the competition of cheaper and more sophisticated British products and by colonial policies restricting such manufacture. However, the struggle for political independence necessitated the establishment of a domestic system of production to fill the demand of households for the previously imported manufactures, especially textiles. The reintroduction of self-sufficient textile production into homes was encouraged along with commodity production using a putting-out system. Although the former caught on briefly as a patriotic fad, it was rapidly replaced by a burgeoning domestic putting-out system and the beginnings of factory production.

Putting-out textile production varied in sophistication from a rural merchant who bartered his wares in return for the spinning, knitting, or weaving of country women, to a city "manufactory" employing as many as 1,200 women and children. The following advertisement describes a putting-out spinning company centered in Philadelphia which offered:

> . . . to employ every good spinner that can apply, however remote from the factory, and, as many women in the country may supply themselves with the materials there and may have leisure to spin in considerable quantities, they are hereby informed that ready money will be given at the factory, up Market Street, for any parcel, either great or small, of hemp, flax, or woolen yarn. The managers return their thanks to all those industrious women who are now employed in spinning for the factory.[31]

The putting-out system of production was particularly suited to husbandless women and their children who were in dire need of cash income yet lacked the capital and entrepreneurial abilities necessary to establish businesses of their own. In fact, many of the first manufactories (putting-out companies) were set up with the combined purposes of providing charity for such poor women and their children, promoting profit-making industry, and freeing the colonies from their dependence on imports. These poorhouse/spinning "schools"/business ventures received government support as well as charitable donations for their original capital outlay and then appealed to the public conscience to sell their finished products. The "Society for Promoting Arts" is an example of such an institution. It placed the following report-advertisement in *The New York Gazette or the Weekly Post-Boy* in 1767:

> *Society for Promoting Arts.*—Whereas it has been found, that the Society for promoting Arts, & c. has answered great and valuable purposes, particularly in the Encouragement of raising Flax and manufactoring Linnen. And besides what has been done by them for that laudable Purpose, there was some Time since, put into the Hands of those Gentlemen and Trustees, the sum of Six Hundred Pounds, to encourage the Linnen Manufactory in this City, which Sum they put into the Hands of Mr. Obediah Wells, to employ Weavers and Spinners; which Trust, they believe, he has honestly and faithfully performed, by employing above Three Hundred poor and necessitous Persons for 18 Months past in this City, in the above Business. As the said Trustees have at present, to the Value of 600 pounds, in Linnens manufactured in this City and Country, to dispose of, which while lying on Hand, disables them from farther prosecuting the benevolent Purposes; they intend therefore to send them about the City, to be sold and distributed, hoping that the good and charitable Inhabitants will purchase them; by this Means, the Linnen Manufactory may again be

carried on, the publick Interest greatly promoted, many penurious Persons saved from Beggary, and great Expence to the Corporation, by relieving Numbers of distressed Women, now in the Poor-House. And the Publick may be assured, that the said Linnens have been manufactured on as low Terms as possible, and are now ordered to be sold with-out any Advance, with the Price of the Cost per Yard, marked on each Piece.[32]

The putting-out system was a major employer of women whose family situations had forced them to find ways to earn cash; hence, while it employed some married women, its major source of labor was single and widowed women. Until the establishment of spinning mills in the late eighteenth century, spinning was the most common put-out activity. Due to the prevalence of husbandless women in spinning, the word spinster, originally appended to a woman's name to denote her occupation, came to mean an unmarried woman.[33]

The development of the division of labor brought other forms of production into a putting-out system in their transition from craft to factory production. Card-making was one such activity: women and their children set the teeth in textile cards for piece rate. The Boston card factory had machinery that cut the leather and cut and bent the teeth; these cards were then put-out to over one thousand women and children who lived in the area.[34] Putting-out production also employed women and children in knitting, sewing, button-making, weaving, and straw bonnet manufacture. With its development as an industry, boot and shoe production was subdivided, and one of its stages—the stitching and binding of the "uppers," a process that had previously been a part of men's craft work—was put-out to women and children in homes.[35]

The driving force behind the development of the putting-out system was capital expansion and not charity. However, the putting-out system did, as advertised, provide many women, impoverished because of the lack of a supportive husband, with the means to support themselves and their families. Although its content changed with the movement of certain stages of production into factories, it continued as a major employer of such women well through the nineteenth century. The seamstresses of the nineteenth century replaced the spinsters of the eighteenth.

A woman with a successful husband was able to care for her family in woman's way, in the home. The lack of a husband and his income forced a woman to orient her work toward the production for cash. In most cases, such a woman did "women's work" for income, work monopolized by women. She became part of a pool of poor women who furnished cheap domestic or putting-out labor, or if she was lucky and ingenious, took up production on her own of homemaking-like goods or services for the market. However, the lack of a husband occasionally put a woman into a position of recognized economic importance in the area of business and "men's work." In the next section, we will analyze this puzzling phenomenon of women doing men's work as widows and as unmarried women.

Women Doing Men's Work

In the colonial economy, the family ownership of business occasionally demanded that a woman, as a family member, enter into men's work, work clearly monopolized by men. Most businesses within the family economy were family businesses owned and run by an individual property owner. Few had an impersonal, corporate status. Usually, most or all of their workers were members of the owner's family. In the cities, families were able to specialize in their business, purchasing their other necessities on the market. In such situtations, a women as a wife and mother (or as a daughter) might be asked to help the men with their work in production or retail. Although her work was oriented toward the market, it was done privately within the family for her husband (or father). The woman worked as a wife, not a wage-earner or petty producer. The husband/father supervised the family business and was its public representative.

The loss of its father/head of household, or his inability to run the family business, placed a family in crisis. Normally, a father developed the family property, and passed it down to his children; if a father died before his sons were able to take the helm, the latters' future property and position, and that of the family, were placed in jeopardy. It was only proper for a homemaker, devoted to the well-being of her family, to step in and take over (or if she was indisposed, an older daughter). She became a "businessman" in the public arena; running the family business became part of her work until a son or male relative could take over. If a woman tried to do men's work for her own self-advancement, she would be shamed and ostracized; but if she undertook the work of men because her family's needs dictated it, her actions were not only condoned, but praised.

Examples of such inheritance of a husband's business are plentiful. Historians, most notably Elisabeth Dexter, have poured over colonial documents to find instances of colonial women in business.[36] Newspaper advertisements are the primary source of information although, unfortunately, they rarely indicate the marital status of the entrepreneur or the origins of her business. ("Mrs." was used for married, widowed, and single women!) However, a striking number of the advertisements were made by women who, as widows, were publicizing their intentions to continue their late husbands' businesses.

Women as widows took over in all areas of commodity production. The following advertisement for a tailoring firm appeared in *The Pennsylvania Gazette* in 1763:

> Mary Cannan, widow of Charles Cannan, late from Manchester, Taylor, deceased, . . . proposes to carry on the business of her late Husband with some sober qualified workmen they brought from England with them, and will esteem it a singular Favour if such, who were so kind to encourage her husband by their Employ in the first setting up in this City, would continue their custom, and will be obliged to any others to favour her with their Employ, as she hopes to be enabled to support herself and Family, and all Endeavors will be used to render her Employers Satisfaction.[37]

Mary Crathorn decided to continue her husband's business of chocolate and mustard production at his mustard and chocolate works "which her late husband went to considerable expence in the erecting, and purchasing out Benjamin Jackson's part."[38] Her advertisement in *The Pennsylvania Gazette* in 1768 began as follows:

> *Mary Crathorn*, Begs leave to inform the public (and particularly those who were her late husband's customers) that she has removed from the house she lately occupied in Laetitia Court, to the house lately occupied by Mrs. Aris, at the corner of the said court, in Market-street, where she continues to sell by wholesale and retail.[39]

In addition to the above, Dexter found the following examples of widows who continued the businesses of their late husbands: Ann Page, turner; Elizabeth Franklin, Crown Soap maker; Margaret Pascal, cutler; Elizabeth Russell, coachmaker; Sarah Jewell, ropemaker; Mary Salmon, horse-shoeing; Sarah Lancaster, "sive weaver"; Hannah Beales, netmaking (her father's business); Martha Turnstall Smith, whaler.[40] In some of these cases, the widow actually worked in production of a commodity; in most, she managed the business. Although such examples have been found in virtually all lines of petty commodity production, such areas were still considered "men's work" and were overwhelmingly populated by men. Women, then, entered them only as stand-ins for male family members.

Women often advertised as merchants, and there are examples of women operating dry goods stores, grocery stores, household good stores, drug stores, hardware stores, and bookstores. Most of these women merchants appear to have been widows or women whose husbands were absent. Below is part of a letter, sent by the widows of New York to their local newspaper in 1773, demanding their rights as property-owners and citizens. It suggests that many of the New York widows supported themselves through shopkeeping:

Mr. Zenger,

We, the widdows of this city, have had a Meeting, and as our case is something Deplorable, we beg you will give it Place in your Weekly Journal, that we may be Relieved, it is as follows.

We are House keepers, Pay our Taxes, carry on Trade, and most of us are she Merchants. . . . [41]

There is no evidence that these widows had themselves established these businesses. Rather, they had inherited family businesses or, at least, the family capital to start one. Some of these were modest stores, some important firms. Widows Grant, Provost, and De Vries each took over large merchant companies from their late husbands which involved them in intercontinental travels and business deals.[42]

Elisabeth Dexter found that women comprised 9.5% of the total number of merchants who advertised during the first half of 1773 in the *Boston Evening Post*. She pointed out that this was significantly higher than the 4.3% figure found in a Census Bureau study of merchants and dealers in 1900.[43] The decline in the prevalence of women shopkeepers was the inevitable product of the decline of the family business which accompanied the development of capitalism.

Women in the family economy occasionally became printers and newspaper publishers. Dexter described the careers of ten women publishers. All of them took on family businesses—eight for their deceased husbands, one for her brother, another one for her son.[44] One of them, Mrs. Green, printed the following in her family's *Annapolis Gazette* along with the notice of her husband's death:

I presume to address you for your contenance to myself and numerous Family, left, without your Favour, almost destitute of Support by the Decease of my Husband, who long, and I have the Satisfaction to say, faithfully served you in the Business of Provincial Printer; and, I flatter myself, that with your kind Indulgence and Encouragement, Myself and Son will be enabled to continue it on the same Footing.[45]

Previously acquainted with the business as family members, these women very capably continued publishing their newspapers.

Women in the family economy even entered the male preserve of agriculture—both as farmers and plantation owners and as managers. The majority of family enterprises in the colonial economy were family farms. We have pointed out the general exclusion, at that time, of white women from agriculture, an exclusion not practiced in England where the wives of wage-workers did seasonal agriculture work in harvesting or weeding. We have suggested that this definition of agriculture as a male domain in North America stemmed from its entrepreneurial character. Except in some very early and short-lived instances (Salem, Pennsylvania),[46] women colonists were unable to acquire land as independent persons.

However, the same entrepreneurial character of early American agriculture occasionally brought women into the male domain of farming. Women inherited responsibilities for the family farm as widows, daughters, or wives whose husbands were absent. In such special cases, it was the woman's duty to provide for the family and run its business until some more appropriate male family member was able to take over—a son, a nephew, or a new husband. Up to 1900, 6% of farmers were women, 73.4% of these widows.[47] Most of the farms such women worked were modest affairs, and these women's accomplishments earned them neither fame nor notoriety. However, in the southern, slave colonies, where farms were expanded into lucrative plantations, a few colonial women were brought into prominence as plantation owners and managers.

The life of the famous Eliza Lucas Pinckney provides us with a striking illustration of the circumstances that could create a woman agriculturalist in the family economy. Her life is well documented, for she copied all her letters into her letter book before sending them. George Lucas, Eliza's father, was a British army officer. He purchased a plantation in South Carolina in the 1730s and moved there in 1737 or 1738 with his wife and daughters. His plans to become a gentleman farmer were dashed when the war with Spain was renewed. He was forced to rejoin his army in Antigua, where he became Royal Governor. Since his wife was in bad health and he had no sons, Mr. Lucas left the family plantation in the hands of his eldest daughter, sixteen-year-old Eliza Lucas.[48]

Eliza Lucas became the manager of the family plantations, then, as a dutiful daughter in service and obedience to her father under the conditions of a family emergency. She accepted this unusual fate as "unavoidable" given the circumstances, as she explained in the following letter:

> . . . I have a little library well furnished . . . in wch I spend part of my time. My Musick and the Garden wch I am very fond of take up the rest that is not imployed in business, of wch my father has left me a pretty good share, and indeed 'twas unavoidable, as my Mama's bad state of health prevents her going thro' any fatigue.
>
> I have the business of 3 plantations to transact, wch requires much writing and more business and fatigue of other sorts than you can imagine, but least you should imagine it too burthensom to a girl at my early time of life, give me leave to assure you I think myself happy that I can be useful to so good a father.[49]

Eliza Lucas aggressively pursued the affairs of the plantations, experimenting in search of lucrative staple crops. By 1742, she had fixed upon indigo and began plantings of it with the help of an overseer sent from the West Indies by her father. By 1744, she had succeeded with her indigo business. Other planters followed her lead, and indigo became widespread in the South as a cash crop.

Yet Eliza Lucas was a female, and, as all "normal" females, sought womanhood and marriage as her goal. She chose and married well—a forty-five-year-old prominent and wealthy lawyer and planter, Colonel Pinckney. Upon her marriage, Eliza's "business" changed from entrepreneurship to wife and motherhood—that is, pleasing Colonel Pinckney. As she wrote to her father, apparently in response to a letter reminding her of woman's place:

> I am greatly obliged to you for your very good advice in my present happy relation. I think it entirely reasonable and 'tis with great truth that I assure you 'tis not more my duty than my inclination to follow it; for making it the business of my life to please a man of Mr. Pinckney's merrit even in triffles, I esteem a pleasing task; and I am well asured the acting

out of my proper province and invading his, would be an inexcusable breach of prudence; as his superior understanding, (without any other consideration,) would point to him to dictate and leave me nothing but the easy task of obeying.[50]

Indeed, she had spent her earlier life serving her father; now she was simply switching masters. Although Eliza, as Mrs. Pinckney, continued to interest herself in her father's plantations, Mr. Lucas' business letters were soon addressed to Colonel Pinckney. Mrs. Pinckney became involved in planting exotic foreign fruit trees in the family garden—for the family, not for export—and soon became a mother.

At the age of thirty-six, with three children, Mrs. Pinckney became a widow, and the responsibility for the family again fell upon her. As willed by Colonel Pinckney, her two sons were left in England to obtain the "proper schooling." Mrs. Pinckney took up the business of the family plantation in America to support them. She wrote to her mother, in her grief, of her dedication to the service of her children now that their father was dead:

> Grant Great God that I may spend my whole future life in their Service and show my affection and gratitude to their dear Father by my care of those precious remains of him, the pledges of the sincerest and tenderest affection that ever was upon earth.[51]

As a widow she reentered the business of plantation manager, this time for her late husband and children. Avoiding remarriage, she remained an active entrepreneur until her death in 1793. We see, in the example of her life, how entering the masculine sphere of agriculture was, in her situation, entirely consistent with her duties as a woman. Eliza Lucas was exceptionally gifted in the womanly art of molding her life to the needs of her family—even when it involved acting as a man in business. Pinckney is but one, famous example of the many women who, as daughters or widows, inherited land which they eventually passed on to their new husbands or children—often after an active period as an entrepreneur. The existence of such women did not, however, dispel the colonial conception of agriculture as men's work.

Thus we see that within the family economy women were, under special family circumstances, recruited into men's work—work that involved the producer/retailer/and/or manager in a business whose goal was the accumulation of wealth. This work life involved a woman in a public existence as a property owner. However, such a woman never became the same as a man, nor was she seen as a man: her primary concern remained the well-being of her family. She did not seek self-advancement in a worldly career, but rather entered and left the masculine sphere as dictated by the needs of her family. Hence, the manly activities of these women did not undermine the sexual division of labor and did not challenge the category of "men's work." Rather, they represented a particular, if somewhat contradictory, expression of the sexual division of labor. Society understood and accepted such a woman as Mr. X's widow or daughter. Her business advertisements appealed to the public's compassion for her unusual and difficult straits.

However, although a family crisis might warrant and even demand a woman's participation in public economic life, she was still denied the political rights of citizenship. The letter quoted above from widow shopkeepers to "Mr. Zenger" included a demand by those women for political rights on the basis of their existences as property owners:

> We, the widdows of this city, have had a Meeting, and as our case is something Deplorable, we beg you will give it Place in your Weekly Journal, that we may be Relieved, it is as follows.
>
> We are House keepers, Pay our Taxes, carry on Trade, and most of us are she Merchants, and as we in some measure contribute to the Support of Government, we ought to be Intituled to some of the Sweets of it; but we find ourselves entirely neglected, while the Husbands that live in our Neighborhood are daily invited to Dine at Court; we have the Vanity to think we can be full as Entertaining, and make as brave a Defence in Case of an Invasion and perhaps not turn Taile so soon as some of them. . . . [52]

These women demanded the rights and responsibilities of citizens which logically followed, as they argued, from their existences as property owners and taxpayers. And it would seem that they had a point. However, only an extreme minority of women engaged in such work and could claim such rights. Perhaps this is the reason they were not recognized.

We have examined above how, in the family economy, women whose families had wealth and position were sometimes called upon to enter into men's work. Here their existence as members of important families elevated them out of womanhood as a private, home-oriented, and disenfranchised existence, conferring upon them (and demanding from them) a kind of temporary manhood. Such occurrences have been even more common in previous aristocratic societies where "blood" and family ties elevated one section of society above all of the rest as an aristocracy. Hence, the daughter of a king would be called upon to rule a country, the ultimate masculine activity, if no male family member was available.

The remnants of aristocratic privilege in colonial America served as a basis upon which some women demanded recognition in the masculine spheres of the economy and polity *in their own right,* rather than as representatives of their husbands. This was a curious example of aristocratic "blood" privilege superseding the sexual division of labor. And we have in history an example of such an occurrence in the famous person of Mistress Brent.

Mistress Brent was one of the first colonists of Maryland. From a prominent and wealthy English family, she arrived in 1638 and established a plantation *of her own.* In 1647, Governor Leonard Calvert appointed her as his sole executor upon his death. She took over his role of attorney for his brother, Lord Baltimore. In this capacity, she once prevented a rebellion of Maryland's army. The army threatened mutiny if they did not receive the pay promised them by the deceased governor. Margaret Brent seized the promised collateral—in the form of cattle—from Calvert's brother, Lord Baltimore, paid the soldiers, and quelled the revolt. This unwomanly and heroic action earned her praise from the Maryland Assembly.[53]

Apparently Mistress Brent chose to remain alone and independent, for we know she had at least one eligible and devoted suitor; at the age of fifty-five, she inherited the estate of a Maryland gentleman, a disappointed but loyal admirer to the end.[54] Mistress Brent, then, forcefully rejected the female destiny of womanhood and, on the basis of her family background, demanded recognition as an important individual. On the basis of this recognition, she worked and achieved prominence in the masculine world.

She could go only so far, however: she was denied rights and recognition as a citizen because she was a female. As a prominent public figure and landowner, Mistress Brent demanded a vote in the Assembly in 1648. This demand for rights was recorded in the Maryland archives as follows (N.B.—"Mrs" did not mean "married" here):

Came Mrs Margaret Brent and requested to have vote in the House for herself and voyce allsoe, for that on the last Court 3rd January it was ordered that the said Mrs Brent was to be looked upon and received as his

Ldp's Attorney. The Governor deny'd that the s'd Mrs Brent should have any vote in the house. And the s'd Mrs Brent protested against all proceedings in this present Assembly unlesse she may be present and have vote as afores'd.[55]

This chapter has examined the work of white husbandless women in the colonial family economy. While some such women were maintained in private homemaking by their extended families or by charity, others turned to self-support by working for income. Work for income took one of two forms. Some women undertook "homemaking for income," a special category of work for the market which resembled homemaking and, as such, usually excluded men. Others were propelled by their family responsibilities to take up men's work, properly speaking, as heads of family businesses. Finally, a very few women claimed men's work as their own, exercising remnants of aristocratic privilege.

The preceding chapters have examined the work of free or indentured women in the colonial economy. But the successful growth of the North American colonies, and of the new United States, was based on the enslavement of black women and men in the southern colonies. While the work of white women on the slave plantations resembled that of others in the family economy, the enslaved woman's work life had a distinctly different content. In the next chapter we will study the sexual division of labor and women's work under slavery.

4

Women's Work and the Sexual Division of Labor under Slavery

The southern colonies developed a slave system of production which employed men and women from Africa. This chapter will investigate the particularities of the sexual division of labor that existed among the slaves and the patterns of women's work that it generated. After a brief overview of the southern slave economy, we will examine the master–slave relationship, the sexual division in slave family life, the sexual division of slave labor, and the concrete work of the slave woman.

The Southern Slave Economy

The development of the colonial economy led to the introduction of slave labor in some of the colonies. A family's search for wealth in the colonial economy was limited both by its productive capacity and by its market. In New England, as we have seen, settlers had difficulty finding commodity products that had markets large enough to free them from self-sufficient production; this frustrated their early search for wealth. The southern colonies, however, were able to produce agricultural commodities—tobacco, indigo, cotton, sugar cane, rice, hemp, and wheat—for which expanding markets existed in England, in continental Europe, and ultimately in the American Northeast. They were, hence, able to profitably invest their surplus in expanded commodity production. However, these southern family farmers ran up against a different limit—the limited size of the family and the labor it could furnish. Indentured servants and wage laborers were one option for the planters, yet both were limited in supply. The employment of slave labor proved to be a profitable alternative.[1] Black Africans had already been employed extensively as slaves in the New World by the Spanish and Portugese.

The seventeenth century saw the introduction of slavery into the West Indies sugar islands as well as the North American South as the solution to the need of expanding farms for cheap and available labor. While early Africans were treated similarly to the white indentured servants, by the mid-seventeenth century Maryland and Virginia had begun to establish legal distinctions between white and black, locking Africans into permanent subordination.[2] Slavery was integrated into the British empire by the lucrative "triangular trade." Cloth, iron wares, and guns were taken from Britain to Africa and traded for slaves; the slaves were brought to the New World colonies and sold to the planters; the planters sold their products to Britain and purchased luxury goods from her.

While the impulse for the establishment of slave labor in the South came from the white planters, its roots in Africa cannot be ignored. The slave trade built on the African form of slavery by purchasing the enslaved prisoners of tribal wars, supplementing its supply through outright kidnaping. Once in the colonies, enslaved Africans still embodied the culture of their West African tribal homelands. Their African heritage was transformed by slavery into a particular, Afro-American culture, but it was not totally destroyed.[3] The sexual division of labor and women's work under slavery were, then, the product of two different, intertwined, and often competing forces: the directives of the slave masters, as inspired by their search for wealth and their conceptions of social life, and this inherited culture of the slaves, transformed and passed down through generations.

The slave man and woman entered into two basic kinds of relationships: relationships with their master's family and his overseer, which centered around their production of commodities or housework, and relationships with other slaves, as family members, friends, and co-workers. The former served to constitute them as subordinated members of society, as slaves. The latter sustained them as family members—husbands or wives, fathers or mothers, parents or children—and reproduced slave culture generationally. We will examine these two types of relationships in the next two sections.

The Master–Slave Relationship

The master–slave relationship determined the life of the slave: as the owner of the slave, the master had, at least in theory, complete control over the conditions of slave life. He was a property owner, and the slave was part of his property. The slave was to the master a means of production, to be maintained and employed to fill the master's need for labor.

The master–slave relationship can be analyzed as the material exchange of physical work for subsistence. Recent quantitative studies of the material conditions of the American slave have found a standard of living comparable to that of the early free working class in Europe.[4] Such claims have disturbed historians, for they seem to suggest that slavery was indeed not an oppressive institution.[5] However, the material exchange between master and slave neither exhausts the content of the master–slave relationship nor is at the heart of that relationship.

While the slave and wage labor relationships are comparable materially, they are disparate socially. Wage labor establishes the worker as a property owner (the owner of labor power), places a value upon that labor power, and allows the expression of individuality by the worker in the choice of job; slave labor, on the other hand, does none of these for the worker. No matter how hard the slave worked, she or he always remained a slave, a piece of property whose human will was denied. The particularity of women's work under slavery, and the heritage of slavery in the post-bellum United States, cannot be grasped by the reduction of slavery to a material relationship. Rather, we must study the peculiar and contradictory constellation of social relationships involved in slavery.

The master–slave relationship was inherently contradictory in that it simultaneously denied and recognized the will of the slave. The master was the owner of the slave and all that the slave produced; he was also responsible for the care of the slave. The slave's will was denied, first, in his or her forcible enslavement, and continually in the exercise of the master's power. Yet at the same time, the slave had to be treated as a human being whose mind and will were recognized. Slaves possessed the capacity for thought and rational action which distinguishes humans from other animals. This capacity made a slave superior to and irreplaceable by livestock. The slave could be taught about a particular production process, given verbal instructions, and expected to carry out such orders under threat or promise of reward. The slave could also be trained as a skilled craftsman or utilized in the master's house as a domestic. However, the slave's productive capacities could be developed only if he or she was taught language, taught to think, taught about the particular production process to be undertaken, and taught to understand the constellation of social relationships in which he or she was to participate. The will of the slave had to be recognized, and his or her ability for self-conscious action developed. Yet this also developed the slave's capacity for conscious resistance, as well as his or her motivation for such resistance, for it gave the slave a will that would, inevitably, conflict with that of the master.

Slave owners labored hard to develop in the slave a will that would accede to its own enslavement. Kenneth Stampp, in *The Peculiar Institution,* analyzes the steps needed in training the ideal slave. The first step was to teach the slave to submit him- or herself unconditionally to the will of the master, to "obey at all times, and under all circumstances, cheerfully and with alacrity" as one Virginia slaveholder wrote. The next steps were to teach slaves that they were personally inferior, as blacks, to all whites, and then to impress upon them a sense of their masters' total power over them, "to make them stand in fear" of their owners, in the words of one North Carolina mistress. Slave owners furthermore tried to develop in slaves an interest in the affairs of their masters, as well as a consciousness of dependence upon their masters. They also used the church, teaching the slaves that slavery was God's will, and resistance against it a sin against God, although the use of the church and Christian ethics occasionally backfired.[6] Ideal slaves, then, willfully suppressed their needs and allied themselves with the will of the master, accepting their inferiority to and dependence upon him.

The master–slave relationship therefore resembled the husband–wife relationship in the free family of colonial times, where the wife suppressed her own needs and took up, as her vocation, the work of filling the needs of her family. One plantation mistress, Mary Chesnut, commented in her diary that "There is no slave, after all, like a wife. . . . All married women, all children and girls who live in their father's houses are slaves"![7] Indeed some southern women, such as the Grimke sisters, so identified with slaves as to become fervent abolitionists.[8] And occasionally masters did fall in love with their female slaves, and live with them as concubines; a few even transformed their slaves into wives through marriage, although they were ostracized for this by their society.[9] However, the "enslavement" of women to men as homemakers was voluntarily undertaken in marriage and involved a true merging of interests; neither of these elements was present in the master–slave relationship. For this reason, good slaves were much harder to find than good wives.

Although slaves, as human beings, were able to perform an invaluable service—labor—masters were unable to fully utilize their potential. Slaves lacked not the capacity to perform labor, but the desire to do so. The will which was essential to their laboring was also led necessarily to oppose such laboring under circumstances that consistently denied it. The wage labor and share-cropping systems that eventually overthrew slavery solved this contradiction by recognizing the property rights of the laborer and establishing a contractual labor relationship that from its origins engaged the will of the worker. Under slavery, laborers spent much of their energies resisting their subordination—indirectly, by slowing down their work pace, destroying crops, tools, or buildings, feigning illness, stealing from their masters, or even injuring themselves, while feigning an obedient, compliant posture, or directly, by fighting their masters or overseers, escaping, or even committing suicide. Masters and their overseers were hence forced to supervise their slaves almost continually; they often resorted to the lash and other forms of physical abuse to motivate such resistant workers.[10] Still, slave owners had difficulty creating dedicated workers out of their slaves. As one slave owner complained to Frederick Law Olmsted, "Faithful service was preached to them as a Christian duty, and they pretended to acknowledge it, but the fact was that they were obedient just so far as they saw they must be to avoid punishment."[11]

Some masters found ways to appeal to the self-interest of their slaves. Slaves were given bonuses for extra work or rewarded for hard work by transfer to a craft job.[12] In the cities, slaves were often hired out and allowed to keep some of their wages; some even lived in homes of their own. However, it was difficult to develop the self of the laborer much without endangering the master–slave relationship. The more a slave's self was developed, the more likely his or her needs would conflict with the will of the master and the less likely he or she would be to accept punishment. One blacksmith, who had taken pride in his work and sought to "distinguish myself in the finer branches of the business by invention and finish," was distraught when his father was physically punished by the master: "after this, I found that my mechanic's pleasure and pride were gone. I thought of nothing but the family disgrace under which we were smarting, and how to get out of it." He eventually ran away successfully.[13] As a slave owner taught at the South Carolina Institute in 1849, "Whenever a slave is made a mechanic, he is more than half freed, and soon becomes, as we too well know, and all history attests, with rare exceptions, the most corrupt and turbulent of his class."[14]

Recognizing the fact that as the slave became equal in social position to the master, his or her subordination was less acceptable to the slave, and less defensible by theories of innate inferiority, the slave masters worked to limit such development. Slaves learned to speak, but were never taught to read and write. As de Toqueville noted:

> The only means by which the ancients maintained slavery were fetters and death; the Americans of the South of the Union have discovered more intellectual securities for the duration of their power. They have employed their despotism and their violence against the human mind. . . . at the present day measures are adopted to deprive him [the slave] of even the desire of freedom.[15]

The enforced ignorance of slaves soon became equated in the southern mind with the innate intellectual inferiority of blacks; and indeed, given that blacks were denied the opportunity to develop their minds, they appeared to be naturally stupid.

Therefore slave masters were required to maintain a delicate balance between developing the sociality of the slave and denying him or her the equality of position that such sociality implied. The slave, with a mind, could think about the slave relationship, recognize its injustice, and plan ways of resistance and escape; the master tried to keep such resistance in control by teaching the slave that blacks were naturally inferior to and dependent upon whites, by limiting the intellectual development of the slave, and by severely punishing the least sign of resistance.

The Sexual Division in Slave Family Life

Within the free family, the sexual division of labor was freely constructed by family members around the husband/household head's position in the larger economy. The husband was a property-owner, struggling to advance himself in the economy; as his position within the economy varied, his wife's work of homemaking adjusted to fill changing family needs. Husband and wife lived out polarized and complementary lives, and the man's position was one of clear superiority and power. In contrast, the slave family was not free to work out its own sexual division of labor; the husband was not free to determine his public activities, nor the wife free to adjust her life to the needs of the family. Both were subordinated to their master, their work determined by his needs and desires. Furthermore, the master's power did not limit itself to slave work. Rather, it continually extended itself into personal, familial relations, for such relationships, under slavery, produced and reproduced Afro-Americans as slaves, property of the master. While the slaves' original African cultures helped shape their lives, they were ultimately subject to the will and whims of the master. Slave society was not freely self-determining, but rather determined in subordination to a society of masters.

We will begin our examination of the sexual division of labor under slavery by examining the black family. But first, a note. Our analysis here necessitates a high level of abstraction and generality. The slave system varied across slave owners. In 1860, over 95% of the slaves lived in the countryside, but on establishments of greatly differing size: 50% had masters who owned over 20 slaves, of which 25% had masters with over 50 slaves, and 25% had masters with fewer than 10 slaves.[16] The large majority of slave owners were small farmers, with only a few slaves, yet they represented only a small portion of cash crop production in the South. Plantations also varied according to their products and according to the particular beliefs, personality, and family size of their masters. Furthermore, the slave system itself underwent important changes in its 200 years of existence in North America, both through its own internal development and with the development of the rest of the continental and world economy. Here we will abstract from these differences to focus on the special nature of the sexual division of labor under slavery.

The first question to answer is why slave owners should recognize and develop the sexual difference in their slaves. In free societies, the sexual division of labor provided the basis for marriage, as a unity of different beings. Combined with the rule of exogamy, it provided for the reproduction of society as a system of families. The slaves originally came from African societies that had a sexual division of labor; male and female slaves were indeed differentiated into man and

woman, different and complementary beings, when they were enslaved. Most of their home societies were horticultural; men engaged
in war, hunting, and clearing the land, and women in hoe-cultivation,
harvesting of crops, and domestic work and child-rearing.[17] Marriage
was based on the sexual division of labor between spouses, exogamy,
and polygamy.[18] Slave owners did not have to recognize and reproduce the sexual division of labor and marriage patterns of the Africans' home societies (indeed, they could not do so exactly, given the
different activities involved and the presence of slavery itself). These
institutions did not directly fill the needs of the slave owner for labor.
However, such familial relationships between slaves were important
to the slave owner, for these provided the basis of the development of
the slave into a self-conscious, socialized human being.

The planters needed social beings for labor and social beings must
be developed and sustained in particular, "familial" social relationships. However, the creation and the sustenance of the sociality of
the slave are two distinct issues. For the slaves to maintain themselves as social beings, capable of performing simple unskilled labor,
they did not need to live in structured families. Once socialized, they
could maintain their sociality through contacts with other slaves and
with their masters. Some West Indies sugar plantations imported
predominantly male slaves, already socialized, worked them to death,
and replaced them with new purchases. However, in the American
South, as well as other areas, slaves were imported in more equal sex
ratios and used both for slave work and for breeding; after the prohibition of the importation of slaves in 1807, breeding increased in
importance.[19] If planters were to reproduce their own slaves as a
means of sustaining and expanding their property, they needed not
only to sustain sociality in their slaves but to engender it in a new
generation. For babies to grow into slaves, they had to be "socialized," turned from human animals into social beings through parenting. As beings whose sociality had to be developed, and who themselves had to reproduce new social beings, slaves had to be granted
some form of private family life, some set of personal relationships
and relationships between families within which their particular personalities could be developed and recognized.

Therefore, while planters were economically interested in the fertility of their slaves, this interest did not lead them to treat their
slaves as breed animals and reduce reproduction to copulation.
Rather, these economic interests led them to recognize familial rela-

tionships among the slaves and to encourage large families. Marriage as a unity of socially differentiated sexes, the practice of exogamy, and parenting by the biological mother and her husband were the only rules of family life known to either slaves or masters. These rules were hence perpetuated when Africans were enslaved; they defined the content of slave family life. Instances of master-arranged marriages or forced breeding reported in the slave narratives are few; for example, only 80 were reported in Escott's study of over 2,300 narratives.[20]

Besides allowing and recognizing slave marriages, most slave owners acknowledged the slave family in the assignment of living quarters and in the distribution of food. In his *Journey in the Back Country,* Olmsted described slave family life on one set of plantations he visited:

> A large part of them lived in commodious and well-built cottages, with broad galleries in front, so that each family of five had two rooms on the lower floor, and a loft. The remainder lived in log-huts, small and mean in appearance. . . . Each family had a fowl-house and hog-sty (constructed by the negroes themselves), and kept fowls and swine, feeding the latter during the summer on weeds and fattening them in the autumn on corn stolen (this was mentioned to me by the overseers as if it were a matter of course) from their master's corn-fields. . . . The allowance of food is weighed and measured under the eye of the manager by the drivers, and distributed to the head of each family weekly. . . . All hands cook for themselves after work at night, or whenever they please between nightfall and daybreak, each family in its own cabin. Each family had a garden, the products of which, together with eggs, fowls and bacon, they frequently sold, or used in addition to their regular allowance of food.[21]

While the standard of living of these slaves appears better than the usual, such family-based arrangements were common to most plantations.

Some slave owners went as far as to specify rules as to the sexual division of labor for their slave families. One slave owner in Mississippi listed the following as one of his Rules for the Plantation:

> 2nd. Each family to live in their own house. The husband to provide fire wood and see that they are all provided for and wait on his wife. The wife to cook & wash for the husband and her children and attend to the mending of clothes. Failure on either part when proven shall and must be corrected by words first but if not reformed to be corrected by the Whip.[22]

An Alabama planter, considered typical of large planters by his biographer, had these rules:

> Men alone are required to feed and perform all lot work [animal care] at the close of every day. The women are required, when work is done in the field, to sweep their houses and yards and receive their supper (communally prepared) at the call of the cook, after which they may sew or knit but not leave their houses otherwise.[23]

Slave owners also attempted to impose their own conceptions of family life on the slaves, discouraging, for example, the polygamous practices of the Africans. At the same time, by recognizing their slaves as particular persons, family members, the owners also granted their slaves a moment of independent self-determination.

The slaves constructed a sexual division of labor in their "free time" activities, even when the master did not impose such a division upon them. This division was a faint reflection of what they had known in Africa. Afro-American women continued their tradition of undertaking domestic work as wives, homemaking for their husbands through cleaning, sewing, child-rearing, and, when it was allowed in the cabins, cooking. Afro-American men hunted for small game and fished, a pale echo of their group hunting excursions in Africa. They trapped or chased with dogs squirrel, possum, raccoon, turkey, and rabbit, and planted gardens, to supplement the family's rations or to sell. Olmsted learned on one of his visits of a slave stock-tender who "had an ingenious way of supplying himself with venison." As he knew from his work where the deer ran, "he lashed a scythe blade or butcher's knife to the end of a pole so that it formed a lance; this he set near a fence or fallen tree which obstructed a path in which the deer habitually ran, and the deer in leaping over the obstacle would leap directly on the knife."[24] In some instances, the slave man was able to act almost as a petty producing head of household. "I know plantations upon which industrious men [slaves] improving their opportunities, sell during the year poultry, stock, and produce of their own raising to the amount of thirty, fifty, and a hundred dollars," wrote the Reverend Charles C. Jones.[25] At the special plantation event of corn husking, activities were also strictly sex-typed: slave men husked the corn, while slave women prepared the meals.[26] The social differentiation of the sexes lived out in slave life, the result both of the masters' directives and the slaves' "free choice," made slave men and women different and complementary; it also underlay their marriage and family life. These institutions were formalized through elaborate courtship etiquette and marriage rituals.[27]

While successful slavery necessitated the slave family, it also led to continual violations of the family's integrity. The free family was recognized as a unit by the other free families. The husband was recognized as the head of household, with charge of as well as power over his wife and children. Similarly, the slave family was recognized as a family by the community of slaves; indeed, given the lack of freedom in the economic and political life of the slaves, family relations gained an added importance, and extended and voluntary family ties were developed.[28] However, the slave family was not guaranteed recognition by the master's family; indeed, the master–slave relationship often violated family ties. First, to the slave master, each family member represented an individual piece of property over which he had complete power. The master's exercise of power over his individual slaves denied the authority of household heads over the members of their families. Second, the daily experience of the master–slave relationship denied the ties of love and unity between family members. The simple living of a slave life was painful for family members to witness; the breaking of the slave's will, the forced labor, the beatings. Attacks on one family member were attacks on the whole family. Slaves, especially women, were vulnerable to sexual harassment and exploitation by masters or overseers whether or not they were married; hence both parental authority and marital ties were constantly threatened and often violated. Slaves who defended the members of their families against such attacks were severely punished, if not killed; yet standing by passively meant ignoring family loyalty. Some slaves fought back in spite of the threat of punishment: Henson tells of his father, who had "beaten the overseer for a brutal assault on my mother." In punishment "his right ear had been cut off close to his head, and he had received a hundred lashes on his back."[29] Certainly, masters and overseers limited their violence in order to avoid such reprisals; one planter included in his "Plantation Rules to Govern Time of an Overseer" the admonition, "above all things avoid all intercourse with negro women. It breeds more trouble, more neglect, . . . and more everything that is wrong on a plantation than all else put together."[30]

One curious result of these attacks was the desire expressed by some slaves to marry slaves from other, nearby plantations. The sacrifice of distance was preferable to witnessing the enslavement of one's family: as one slave man wrote, "No colored man wishes to live at the house where his wive lives, for he has to endure the continual misery of seeing her flogged and abused, without daring to say a word in her defence."[31] Of the marriages reported in the slave narratives, 27.5% were of this type; Escott suggests that many such marriages were forced by the limits of the individual plantation's slave force combined with the rule of exogamy.[32]

An area of direct conflict between slavery and the slave family was the sale of slaves away from their family members. While slaves could be exchanged in families, they were also productive as individuals. As means of production, slaves were often sold—when the labor needs of the plantation changed, if new family members were not needed, or if the slave owner was in debt. Simply the normal division of the free family's property among its heirs often necessitated the dividing up of slave families. Even if the owners tried to sell the family as a unit, a purchaser for such a combination of slaves might not be found. Certainly, once family ties existed, there were incentives for the owner to respect them. Slaves forcibly separated from their families often ran away or refused to work; conversely, slaves who wished to run away were often dissuaded by their family ties, or caught because they returned to see their families. One overseer explained to Olmsted that few slaves escaped his plantation permanently since "they almost always kept in the neighborhood, because they did not like to go where they could not sometimes get back and see their families." Escaped slaves "would come round their quarters to see their families" and he would catch them.[33]

Nonetheless, economic considerations often led owners to separate slave families. One poll of ex-slaves in Mississippi found that 35% of their marriages had been terminated by force, 41% by death (some of these also counted in first category), and only 9% by mutual consent or desertion.[34] A different study of 2,888 slave marriages in Mississippi, Tennessee, and Louisiana had similar results: of broken marriages, 37.5% had been terminated by the master, 46% by death, 3.7% by war, and only 12% by personal choice.[35]

Although the needs of the slave owners led them to violate as well as recognize the family life of their slaves, this tension did not prevent the slave family from being of great importance in the slave community. While it is certain that the response of some slaves to slavery's pressures on family life was to avoid forming strong family ties, slave narratives attest to the fact that, for most slaves, family life was of central importance and attacks on the integrity of the family were both mourned and resisted. As Escott concluded from his study of the slave narratives, "The narratives make clear that families were a vital institution and a towering source of strength for the slaves . . . threatened with destruction, slave families grew closer together. An abundance of testimony detailed the devotion that husbands and wives and fathers, mothers, children, and grandparents felt for each other, while only a few former slaves suggested that family life had lost its meaning."[36]

The Sexual Division of Slave Labor

We have claimed here that the necessity of constituting his slaves as social beings led the master to recognize, at least to some extent, marriage and a sexual division of labor among the slaves. It is now necessary to examine the question of the sexual division or sex-typing of slave labor, labor done explicitly for the master.

Slaves were "employed" by patriarchal, slave-owner families (or by the manager families of absentee owners), families organized like those of the family economy we have studied in the previous chapters. The goal of such families was to expand their wealth through expanding production of commodities; toward this end, they engaged in both commodity and self-sufficient production. The master was the recognized property owner and headed the activity of commodity production. His wife, the "mistress," was the homemaker; her responsibilities centered in the private sphere of the home, including undertaking and/or supervising self-sufficient production for the consumption of the family, and, occasionally, for the slaves. Under slavery, both husband and wife had the energies of slaves to aid them in their respective activities.

Therefore while all slaves were owned, in the typical family, by the master as property owner, they were not all under his direction. Slaves in the fields, engaged in commodity production, were under the master's direction; those working in self-sufficient production for the household and in housework fell predominantly under the control of the mistress. The slave artisan fell somewhat in between these two, for such slaves produced for the plantation and also occasionally for sale.

WORK IN THE FIELDS

Let us begin by considering field work, the backbone of the plantation economy, the work of 70 to 90% of plantation slaves. As we have seen, free American women were rarely employed in the fields, for such work was in the sphere of commodity production and, as such, men's work. However, slave owners employed women in the fields, equally or even to a greater extent than men: Fogel and Engerman estimate that in the agricultural sector, about 75% of slave men and 80% of slave women were employed as laborers in the field.[37] It is not difficult to understand why planters worked women in the fields, given the preponderance of such work on the plantation. Furthermore, field work had been predominantly women's work in the slaves' African homelands.

Were work assignments or jobs in the fields sex-typed? One can find examples of clear sex-typing of work: on one Virginia wheat farm, men scythed and cradled the grain, women raked and bound it into sheaves, and children gathered and stacked the sheaves. A Sea Island planter made ditching men's work and moting and sorting cotton women's work.[38] On the other hand, it was not unusual for a plantation-owner to assign men and women to common tasks. As Austin Steward recalled that in his *Twenty-two Years a Slave,* "it was usual for men and women to work side by side on our plantation; and many kinds of work, the women were compelled to do as much as the men."[39] Both sexes and all ages were employed in the rush to get in the harvest; both sexes worked in hoeing gangs. Olmsted, in his travels in South Carolina, saw thirty men and women at work repairing a road, and "the women were in majority, and were engaged in exactly the same labor as the men; driving the carts, loading them with dirt, and dumping them upon the road; cutting down trees, and drawing wood by hand, to lay across the miry places; hoeing and shoveling."[40] According to one slave woman, "the women had to split rails all day long, just like the men" on the farm where she had worked in Mississippi.[41] Women could even be found doing the stereotypically masculine work of plowing—an occurrence so shocking it was often remarked by travelers. Olmsted, visiting Mississippi, noted on a series of plantations that "the plowing, both single and double mule teams, was generally performed by women, and very well performed, too. I watched with some interest for any indication that their sex unfitted them for the occupation . . . they twitched their plows around on the head-land, jerking their reins, and yelling to their mules, with apparent ease, energy, and rapidity."[42] A former slave explained in an interview, "In slavery time de wimmen plowed jes lack de men."[43] This breakdown of the sexual division of labor fascinated and perplexed observers, both slaves and free. "In the winter she sawed and cut cord wood just like a man," one slave testified of her grandmother, explaining, "She said it didn't hurt her as she was strong as an ox."[44] A white female visitor observed that men and women "promiscuously run their ploughs side by side, and day after day . . . and as far as I was able to learn, the part the women sustained in the masculine employment, was quite as efficient as that of the more athletic sex."[45] As Fanny Kemble wrote of a Georgian plantation, "On Mr. ——'s first visit to his estates he found that the men and the women who labored in the fields had the same task to perform. This was a noble admission of female equality, was it not?"[46]

Indeed, the demands of the plantation economy led planters to acknowledge the equality of physical strength between many males and females. The sexual division of labor, supposedly the result of natural differences between the sexes, often broke down in unskilled agricultural labor precisely because slaves were employed solely on the basis of their physical capacities. The more slaves were treated as bodies, the less their social sexual differentiation mattered. In the fields, the slaves were classified as "hands:" although many women were only counted as 3/4 hands, due to smaller size, some were classified as 1's, and men were classified as both, according to their size and strength. Woman's special ability to bear children was of import only when she actually was pregnant or recovering from her delivery. Slaveholders usually followed the rule that "pregnant women should not plough or lift but must be kept at moderate work until the last hour if possible"; after delivery, women were usually given three weeks with their infants before returning to work.[47] Once hands were classified, they all did the same work, just different amounts. Due to the importance of physical strength and stamina, factors such as age, size, and state of health often outweighed sex in determining the division of labor.

The same thing happened in industrial slave labor. Women were employed extensively in the very demanding work of building levees, roads, railroads, and canals. One Carolinian noted that "in ditching, particularly in canals . . . a woman can do nearly as much as a man." Slave women (and children) were also employed in textile, hemp, and tobacco factories, as well as in sugar refineries and rice milling. Industrialists, encouraged to employ slave women and children because they were cheaper, found them adequate to most tasks. In fact, Robert Starobin notes that in industrial slave work, the division of labor was just as often made on the basis of age as on the basis of sex.[48]

So in most agricultural labor as well as unskilled industrial work, the sexual division of labor was often revealed to be an economically inefficient social artifact, and was erased in the slave system's drive for efficiency. Given that the majority of slaves were employed in the fields, this curious sharing of work by men and women must have shaken both slave and free conceptions of the physical differences between the sexes. It also served to widen the differences between blacks and whites. Still, this attenuation of the sex-typing of slave field work did not eliminate the social differences between the sexes; indeed, it probably caused slaves to intensify their wish to sexually divide their free activities.

While the sexual division of labor often broke down in field work, the social difference between slave men and women was maintained in other areas of slave work. Indeed, in the fields, the driver's job, that of overseeing fellow slaves, was typed as men's work; it demanded the ability to direct both men and women, a quality which both master and slave cultures attributed to men. Furthermore, slave work outside of the fields was also sex-typed, as we shall now see.

EMPLOYMENT OUTSIDE OF THE FIELDS: CRAFTS AND DOMESTIC SERVICE

Although field work constituted the main employment of slaves in southern agriculture, there were other tasks to which slaves were assigned. The needs of the master's household included the need of the plantation for means of production, the needs of the master's family for meals, clothing, nursing, entertainment, housing, *and* the needs of the slaves for at least a minimum of clothing, housing, and food for meals. The manner in which these needs were filled, and hence indeed the content of these needs, depended upon the success of the household in profitably producing commodities, as well as the accessibility of markets to supply their commodity needs.

The master's household needs could be filled either by the purchase of commodities or services outside of the household, by the assignment of his own slaves to the production of such commodities or services, or by the energies of the free family members. Wealthier households purchased sophisticated craft manufactures from Europe or the North, and had as well a retinue of slaves who worked to fill household needs through production and service. Such a combination allowed them to attain standards of wealth and luxury surpassing that available to free families without slaves. On the more modest plantations, the work of masters and mistresses could include the provisioning of their slaves, while the latters' energies were concentrated in the fields. The son of a small planter recollected:

> My mother spun, wove cloth, cooked and occasionally went to the cow pen to milk the cows, father plowed and drove the wagon, made shoes and did other work. My mother always seed to her cooking and did a good deal of it, had her spinning and weaving done for the whole plantation white and black, no cloth or negro shoes were bought wilst father and mother lived, father made his own negro shoes and mother made the clothes.[49]

The employment of slaves in commodity production provided the southern household with a means to replace self-sufficient production with purchased commodities; at the same time, given that much of the provisioning of needs was not yet commoditized, the provisioning of the slaves itself required additional self-sufficient production in the household, employing slaves and taxing the mistress. The plantation garden and livestock were used to produce food for both the free and slave members of the household; the kitchen often cooked for both; the mistress of the plantation often nursed the whole household, along with the slave conjurers and herb doctors. While slave cloth was originally purchased from Britain and the North, when the Revolutionary War cut off the textile supplies and when the price of their cash crops plummeted, many southern ladies took up spinning and weaving, just as did their northern counterparts. However, in the southern case, home-makers worked to fill the needs of both free and slave members of the household, and they had women slaves to train and use as workers.[50] Hence the plantation's employment of slaves both represented specialization in a cash crop and encouraged more self-sufficient household production. It is for this reason that some slaves were employed outside of the fields, in craft and domestic work.

A small percentage of plantation slaves possessed special skills which they used in their slave work. Some of these skills had been acquired in Africa; others were gained through training as slaves.

Some plantations purchased slaves who had been apprenticed to free craftsmen in the cities and used these trained slaves to train others;[51] others were trained on the plantation by their masters or mistresses, or by overseers and their wives.

An elite of slave men was trained as carpenters, coopers, stone-masons, millers, and shoemakers; some masters used such promotion as a reward for good field work. Slave women were trained for feminine occupations, such as sewing, spinning, and dairy keeping, by their mistress homemaker, by white women bond servants, or by the wife of the overseer.[52] Peter Wood notes an incident where a slave girl was boarded out to a free woman for a year by her master to be taught sewing.[53] Both men and women slaves were trained and employed as cooks on the plantations; cooking for the household was feminine, part of homemaking, yet fancy cooking for the entertainment of "society" at large was a masculine craft.

The sexual division in skilled slave work seems to have been quite strict: I have yet to find an example of a slave woman employed in one of the above-mentioned masculine crafts, or of a slave man working at spinning, sewing, or milking. One slave owner recounted that his male slave, when asked because of the illness of his mistress to milk the cow, refused on the grounds that "everybody knew that to be 'woman's work' and therefore impossible for him to undertake."[54] Data on the occupations of slaves from *The Census of Occupations of Charleston for 1848* indicates the degree to which skilled slave occupations were sex-typed in the cities: of the forty-three occupations listed other than domestic servants, unspecified laborers, and apprentices, men alone were employed in thirty-four, women alone in eight; only under "cooks" were both men and women listed.[55]

Hence craft or skilled slave work was not only clearly sex-typed, it was sex-typed in the same manner as among free men and women. Indeed, in our search for the reasons behind such sex-typing, we must begin with the prejudices of the slave owners and free craftsmen. To them, blacksmithing and stone-masonry were men's work, spinning and needlework, women's; they applied such sex-typing to slave workers as well as to free. Slave owners were not forced by demands of seasonal harvest or shortages of available recruits to discard their sexual stereotypes, as they were in agriculture. As a small minority of the slave population—Genovese estimated that 5% of the (male?) slave population was comprised of "*men* of skill," as he called them—skilled slaves represented an elite saved from the burden of field work.[56] There was, therefore, usually an abundant supply of potential trainees of the correct sex, and little pressure on slave owners to revise the sex-typing present in white society. Hence, although the device responsible for the sex-typing of these crafts among free families—the difference between skilled work for income, men's work, and skilled work for the family, women's work—was absent among those men and women employed equally as slaves, craft work was nonetheless sex-typed for slaves.

The second major category of employment of slaves outside the fields was that of domestic service. This category blended into that of skilled and craft work described above, for both, under slavery, directly catered to household needs. Women slaves often combined personal service with skilled production—caring for children, cooking, minding the dairy, and sewing clothes—just as free homemakers did. On small estates, they often worked part-time in the fields. Slave craftsmen were less often employed as domestics; in the masters' minds, craft production was distinct from homemaking. As in free families, slave craftsmen tended to specialize in one particular craft, whereas slave craftswomen mastered a range of skills—such as spinning, weaving, and sewing—and this work was merged into a broader set of domestic duties. However, there was a major difference between slave and free sex-typing found in domestic work: unlike among free families, slave men were extensively employed in domestic service. The Charleston Census of 1848, which we looked at earlier, found that over one-third of the adult domestic workers were men.[57] But while domestic work as a whole was not a sex-typed occupation for slaves, jobs within domestic service were commonly sex-typed.

Household service had a personal quality absent from craft or field work. Due to their personal contact with their owners, servants needed to act in a "civilized" manner, as social beings respecting the social ways of their owners. In order to perform their work of serving the personal needs of their owners, house servants needed intimate familiarity with their ways and needs. It was this involvement of domestic or household servants in personal relationships with the master and mistress that necessitated the sex-typing of much domestic work. The strict sex-typing of the world of the slave-owners projected itself through their personal needs to sex-type domestic service.

Slave owners believed, as did all free American society, that parenting of the young was woman's natural work. Hence caring for the master's children was the work of the slave woman; such work could even include nursing them in infancy. The jobs of driver, protector, and gatekeeper to the home were masculine in free society, and slave men performed the slave analogues to such work, as coachmen, footmen, and butlers.

The intimate work of personally serving master or mistress was, of course, sex-typed. A woman's or girl's personal servant was a woman or girl. Only women possessed the necessary knowledge to thus serve women; furthermore, the intimacies involved with such service were unfitting a strange man. Likewise, a man's or boy's servant was a male "valet." A good personal servant needed to develop personal knowledge of the master or mistress so as to anticipate his or her needs; in some slaves this brought ties of loyalty, in others an opportunity for sabotage and stealing. Many personal servants were assigned to their masters or mistresses from childhood; some were passed from mother to daughter or father to son.

> She was never sold, since she was given to her mistress by that lady's mother who owned "Grandma's" mother, when she was only 10. . . . Her earliest work was to wait on the table in her mistress' home. She was so small then that she had to stand on a little bench in order to reach the top of the table. Later, she did housework, sewing and cooking, and acted as nurse to the children in the plantation family. She also did a little work in the fields.[58]

Very young children were employed in domestic work, as among free families; once they became adolescent, they were "apprenticed" to work appropriate to their sex, at home or in the fields.

The personal service of concubine or male prostitute was, of course, sex-typed, as it involved direct sexual service. We have discussed earlier how occasionally the intimacy involved in such relationships led some masters to set up household with their slave-concubines as equals. But for most slave women and men, this represented a traumatic denial of their own family ties and slave relationships.

On the other hand, there existed household work, such as house-cleaning and cooking, which did not involve personally relating to the master or mistress as a sexual being: such work was not sex-typed, or was sex-typed according to the whims or labor supply of the particular plantation. The work of serving the table was also not consistently sex-typed; the performance of this traditionally feminine work by a man gave extra status to those served.

Hence, we find that slavery did produce and reproduce a sexual division of labor among the slaves, both in their free family activities and in some aspects of their slave labor. A social differentiation of the sexes existed among the slaves, but it was ignored in those instances where it was both insignificant and unprofitable for the slave owners.

The division of labor in the slave marriage was superseded by the demands of the slave owner. Whereas in the free family, the white homemaker interacted with the public sphere through her husband, and had her work life determined by him, the enslaved Afro-American homemaker was directly subordinated to and determined by her owner, a non-family member. This perpetuated the relatively independent position she had known vis-à-vis her husband in her previous horticultural society. The equal enslavement of husband and wife gave the slave marriage a curious kind of equality, an equality of oppression. Both were subordinated to the will of the master and his family, and hence responsible for fending for themselves. Thus, although the slave owners imposed their conception of the family upon the blacks, the very fact of enslavement created in the latter a distinct family form. This partially accounts for the racial differences in the labor-force participation patterns of homemakers after emancipation, which we will study in Part II.

The Work of the Slave Woman

The slave woman was, due to her status as a slave, necessarily "employed" outside of her family, outside of homemaking. She was forcibly made a member of the public, economic sphere—not as a property owner, but as a piece of property.

As a slave, she was put to work in the fields, for the homemaker, or both. She worked in the fields next to slave men. In the master's house, she did homemaking for her mistress, and often for her fellow slaves. As one woman described her work as a slave, "What did I do? I spun an' cooked, an' waited, an' plowed; dere weren't nothin' I didn't do."[59]

As a member of the "public" slave sphere, the black woman was forced to fend for and defend herself. Slave narratives contained the following descriptions: "She'd git stubborn like a mule and quit," or she took her hoe and knocked the overseer "plum down" and "chopped him right across his head."[60] She was treated as an individual and punished as an individual, often brutally: visitors' journals are full of surprised references to the cruel beating of slave women, an occurrence that so clearly violated the "normal" protection (and punishment) of women by their husbands or fathers.

Yet slave women also undertook the majority of housework and child-rearing in their own families. Henry Baker, an ex-slave, described the work of the female field slave: "In slavery time de wimmen plowed jes lack de men. On Wednesday night dey had tu wash en aftuh dey washed dey had tuh cook suppah. De nex' mornin' dey would get up wid de men en dey had tuh cook breadfus 'fore dey went tuh de field 'en had tuh cook dinner at de same time en take hit wid 'em."[61] Another slave described the work of his mother, a house servant:

> My mother's labor was very hard. She would go to the house in the morning, take her pail upon her head, and go away to the cow-pen, and milk fourteen cows. She then put on the bread for the family breakfast, and got the cream ready for churning, and set a little child to churn it, she having the care of from ten to fifteen children, whose mothers worked in the field. After clearing away the family breakfast, she got breakfast for the slaves . . . which was taken at twelve o'clock. In the meantime, she had beds to make, rooms to sweep, & c. Then she cooked the family dinner, which was simply plain meat, vegetables, and bread. Then the slaves' dinner was to be ready at from eight to nine o'clock in the evening. . . . At night she had the cows to milk again. . . . This was her work day by day. Then in the course of the week, she had the washing and ironing to do for her master's family . . . and for her husband, seven children and herself. . . . She would not get through to go to her log cabin until nine or ten o'clock at night. She would then be so tired that she could scarcely stand; but she would find one boy with his knee out, and another with his elbow out, a patch wanting here, and a stitch there, and she would sit down by her lightwood fire, and sew and sleep alternately, often till the light began to streak in the east; and then lying down, she would catch a nap, and hasten to the toil of the day.[62]

Mothering conflicted with the demands of the mistress's house, or of the fields. Although treatment varied between plantations, slave mothers were forced to labor through most of their pregnancies and were put back to work, on average, within three weeks of their delivery. During the work day, their children were cared for by older slave women. If her work was "mammying" her owner's children, a black woman could be engaged in mothering two sets of children, homemaking for two families at once!

The forced participation of the slave mother in labor outside of her home meant that she lived the "double day" long before it became common among free families. The cruelty of this double burden was noted by one plantation mistress, Fanny Kemble, in her diary: "In considering the whole condition of the people . . . it appears to me that the principal hardships fall to the lot of the women—that is, the principal physical hardships."[63] A well-known statement by an ex-slave describes the beating of nursing mothers "so that blood and milk flew mingled from their breasts."[64] The calculated exploitation of women slaves most clearly conflicted with free white norms when it forced slave mothers to work outside their homes.

While mothering was hence a tremendous burden to the slave woman, it at the same time represented one of the strongest relationships in the slave community, one in which the particular personalities of mother and child were expressed and affirmed. Slave mothers begged and fought to be kept with their children. Moses Grandy recalled that "my mother often hid us all in the woods, to prevent master selling us."[65] If the master was bent on selling the family off, a mother's pleadings with potential owners sometimes convinced the latter to purchase both mother and child: a record of one sale read "Hannah had a young child [a boy three months old], and her distress at the separation from it induced Read to propose to purchase it."[66] Slaves' narratives are full of exclamations of love and appreciation for their mothers. One slave wrote, upon being reunited with his mother, "She was a good mother to us, a woman of deep piety, anxious above all things to touch our hearts with a sense of religion. . . . Now, I was once more with my best friend on earth, and under her care."[67] The freedom of home relations under slavery, relative to slave labor, accentuated the positive qualities of the black woman's homemaking work, and in particular those of mothering.[68]

The institution of slavery in America clearly differentiated white and black womanhood. The white woman's marriage contract and position as mother were recognized by society at large, while those of the enslaved black were often violated. While both communities formally placed married women under the authority of their husbands and fathers, the black woman was furthermore enslaved to her master and his family. At the same time, her enslavement to the master forced the black woman to act independently, to individuate herself from her husband; therefore, unlike the white homemaker, the black homemaker's work was not determined by her husband.

Compared to the enslaved man, the slave woman was more burdened; she served two masters instead of just one. However, it is likely that her work was also more fulfilling than his, for in it she could sustain the essense of the feminine identity, that of the homemaker. Her male counterpart was denied a public arena where he could, with other men, act out his masculinity. The masculine public sphere was, for the slave, almost exclusively one that denied his manhood and personhood. Furthermore, the presence of his wife or daughter in the sphere of slavery prevented him from consistently acting as the masculine head of household, as her provider and protector.

The particularities of womanhood and the family for the Afro-American slave have left, after abolition, a heritage that has continued to differentiate the economic life of the black woman from that of white women up through the twentieth century.

The family economy was, historically, a stage in the transition from feudalism to capitalism. The full development of capitalism abolished slavery, replaced the family firm with the factory, and replaced work within the family with wage labor. The next part of this study will investigate these developments and their effects on homemaking and women's work.

Part II

WOMEN'S WORK AND THE SEXUAL DIVISION OF LABOR UNDER THE CULT OF DOMESTICITY

5

The Development of Separate Sexual Spheres of Activity and of Masculine and Feminine Self-seeking

The family economy of colonial times was not, by any means, an equilibrium state. It contained a dynamism—the seeking of wealth by individuals—which propelled it across the North American continent, transforming the "wilderness" into a growing, integrated economy in the space of two hundred years. But while it was expanding geographically, the family economy was also transforming itself into the factory system. The rise of the factory system in the nineteenth century brought the separation and development of economic and family relationships, constructing separate spheres of social life. This chapter will analyze this transformation, focusing upon its effects on the sexual division of labor.

The Development of the Capitalist Economy and of Masculine Self-seeking

As the accumulation of wealth proceeded, it came up against limits inherent in the family economy; these limits were transcended with the development of the factory system. As we have explained, the family economy was, in its essence, based on a division of labor between property-owning families, each specializing in the production of a particular commodity, which was exchanged for the commodity products of other families through the impersonal market. The extension of money relationships or of the market into social life was the other side of this division of labor between property-owning families. However, in the family economy, the division of labor within the producing family was not mediated by exchange. Family members, along with servants, apprentices, domestics, or slaves, made up a household unit, which cooperated in the production both of goods for home use and of commodities for the market. Their joint product of home goods and income was redistributed among them by the head of the household. The household production unit used a family labor force limited both in its size and in its abilities. Yet the goal of men, as petty commodity producers, was to gain wealth through expanding their production and sale of commodities. Wage labor began to replace family and servile labor, and the factory took the place of the household as the commodity production unit. In the early nineteenth century, manufacturers in the Northeast began to take advantage of the growing wage labor force and establish factories. The triumph of the North in the Civil War of the 1860s brought the legal abolition of slavery, guaranteeing the hegemony of production based on wage labor.

The development of industrial capitalism in the United States was a long, drawn-out, and uneven process; it involved the expansion of the frontier, the absorption of large numbers of immigrant workers, and the elimination of slavery. It is not the aim of this chapter to trace out this process of the uneven development of capitalism in the United States. Instead, we will look at the way in which the development of industrial capitalism affected the relationship between the family and the economy. This will allow us to pinpoint its affect on men's work and women's work, and on masculinity and femininity.

Looked at from this point of view, the nineteenth century brought the gradual freeing of the production of wealth from the limits of the family. In its struggle for wealth, the property-owning family was forced to transcend itself, to transfer its entrepreneurial spirit to an increasingly impersonal corporation. In the family economy, the family had owned, managed, and worked in its business, in most cases, a family farm. As the new nation began to develop consistent and expanding markets, the family firm found its expansion limited by its labor force—the family (including its property, e.g., slaves) could not guarantee itself a labor supply that was either quantitatively or qualitatively optimal. At the same time, competition between families had, by the nineteenth century, begun to create a class of families without means of production who were willing to work for others, a class augmented through the century by waves of immigration. This conjuncture allowed growing family enterprises first to supplement, and eventually to replace, family workers with non-family wage workers. Moreover, as the firm grew both in its labor force and its technology, it outgrew the household and moved into the factory, a separate, non-family place.[1] By mid-century, the family was also beginning to prove itself inadequate to the management of the most prosperous and geographically dispersed firms, the railroads; the development of salaried (non-family) management began. By the first decades of the twentieth century, "managerial capitalism" dominated the economy.[2] In the large, quasi-public corporations, the family's role was reduced to that of an owner, one of many. The freeing of the firm from determination by family relationships was complete; the firm had gained a life of its own, becoming, legally, a person. Wealthy families initiated this process themselves, for incorporation of their firms allowed them to seek needed capital from others, while limiting their liability for these debts, thus protecting the family against the risks involved in big business. The transformation of family enterprise into managerial capitalism has been a gradual one, not yet completed today. While family firms live on in farming and small businesses, the economy has become increasingly dominated by large corporations who carry on, in an impersonal way, the struggle for wealth initiated by families in the colonial economy.

While commodity production increasingly left the control of families or individuals, becoming determined by the competition between corporations, men, as property-owning wealth seekers, gained rather than lost freedom. The development of capitalism established equality of rights between all white men, extending to all the freedom to self-advancement.[3] The new democracy of the nineteenth century was based on equality between men as property owners, an equality which emerged with the institution of wage labor. Certainly, wage labor represented the demotion of petty producers who lost the contest for wealth; Marx described the rise of wage labor as proletarianization, emphasizing the fact that it deprived men of ownership and control over their tools and product.[4] However, the development of wage labor also brought the elimination of servile and, eventually, slave labor. Men born without means of production, or of slave parents, were no longer doomed to live as second-class family members in another household. The rise of wage labor and the concomitant elimination of servile and slave labor extended to all men the right to establish households of their own with their wages, and the possibility of advancing themselves economically through hard work and shrewd dealing.

Hence the freeing of commodity production from the family, and the concomitant rise of wage labor, also freed men from their "lineages," from determination by their fathers. As long as ownership of means of production was necessary to the earning of wealth, a man's position in the economy was greatly influenced by that of his father: the son of a landowner or urban entrepreneur inherited the family business, while the son of a propertyless father was usually doomed to servile labor. And, of course, the son of a slave inherited his father's slave status. But as the family economy and slavery broke down, there were increasing opportunities for individuals to earn wealth, regardless of the legacies of their parents; the power of family ties to determine one's economic position gradually declined.[5] The freeing of men from determination by their fathers freed masculine self-seeking from the constraints of lineage and allowed it to emerge as the dynamic motor of the new, capitalist economy.

The freedom to better themselves motivated American men into a frenzy of economic activity. In the first part of the century, the prevalence of petty commodity production gave every free man the dream of achieving economic independence and motivated a vast migration to the West. "Like most new States," wrote the governor of Michigan, "ours has been settled by an active, energetic and enterprising class of men, who are desirous of accumulating property rapidly."[6] Later in the century, as capital concentrated itself into fewer and larger concerns, self-advancement came predominantly as an increase of one's wage or salary and an improvement of one's position. Instead of fighting for the growth of a business of his own, a man was to work to better the position of his employer: "Eliminate your personal self. Endeavor to become to your employer a thoughtful machine, and the meed of respect and confidence that will be yours will amply compensate."[7]

The freedom of men to advance themselves was not, however, a guarantee that all would do so, or even that all could do so if they worked hard enough. Although self-employment was very common throughout the century, again particularly in farming, it has been estimated that as early as 1860 almost 60% of the American labor force was employed in some way, that is, not economically independent.[8] As the century advanced, petty producers were eliminated by capitalist firms, and smaller capitalists by larger ones, both processes increasing the wage labor force. The struggle for self-advancement was, in reality, a competition between men, all of whom could not advance to, and remain at, the top. The developing equality of rights between men which emerged in the nineteenth century did not eliminate the hierarchy of wealth and income. However, the economic hierarchy did grow flexible: one's economic position was not inherited from one's parents, but rather earned by one's action.

A man's wealth became, therefore, a measure, not only of his abilities, but of his abilities relative to other men. The nineteenth-century obsession with the self-made man was not simply the approval of one who had advanced himself without the help of an inheritance; it also implied that all men were, to some extent "self-made" and was an implicit condemnation of the poor man for having remained in poverty. As one Republican senator put it in 1857, "let him labor in the same sphere, with the same chances for success and promotion—let the contest be exactly equal between him and others—and if, in the conflict of mind with mind, he should sink beneath the billow, let him perish."[9] Later in the century, this philosophy gained preeminence as "Social Darwinism." In the eyes of society, wealth became the sign of individual success, and poverty that of failure, in the masculine economic competition.

In this way, all men were not only given the opportunity to improve their economic position but also challenged to do so. Manliness became equated with success in the economic competition; indeed man's position in the household came to be described as "bread*winner*."[10] The development of capitalism did not eliminate the effects of a man's birth on his probable future position. The inheritance of wealth continued to create capitalists, while that of black skin to subject one to the virulent racism of whites. Class and race, by affecting one's upbringing, further influenced one's chances to reach the top. However, by his own actions, a man could either improve or worsen his economic position; if he was more able than those above him, he could take their place and move ahead. Society, therefore, held him responsible for his advance or decline and, ultimately, for the amount of wealth he was able to earn. In the family economy, men had been incited to struggle for wealth to maintain and improve the status of their families, or for simple economic survival. Under capitalism, men's striving in the economy became, literally, a seeking of their selves, a struggle to establish their own identities by economically competing with other men:

The money wage provides both the means to the acquisition of commodities capable of satisfying needs, and a quantitative measure of the *relative* worth of a laborer himself. . . . This quantification of the social hierarchy is of decisive importance. It sustains the idea of equality of property owners *as* property owners within a structure of inequality in amount of property. Since status within the social hierarchy is an element of personality structure, the relationship of inequality becomes a necessary part of the sustenance of personality.[11]

By making the hierarchy of wealth and position a fluid one, in which men rose or fell according to their own abilities and decisions, the development of industrial capitalism drove men to intensify their work efforts, harnessing men to the accumulation of capital. With the passing of the nineteenth century and the advance of the twentieth, the motivation of economic self-seeking, of establishing oneself as a man through competition for advancement with other men, has become the predominant masculine ethic, wiping out the competing ethics of loyalty to firm or family, and religion.[12] In this way, the capitalist economy developed masculine competition and harnessed it to the process of capital expansion.

The Development of the Home as a Separate Feminine Sphere and of Feminine Self-seeking

The separation of commodity production from the home and its development into a distinct, masculine sphere was not without effects on family life and womanhood. Rather than emptying the home and family of their content and eliminating homemaking, this separation allowed for the emergence of family life as a distinct sphere of social relationships, a sphere assigned specifically to women. This was a complicated and striking process, which we will trace out in this section.

First, the rise of industrial production and of wage labor allowed the household to become more of a family unit. Indeed, while we have analyzed the separation of economy from family as part of the economy's development, this process can also be understood as necessary to the full development of the family. In the nineteenth century, the family began to free itself from economic determination and limitation, and in doing so, to become *more* of a family. In the family economy, households consisted of the members of the nuclear family and of servants or slaves who were members of other families, strangers to the family. Families that owned means of production could establish households and often enlarged their households with non-family members. Families without their own means of production were forced to split themselves up and send their children to other households: family members could not live together as a family but were forced to live apart from one another in the households of strangers. By moving its business out of the household and into the factory, and by replacing servile or slave labor with wage labor, the commodity-producing family freed its household both from economic activity and from the presence of non-family members, making it a more familial place, a home. By transforming the family business into an impersonal corporation, the entrepreneur was able to limit his family's liability for business debt and free his sons from the obligation to continue in his work. Similarly, by engaging in wage labor, workers who did not own their own means of production were able to limit the hours spent in their place of work and to establish homes and families of their own.

In this way, as wage labor developed and commodity production moved out of the household, families freed themselves from economic restrictions and households became homes, centers for such familial relationships. Let us examine the way which familial relationships developed.

First, the development of capitalism affected the parent–child relationship. We have discussed the way in which capitalism transformed the laborer from a dependent, second-class family member to an independent wage laborer. The child in the family economy had been treated, essentially, as a little worker, whose training meant simply engaging in his or her future work. But now that men's work had left the household, were boys to follow it in order to acquire their training, and were girls to continue in their domestic training under either their mother or some other homemaker?

Parenting continued to mean preparing the child for adult life, as the heir to the family name; however, with capitalism, the way to do so changed. Unlike in the family economy, the child's future work could no longer be simply determined by the father, through the bequeathing of property, apprenticeship, and the arrangement of marriage. A son's future depended upon his performance in the labor market; a daughter's not only on her success in the marriage market, but also upon her husband's success. In poor families, where parents expected no upward mobility for their children, boys and girls were "put out" to wage laboring in unskilled or menial work; they were put to work for the family much as they had been in the family economy. However, fathers who were more successful wanted their sons to follow in their footsteps, and their daughters to marry well; they, also, did not need income from their children. Because successful marketplace competition meant shaping oneself to the needs of capital as they arose and advancing oneself through a series of jobs, preparing a son for economic success could no longer mean instructing him in the skills of a predetermined trade through employment as a little worker. Rather, the parenting of a son came to mean teaching him to be a self-seeking competitive individual, instilling in him the drive to succeed and the belief in his ability to do so. Such parenting was inextricably linked to the development of capitalism as the necessary preparation for success in the economic competition. The parenting of girls changed with that of boys for it meant, first and foremost, preparing them to be mothers and wife/supporters to these new individuals. It was, then, in the late eighteenth and nineteenth centuries that the conception of childhood as a distinct life stage emerged, first among the middle and upper classes. The child was no longer immediately assigned to a life work by his or her parents and then trained for it as an apprentice. Rather, childhood became the period in which the child developed the basis for his or her future individuality, future self-seeking.[13]

Parenting became a distinct social and familial activity centered in home life. Parenting no longer meant putting the child to work; parents (along with the school system) were expected to instill an ethical sense in their children, to develop their abilities to act correctly, productively, and responsibly, in society at large. Through its parenting activity the family was recognized as determining the future character of individual social members, and hence the future of society. The following selection from *Woman's Influence and Woman's Mission*, written in 1854, is a good example of this growing awareness of the distinct importance of parenting:

> The "little morals" of life should be most scrupulously required of children in a family circle, rights of property and a faithful observance of the truth should be observed, all prevarications punished, and they taught to consider a falsehood as not only a mean subterfuge, but a sin. . . .

It is in the daily and hourly family intercourse that these "little morals" must be cared for by the watchfulness of parents. When their children go forth into the world, they will be called upon to exercise self-denial, patience, and self-command, under most trying circumstances; if not fortified by home discipline, how can they practice them when beset in their daily walks? . . .

No station in life is exempt from them; evil passions must be conquered, temptation resisted; it matters not where the struggle is sustained, in the marble palace, or the humble shed, the evil promptings are ever at work. So far as parents can control circumstances, they could choose that position for their offspring that will give virtue most advantage; in this age, the "post of honor is a private station": but then parents cannot always select the niche for their children; therefore they must fit them for all, by doing all in their power while under the parental roof, to strengthen their moral nature. For they are responsible to society for the beings they send forth from the parent nest.[14]

This quote captures the new conception of family life as the ethical training of the child and also links it explicitly to the freedom of the child in the new capitalist economy. Such a responsibility could not be entrusted to hired servants, who had shown themselves incapable of success; therefore, parenting became a clearly familial activity. Separated from work in the economy, tied to the family, parenting was to find its sphere in the home, where the child's individuality could develop in privacy and love.

Home and family life had another specific mission in capitalism: to shelter and rest man, as husband and father, after his day's work in the world. While his wage work allowed the man to support a home of his own, it also made him need a sphere freed from the competitive pressures of the labor force. The home began to become a special place where his particular personality could be expressed and nurtured:

The very idea of home is of a retreat where we shall be free to act out personal and individual tastes and peculiarities, as we cannot do before the wide world. . . . Our favorite haunts are to be here or there, our pictures and books so disposed as seems to us good, and our whole arrangement the expression, so far as our means can compass it, of our own personal ideas of what is pleasant and desirable in life. This element of liberty, if we think of it, is the chief charm of home. "Here I can do as I please," is the thought with which the tempest-tossed earth pilgrim blesses himself or herself, turning inward from the crowded ways of the world.[15]

A similar vision of home tormented the hero of the best-selling novel *The Reveries of a Bachelor:* "Sending your blood in passionate flow, is the ecstasy of the conviction, that *there* at least you are beloved; that there you are understood; that there all your errors will meet ever with gentlest forgiveness; that there your troubles will be smiled away; that there you may unburden your soul, fearless of harsh, unsympathetic ears."[16] For a man, the home was a needed antidote to the economic world where he was forced to rule his actions according to the dictates of competition, and where his value was constantly at question.

So when the development of industrial capitalism separated commodity production from the household, the family was freed from the function of organizing this production, and it was freed from the presence of strangers in the family. The household became a home, a private family place. Family relationships—between husband and wife, between parents and children—began to gain a content of their own. The sharing that had characterized the household developed an emotional underpinning—love and personal attachment between family members—when the household became a home. This new type of social relationship was a necessary complement to the new freedom and competition in the economy.

How did these changes in family life affect women, assigned, even restricted, to the domestic sphere in the family economy? In the family economy, woman's work of homemaking had constituted her as a "natural" being, clearly socially inferior to men. Her work of serving the family had included a primitive form of production (replaced by commodities or servants when possible), the physical bearing of children, and the training of girls in the same work. These were all seen as physical or natural activities, which all women as females were equally capable of performing—except for child-rearing, which for reasons of kinship, had to be performed by the homemaker. Compared to man's explicitly social work of earning wealth and being a citizen, woman's work of homemaking had appeared as crude and natural. And due to this, woman had not been considered man's social equal, but rather an inferior, natural being unqualified for social life as a property owner or citizen.

The movement of man's work of commodity production out of the household allowed family life to emerge as a distinct and specific social process. Children had to be formed as ethical, self-motivated individuals in the home to prepare for their launching into the world of self-seeking. Husbands had to be ministered unto and cared for after their day of work in the economic sphere. As family life emerged as distinct, its social content of forming and sustaining the personalities of family members became explicit.

Which sex was to do this important social work of parenting? Certainly, the bearing and nursing of a child were necessarily the work of the female. Yet the socialization of infants and children in no way required a female biology; indeed, in colonial times, men had taken an active, even leading role in parenting. Furthermore, the new parenting necessitated a social being, familiar enough with the public sphere to be able to prepare the children for success. Women, as private, almost natural beings, were clearly not qualified. Should parenting not then be assigned to men, who were clearly more conversant with the ways of the world? But men had seen their primary work, the accumulation of wealth, transferred out of the home to a sphere of its own, the economy; masculinity now meant competing in the labor force or as a capitalist. Men were developed as competitive, self-advancing individuals, seeking to dominate others; such a personality clashed with the notion of parenting as the nurturing of individuality in others. Indeed, the new kind of parenting more resembled woman's traditional role of serving the needs of her family, redefined as serving the child's needs for self-development.

So as parenting became a recognized social activity, it was not taken away from woman; it did not become fathering, part of man's work. Rather, it remained strongly connected to woman, as motherhood. This fact expressed the paradox of the sexual division of labor as a social division built on a natural difference between the sexes. A female was assigned to woman's work on the basis of her distinct biological capacity to bear children; her biology qualified her for the supposedly natural activities of child-rearing and homemaking. And while this work of homemaking was a social activity, the fact that only females were prepared for and assigned to these activities transformed them into particular social beings, women, who *were* "natural" mothers and homemakers, trained to subordinate their actions to the desires of others. Meanwhile, the exclusion of males from such activities, and their training for lives as property owners, made them unsuitable for such servile, private work; they seemed "naturally" unfit for it. As capitalism developed, masculine competitive self-seeking was sharpened and its sphere separated from that of the home and children. In spite of man's superior knowledge of the social world, masculinity became more, not less, antithetical to active parenting.

Therefore the transformation of parenting into an important social activity did not replace mothering with fathering, but rather transformed the content of mothering and, hence, of womanhood. When the sociality of the parent–child relationship was discovered, it was discovered as the social content of mothering. The result of the emergence of the family as a social sphere was not only the constitution of homemaking as an important social vocation, but also as a social vocation reserved exclusively for woman. This elevation of family life and of woman as its keeper has been aptly labeled by historians "the cult of domesticity."[17]

The constitution of homemaking as a profession for woman allowed the development of feminine self-seeking. Woman's work, as homemaking, was still the process of subordinating oneself to the needs of the family, of emptying oneself of one's own needs and of taking on instead the task of filling the needs of others, one's family members. But this was no longer a passive process. It demanded the active self-seeking of women as homemakers, their creative and individual responses to the needs of their families. First, the homemaking vocation had yet to be clearly defined. The movement of commodity production out of the home and the development of masculine self-seeking had only brought to social awareness the specificity and social importance of family life. It was up to women, as vocational homemakers, to develop their vocation, to articulate the needs of their families, and then to fill them. To the extent that social institutions prevented healthy family life, it was up to women to fight for their transformation.

Second, once homemaking had been defined as a social rather than natural activity, its content delineated, and the measures of its success indicated—for example, successful children or husbands—it became the expression of a woman's self, of her particular individuality. Whereas men's selves were sustained and measured in the labor force competition, women's selves were sustained and measured in their performances as homemakers. Once homemaking had been defined as a social vocation, successful homemaking was not the result of superior physical abilities but of sound judgment and superior dedication to one's family. Women were responsible for their success or failure as homemakers, as measured by the success and happiness of their husbands and children. Scores of books were written on the mothers of great men, all starting from the basic premise that the latters' greatness derived from the formers' mothering abilities. J. C. Abbott, in his *Mother at Home: Or the Principles of Maternal Duty* of 1833, described society's growing awareness of the importance of mothers, linking it to the discovery of the importance of childhood:

> The efforts which a mother makes for the improvement of her children in knowledge and virtue, are necessarily retired and unobtrusive. The world knows not of them; and hence the world has been slow to perceive how powerful and extensive is this secret and silent influence. But circumstances are now directing the eyes of the community to the young, and the truth is daily coming more distinctly into view, that the influence which is exerted upon the mind during the first eight or ten years of existence, in a great degree guides the destinies of that mind for time and eternity. And as the mother is the guardian and guide of the early years of life, from her emanates the most powerful influence which is exerted in the formation of the character of man.[18]

Woman's grave responsibility as mother was elaborated by Mrs. Coxe in her 1842 book, *The Claims of the Country on American Females:*

> To American mothers . . . is then committed, in a special manner, the solemn responsibility of watching over the hearts and minds of our youthful citizens who are soon to take their places on the public arena, and to give form and individuality to our national character.[19]

A woman's subordination to the needs of her family was hence an active, self-seeking process, pursued aggressively and rewarded with the approbation or criticism of her husband and peers. Femininity began to involve as much self-expression and choice as masculinity— but whereas a man's self-seeking meant striving to subordinate other selves, a woman's self-seeking meant striving to subordinate herself to the self-advancement of her husband and children.[20]

Finally, the development of homemaking and of feminine self-seeking brought the development of woman. To perform the important social vocation of homemaking correctly, a woman had to develop her own self, her own skills and social knowledge. The socialization of family life, and the concomitant assignment of this task to woman, set loose a powerful dynamic that transformed both homemaking and woman herself.

The development of capitalism brought the development of home-making as woman's vocation—the search after its proper and universal content, and the development of women's education and freedom as homemakers. This process affected all women, all homemakers. At the same time, the class and race division inherent in American capitalism differentiated the requirements of homemaking for women, for it differentiated the lives of their husbands and the opportunities of their children. In particular, financial necessity, combined with limited economic opportunities, held back the development of the cult of domesticity in the family among the poor. Womanhood and home-making developed, hence, in a dialectical manner, the search for a common conception interacting with the differentiation of needs across families. This process will be examined in detail in the following chapters.

Economy and Family as Separate Sexual Spheres: Man and Woman as Separate but Equal

In the family economy, economic and family life had been merged in the household production unit. Men and women had jointly occupied this sphere, the husband centered in commodity production and the wife in the private provisioning of family needs. With the development of capitalism the family economy's distinction between self-sufficient homemaking and commodity production was developed into a separation of social spheres of activity. Family and economy began to emerge as distinct spheres characterized by distinct relationships. Each had a positive content of its own and was recognized as an important and integral part of social life. The sphere of commodity production was characterized by exchange relationships between property owners; it was a sphere in which individuals sought their fortunes and determined themselves, a sphere of impersonal, quid pro quo relationships and competition. The home became a familial sphere; it became the sphere of personality formation and of the emotional bond of love, the sphere where particular personalities mattered and were appreciated, the sphere of sharing rather than competition.

With the development of capitalism, the sexual division of labor became more consistent and clear as men and women gained distinct spheres of work, economy and family respectively. Home and economy became respectively, woman's and man's spheres of work, woman's and man's vocations. This difference of spheres was asserted as natural and God-given by nineteenth-century writers:

> The intellectual and moral constitution of the sexes, as well as the Bible, instructs us that all the affairs of state, both civil and political, all the affairs of the church as respects both the government and public teaching, all the enterprises for evangelizing and reforming the world, all the more public, literary, and religious institutions, especially those embracing both sexes, should be headed and controlled by man; while the more modest and retiring, though not less valuable and powerful, influences of her personal character and conversation upon her domestic circle, her neighbors and associates, and through them upon the world, together with the fruits of her intellect, imparted not in public lectures, but by private instruction, or communicated to the world through the medium of the press, belong to woman.[21]

Or as Mrs. Ellet put it simply in her "Cyclopaedia of Domestic Economy," *The Practical Housekeeper*, written in 1857: "As it is the business of man to provide the means of living comfortably, so it is the province of woman to dispose judiciously of those means, and maintain order and harmony in all things. On her due performance of her part rest the comfort and social peace of home."[22]

The participation of the sexes in different spheres of activities gave them distinctly different personalities. Men, as participants in the capitalist economy, the sphere of self-advancement and competition, acquired the personal characteristics of self-seeking, competition, and even ruthlessness. Women, on the other hand, emerged as guardians of the family, creators of the home; they acquired the personal characteristics of generosity, sensitivity to the needs of others, and self-sacrifice. Yet this difference, even polarization, of personalities did not drive the sexes apart; it made them need each other, need their other, complementary half. The competitive and selfish man needed a woman to create a home for him, to care for his children, and to love him without competitively challenging his abilities. The selfless and home-centered woman needed a man to support their home financially, to provide her with legitimate children, and to give definition to her work. So great a polarization of the sexes was achieved by the separation of their spheres of activity that:

. . . all the moral virtues of either sex, though they bear the same name in each, are to assume the masculine or the feminine character according to the sex in which they exist. The same act which would be modest and delicate in a man would not always be so in a woman; while, on the other hand, what may be very bold and energetic in a woman, might be very tame in a man. It is on this principle that we are accustomed to say of the man who partakes of the character appropriate to females, that he is effeminate; and also of the woman who partakes of the character appropriate to males, that she is masculine. These terms, we all know, are intended to designate something out of place, something undesirable and unlovely. We tolerate here and there an anomaly of this kind; but we wish to see such cases "few and far between." We should wisely consider the end of all things not far distant should they become universal.[23]

The new relationship between man and woman was one of equality and difference, not superior and inferior. Woman, acquiring for the first time a clearly distinct and social sphere, acquired a distinct and different existence from man, and from her husband. The idea of woman as inferior, which was part of the family economy, was based in the dependence of woman's work and self-definition on her husband, and on the seemingly natural and crude nature of her work; the cult of domesticity, by distinguishing and elevating woman's work, made way for a conception of the sexes as different but equal, heading two different but important spheres. Hence woman was no longer considered to be inferior to her male partner, but rather became different and "equal." This emergence of separate sexual spheres led writers and philosophers to dismiss the Enlightenment question of comparative intelligence upon which the argument of woman's inferiority had been based. As Sigourney wrote:

There was in past times much discussion respecting the comparative intellect of the sexes. It seems to have been useless. . . . The sexes are manifestly intended for different spheres, and constructed in conformity to their respective destinations. . . . But disparity need not imply inferiority.[24]

Burnap made a similar point in his treatise, *The Sphere and Duties of Woman*, written in 1841:

The question has been raised, and often discussed, whether the original intellectual endowments of woman are as great or rather the same as those of man. It is a question, however, which never can be settled and which is unimportant to decide one way or another. . . . But whatever may be the original equality of the sexes in intellect and capacity, it is evident that it was intended by God that they should move in different spheres, and of course that their powers should be developed in different directions. They are created not to be alike but to be different. . . . This radical and universal difference points out distinctly a different sphere of action and duty. . . . [25]

The sexes, placed as they were, by God or nature, in different spheres, were no longer comparable; hence woman could not be measured as less social than man. Rather this difference, it was argued, was the basis of an emerging equality between the sexes.[26]

In the family economy, a man's freedom to express himself in the search for wealth had been restricted by his parents and their legacy, while the crude and natural character of woman's work had practically denied her recognition as a social self. As capitalism developed, so did the individual's freedom to self-seek, to determine his or her actions according to his or her own personality. However, this freedom developed in a bifurcated manner: men expressed their selves in the economic struggle for increased wealth whereas women expressed their selves as homemakers, in their creation and sustenance of their homes, and in their furthering of the selves of the members of their families. Masculine individuality emerged as self-expression through economic self-advancement, and ultimately, as competition with and subordination of other (masculine) selves, while feminine individuality developed as self-expression through seeking the advancement of one's family members, and ultimately as the active subordination of self to others. Two different and complementary ethics or life principles thus emerged in the nineteenth century: for men, an impersonal, public, competitive one; for women, a personal, private, charitable one. As we will see in Chapter 8, this difference of ethics led homemakers to leave their private homemaking and seek to humanize the masculine sphere.

The development of the freedom and equality of men and women was expressed in the development of romantic love within marriage. As wage labor replaced household commodity production, marriage was no longer contingent on the couple's ownership of sufficient property to engage in commodity production. Children did not have to wait for an inheritance, to depend on their father's whim, nor did they have to choose a spouse simply on the basis of property. It was no longer necessary for a father to protect his business by literally keeping it in the family through arranged marriage; a corporate identity allowed the firm to belong to more than one family. As the external economic and extended familial reasons for marriage eroded, the choice of a marriage partner could become the choice of an individual on the basis of his or her own merit, rather than his or her family's economic position. Since part of a wife's work was to understand and support her husband, she had to love and respect him; since parenting now meant instilling certain principles in one's children, a couple had to share similar world views. A proper nineteenth-century marriage had to be constructed on the basis of the personalities of the spouses, on their attraction and love for one another. One manual advised young men and women to "select for a companion one whose feelings, desires, sentiments, objects, tastes, intellect, and moral qualities, &c., harmonize with your own, at least in all their leading elements."[27] Marriage was to be a personal, close relationship, a relationship of mutual respect and sharing in which two particular, distinct, and equal personalities embraced in love. As Harriet Beecher Stowe insisted in her *House and Home Papers* of 1865: "No home is possible without love. . . . All business marriages and marriages of convenience, all mere culinary marriages and marriages of mere animal passion, make the creation of a true home impossible in the outset."[28]

The conception of family life that developed in this "cult of domesticity" was a peculiar one. Although husband, wife, and children made up the nuclear family, husband and wife did not participate equally in family life. Family life emerged with man's separation from the household and his engagement in a distinct, economic sphere. It emerged as woman's sphere, as woman's work; for man, family life represented not work, but a retreat from the world of work, where man could relax and be rejuvenated by the ministrations of his wife. Since the husband centered his life around self-seeking competition in the economy, women as wives became complements to this process of masculine self-seeking, and family life itself became oriented around his struggle in the economy. Husband and wife cooperated in the formation of man's labor-force identity and in his perpetuation through his children. While man could correctly claim that, in the labor force, he was working to support his family, it is also true that the whole of family life, and of woman's work, was at the service of man's economic success. Man and woman were dependent as husband and wife, each filling the needs of the other, but in this process man's labor-force activity dominated as the determinant of the activities of his wife and family. Furthermore, given that success in the economy was gained through loyal service to capitalists and capital, one could say that family life had begun to order itself according to capital's need for expansion, even though capital did not interfere directly with family life. Similarly, the centering of caring for others in woman and in home life meant that capital expansion could take on a heartless character, ignoring the suffering of its workers or consumers, without being challenged by its masculine personifiers. Men could become open and feeling again when they came home, to their "haven in a heartless world."[29] As Reverend Weaver wrote in 1875:

> In our intercourse with the world we are barricaded, and the arrows let fly at our hearts are warded off; but not so with us at Home. Here our hearts wear no covering, no armor. Every arrow strikes them; every cold wind blows full upon them; every story bears against them. What in the world we would pass by in sport, in our Homes will wound us to the quick.[30]

We have traced, here, with broad strokes, the vast changes that occurred in family and economic life with the development of capitalism in the nineteenth century, and shown how they transformed the sexual division of labor to a division of clearly distinct and equal spheres of activity. The next chapters will discuss in detail the way in which these changes affected womanhood and woman's work of homemaking.

6

Homemaking under the Cult of Domesticity: Unity and Diversity

The developments outlined in the previous chapter happened gradually in the nineteenth century. The emerging capitalist economy inherited past differences between families—between wealthy and poor, urban and rural, exchange-oriented and self-sufficient, and between white and black. Into this already diverse assembly of families poured waves of immigrants from various European cultures. Due to these differences between families, the development of homemaking as a vocation was very uneven. In this chapter we will study how the content of homemaking continued to vary according to race, class, and the presence or absence of a husband/provider. The first two sections will examine the content of homemaking among free white families. The third will show the particularity of black homemaking, and the fourth will examine the lives of husbandless homemakers. The last section will discuss homemaking for the privileged homemaker.

White Homemakers: Unity and Difference

White homemakers in the nineteenth and early twentieth centuries had one essential thing in common: they did not participate in the labor force. Married white women did not flow into the labor force with the rise of capitalism; rather white homemakers, both native and immigrant, remained in the domestic sphere in low-income as well as wealthy families.[1] Through the 1920s and 1930s, homemakers whose husbands were present rarely participated in the labor force. In 1890, only 4.5% of all married women were engaged in "gainful occupations," that is, work for income in the factory or in the home. By 1900, this percentage was still only 5.6%, and by

1920, only 9%.[2] Furthermore, many of these women, an estimated 40%, were not actually living with their husbands, and hence were effectively husbandless.[3] Finally, if we eliminate the black homemakers from this statistic, who, as we shall see, did not clearly share the domestic ideal of womanhood, the percentage of married women in the labor force falls to 3.2% in 1900 and 6.5% in 1920.[4] This pattern was equally prevalent among white immigrant families. In 1900, for example, 3.6% of first-generation immigrant married women and 3.1% of second-generation married women were gainfully employed, as compared with 3.0% of native white women.[5]

This domesticity should not be surprising, for it represented simply the continuation of the homemaker's restriction to the home sphere in the family economy. The homemaker's absence from the labor force in the nineteenth century was simply the perpetuation of her relative absence from commodity production in the family economy. However, the homemaker's domestic presence gained new force under the cult of domesticity, for it became the symbol of her husband's masculinity. We have seen how the development of capitalism extended property rights to all men and made the struggle for economic self-advancement the essence of their masculinity. The income a man earned indicated his success or failure in this competition for wealth. But being a man meant not only competing in the economy; it also meant acting as the head of household, married to a feminine, private homemaker. Since a homemaker would enter the labor force only if her husband's income was insufficient to provide for family needs, her labor-force presence signaled his inability as head of household. Only if he earned sufficient income to provide for the family's basic commodity needs could she specialize in domestic homemaking, allowing the couple to live out clearly polarized masculine and feminine lives. For these reasons, being able to support a homebound wife became the cornerstone of manhood. Men took up as an essential part of their labor-force struggle the demand for a "family wage," the demand for a wage sufficient to support a family, and hence allow for a homebound homemaker, and couples postponed marriage until their savings and the husband's income would allow the homemaker to remain at home. In poor families, husbands whose meager incomes branded them as relative failures were all the more eager to have their wives stay out of the labor force, showing without a doubt who was "wearing the pants" in their families. If a husband was absolutely incapable of supporting his family, the marriage was likely to dissolve due to his desertion or his wife's sueing for divorce.[6] The state supported this strict division of labor in marriage by passing laws requiring husbands to support their families and by making nonsupport by the husband grounds for divorce. Feminine domesticity was no longer a negative expression of woman's incapacity to function in the public sphere, of her inferiority; it had become a positive sign of equality between men as property-owning husband/providers, as well as an essential aspect of the social differentiation of the sexes. Although, as we shall see, poor homemakers could not completely live out the cult of domesticity's ideal of homemaking, they did work to achieve one of its primary elements, a domestic presence.[7]

The domestic ideal of womanhood was expressed in the homemaker's attempts to work within her home and/or for her husband if she was forced to work for income. Statistics on gainfully employed married women show that a substantial number of them were not fully employed in the masculine economic sphere. Their desire for domesticity was exploited by nineteenth-century capitalists in two ways. First, a few early factories built on the family economy by hiring male heads of household to employ their families in the factory. This family-based hiring allowed for children and wives to earn income for their families, while still remaining under the protection of the male head.[8] Second, the putting-out system allowed a wife to remain under her husband's roof; in some instances, for example in shoe-binding, the wife's payment was received through her husband, who also worked in putting-out shoe production.[9] These systems allowed for the persistence of family-based employment of homemakers and children.

In the nineteenth century, then, a commonality had emerged between white homemakers, a common domestic existence, a common exclusion from the labor force. The commonality between white homemakers ended there, however; the stratification of husbands' incomes and the domestic ideal of womanhood retarded the emergence of a common conception of family life and of the requirements of homemaking. While all homemakers shared an exclusion from the labor force, the inequality in the incomes of their husbands prevented them from providing their families with the same standard of family life. Therefore, the movement of commodity production out of the home only established the preconditions for the development of family and home life as a distinct social vocation for women; the actual emergence of this common domestic vocation was a very uneven process commenced among the wealthy and only slowly diffused to (and imposed upon) the poor.

Wealthy and middle-class homemakers were able to explore the distinctiveness of family and home life. They had sufficient income to purchase commodities to fill many of the family needs; the drudgery work that remained in the home could be done by hired domestic servants, if the family's resources allowed. The wealthier her husband, the more the homemaker was able to center herself on this new and intangible object—creating and sustaining family life, being a good mother and wife, maintaining a home. These women's efforts to define and perfect vocational homemaking brought mothers' groups and a scientific homemaking movement (their work to develop homemaking will be discussed in Chapter 8). Wealthy homemakers were able to realize the cult of domesticity as more than a domestic presence—as the development of a distinct and important social vocation.

Poor homemakers, on the other hand, were financially strapped. Their husbands' limited incomes prevented them from hiring servants or purchasing many of the commodities accessible to their wealthier counterparts. They were forced to provide for their families' basic needs with their home production. As the wives of unskilled laborers who remained at the bottom of the income hierarchy, they were largely unfamiliar with the promise of upward mobility and freed from the charge of raising upwardly mobile children. Rather than recognizing their children as little individuals whose selves needed developing through the special attentions of the homemaker, poor families often continued the family economy practice of treating children as little workers and sent their children into the labor force to supplement the family's income. For them, family life continued to resemble that of the family economy, in which the essence of homemaking was self-sufficient production, and the essence of childhood was apprenticeship. Poor homemakers could not participate in the cult of domesticity's search for a special content for homemaking; their energies were absorbed in trying to survive on their husbands' meager incomes. But they did obey the essential principle of the cult of domesticity; they did stay out of the labor force. A 1927 study of poor families found them more likely to seek aid from charity than that the homemaker would seek outside employment. [10]

So the development of capitalism did not automatically erase the differences between homemakers of different classes; indeed, in many ways, it accentuated these differences. Neither did it immediately purge the home of economic activity, or transform child apprentice-ship into "mothering." The cult of domesticity's active proponents were wealthy and middle-class homemakers; homemaking retained more precapitalist elements among the poor. However, the develop-ment of man's self-seeking in the economy did establish domesticity as the cornerstone of successful womanhood for all white women. This made homemaking for the poor woman a struggle to "make ends meet."

Making Ends Meet: Homemaking in Poor White Families

We have argued that a cornerstone of homemaking among white married women was a domestic presence. This conferred upon their husbands the position of family provider, the essence of emerging manhood. Accepting her husband's income as the family's income, the poor white homemaker's work became the adjusting of the needs of her family to this amount. While wealthy homemakers were free to seek out new and superior ways to spend their ample incomes, poor homemakers were forced to invent ways to make ends meet. This was a challenging task for, even if marriages were begun with an adequate flow of income, vacillations in husbands' incomes due to unemploy-ment or illness combined with necessary increases in family expendi-tures through the life-cycle (due especially to having and raising chil-dren) to present most working-class homemakers with times of cash deficits.[11] Here we will examine the different ways in which home-makers resolved this problem.

A straightforward and essential way that poor homemakers made ends meet was by, literally, saving money—not by putting money into saving, but by reducing family expenditures. A homemaker did so by denying her family many "luxury" commodities and by substituting her own home production for as many essential commodities as possible. At the turn of the century, many families were living on extremely limited budgets.[12] They did so by, (1) limiting their families' consump-tion of commodities, (2) filling as many family needs as possible with their home work, and (3) finding other sources of income.

The first two tricks of homemaking were interrelated: a homemaker could substitute for commodity purchases with her own home efforts, as she had in the colonial economy. Needless to say, she would save money by not hiring a domestic and instead doing the drudgery housework herself—cleaning, food processing, heating the home, carting water and sewage, cooking. She could, furthermore, avoid purchases of food for the family by maintaining a family garden, even livestock. This was done in factory towns and city tenements as well as in rural areas through the early twentieth century. Although most cloth was purchased by the mid-nineteenth century—home-spun being unacceptable—homemakers could sew the family's clothes. Through such self-sufficient production a homemaker could fill many of her family's most basic needs.

However, even in the colonial family economy, families had needs for commodities that could not be satisfied by woman's home production; by the mid-nineteenth century, and increasingly as time went on, there were indispensable commodity purchases to be made. Home-spun and -woven was no longer acceptable in clothing, accommodations in factory towns or cities had to be rented, coal had to be purchased for heating the home, life insurance had to be bought to cover burial expenses, medicine or doctor services were needed in case of illness, and utilities—running water, electricity, sewage—were introduced. Only income could fill her family's need for such things. If, after the substitution of home production for commodity purchases wherever possible, the husband's income was inadequate to fill the remaining commodity needs of the family, the homemaker had to seek out sources of additional income for the family.

A number of low-income families resolved the conflict between the need for more income and the need for the homemaker to be at home by taking in boarders, an activity halfway between labor-force participation and homemaking. Like the tavern keeper of colonial times, the homemaker who took in boarders did homemaking in her own home—but for a non-family member, and in exchange for money. She was clearly doing women's work, but she was doing women's work for income. As in the family economy, the family extended its household, taking in strangers, for economic reasons; but whereas in the family economy this practice had been centered in wealthy families, in industrial capitalism it was practiced by the poor. Taking in boarders allowed homemakers to remain in the domestic sphere at their "natural" work of homemaking. Not all boarders were strangers to the family; many poor families charged their older children "board." The service provided by homemakers varied from simply renting out a room to providing meals and homemaking services. Given the flow of new laborers into the cities, from abroad and from the countryside, there were many single and homeless individuals who needed the services of a homemaker. Studies have shown that taking in boarders was a common method of supplementing a husband's income. John Modell and Tamara Hareven estimate that up through the 1930s from 15 to 20% of urban households had boarders or lodgers *at any one time*, and point out that the proportion that *ever* had boarders must have been much higher.[13] Studies of wage-earners' budgets in New York City in 1907 and 1909 found boarders in 31 and 29% of families, respectively; the former study noted that a full 9.2% of the total income of these families came from this source.[14] The prevalence of the practice of taking in boarders varied greatly between ethnic groups: the 1909–10 survey of immigrant families in cities found the percentage of families taking in boarders varying from 2.9% of Syrian families to 56.6% of north Italian families (see Table 6-1). While its conception of home life as well as the availability of boarders certainly played a role in determining whether or not a family would take in boarders, financial need was the basic motivator. The middle class was able to expel non-family members from its households as the cult of domesticity ideal of privacy developed; the financially strapped working-class family, holding to the ideal of domestic womanhood, most often preferred to disturb family privacy with boarders rather than to send the homemaker into the labor force—although some were forced to do both. The progressive reformers' attacks on the "lodger evil" were, hence, misplaced; only rising and more stable standards of living in the twentieth century would allow working class families to enjoy both domestic womanhood *and* family privacy.[15]

Another source of income for the homebound homemaker was putting-out work, which we have already discussed. As spinning and weaving were moved into the factories and the production of cloth was mechanized, the sewing of clothes became a putting-out activity. Needlework done at home for a merchant-capitalist was a common source of additional income for homebound married women. Putting-out work was popular among homemakers because they could earn income while remaining in the domestic sphere. The willingness of homemakers to do such work for very low wages allowed putting-out production to persist into the twentieth century, in spite of its technical inferiority to factory production. It also kept wages at a level sufficient only to supplement a husband's income, making life difficult for the widows and deserted women who tried to survive on needlework.

In most instances, a family would not be started until the husband's income, plus these supplements, was adequate to its financial support. However, even with careful planning, a sudden reduction in the husband's income caused by his unemployment or underemployment, or increases in the necessary expenditures of the family due to the birth and maturing of the children or to family illness, could cause these home methods of earning income to be inadequate. Here the only remaining options of the family were sending the children or the homemaker out into the labor force. The domestic ideal of homemaking, combined with the vestiges of the family economy conception of the child as a little worker, meant that many families chose to send their children rather than the homemaker to seek such income in the labor force.

Poor families had not had the opportunity to develop the cult of domesticity conception of childhood as the special right of the young; rather, they adapted the family economy idea of the child as a little worker to capitalist factory production. And, since most of the poor envisioned their sons' and daughters' futures as unskilled laborers or as home-makers, respectively, unskilled work in a factory or domestic service in the home was indeed appropriate training. Carroll Wright's 1875 study of outdoor laborers and mill operatives in Massachusetts found that children represented 44% of the workers, earning 24% of income earned—as compared to wives, who were 1% of the workers, contributing only 0.8% of the income earned.[16] The 1911 government study of immigrants in cities showed that, for most ethnic groups, it was more common to employ children than homemakers.[17] A 1923 study of poverty level families, *The Share of Wage-earning Women in Family Support*, found labor-force participation rates of family members which ranged from 96.3% of fathers, 96.6% of sons, and 95% of daughters, to only 25.9% of wives or mothers.[18] The employment of children, including daughters, in the support of their families meant a relatively high labor-force participation rate for single women. In 1890, over 40% of single women were in the labor force, many of them helping their mothers to remain in the home; 70.4% of foreign-born white single women worked for income.[19] Among women in the working class, the life-work cycle was most often employment in childhood or adolescence, which would be terminated at marriage.

Table 6–1: Percent of Families Having an Income from Husband, Wife, Children, Boarders or Lodgers, and Other Sources, by General Nativity and Race of Head of Family

	Number of selected families[a]	Earnings Husband	Wife	Contribu-tions of children	Payments of boarders or lodgers	Other sources
Native-born of native father:						
White	374	86.6	16.0	21.9	14.4	9.4
Negro	179	73.2	64.2	9.5	32.4	5.6
Native-born of foreign father, by race of father:						
Bohemian and Moravian	33	100.0	45.5	6.1	6.1	3.0
German	169	83.4	16.0	25.4	11.8	10.1
Irish	222	86.9	20.3	24.8	12.6	6.8
Foreign-born:						
Bohemian and Moravian	472	81.4	34.7	33.5	15.3	9.3
German	431	77.0	20.2	42.0	10.7	22.0
Hebrew, Russian	721	85.3	7.8	35.6	43.0	9.3
Hebrew, Other	149	77.9	12.1	34.2	31.5	8.7
Irish	599	77.5	19.6	41.9	17.5	7.8

Italian, North	53	88.7	13.2	28.3	56.6	7.5
Italian, South	1,269	93.8	16.8	21.6	27.0	5.0
Lithuanian	260	96.2	6.5	8.8	77.3	4.2
Magyar	182	90.1	22.5	9.3	52.7	4.9
Negro	37	94.6	67.6	5.4	51.4	5.4
Polish	959	90.9	10.7	21.9	38.1	13.9
Slovak	308	93.5	14.6	14.9	44.8	10.7
Slovenian	100	98.0	.0	11.0	36.0	8.0
Swedish	113	77.9	20.4	36.3	42.5	12.4
Syrian	34	85.3	11.8	8.8	2.9	11.8
Grand total	6,700	87.0	17.7	26.0	30.3	9.4
Total native-born of foreign father	441	86.6	20.6	23.1	11.8	7.7
Total native-born	994	84.2	26.8	20.2	16.5	7.9
Total foreign-born	5,706	87.4	16.1	27.0	32.7	9.6

SOURCE: U.S. Senate, *Immigrants in Cities* (1911), Vol. I, p. 139.

a. Sample of 10,000 households from the most congested (and poverty-ridden) sections of New York City, Chicago, Philadelphia, Boston, Cleveland, Buffalo, and Milwaukee. This table includes only races with twenty or more families reporting. The totals, however, are for all races. Families are excluded which reported income as "none."

Table 6–2: Labor-force Participation Rates of Females[a] over 15, by
Marital Status and Age, 1890

		Marital Status			
Age	All marital status	Single and unknown	Married	Widowed	Divorced
all ages	18.9	40.5	4.6	29.3	49.0
15–24	29.0	37.3	6.4	53.5	50.0
25–34	17.2	55.0	4.8	55.0	56.0
35–44	13.2	48.1	4.5	50.1	54.2
45–54	12.9	41.0	3.9	37.0	44.5
55–64	12.0	32.3	3.0	24.5	32.9
65	8.3	17.7	2.3	11.0	18.1
unknown	30.8	44.0	14.2	39.2	58.2

SOURCE: U.S. Department of Commerce, Bureau of the Census, *Statistics of Women at Work, 1900,* p. 14.
a. The number of women in the labor force divided by the number of women in the population.

The domestic homemaking of married women was supported by the labors of their daughters (we will discuss the working girl more in Chapter 7). The resulting difference in their labor-force participation rates is shown in Table 6-2.

In some poor families, the children were too young to be employable; in other, homemakers were determined to allow their children to finish school. In these cases, homemakers chose to work to fill commodity needs of the family, even though their employment outside of the home under the cult of domesticity represented an unhealthy or failed family. While this brought extra income into the family, it also threatened the husband's ego by branding him as an inadequate husband and depriving him of his special role in the family. Louise More described the effects of the homemaker's employment on her husband in her 1907 study of wage-earners in New York City: "As soon as he sees that the wife can help support the family, his interest and sense of responsibility are likely to lessen, and he works irregularly or spends more on himself. . . . Charitable societies generally deplore the prevalence of this custom because of its economic and moral results on the head of the family."[20]

Most married homemakers in the labor force were there to supplement the inadequate wages of their husbands, or because their husbands were unemployed, ill, or injured. Gwendolyn Hughes' 1925 study of wage-earning mothers in Philadelphia revealed that the insufficiency of the husband's wage accounted for the entrance of married women into the labor force in 90% of the cases. Sixty percent of working mothers had no income at all from their husbands, due to his illness, desertion, or death. Another 29% worked because the husband's wage was "insufficient." The 11% who said that they worked out of personal preference cited the needs of the household for additional income: "The money which the wife earns is usually spent for 'extras' which the husband cannot supply. These additional commodities, however, would be regarded as necessities in more fortunate households."[21]

Most often married women were brought into the labor force by unexpected drops in their husbands' earnings, due to seasonal work or unemployment. In the nineteenth and early twentieth centuries many of the lowest paying jobs were also the least stable. In one study of immigrant women in the labor force, the employment of their husbands was often so unstable that the working wives were unable to describe their husbands' jobs with anything more than the name of the employing firm. According to the study, "The complaint of 'work not too much' was heard again and again in the home visits."[22] Another major cause of unemployment was illness of the husband. In all these cases, the employment of the homemaker provided earnings to fill unexpected gaps in family income or to lay aside a bit of savings for such emergencies. Thus, periods of general economic recession, by decreasing male wages and increasing unemployment, brought homemakers into the labor force.

Immigrant homemakers were found to share the general pattern of labor force participation described here: they entered the labor force as supplementary workers in order to make ends meet. Caroline Manning's study of immigrant women in the labor force found that 67.8% of married women workers studied worked becuase their husbands' support was "inadequate"; 47.1% stressed the inadequacy or vacillations of their husbands' wages; 20.7% stressed their own inabilities to homemake given the limited family income. The other major reason for entering the labor force, given by 21.0% of these women, was an interesting one—"to buy home or furniture." Apparently, owning their own home was a goal shared by many families.

According to Manning, a period of steady earnings by the husband encouraged a family to begin this investment; vacillations in the husband's earnings then forced the homemaker into the labor force to meet the monthly payments.[23]

As Mary Winslow wrote in her Women's Bureau Report of 1924, *Married Women in Industry:*

> From the material on married women wage earners which we have assembled in this report, we have reached one definite conclusion: whatever may be the extent of their earning capacity, whatever may be the irregularity of their employment, married women are in industry for one purpose and, generally speaking, for one purpose only—to provide necessities for their families or to raise their standard of living. In one study we found that practically all women who were wives and mothers—95% of them, to be exact—contributed all of their earnings to their families. And although these earnings were not as a rule large, they often brought the family income up to a level which was adequate for the maintenance of a satisfactory standard of health and education for the children.[24]

This claim that homemakers worked in order to bring their families' incomes up to some basic, shared minimum standard is substantiated by the 1923 Women's Bureau study of *The Share of Wage-earning Women in Family Support.* This study found that the homemakers' earnings raised the median per capita family earnings "from $438, which is considerably below the median for all families, to $641, which is considerably above . . . with the wives' earnings included, only 35.4% of the families fell below per capita earnings of $500, while the exclusion of the wives' earning would result in 60.2% of the families falling below this level."[25]

Although the inferiority of their husbands' incomes pressured poor homemakers to enter the labor force, in some sense to achieve some accepted standard of living, we must remember that the striking quality of nineteenth- and early twentieth-century family life was the absence of such a common standard of living, the lack of a common conception of the commodity needs of the family, or of the place of the children in the home. Poor families used self-sufficient home production, putting-out, boarding, or child employment to get by with a minimum of commodity purchases; wealthy families could free themselves from self-sufficient production, purchase commodities, hire servants, and pamper their children. Furthermore, among the poor there was considerable variation in the ways in which families coped with the poverty of their head of household. The taking in of boarders or of home work, the employment of children or of the homemaker herself, were all options for families; a couple's sense of family life and its priorities informed its choice between these methods of supplementing the husband's income. To some extent, conceptions of family life and responsibilities can be traced to cultural heritages: income sources differed significantly between ethnic groups (see Table 6-1).

White native and immigrant families, rich and poor, shared the domestic ideal of womanhood, the ideal of the homebound homemaker. The family of the man at the bottom of the income scale fought to maintain the domestic ideal of womanhood (and hence the manhood of its husband/household head), and most often succeeded. The price paid for this was not only a more limited family budget, but also the inability to transform the household into a personal, family sphere. The presence of boarders prevented the home from being a family place, and the necessity of child labor kept homemakers from mothering and from allowing for the full individual development of their children. Boarders and child labor were absent from the homes of privileged homemakers; indeed, as we will see in Chapter 8, these women fought against child labor as antithetical to their conception of the family and fought to commoditize homemaking so as to free their homes from the presence of strangers. So although poor families and wealthy families shared domestic homemakers, they lived out very different kinds of family life. These differences were part of the absence, in society at large, of a clear conception of the requirements of healthy family life.

Homemaking in the Black Family

We have mentioned that a significant percentage of black homemakers did not share the domestic ideal of native and immigrant whites. In 1900, 22.7% of black married women were in the labor force, as compared to only 3.2% of whites.[26] In the 1911 *Immigrants in Cities* study of poor families, black families were the most likely of all ethnic and racial groups, native, first- and second-generation, to have earnings from the homemaker (64% of them did; see Table 6-1).[27] On the other hand, although domesticity was less prevalent among blacks than among whites, the majority of black homemakers was indeed absent from the labor force, supported financially by husband/providers in the white pattern.

The relative weakness of domesticity in black families does not in itself mean that the domestic ideal held there any less strongly. It could have been simply the result of the lower wages that black men provided to their families. Although abolition formally gave black men property rights equal to those of whites, black men have remained in an inferior economic position up through the twentieth century. Rather than working to bring blacks out of the ignorance and poverty inherited from slavery, white society as a whole worked actively to exclude blacks from the white world with Jim Crow laws, racist union policies, segregated institutions, and, if necessary, lynch mobs. Kept out of white jobs and living areas, black men remained concentrated on the land, as poor share-croppers: in 1900, 58% of black employed males were working in agriculture, compared to 27% of white males.[28] If they moved out of agriculture, they were excluded from higher-paid jobs, concentrated in domestic service and in unskilled and semiskilled work, and hardest hit by unemployment. Certainly the restriction of black men to low-paid jobs and their higher rate of unemployment explains some of the difference between the labor force participation rates of black and white homemakers.

Yet careful comparisons of black and white families show that more than poverty was at work here. When black and white families in which the husband's income and the number of children are the same are compared, black homemakers were still more likely to be gainfully employed; this difference has been documented from the turn of the century through the post–World War II period. For example, in the *Immigrants in Cities* study we have already cited, black families were four times more likely than foreign born to have income from homemakers (64.2% versus 16.1%) in spite of the fact that the average earnings of the male family heads were slightly higher for the blacks ($465 versus $452).[29] Recent econometric studies have found that black homemakers had higher labor-force participation than whites, even when economic and demographic variables were controlled for.[30] Black homemakers were more likely to respond to the poverty of their families by taking responsibility for earning income. Why?

Slavery and its heritage of racism worked against the establishment of a domestic ideal of womanhood in the black family by excluding the black man from the white conception of manhood and by forcing the black woman to retain the independence and responsibility forced upon her under slavery. We have traced the push for domesticity among poor whites to the family's efforts to establish the manhood of the husband/head of household, to signal his membership in the community of property-owning, competing men. Yet black men were forcibly excluded from this community, denied acceptance as equals in the white competition for manhood. They were prevented from entering jobs that allowed for competitive advancement and provided a family wage. It was the struggle to show success in this masculine labor-force competition that underlay efforts to keep homemakers at home; yet black men were excluded from this whole process. And, unlike immigrant men, all their efforts to fit in could not erase their stigmatizing quality, their skin color. Unemployment and restriction to the lowest-status jobs made the black man's labor-force participation an experience of subordination and degradation as much as one of masculine self-assertion. Further pressure against the domestic ideal came from the black woman. Slavery had cut her and her children off from the protection of her family and often forced her to take sole responsibility for children. She had been forcibly "individuated," forced to deal on her own with "the (white) man." Under slavery, she had lived both roles, homemaker/mother and "provider." After abolition, the white homes and factories that had employed her as a slave now offered her paid employment; moreover, it was often easier for her to find employment than for her husband.

When slave families were freed, they did not simply adopt the white pattern of husband in the labor force, wife in the home. Yes, the withdrawal of homemakers and children from the fields during Reconstruction was much remarked. One ex-slave vowed "to support his family by his own efforts; never to allow his wife and daughters to be thrown in contact with Southern white men in their homes."[31] However, although black men may have wished to become husband/providers and support homebound wives, their low wages and unstable employment prospects made such a transformation difficult. Black men faced tremendous difficulty establishing their manhood after abolition. Racism combined with the ravages of slavery to make their achievement of the white ideal of manhood virtually impossible. Their wives, faced with the prospect of family poverty, aware of their own abilities to earn income, and feeling an individual responsibility for their children, did not always sit by passively. Some persuaded their husbands to accept their help.[32] Upon abolition, therefore, a new family form emerged among the more oppressed blacks—a family where both husband and wife worked in the labor force.

A second difference existed between poor black and poor white families: their treatment of their children. Perhaps due to their goal of upward mobility, and the difficulty of such a struggle, poor black families kept their children out of the labor force more than their white counterparts. The *Immigrants in Cities* study showed that while 26% of the families studied had income from their children, only 9.5% of black families did (see Table 6-1). Elizabeth Pleck found that school enrollment rates of black children were twice those of Italians: it seems that blacks valued the education denied them as slaves, seeing it as the key to their escape from oppression.[33] The greater reticence of blacks to take their children out of school further pressured the black homemaker into the labor force. When the black child grew up, however, he or she quickly sought work, left home, and began helping the parents.[34] The labor force participation rate of single black women in 1900 was 60.5% compared to 31.4% for native, 49.1% for second-generation immigrants, and 69.4% for first-generation immigrants.[35]

Hence the sexual division of labor was less pronounced among black families. However, the two-earner family was not to be the source of joy and equality among blacks—rather, it was a sign of oppression as well as a source of tension between husband and wife. While her labor force participation represented the black woman's commitment to her family, it also signified, by white society's standards, her husband's failure to achieve manhood. Her efforts to help her husband and family were at the same time resented as depriving her husband of his manhood, his ability to provide. Slavery and racism have prevented many black men from achieving masculinity and encouraged black women to share man's role. Yet this has not meant liberation of the sexes, but rather anger, mistrust, and a weakened marital bond. By depriving the poor black man of a means to support his family, and simultaneously schooling his wife in the world of work, white society has, effectively, castrated him.

Husbandless Homemakers

While the cult of domesticity pressured married homemakers to remain in the home, it simultaneously pressured the husbandless

homemaker into the labor force. With the decline of family businesses, widows of capitalists were less likely to inherit the management of a business; instead, they lived off the firm's earnings. As in
the family economy, husbandless women left without wealth first
sought remarriage or support from their children or relatives. If a
homemaker was left without wealth or family support, she was forced
into the labor force, or to seek charity. A large part of employed
married women were, in fact, without husbands: 41.8% in 1900,
37.6% in 1920. As the study puts it, "If, therefore, the normal home
life for a married woman be defined as living with her husband in a
home of her own, then somewhat more than one-third of these married women gainfully employed did not have a normal home life."[36]
Hughes' study of working mothers found that 60% of them had no
income from their husbands because of his illness (14%), desertion
(13%), death (22%), or nonsupport (11%).[37]

Homemakers who lacked husband/providers were, then, often
forced to be both husband and wife, to earn income for the family and
to care for the family. They were the casualties of the sexual division
under the cult of domesticity. The loss of one's husband and provider
was the worst tragedy a homemaker could experience. The plight of
one such woman was described in a *New York Tribune* article in
1845: "It was but a week or two ago that a respectable woman,
reduced from competence to poverty by a sudden calamity, traversed
the streets of our city for 2 or 3 days in search of some employment
by which she could earn bread for herself and children." In this case,
the woman found paid home work as a seamstress, worked for a
week, and received only "credit": "With this she was to return to her
desolute, destitute home. Such scenes are occurring daily in our city
and in all cities; . . . not alone those inured to famine are doomed to
such destitution, but many who dance in jewels one year are shiver-
ing in garrets the next, willing to labor for the humblest fare, yet
unable by labor to procure it."[38]

As in the family economy, women in such situations were suddenly
forced to seek money income through employment or charity, unless
their husbands had left them a sizable amount of capital. By 1830,
they were crowding the cities. In a study of poor women in Philadelphia in 1830, Matthew Carey found that of the city's 549 "out-doors
paupers," 498 were females, of which 406 were widows. He inquired
of the Secretary of the "Female Hospitable Society," a charity that
provided paid work to paupers, about the nature of the women who

came to them. According to the Secretary, these women were, over-whelmingly, homemakers without husbands: "As to the number of widows, the proportion is as 75 to 100; the remainder are, chiefly wives, deserted by their husbands, or whose husbands do nothing for the maintenance of their children, who are too young to do anything for themselves."[39]

Clearly, the homemaker without a husband/provider was much more likely than an actively married woman to enter the labor force, and most likely to do so if she had children to support who were themselves too young to be able to support her. Her only alternative to entering the labor force was to fall back upon the charity of her family or of strangers. The labor force participation rates of widowed and divorced women were 29.9% in 1890, 32.5% in 1900, and 34.1% in 1910.[40] The 1907 study of women in wage work, compiled from the Twelfth Census, lists labor-force participation rates by age and marital status (see Table 6-2, p. 130). Widows were more likely to work when they were younger: this was explained by "their necessity of support-ing not only themselves but their dependent children. As the years go by, the children grow up and are able to support their mothers."[41] Furthermore, women widowed at a later age were more likely to have sufficient inheritance from their husbands to support them-selves. Divorced women were the most likely to be in the labor force, but they formed only a very small percentage of women, less than one-half of one percent in 1890–1900: the 1907 study claims that their very high labor-force participation rates resulted from the fact that only financially independent women were able to get divorces.[42] Most women who lived apart from their husbands were only informally separated, and hence still listed as married—causing a misleading inflation in the labor-force participation rates of married women.

By the early twentieth century, the development of the govern-ment sector and its growing role as guarantor of the welfare of its citizens brought the introduction, first in some states and eventually on the national level, of programs supplying financial support for "female heads of households." Such programs attempted to solve the cult of domesticity's major problem: the problem of the "broken home" where the absence of a husband/provider prevented the homemaker from concentrating on her private homemaking. Concern for the poverty of fatherless children, combined with a desire to have them raised in homes rather than in charitable institutions, prompted the state to begin to step in to prop up the family by acting as a husband-replacement.[43] Certainly, other ways of rescuing such children were imaginable, such as providing their mothers with job training, jobs and subsidized day-care facilities. The state's decision to provide cash child-support payments to female heads of households reflected the prevailing conceptions of family life as woman's vocation and proper parenting as mothering within the home. Ironically, the welfare system, which was set up to buttress the ideal family, actually may have contributed to its disintegration among the poor by providing them with a strong disincentive to marriage.

Privileged Homemakers and Their Mission

The homemaker whose husband was at the middle or top of the income hierarchy was in a very different position than the poor homemaker, that of finding and defining her work. A need for income did not force her to send her children into the labor force, nor encourage her to take in boarders to make ends meet. She was able to hire domestic servants to perform the household drudgery that could not be lightened by commodity purchases. For these women, the home sphere and homemaking were largely freed from crude production, and the specificity of family life had room to emerge. They had no need to use their children as little workers, but rather could afford to explore the profession of mothering as a personal and private matter. Neither did homemaking mean labor force participation; their husbands' successes as husbands/providers not only necessitated but comfortably allowed for their domestic confinement. Yet these women faced another task, defining the content of homemaking, making it indeed into a vocation. The cult of domesticity sent such women on an active search for their homemaking profession.

A vast field lay open to these privileged women. The care of the family, the creation of the home, the service of others, and the cultivation of ethical children, as women's work, were their work; yet it was unclear what they involved. It became the task of privileged women to define and perfect woman's emergent vocation. The nineteenth century saw a tremendous flurry of middle-class feminine activity directed toward this end. While much of this was restricted to woman's private home sphere, the masculine and hence heartless quality of economic and political life cried out for complementing by the feminine principle, drawing many women into "social homemaking," homemaking for society at large. The inability of poor home-makers to achieve the middle-class homemaking ideal inspired these vocational homemakers to take up the task of helping their poorer sisters, and their children.

The process of defining woman's homemaking work had the indi-rect effect of developing woman as homemaker. Woman's desire to fulfill her vocation led her to demand her own training and social development. Her desire to homemake for the world brought her push for political rights. And this development of woman occasioned by the cult of domesticity began to lead her into the masculine sphere itself. We will examine these three aspects of the development of the homemaking profession by middle-class women in Chapter 8. But first we shall investigate another result of the cult of domesticity, the complement to the domestic homemaker—the working girl.

7

The Working Girl

While the cult of domesticity kept the married women in the home if possible, it did not exclude all women from the labor force. Table 7-1 shows that although women's labor-force participation rates were significantly lower than men's in the nineteenth and early twentieth centuries, they were by no means insignificant. Hence, females, although not proportionally represented in the labor force, made up 17.1% of the labor force in 1890 and 20.4% in 1920.[1]

The development of wage labor and the movement of commodity production out of the home, did draw women into the labor force; however, the development of the female labor force was an uneven and complex process. The rise of factory production left the large majority of homemakers in the home—indeed, the new conception of manhood put extra value on a wife's domesticity. It also drew unmarried women into the labor force, however, making working for wages part of adolescence for many women. We will study the development of the working girl in this chapter.[2]

The Woman Worker as "Working Girl"

Female labor-force participation rates were highest in the fifteen to twenty-four age group (see Table 7-2). Women in the labor force were so often young that early studies of them actually had titles such as *Working Girls in Large Cities* and *The Working Girls of Boston*.[3]

The use of the word *girl* to describe females in the labor force, however, was misleading: labor force participation rates by age and marital status reveal very *low* rates for young married women and very high rates for older unmarried, widowed, or divorced women (see Table 6-2, p. 130). Statistics for 1890 and 1900 show the labor-force participation rates of single women at 40.5 and 45.9% respec-

Table 7–1: Labor-force Participation Rates by Sex,[a] 1890–1930

	Males	Females
1890	84.3	18.2
1900	85.7	20.0
1920	84.6	23.6
1930	82.1	23.6

SOURCE: U.S. Department of Commerce, Bureau of the Census, *Historical Statistics of the United States: Colonial Times to 1970*, p. 132.

a. The number of women (men) in the labor force divided by the number of women (men) in the population.

Table 7–2: Labor-force Participation Rates of Women[a] by Age, 1890, 1900, 1920

	Age				
	10–15	15–19	20–24	25–44	45–64
1890	10.0	29.7	30.3	15.0	12.0
1900	10.2	32.3	31.8	17.6	13.8
1920	5.6	34.5	37.6	21.7	16.6

SOURCE: U.S. Department of Commerce, Bureau of Census, *Historical Statistics of the United States: Colonial Times to 1970*, Series A 119–134, p. 15, and Series D 29–41, p. 131. For the 10–15 age group, *Census, Population*, 1930, Vol. V, General Report on Occupations, p. 45.

a. The number of women in the labor force divided by the number of women in the population.

tively, versus rates for married women of 4.6 and 5.6% respectively.[4] Marital status, not age, was the variable that determined women's labor-force participation. An unmarried and hence "immature" woman was likely to be in the labor force; marriage and maturity meant leaving the labor force. The "spinster" who had continued on in the labor force past her girlhood years without marrying remained a perpetual "working girl." Hence, never-married women comprised the majority of the female labor force in the nineteenth and early twentieth centuries: 68.2% of the urban female labor force in 1890, and 66.2% in 1900, and 77% in 1920.[5]

Working girls not only constituted most of the female labor force, their labor was essential to the early development of factory production. The early textile factories, established on the rivers of New England in the 1820s and '30s, were unable to attract many men away from the agricultural sector. Concentrated in farming, men were reticent to give up the status of independent commodity producers. Women, especially single women, provided these early factories with much of their labor force; wage work, we will see, fit into their obligations as daughters. As the factory system gained hegemony and centered itself in cities, men joined women in the labor force, yet working girls remained an important part of it.

The Roots of the Working Girl Phenomenon

When capitalist development brought wage labor, single women or girls were drawn into it. Why? The working girl resulted from a combination of factors: the colonial economy's conception of children, the struggles of families to keep their homemakers out of the labor force, and the conception of femininity as the subordination of one's self to the service of one's family.

Among the poor, the phenomenon of the working girl was a carry-over of the family-economy conception of childhood. A single woman was socially defined as a daughter, a child, her life determined by the mutual responsibilities of the parent–child relationship. Children in the family economy had been put out to other families when their own parents could not afford their support or could not provide them with adequate training. This practice freed poor parents from the obligation of supporting their children, although it rarely brought them additional income. The early factories used two systems of employment that built upon and transformed the family economy's use of children. Some early mills hired entire families, including children, through the father and household head; others provided dormitories for the young workers, complete with supervision and rules of behavior that substituted for the supervision of a household head. In each case, the child labor was now rewarded with money wages which the parents received, either directly from the employer or indirectly through their children. As the system of child labor for wages developed, it lost some of its paternalistic qualities; in the cities, children lived at home or in boarding houses and labored in factories just like adult workers.

Such work fit in with the life cycle of the family income and expenditure. As children grew to adolescence, their growing needs made increasing demands on the family budget: wage work by adolescents allowed poorer families to provide for this increase in expenditures. As Robert Chapin explained in his study of New York City in 1909:

> Where the father's earnings are low say under $800, the children have to go to work as soon as the law allows—sometimes earlier—if the standard of living is not to be lowered in the effort to make the same income meet the wants of children who, as they grow, must have continually more to eat and wear.[6]

Of course, the same was true for the children of widows.

The family-economy conception of children as little workers, under the complete power of their fathers, was thus grafted onto the factory system. While middle- and upper-class families were concerning themselves with the proper education of their children, working-class families were using their children to make ends meet.

The desire of poor families, like others, to keep their homemakers out of the labor force limited their incomes and pressured them to use their children as sources of income. We have examined this phenomenon in detail in the previous chapter. The poor family's decision to employ its children rather than the homemaker illustrated both its adherence to the cult of domesticity notions of manhood and womanhood, and its conception of children as lacking wills or rights of their own. The child's schooling or femininity was sacrificed in order to allow the parents to sustain a sexual division of labor.

In the 1820s, '30s, and '40s, the early textile mills employed single women who worked as daughters for the benefit of their families. The experience of these "mill girls" is well-documented; mill owners anxious to establish a good reputation for their mills so as to attract workers commissioned books and articles to be written describing the experience of the mill girls;[7] they even started a newspaper, *The Lowell Offering,* which published articles written by the mill girls themselves. Their attempt to portray the mill girls' experiences as both educational and enjoyable actually succeeded in confusing historians for some time. In 1845 a *New York Daily Tribune* article, "Visit to Lowell," contained one such description:

> Thank God, those fresh spirits gathered down from Granite Hills and from green peaceful valleys by their own wills, to the carnival of spindles and looms, and iron arms, heaving with their titan best, are nonetheless, but more beautiful, while pure, they stand up and vindicate the sacredness of Toil. They are not called by imperious wants.[8]

A careful reading of primary sources, however, reveals that, without a doubt, the mill girls were not working for their own edification, but for their families. As the first American workers' magazine, *The Voice of Industry,* aptly asked, why, if the mills were as attractive as depicted in these books, were not the "ladies" found there:

> The only wonder, seeing what a prodigality of advantages are prepared for the factory laborers, seeing too what immense fortunes they accumulate, is that the wives and daughters, the sons and uncles of the owners, have not been attracted to enter into such an enviable condition. Are there any records of ladies leaving their silken and perfumed saloons to become factory girls from the mere love of luxury? Has any youthful exquisite, satiated with the ordinary pleasures of wealth and elegance, sought for newer and intenser enjoyments in twelve hours a day steady toil, amidst the hum of spindles and the jar of machinery?[9]

There was clearly a class difference between mill girls and ladies: girls who "chose" to go to the mills were from poor or declining families in dire need of cash incomes:

> Do they from mere choice leave their fathers' dwellings, the fireside where all their friends, where too their earliest and fondest recollections cluster, for the factory and the corporation's boarding house? By what charm do these great companies immure human creatures in the bloom of youth and first glow of life within their mills, away from their homes and kindred? A slave too goes voluntarily to his task, but his will is in some

manner quickened by the whip of the overseer. The whip which brings laborers to Lowell is Necessity. They must have money; a father's debts are to be paid, an aged mother is to be supported, a brother's ambitions to be aided, and so the factories are supplied. . . . Is there any one such a fool as to suppose that out of six thousand factory girls at Lowell, sixty would be there if they could help it? Everybody knows that it is necessity, alone, in some form or another, that takes them to Lowell, and that keeps them there.[10]

The Lowell Offering, when carefully examined, reveals the same harsh reality: girls came to the factories because their families desperately needed money. While The Offering's articles about mill work (written by the mill girls themselves) were used for public relations by the mills owners, the poverty of the girls' families consistently emerges in its pages. The reasons for coming to the mills mentioned in its stories were almost always some type of family catastrophe: a failed father, the death of the father or of both parents, illness of family members, a bankrupt family farm. In one story a girl complained that the sudden death of both of her parents catapulted her into destitution, sending her into the mills to support her sick brother. Her boarding-house mate responded, "Why, Alice, there is hardly a girl in this house who has not as much trouble, in some shape, as you have."[11] Family poverty forced girls into the mills where they worked as daughters, sending back their meager pay to aid their families. They were not independent young women seeking their fortunes, but rather poor and burdened daughters. Girls employed in the eastern mills provided needed income for their parents' family farms, which were suffering from competition from the west. The employment of daughters in this case eased the process of agricultural concentration and the rural–urban migration which accompanied it.

The phenomenon of the working girl did not disappear when factories moved to the cities. An 1880 study of 1,032 Working Girls of Boston found that 90% were unmarried. Interviews of the girls' families revealed insufficiencies in the fathers' incomes and the dependence of the families on their daughters' earnings:

The information furnished by the working girls shows that the wages earned by them constitute in many cases the chief, and sometimes the entire support of the family, the parents looking to the earnings of one, two, three, and four daughters to pay household bills; the father often being reported not able to work much or always, on account of disability, from lack of steady work, or possibly, from disinclination to work while there is revenue from any other source. In large families, the earnings of the girls, together with the wages of the father, when all are working, do not more than cover living expenses.[12]

Of the unmarried working girls, almost one-half had lost their fathers. A 1927 study of *The Young Employed Girl* interviewed 500 of Philadelphia's 3,867 working girls aged fourteen to sixteen years and visited 263 of their homes. All but ten of these girls turned their entire paychecks over to their families. Of the 263 families interviewed, 209 were in dire need of income—half because of death or illness of parents, the other half because the father's income was simply insufficient to buy necessities for the family. Many families cited the increasing costs of their growing children: they needed extra income to maintain their present standards of living "for the sum of money necessary to supply the demands of a growing daughter at a given age is not sufficient to supply the demands of that same daughter later." None of the families interviewed was well-off.[13]

The working girl was part of the larger phenomenon of the working child. Through the early twentieth century, it remained common for poor families to send their children to work to supplement their incomes. In More's study of the budgets of wage earners in New York City in 1907, 37% of the families studied received income from working children: 32.4% of families with native American fathers, 42.1% of families with foreign-born fathers. These working children contributed a total of 11.5% of the total income of all these families.[14] Other studies found similarly high percentages of children employed: Chapin (New York City "workingmen," 1907) found children at work in 81 of the 391 families studied, about 20%; Houghteling (Chicago unskilled laborers, 1927) found children adding to family income in 108 of 467 families, over 25%.[15] In 1920, nearly 88% of the children at least sixteen years old of Chicago unskilled workers were employed.[16] Claudia Goldin's econometric study of Philadelphia in 1880 found a clear negative correlation between the father's full-time wage and the probability of labor-force participation for both sons and daughters, supporting our contention that children worked to help financially needy parents.[17]

However, the working girl's experience was differentiated from that of her brother in two important ways. First, the daughter's labor-

Table 7–3: Labor-force Participation Rates
of Men and Women[a] by Age, 1900

Age	Male	Female
10–15	26.1	10.2
16–20	76.8	32.3
21–24	93.1	30.8
25–34	96.3	19.9
35–44	96.6	15.6
45–54	95.5	14.7
55–64	90.0	13.2
65	68.4	9.1
age unknown	59.6	24.2
total	90.5	20.6

SOURCE: U.S. Department of Commerce, Bureau of the Census, *Statistics of Women at Work, 1900*, p. 14. For the 10–15 age group, *Census, Population, 1930*, Vol. V, General Report on Occupations, p. 45.
a. The number of women (men) in the labor force divided by the number of women (men) in the population.

force participation was only a temporary stage to be superseded, it was hoped, upon her marriage, by the practice of homemaking; the son's was an apprenticeship of sorts to his future as a laborer and head of household. Hence families were most likely, when needing a child's income, to send their sons into the labor force: Table 7-3 shows that, in the ten to fifteen year age group, 26.1% of males were in the labor force in 1900, versus 10.2% of females; for the sixteen to twenty year age group, the percentages were 76.8 and 32.3, respectively. As both sexes grew to adulthood, the disparity in labor-force participation widened: for a man labor-force participation meant adulthood; for a woman, it meant immaturity.

A second difference between men and women had the opposite effect on their labor-force behavior as children. The girl's life was to be dedicated to the service of her family, first as a daughter, later as a homemaker, whereas the boy's life was subordinated to his family's needs only during childhood. As an adult he would become an individual competitor in the labor force, a head of household served by his wife and children. Since she planned to be a homemaker, the daughter's claim on self-development was weaker than that of her brother, while her obligation to serve their parent family was greater. Working-class families kept tighter control over their daughters' earnings than their sons'.[18] And it was not uncommon for daughters to be sent into the labor force instead of their brothers. *The Lowell Offering* contains many stories of girls working to allow their brothers to remain in school. In "The Sister," a boy achieved upward mobility through the toils of his sister, whom he then would not visit for fear of losing his respectability.[19] According to Harriet Robinson's account of her experiences as a factory girl, *Loom and Spindle*, the education of male family members was the girls' most common motive for entering into the mills:

> Indeed, the most prevailing incentive to our labor was to secure the means of education for some *male* member of the family. To make a *gentleman* of a brother or a son, to give him a college education, was the dominant thought in the minds of a great many of these provident mill-girls. I have known more than one to give every cent of her wages, month after month, to her brother, that he might get the education necessary to enter some profession. I have known women to educate by their earnings young men who were not sons or relatives. There are men now living who were helped to an education by the wages of the early mill-girls.

She quotes Mr. Thomas Wentworth Higginson on the subject:

> I think it was the later President Walker who told me that in his judgment one-quarter of the men in Harvard College were being carried through by the special self-denial and sacrifices of women. I cannot answer for the ratio; but I can testify to having been an instance of this myself, and to having known a never-ending series of such cases of self-devotion.[20]

The same self-sacrifice drove a New York Italian girl to work as an artificial flower maker to help her brother through a medical course. She explained, "I often say to my mother that we treat my brother as if he were a king. But I can't help it."[21] Such behavior was very much a part of the general conception of femininity toward which females of all ages and marital statuses strove: "The one quality on which woman's value and influence depend, is the renunciation of self—the fundamental principle is right—'that women were to live for others.' "[22]

The phenomenon of the working girl highlights the conception of womanhood under the cult of domesticity, but in a contradictory manner. It was the combination of the homemaker's need to remain in the home and the conception of children as in their parents' service which resulted in the working girl. Yet working girls were immature women; their goal was not to make careers for themselves in the labor force, but to marry and take up homemaking. As Lucy Larcom, an ex-mill girl, wrote in her book on the mill girls, *An Idyll of Work:* "Home Dreams, as in all womany souls, made undertone to her life's music."[23] Most working girls succeeded in terminating their working lives in marriage. The average stay of a working girl at the Lowell mills was four and a half years, and most girls left the mills to marry.[24] As the 1920 study *Women in Gainful Occupations 1870–1920* observed:

> To a woman marriage normally supersedes or precludes the pursuit of a gainful occupation, in that it involves the establishment and care of a home, with the housework or household duties incident thereto, and at the same time provides her with a livelihood [i.e., from her husband]; so that, as a rule, the woman who marries is not as free to follow a wage-earning occupation as she was before marriage, nor under the same necessity for doing so.[25]

For most females, then, labor force participation was an adolescent "stage" which, they hoped, would pass. Maturity, for a woman, was marriage, and marriage meant undertaking the vocation of homemaking and motherhood.

Unlike during colonial times, however, a girl's work was not an apprenticeship to homemaking, unless it involved working as a domestic. Tending a loom in a mill did not prepare a daughter for her future homemaking work in the way that domestic service had in colonial times and even in the nineteenth century. Work for wages was not homemaking; its technology was becoming more and more distinct from the activities involved in homemaking. Helen Sumner described this phenomenon in her *History of Women in Industry* in the United States, written in 1910, as "the divorce of marriage and skill":

> Girls [are] forced to undertake tasks which have no direct interest to them as prospective wives and mothers; there has grown up a class of women workers in whose lives there is internal contradiction and discord. Their work has become merely a means of furnishing food, shelter and clothing during a waiting period which has, meanwhile, gradually lengthened out

as the average age of marriage has increased. Their work no longer fits in with their ideas and has lost its charm.[26]

The same was not as true for a son; unless he was oriented toward the professions, wage work for a boy was a preparation for his future work in the labor force (although its early practice, by cutting short his schooling, did limit his upward mobility). The separation of commodity production and homemaking necessarily brought this disjuncture between a girl's labor-force participation and her future homemaking vocation. Training for homemaking had become schooling, the development of the future mother's socializing skills—not working for others—yet among poor families, schooling's ephemerous benefits were quickly sacrificed when a daughter's earnings were needed.[27]

Not only did wage labor fail to develop a girl's homemaking skills, it also often prevented her from becoming a homemaker. Very poor families often depended upon daughters' earnings for their survival, forcing some devoted daughters to remain in the labor force. Since, according to the cult-of-domesticity conception of womanhood, labor-force participation precluded marriage and homemaking, these women were forced to sacrifice their own marriages for their families. Their fate was eloquently described in a study of "The Gainfully Employed Women of Brattleboro, Vermont" done in 1925:

> A critical period in the lives of these working women comes in the decade between 20 and 30. Fathers have not yet lost their earning capacities; brothers and sisters may be contributing to the family budgets; so that daughters of more prosperous families may marry without feelings of disloyalty to the older family groups. But there are many unselfish women who must face the necessity of suppressing the mating instict because they realize that their services are indispensable in the care of widowed mothers, younger brothers and sisters, or disabled members of their families. . . . Daughters of families with such inferior members [suffering from mental or physical ailments which made it impossible for them to earn a living] are often confronted at the threshold of life with demands for unselfish devotion to the family derelicts.[28]

Woman's predisposition for self-sacrifice, her lesser claim on individuality, made service to her parents as an adult more bearable for her than her brother, even though marriage and continued financial support of one's parents conflicted less for a man: "Their [females'] vocational careers do not seem so important as those of sons, and less imperative sex needs permit the acceptance of the celibate life of service to which they resign themselves fully as the years pass."[29] These females were unable to make the transition from adolescence to adulthood, from daughter to mother/wife; the needs of their parents kept them in the role of the daughter and prevented marriage. They remained "working girls" who aged in years but were doomed to a state of permanent adolescence.

Conversely, girls who had worked to aid their families by being self-supporting were forced to remain in the labor force if they were unable to find husbands. Single women did not have control over their marriages—they had to wait until some man asked for their hand. If they failed to find a husband, and their parents could not support them, daughters were still obliged to support themselves. The period of employed daughterhood could extend itself indefinitely. The movement of young men to the frontier in the nineteenth century created a surplus of young women in the East and increased the numbers of spinsters who were forced into self-support and deprived of mature, domestic womanhood. A *New York Daily Tribune* article in 1853 deplored the difficult position of such girls:

> To tell our hundreds of thousands of poor Young Women, who are constantly looking this way and that for opportunities to earn an honorable and comfortable living, that the end of their existence is to be good wives and mothers, is to insult them most stupidly. What prospect have they, or the half of them, to become wives at all, while so many men spurn the restraints of marriage and riot in dissolute pleasures, and when so many thousands after thousands of our young men are lured away by the still increasing spirit of adventure to California, Central America. . . . It is a decree of Fate that a very large proportion of the Young Women of our older and more easterly States must remain single, while necessity and self-respect alike forbid that they shall eat the bread of idleness.

The author goes on to deplore the lack of suitable jobs at which such women can earn their bread and urges society to do something about it:

> Society must either secure her the opportunity of earning an independent subsistence or shield her from famine and shame with the protecting though degrading mantle of Polygamy and virtual Slavery—assuming Marriage to be the sole condition wherein Woman may live usefully and worthily, the polygamist becomes a public benefactor, especially of the dependent sex.[30]

The Transformation of the Working Girl

While most daughters entered the labor force as dependent and self-less children serving the needs of their families, their experiences in the labor force gave them a degree of independence and freedom as yet unknown to women. For unlike work in the family economy, wage labor rewarded the worker with income and gave her the possibility of living independently of a father or father figure. In the family economy, the employed daughter had worked in the household of a strange man, under his authority, and without pay. As time passed, daughters' employment gradually shifted from self-sufficient home-making for their own families or for families as live-in domestics, to putting-out work for income for their own or other families within a home, to wage labor outside of the home in the factory. Even in the factory, a girl was not always employed as an individual. We have discussed the family labor system, in which the husband and house-hold head contracted jointly for the labor of himself, his children, and occasionally, his wife. As the nineteenth century advanced, the direct employment of children in wage labor grew in prevalence. As a wage laborer a girl was employed by a firm which payed her money that was her own (unless the contract had been drawn between her father and the employer). She had at least some say over how this income was spent, some latitude to use it to fill her needs. Furthermore, her employer no longer automatically provided her with lodgings; if she did not live at home, she used her wages to live on her own. Finally, working as a wage laborer provided a woman with an individual public existence, a public identity of her own, and a sense of her own worth. These ingredients made the working girl more than a simple continuation of the family economy experience of daughtering; they made it an experience which developed a woman's individuality during her unmarried, adolescent life. We will examine these different factors in turn.

Although daughters worked, in most cases, to increase the incomes of their families, and loyally turned over their incomes to their parents, their earnings still were, in some sense, theirs, and they were able to exert some claim upon them. One of the pressing claims upon a girl's wages was her need for a dowry to prepare herself for marriage. A poor girl's parents could not provide her with advanced education in school and in homemaking, a wardrobe of clothes to make her attractive to prospective husbands, time for social life, and a dowry of money and/or household articles to help in the establishment of her home as could wealthy parents. Working girls from poor families often used part of their wages to accumulate dowries and increase their prospects of marriage. Given that a girl's entire future would be colored by the financial success and emotional loyalty of her husband, an "investment" by an adolescent girl in clothes to increase her attractiveness to men of means could result in the life-time "payoff" of a financially secure home. Liberal reformers of the nineteenth century commonly complained about expenditures by poor working girls on clothes, which seemed extravagant relative to their limited incomes: these expenditures are comprehensible, however, as a means to the realization of the life goal of marriage. Such wage work could continue after a girl became engaged; as we have already made clear, most couples postponed marriage until the husband's earnings and the couple's savings would be sufficient to allow the wife to lead a domestic life. If the wife-to-be worked, she could add to the couple's savings and reduce the delay until marriage. Future wives also worked to support the education and advancement of their fiancés. In one *Lowell Offering* story, a girl entered the factory to put her fiancé through school, a reasonable action given that his increased earnings would make her married life an easier one. In this case, however, the plan backfired. His upward mobility and her degradation as a factory girl made it more and more inappropriate for him to marry her. Out of a sense of duty he asked her to marry him, but she, sensing his sacrifice and reticence, refused for his good, remained in the factory, and eventually pined away and died.[31]

Some girls used their wages to prepare for their futures in yet another way: to pay for their own educations. Lucy Ann, who worked at the mill to send herself to Oberlin College, wrote to her cousin, "I have earned enough to school me awhile, & have not I a right to do so, or must I go home, like a dutiful girl, place the money in father's hands, & then there goes all my hard earnings. . . . Others may find fault with me, and call me selfish, but I think I should spend my earnings as I please."[32] Thomas Dublin uncovered this desire for independent self-advancement in the lives of the mill girls in his excellent study of "the transformation of work and community in Lowell."[33]

Although many working girls, particularly in the cities, lived at home, wage earning allowed, and sometimes required, them to live away from home, outside the orbits of their parents, or of substitute parents. This was quite a radical change for daughters, so much so that the early textile mills had to provide supervised dormitories for the mill girls in order to allay parents' fears. When wage work moved to the cities, however, daughters of rural families were often sent to seek work on their own. If no extended family member was available, they lived on their own, in boarding houses. Freed from the supervision of their parents, they could live their social lives as they pleased, choosing their own friends and boyfriends. This freedom was also dangerous: editorials often complained of how country girls working in the city were tempted into prostitution by its romance and seeming glamour when compared to the factory. Even for the working girl who lived at home, the experience of working outside the supervision of parents or teachers brought a degree of social freedom. The experience of working in the "public" sphere, as well as the leverage their wages gave them over their families, led working girls to demand and win more freedom to determine their own actions after work hours.[34]

We have centered our discussion of the working girl on the daughters of families at the bottom of the income hierarchy; however, daughters of middle- and upper-class families were also drawn into the labor force by the development of capitalism. In the colonial economy, these girls had helped their mothers in the home, learning the skills of homemaking, until marriage brought them homes and families of their own; those unable to find husbands had been condemned to lives of dependency upon relatives, often spent in helpless idleness. The cult of domesticity developed the notion of homemaking as a vocation and prescribed women's higher education as preparation for her social duties of mothering; secondary school and even college became important to a privileged girl's upbringing. Furthermore, the developing social homemaking movement drew women, especially single women, into political work, as well as paid work, which would serve society's families. Hence, for privileged daughters as well, daughterhood began to mean a period of participation in the public sphere, particularly in the labor force, a period that allowed for some development of her individuality. We will examine social homemaking, and its effect on single women, in the next chapter.

The development of capitalism in the nineteenth century drew single women from all classes into the labor force. At any one time, from 40 to 50% of single girls were in the labor force, suggesting that an even greater percentage of women had some labor-force experience before their marriages. Sent into the labor force to serve her family or society at large, the working girl nevertheless achieved a degree of financial independence and public recognition denied to married women. As the nineteenth century advanced and was replaced by the twentieth, the individualistic, independent qualities of the single girl's working experience were accentuated. Increasingly stringent child-labor laws and compulsory education raised the average age of the working girl, while the opening up of colleges to women allowed for an extended period of higher education. A girl's working experience changed gradually from an experience of childhood oppression to one of girlhood freedom and independence. The period of singleness changed from a time of waiting, immaturity, and responsibility to one's parents to a period of independence and self-expression.[35] Most young women continued to plan to leave the labor force in order to take on their real vocation, homemaking. However, their labor-force experiences had become an important and special interim, a time where they were devoted neither to their parents nor to their husbands. This experience colored their future lives as homemakers; in particular, it facilitated their entrance into the labor force as homemakers in the twentieth century.

8

The Development of the Homemaking Profession, and of Women as Homemakers

Wealthy and middle-class homemakers became the activists of the cult of domesticity. Freed from the drudgery of housework by commodities and domestics, they took up the challenge of defining their vocation. What was homemaking? How was it best carried out? What were the needs of the family? What did enlightened child-rearing involve? The attempt to answer these questions for themselves, and for other women, led these women to take new initiatives in their homes and with their families; the need to defend and realize these changes drew them into the larger, political sphere, and these efforts, together, transformed women.

In the next two sections, we will discuss two distinct but interrelated tangents upon which women embarked in their efforts to socialize and professionalize their homemaking work: scientific homemaking and voluntary motherhood. Then we will go on to investigate the movements of women outside of the private home sphere in the social homemaking movement, and finally the manner in which women developed themselves in this whole process.

The Development of the Homemaking Profession: Scientific Homemaking

In the nineteenth century, middle-class and wealthy homemakers took up the task of defining and perfecting woman's new homemaking vocation. In the family economy, the merging of economy and family had left woman's homemaking work with little particular familial content. Homemaking resembled crude production, both of goods and of children, more than distinctly familial activity. This impersonal quality was reflected in the homemaker's willingness to hire domestics to perform, not only the physical work of self-sufficient production, but also the "work" of mothering. In the nineteenth century it became the job of homemakers to purify homemaking, to develop it as a distinct social vocation; they did so in two disparate but interconnected movements. One focused on understanding, improving, and protecting the particular familial aspects of homemaking, while the other concentrated on rationalizing those aspects of homemaking that resembled commodity production. As it was the rationalization of the production-like aspects of homemaking that allowed its personal side really to emerge, we will begin by examining this first process.

The scientific homemaking movement was begun by Catherine Beecher in the nineteenth century and reached its zenith in the early twentieth century.[1] It was dedicated to the rationalization of the homemaker's productive work. This meant both researching the proper, scientific methods of homemaking and teaching young women these methods. The establishment of homemaking as a profession or vocation for which women were responsible in society created in homemakers an active, thoughtful, willful, professional attitude toward homemaking. Women could homemake well or poorly, and they desired to do it well. This meant scientifically studying it, finding out the best way of doing it, and training themselves in the science of homemaking. Ida Tarbell, one of the scientific homemakers, described this need for professionalization in an article in *Annals* in 1913:

> Housekeeping is a many sided business calling for training in theory and practice for scientific management. It needs as varied qualities as any business known to humans beings, and yet as things are now girls and women are getting only the most superficial and artificial training in it. *It needs to be formulated and professionalized* and every girl rich or poor should be taught at least its principles: at the same time she should be taught its relation to all economic and social problems and in particular to the problem of the cost of living [emphasis added].[2]

When scientific homemakers took up the challenge of professionalizing homemaking, much of homemaking still involved the participation in or supervision of "work" in the home. This work, analyzed as a physical process, resembled man's work in the factory. Since capitalism was rationalizing men's work of commodity production, homemakers sought to rationalize the different processes which the home-maker undertook or supervised. Catherine Beecher's widely read book, *A Treatise on Domestic Economy*, first published in 1841, included discussions of the principles of medicine, architecture, horticulture, and psychology, as well as the more traditionally feminine fields of sewing, cooking, and cleaning.[3]

Homemakers logically sought the key to scientific homemaking in the sphere of capitalist production, interpreting their mission as the application of economic principles to the home. At the time that women were seeking out a scientific content for homemaking, commodity production was being increasingly subjected to scientific analysis. The desires of competing firms to minimize production costs had led them to the scientific study of the process of commodity production. They initiated "time–motion" studies, examinations of the labor process which charted in detail the movements of workers. Efficiency was achieved by subdividing production into simple tasks that could be performed by machinery and unskilled labor. Major technological breakthroughs were achieved in the early twentieth century by this school of scientific management, culminating in the introduction of the assembly line. The search of homemakers for a science of homemaking, necessary to the constitution of their profession, brought them to this science of commodity production. One of the more famous of these "scientific homemakers," Lillian Gilbreth, was the wife of the pioneer of time–motion studies, Frank Gilbreth. She worked at applying to the home the principles her husband used in the factory—if scientific management made *commodity* production rational and efficient, it could do the same for *home* production. The result was "scientific homemaking" or "home economics," a movement which treated the home as a factory and the homemaker as a worker and/or administrator. C. W. Taber's book *The Business of the Household*, written in 1918, exemplifies the equation of family and economy, of home and factory, which was the basis of the home economics movement. According to Taber, if the homemaker were to be a professional, she had to realize that homemaking was a business enterprise: "Household management is both a practical art and a trained profession. Not until it is recognized as such will the average home be maintained upon an efficient and economical basis. It is as much a business enterprise as is the running of a store or office, or as is the operation of factory."[4] He continued, describing homemaking as "a highly specialized industry":

As in the factory, so in the home, raw material must be purchased and converted into finished products; countless operations must be supervised and directed; various seemingly detached enterprises must be fostered and developed and made to coordinate with all of the general family activities. The labor problem must be considered and dealt with; hearing and illuminating factors must have attention; capital must be invested and turned to the best possible advantage. Overhead costs, running expenses and depreciation insistently demand intelligent attention and with all these problems, the human equation of relationships, of intimate family ties combined with the perplexing questions of education, ethics, religion and society, demand serious thought.[5]

So women were the managers or administrators (and most often also the "workers") in the home business. Just as the manager learned and applied the scientific principles of economics and natural science to his business in order to achieve success in the business world, a homemaker needed to learn and apply these same scientific principles of business to her homemaking. Articles on scientific homemaking clearly acknowledged that the source of their "science" was in the economy, in the scientific management movement. The goal of the scientific homemaking movement was to introduce these principles into the home. Mrs. Pattison began her article, "Scientific Management in Home-Making," with the following statement:

The purpose of this paper is to show that not only are these same principles [those of scientific management] definitely translatable to her world of activity, but that in the present status of the home the only sure progress toward the solution of the so-called "servant-problem," as well as the high cost of living, lies in the ability to apply just this system of scientific management from the survey, the budget, the index and card-catalogue to the required time, motion, cost and temperature in boiling potatoes, making bread or washing a garment.[6]

These principles were illustrated and applied to homemaking in a series of articles on home economics beginning in the teens and continuing up until the present. They were also taught in home economics courses that became a standard part of a young woman's education. Christine Frederick wrote one of the first series of such articles in the *Ladies Home Journal* in 1912, entitled "The New Housekeeping." Each article started with this example of a labor-saving improvement in industry:

A bricklayer used to lay 120 bricks in an hour. A man who studied the subject prepared an adjustable table to be placed at the bricklayer's side, so that he wouldn't have to stoop, and had the bricks delivered on it in just the right position, so that the bricklayer wouldn't have to turn every brick right side up. The result is that the same bricklayer who laid only 120 bricks an hour under the old method now can lay 350 bricks in the same time without any more exertion. This is a good sample of what modern "efficiency" and "scientific management" are doing in factories, stores, and offices, revolutionizing all kinds of work.

It is housework's turn now to become revolutionized, and these articles have told in detail how it may be done.[7]

The above suggested the application of time–motion studies to home-making. Another principle Frederick wrote of was that of specialization: "In ironing I followed the same idea of specialization [as in dish-washing and cleaning]: all starched pieces first, all flat pieces last. It is this separation and specialization that enables the worker to "speed up" as no other plan allows."[8]

Frederick also taught women how to use elaborate filing systems to organize their knowledge of homemaking—another idea borrowed from business. The goal of business was to so rationalize a production process as to make it indifferent to the particular personality of the worker and hence truly objective. The home "business," according to scientific homemaking, was best organized when the homemaker was replaceable by any stranger:

> Every woman can very readily adapt these ideas to her own needs and develop filing systems of her own. I know that any woman who has once felt the comfort, satisfaction, and pride that come from the use of a system-atic filing method will never return to the slipshod ways of the past. She will feel that it is just as commendable to have her home run in such a manner that a stranger can run it in the same grooves as herself as it is desirable to have the cogs in the wheels of a great railway system go right on moving, even though the fingers of the president of the road cease to write his dictates.[9]

The home economics movement was contradictory: while its goal was to professionalize and elevate the homemaking vocation, its logi-cal development violated the conception of vocational womanhood. Instead of illustrating the unique importance of the homemaker's work, it made the homemaker replaceable by "any stranger." Instead of developing the home into a distinct, familial sphere, it reduced the home to a factory. Christine Frederick was criticized for so reducing homemaking to impersonal factory-like production; her answer:

> Housework should not be drudgery. . . . Some women may say that because I do sewing and other tasks in this apparently formal matter [i.e., specialization of tasks] I am reducing them to bare mechanical processes, and robbing them of their beauty and the "home touch" which has been praised for ages. That is just what I do not do. I put into these things all the inspiration and love and joy I feel as a home-maker and mother. Because I do them more quickly and scientifically does not rob them of any ideal, esthetic touch which any task must receive in order to be other than factory work. . . . I don't want to run my home like an office or a factory, and I don't do it. I want it to be home, and it is.[10]

Frederick was caught within her own contradictory conception. She wanted homemaking to be a profession, scientific et al., and hence applied to it the rules of science as they existed in the economy. By doing this, however, she was forced to deny the personal aspects of the home and of homemaking, something she did not wish to do.

The end result of the scientific homemaking was not to equate home and factory life but rather to further differentiate them by moving many impersonal activities out of the home. First, economically efficient homemaking—a reduction of the time taken to perform productive activities in the home—was best achieved by using labor-saving devices, devices which reduced the quantity of a housewife's time that went into the performance of a certain task. The "House-keeping Experiment Station" of the New Jersey Federation of Women's Clubs did efficiency studies of work in the home. It found that the best methods unfailingly involved the use of power tools and machines:

> Objectively, it became a matter of employing the best known machinery, and through tests in efficiency, economy, time and motion, proving its value in doing the work from both the practical and educational standpoints. Each household operation was reduced to the effect or result desired, and an untiring search made for the best device, tool or material to produce these results—automatic electric being our standard.[11]

Second, scientific homemaking urged the replacement of "home-made" with "store-bought" goods. When judged by the criterion of efficient production, commodity production was clearly superior to home production, for it involved a highly developed division of labor both between and within firms which could not be matched by the efforts of an isolated housewife, however well-intentioned or aided by domestic servants. As soon as she could afford it, the dedicated home-maker would replace her home products with fancy, store-bought goods. Hence the professional homemaker, by trying to act effi-ciently, by trying to treat her home as a factory, turned herself into a consumer of commodities and voided the home of more and more of its "productive" activities. These developments went hand in hand with the development of commodity production, capital actively penetrated into the home, offering commodities to the homemaker which would replace her home product or reduce her housework. Already by 1873, a writer could look back with amazement upon the productive efforts of her grandmother: "The feminine world, worn and jaded with their daily duties, consider the marvels that were wrought by the matrons of that golden age—the yards of cloth they wove in their stout looms, the skeins of yarn they spun, the stockings they knit, the quilts they sewed, the cheeses they made, the butter they churned, and can only murmur in wonder, 'They were giant-esses in those days.' "[12]

However, many activities that could have been commoditized re-mained in homes because the homemaker was there, and because she felt a need to be physically active and "productive." Anna Richard-son, a home economist, asked herself "why economic activities persist in a modern home" in her 1929 article on the "modern" homemaker. After citing the inavailability of family income to purchase commodity equivalents, and the lack of part-time jobs consistent with homemak-ing which could give homemakers this income, she added that the women themselves were invested in these activities as part of their vocation:

> There is a considerable number of women who enjoy housework and prefer it to other forms of occupation. They get intellectual and emotional satisfaction from it. This fact is frequently overlooked in discussions which present only the attitude of the women who honestly detest housework and who feel that they are demeaned by doing it.
>
> Tradition holds most women in the home as the legitimate place for the use of their talents. This idea is strengthened by the attitude of many men who are still strongly in favor of women making their economic and social contribution through the work of the home.
>
> There is still a profound belief on the part of a large majority that home

life is closely bound up with the doing of these tasks, and that much of the hominess is lost when the production activities are taken away.[13]

The technological developments of the twentieth century have been affected by women's desire to remain in the home: for example, mechanization ultimately allowed home washing machines to triumph over socialized laundries and home ovens to replace community bakeries.[14] Such concrete tasks gave a definite content to homemaking by giving it a tangible, physical product. Hence, there were counter-currents operating: while homemakers could fill family needs better through the purchase of commodities, and the purchase of such commodities allowed them to concentrate on the special, personal aspects of homemaking, their investments in homemaking as a vocation pressured them to hold onto their "work," even to reintroduce home production into the family. It would take the end of the conception of homemaking as a vocation to move production out of the home completely.[15]

The scientific homemaking movement cooperated with the development of capitalist commodity production to transform the homemaker from a home producer of goods to a purchaser of commodities, a consumer. The homemaker retained her role of filling the family's needs, but began to do so, increasingly, through the purchase of commodities on the market, with money earned by her husband, rather than by her own productive activity. Richardson, in her book *The Woman Who Spends*, hailed this transition as liberating women from the "yoke" of production:

> In the relationship of women to the getting and spending of money, the world has seen a most interesting change. Years ago, when our nation was a nation of country folk, women did little of the spending, but helped much in the production of wealth. . . . Production of most of the needs of life centered around the home. Women very naturally came into close touch with this production. . . . The country has moved to town. Women can now buy all the necessities they at one time had to manufacture. Consequently, living is easier. Today women are not spinning and weaving; they are buying dress goods by the yard and linen by the bolt. They are not producing; they have thrown off the yoke of economic production. They only spend.
> . . . On account of the change in the economic conditions of production, however, women have gained a whole new field of economic activity, that of consumption. For women, economic consumption is the spending

of money. Their problem is not, What shall be produced to satisfy my needs? but, How shall I spend to satisfy my needs? The greater the opportunities for spending, the wider is the field of choice; and the very complexity which the many sides of life present makes us realize the importance of recognizing the things that are vital and therefore needed.[16]

The transformation of woman's work from production to consumption brought her a specific, feminine sphere all her own. In the family economy, before production was truly socialized, the masculine/feminine division was one between public and private production. Woman's work of filling family needs through home production had appeared as a crude, natural form of man's work of commodity production. When the extension of commodity production into the home emptied homemaking of productive work, it also created a new and clearly feminine job: that of filling the particular needs of the family through the purchase of commodities with the earnings of the head of household. This work was clearly social, tied, as it was, to the process of commodity production. The husband earned income, value in the abstract, in his masculine labor-force competition; his wife, the homemaker, transformed this abstract wealth into particular commodities which filled the needs of the individual family members. As Mrs. Julian Heath, founder and President of the National Housewives League of New York, wrote in 1913: "Marriage is a contract by which a man becomes the producer and the woman the dispenser."[17]

The scientific homemaking movement was logically followed by the glorification of consumption as the distinct vocation of woman. Homemakers did not see consumption as a passive process but as a willful activity with social import. Clearly, consumption, as the exchange of commodities for family income, had an economic content. But this alone was not sufficient to constitute a vocation. Consumption as a vocation implied that consumption was social in some special sense, valuable not only to the family but also to society at large. As a vocation it had to fit into the larger social division of labor; it had to make the housewife's work an integral part of this division of labor. The consumer movement attempted to constitute consumption as a productive vocation through which woman as homemaker could realize her individuality and social importance. It therefore demanded that woman's work of consumption be professionalized and valued. The President of the Housewives League described the work of that organization as follows:

If the American woman has failed at any one point it has been to recognize her economic position as the spender of the family income. We have demanded that the man be trained to produce, but we have not demanded that the woman be trained to spend, yet it devolves upon her to so spend what the man produces that the family shall be properly fed, clothed, housed and educated to take their place in the world.

. . . This newly awakened class consciousness of the housewife has changed the entire viewpoint of women toward housekeeping and of the public toward the housewife. Housewives are at last recognizing that they are a great factor in economic life and have taken their right position.[18]

Much of the literature attempting to analyze consumption economically has been motivated by this desire to establish consumption as a true vocation for woman. A group of social scientists analyzed consumption as a productive economic activity. In his 1929 article, "The Home Woman as Buyer and Controller of Consumption," Benjamin Andrews redefined production to be the production of utility rather than the production of commodities.[19] Since women's work of consumption created utility, it was an integral part of the production of wealth.

Retail buying is a productive act, for it can multiply many fold the satisfactions from a given income. Retail selling is necessary in the production process; retail buying which precedes the act of consumption is as essential as retail selling and has evidently the same productive power for wealth creation. . . . The family buyer's responsibility is a widening function, for as old-time production of material commodities for sale or use leaves the home, new activities arise there related to spending that have productive advantage, such as health conservation, child guidance, economic administration, family leadership, income spending, and consumption direction—all these are really productive since they increase the utilities enjoyed, which are the real purpose of the productive process. Under the present price system, money income and money spending are both equally important.[20]

Note that the conclusion of his argument is that the two functions are "equally important." The redefinition of production serves the purpose of constituting woman's and man's works or vocations as, again, separate but equal.[21]

The ultimate result of the scientific homemaking movement was to further distinguish home life from the world of the economy, to allow its distinctive features to emerge. In this, it aided the other main aspect of the professionalization of homemaking: the development of family life. As Anna Richardson, an advocate of scientific homemaking, wrote in her article of 1929:

> The home, with family life as its nucleus, furnishes opportunities for development, through experience, which no other enterprise has been able to substitute. Women will be foolish indeed if they do not release every activity which can be carried on as well or better, outside of the home, but the woman will sell herself who does not hold tenaciously to her share in those functions which give the home its unique place in the building of human personality and character.[22]

The Development of the Homemaking Profession: The Particularization of Family Life

The elimination of impersonal, productive activities from the home not only developed consumption as woman's work but also allowed for the development of homemaking into the sustenance of family life. Therefore, although the purchase of commodities was "labor-saving" for the homemaker, it did not reduce homemaking time, for homemaking was not labor. As Hazel Kyrk noted in her 1933 book, *Economic Problems of the Family:* "We have shown a tendency to use the time freed by labor saving machinery not for more leisure, but for more goods or services of the same general character. . . . The invention of the washing-machine has meant more washing, of the vacuum cleaner more cleaning, of new fuels and cooking equipment, more courses and more elaborately prepared food."[23] An increase in income, by allowing for an increased standard of living, could in fact increase the hours a homemaker spent at work, both by raising her standards and by expanding her work into other areas of homemaking:

> One can easily explain why the home-maker with children and low income, especially if she lives on a farm, must work long hours. She can hire little or no assistance, she must make rather than buy so long as money-saving is effected thereby, she can buy little of the more expensive equipment. Her house is likely to be poorly planned. If she lives in the city it is likely to be in more grimy districts. What happens if the family income increases materially? They move to a cleaner district, into a house more conveniently and efficiently planned; they buy labor-saving utensils and equipment; they employ hired workers; they patronize dry-cleaner and

laundry; they buy goods previously supplied at home. But their house is larger, the furnishings more abundant and elaborate; in time if not immediately their standards rise; time released at one point as in cooking and cleaning goes into care of children, buying and management, and the home-maker's week may be not far below that under the living conditions of the earlier years.[24]

Kyrk's own studies found that city women spent more time homemaking than country women—the former averaged eighty hours per week compared to the latters' sixty hours. More recently another home economist, Kathryn Walker, found that the total amount of time spent weekly on homemaking in urban areas increased through the twentieth century from 51.1 hours in 1926–7, to 51.8 hours in 1952, to 56 hours in 1967–8.[25]

Homemaking did not, then, disappear with the commoditization of home life. As Kyrk emphasized, standards of "good housekeeping" were tightened as these new commodities were marketed. But furthermore, and importantly, the commoditization of the housework allowed the personal and distinctive aspect of homemaking to emerge. As one writer noted in 1838,

> We smile with condescending piety at the blinded state of our respected grandmothers, and thank God that we are not as they, with a thanksgiving as uncalled for as that of the proud Pharisee. On abstract ground their education was better than ours; it was a preparation for their future duties. It does not affect the question, that their notion of these duties was entirely confined to the physical comfort of husbands and children.[26]

The scientific homemaking movement contributed to the development of home life as a particular familial activity. The movement to professionalize homemaking, to develop the homemaking profession, held at its core the search for a distinctive social content to homemaking. Although scientific homemakers mistakenly grasped this content as an economic one, their efforts in fact helped to reduce the similarity between homemaking and commodity production. The development of consumerism led the homemaker to focus on the particular needs of her family, to work to define these needs. It furthermore allowed privileged homemakers to make the home a truly familial place by substituting commodities for domestic servants. As Lucy Salmon wrote in her 1906 book, *Progress in the Household:*

The domestic employee is not, and cannot be, a part of the family; she never in all her history has had more than a semblance of such a relationship and even that semblance has long since disappeared. The presence of the domestic employee in the family is not essential to the existence of the family; the domestic employee comes and goes, but the family remains. More than this, it must be said that the presence of the domestic employee does something to destroy the integrity of family life. Family life presupposes the existence of congenial tastes and sympathetic relationships.[27]

The movement to define family life and the scientific homemaking movement were, thus, bound up together—intertwined aspects of the professionalization of the homemaking vocation by privileged women. Although the more complete commoditization of housework achieved in the early twentieth century aided the acceptance of the particularity of family life, the movement to vocationalize family life did not wait for these developments, but rather proceeded energetically from the early nineteenth century.

What is meant by the vocationalization of family life, of the caregiving aspect of homemaking? We have seen the separation of spheres in the nineteenth century and the emergence of freedom within the economy—in the choice of mate and in woman's practice of homemaking—and we have connected this to the socialization of homemaking. Woman's work of filling the needs of family members was transformed from the physical provisioning of their needs to the attempt to fill their needs for individuality, for personalities of their own. In particular, mothering began to be recognized as the eminently social process of cultivating the particular individuality of the child. This was especially important in middle-class families, where well-motivated and prepared young men had a good chance of upward mobility. Middle-class homemakers were responsible for their children's successes or failures—a responsibility which they embraced as their special power.

One of the clearest expressions of the transformation of mothering into a social process was the decrease in average family size through the nineteenth century. In the course of the nineteenth century, the average number of children per (white) woman fell by half, from 7.04 in 1800 to 3.56 in 1900.[28] The reduction in and control over the number of children she bore was integral to woman's enlightened practice of her mothering vocation.[29] As we would expect, poorer families remained larger than wealthier ones; they were forced to retain the old conception of the child as worker for the family in their fight to realize domestic womanhood. But for the middle-class home-maker, who did not need her children's wages for family income, a reduction of family size was necessary: how else could a woman as mother care properly for each individual child? As Ida Craddock explained to fellow women in her 1897 book, *Letter to a Prospective Bride:* "To create a few, a very few children who shall be an expres-sion of the noblest thoughts of yourself and your husband and to give those children all possible advantages of education, travel, and soci-ety, is not this doing your duty as a wife and mother better than if you create children at haphazard and by wholesale to such an extent that you can scarcely secure for them a decent living?"[30]

The reduction in family size achieved by families in the nineteenth century can be attributed to women's efforts to control their vocation. These efforts happened on many levels. One was women's efforts to limit sexual intercourse with their husbands, expressed in the Volun-tary Motherhood movement, a movement womaned by suffragists, free lovers, and moral reformers. These women took motherhood seriously, as woman's vocation, and argued that the proper practice of mothering necessitated woman's control over the number and timing of births. Voluntary motherhood was advocated, not simply to ease the individual homemaker's burden, but as necessary for the health of society. As Elizabeth Cady Stanton argued in an 1870 speech, "When people begin to weigh the momentous consequences of bringing badly organized children into the world there will be fewer still . . . when a mother can give the world, one noble, healthy happy man or woman, a perpetual blessing in the church and the state, she will do a better work for humanity than in adding numbers alone, but with little regard for quality."[31]

The method of controlling family size recommended by the Volun-tary Motherhood movement was simply abstinence from sexual rela-tions. They opposed contraception, claiming that it disconnected sex from reproduction and increased men's freedom to have wanton sex.[32] Although few Voluntary Motherhood advocates openly supported contraception or abortion, both methods of birth control were widely practiced in the nineteenth century by women attempting to control the size of their families. Women learned about methods of birth control not only from books but from each other: Carl Degler's study of correspondence between women in the nineteenth century reveals an "underground" information network among women friends.[33] In 1873, the Comstock Law formally prohibited the diffusion of information on birth control through the mails, but this did not keep women from practicing contraception and abortion.

The control of family size was, of course, only the very first step in the professionalization of mothering; the concentration of the efforts of nineteenth-century women on family size revealed how new the conception of vocational mothering really was. In the nineteenth century, manuals instructing women about the proper psychological and moral content of mothering replaced the colonial economy's advice books to fathers. Breast-feeding by the child's mother was considered a must, unlike in the colonial times, when wet-nurses had been commonly used. Moral training was to begin immediately; the concern for the impact of mothering on the personality of the child was fervent, although the understanding of the developmental stages of childhood was far from perfected. Women were warned that once a child reached the age of four to six months, his or her character was shaped by mother's every action: "While the tenderest affection beams from her own eye and plays upon every feature of her countenance she contrives by the soft and winning tones of her voice to overcome the resistance of the child, too young indeed to know why it yields but not too young to feel the power by which its heart it so sweetly captivated."[34] In the 1830s and '40s, women met locally in maternal associations to "renew vows of devotion to their children and to devise ever more elaborate and demanding methods of child care."[35] As historian Nancy Cott observes, "women who created maternal associations seemed burdened with the weight of responsibility in motherhood as well as impressed by its power."[36] Mothering continued to form the center of vocational homemaking into the twentieth century, increasing in its sophistication as the science of psychology developed. By 1929, mothering was described in the following, sophisticated manner:

As the home is the environment responsible for shaping the early years of our children, it is imperative that we recognize the importance of the influences of the everyday experiences in developing their physical, social and emotional life. Those homes which give to the child his rightful opportunity provide experiences which enable him to develop sound habits of physical behavior, such as eating, sleeping, elimination, cleanliness, good posture and muscular control; good habits of social behavior, such as ability to make friends, express himself adequately, assume responsibility, have respect for the property of others; character traits, such as honesty, fair play, perseverence, respect for authority; religious ideals which help him to understand the concept of God, the use of prayer; and stimulate intellectual and aesthetic tastes, through pleasure in good literature, in the arts, and in creative work and play.[37]

The Dr. Spock manuals later in the twentieth century were simply the end of a long process initiated by vocational homemakers in the early nineteenth century.

Another part of the transformation of homemaking into a familial vocation was the efforts of homemakers to exert moral influence over their husbands. The Voluntary Motherhood movement urged men to control their sexual impulses in order that family size could be limited—in the name of their prospective children. Women also directly worked to influence the morality of their husbands. Men, relegated to the economic sphere of competitive self-seeking, seemed to women to be peculiarly devoid of morality and ethics. Ministers taught that husbands, as well as children, needed the influence of feminine morality.[38] Women who fought to reform their men did not argue on the basis of their own needs, as homemakers, for this would contradict the feminine vocation of filling the needs of others. Rather, they touted high moral principles which their husbands needed but lacked; they militated on the basis of the needs of their husbands and children, not their own. Sarah Joseph Hale, editor of the popular *Godey's Lady's Book,* called woman "God's appointed agent of *morality,*" with the responsibility to refine man's "human affections and elevate his moral feelings."[39] Wives worked to exert moral control over their husbands' sexual freeness and drinking habits. Women's increased demands on marriage led to more divorce, particularly more wife-initiated divorce.[40]

In the nineteenth century, wealthy and middle-class women transformed homemaking from an impersonal, crude process to a particular and familial vocation by moving production out of the home and by taking control over their children and husbands. Anna Richardson analysed the change in this way:

We are more and more subordinating all other functions of the home to attaining its fundamental raison d'etre which is to give refreshment and strength to body and spirit through experience which family life alone is able to furnish, to provide activities, experiences, and relationships, essential for the continued growth and all around development of both children and adults.[41]

By 1912, Ida Tarbell could describe *The Business of Being a Woman* as follows:

> To socialize her home . . . to put the stamp of affectionate, intelligent human interest upon all the operations and the intercourse of the center she directs . . . to make a place in which the various members can live freely and draw to themselves those with whom they are sympathetic—a place in which there is spiritual and intellectual room for all to grow and be happy each in his own way.[42]

Homemaking Out-reaches the Home: Social Homemaking

The professionalization of private homemaking we have studied above was an important part of the development of the homemaking vocation. The requirements of good homemaking were studied, rationalized, and then taught to women through a proliferating literature.[43] But there was another, connected aspect of the professionalization of homemaking: the movement of homemakers out of the private home sphere to reform the world. Even after a homemaker had learned of all the most scientific ways to carry out her profession, she was foiled by social institutions that threatened the security and health of home life. This encouraged women as present or future homemakers to move into the public sphere, a phenomenon historians have termed "social housekeeping" or "social feminism," which we will call "social homemaking," homemaking for society at large.[44] Social homemaking, like the scientific homemaking movement, was predominantly the work of privileged women. It was not limited to white women, however. Gerda Lerner has recently drawn attention to the social club movement among middle-class black women, which undertook projects to aid the black community.[45] Since the organizations and charitable institutions created by white social housekeepers usually excluded blacks, black women organized a distinct and somewhat parallel movement to protect their families. Social homemaking's most active workers were women who had not yet begun their own homemaking vocations and were not needed as helpers by their mothers; hence, they were not from poor families. The homemakers who participated in social homemaking were also, necessarily, women whose husbands' affluence freed them from the struggle for mere survival and allowed them to cultivate a distinctive home sphere. This movement of women outside the feminine domestic sphere was not undertaken as a rejection of the demands of vocational homemaking; rather, women saw such action as a holy duty demanded of them as vocational homemakers. As Carry Nation, a nineteenth-century reformer, explained in her autobiography:

> We hear "A woman's place is at home." That is true but what and where is home? Not the walls of a house. Not furniture, food or clothes. Home is where the heart is, where our loved ones are. If my son is in a drinking place, my place is there. If my daughter, or the daughter of anyone else, my family or any other family, is in trouble, my place is there. [A woman would be either selfish or cowardly if she] would refuse to leave her home to relieve suffering or trouble. Jesus said, "Go out into the highways and hedges." He said this to women, as well as men.[46]

Another woman called others to such service as mothers: "Oh, women of the world, arise in your strength and demand that all which stands in the path of true motherhood shall be removed from your path."[47]

There were three essential ways in which vocational homemaking developed into social homemaking of one kind or another. First, social homemaking was driven by the homemaker's need to protect her home; special emphasis was put on ensuring that her husband, upon whom her family's livelihood depended, properly carried out his duties. Second, homemakers worked to correct the masculine and heartless impersonality of their husbands' capitalist sphere, particularly to remedy the fact that it prevented many families from achieving a healthy family life. Third, women directly "mothered" the needy outside of their homes; they saw to the nursing of war-injured men and the teaching of children.

One of social homemakers' reasons for leaving the domestic sphere was, ironically, to protect homemaking and family life. These efforts were concentrated in two directions: the fight to control their husbands, so as to guarantee their performance as husbands/providers for the family, and the consumer movement, which worked to protect the family against poor and overpriced commodities.

The work of women to reform their husbands had its roots in religous beliefs. Nancy Cott has noted how women emerged from the religious revival of the early nineteenth century ready to reform the world.[48] Indeed, throughout history, women have justified stepping out of the domestic sphere as the will of God. The cult of domesticity's acknowledgment of the special abilities of woman encouraged women to moralize to their husbands and to the rest of society. From the Second Great Awakening through the 1920s, women went on a powerful crusade to save American morality, particularly that of men, their husbands or potential husbands. In their calling to "rehabilitate mankind," women fought against prostitution, which tempted their husbands into sin and ruined the lives of young women, potentially their daughters. They formed "Female Reform Societies" and the "Social Purity" movement to this end, using innovative tactics like petition campaigns (they as yet had no vote) and the shaming of men who thus indulged. They fought actively against men's consumption of alcohol, which not only threatened the livelihood of the family but was immoral in its own right. The Temperance movement, advertised as a campaign for "home protection," fought against individual saloon keepers as well as more broadly with petition drives and later with the vote to prohibit the sale of alcohol; by 1920, it had an estimated 800,000 members.[49] These organizations had developed from local women's discussion groups to national political movements. In the course of the nineteenth century, they shifted their focus from immoral individuals and enterprises to law and legislatures. They were able to permanently prevent the regulation (and hence legalization) of prostitution and to pass Blue Laws which remain to this day.

Another way in which women organized to protect and better their homemaking was in the consumer movement, which developed strength in the early twentieth century. Women had the responsibility for filling the commodity needs of the family through consumption; they took on the responsibility of seeing that the commodities they purchased were of good quality, "worth it." Mrs. Julian Heath organized the Housewives League on this principle: organizing their consumption would allow women, as consumers, to exercise their power to determine production. She explained this philosophy in her article on "The Work of the Housewives League," written in 1913. First she blamed women for the fact that poor-quality products were being sold in violation of rules set by the Department of Agriculture. She asked, "Who is to blame? Those who purchase these impure foods and no one else. This is purely a question of supply and demand. If no adulterated foods were bought, none would be manufactured."[50] The solution to this problem, according to Heath, was the further development of the housekeeping profession, which had been "exploited" by business precisely because housewives had been ignorant of their power, had not been "class conscious," as she called it.

> The profession of housekeeping has been exploited as has no other profession. Exploited by the use of dishonest weights and measures, by the unsanitary condition of our commercialized home industries, the bakeries, the laundries, the canneries, and last but by no means least, by the manipulation of food prices until the American home itself is in danger. Housewives have not realized this before because they have not been class conscious. All that, however, is changing, and the housewives are seeing these things from a different viewpoint, recognizing the power of concerted action.[51]

Mrs. Heath's enthusiasm and sense of political and social responsibility inspired the formation of the Housewives League and were part of a broader social movement of women consumers in the twentieth century. By organizing collectively and boycotting certain products, homemakers were able to have an impact on profit-conscious firms. Their boycotts were applied, not only to poor quality goods, but also to those whose production took place under unhealthy working conditions, especially when women workers were involved.

A second and related kind of social homemaking undertaken by women was their struggle to reform capitalism. The masculinity of the economic world urged women to enter and reform it. If their husbands, or other husbands, were acting immorally, women saw it as their duty to enlighten these men. If men, in the early and heartless stage of capitalism, formed a system that forced children into the factories and enslaved black people, this also needed to be corrected by homemakers. Capitalism in the nineteenth and early twentieth centuries was harsh, as destructive of individuals as it was productive of wealth. Its slave economy denied the humanity of those enslaved. Its factory system was inhumane: it employed children, denying them childhood; it exploited married women with low wage payments; its work conditions were atrocious; it denied many men the family wage they needed. Since capitalism was not filling the needs of many men, women, and children and was preventing them from attaining the standard of home life that professional homemakers saw as essential, the latter took it upon themselves to minister to these "needy."

In the late eighteenth and early nineteenth centuries, wealthy women organized orphan asylums and homes for indigent women. By the 1830s, such female-run institutions had become an indispensable component of city life.[52] In the antebellum period, women organized and actively participated in the movement to abolish slavery. Later in the nineteenth century, women began serving the poor immigrant populations in the cities with "Settlement Houses." As experience taught them that the basic cause of such social problems was poverty, they began to work to unionize women workers, something male unions had shunned.[53] They formed the Women's Trade Union League, which united working women with social reforming sisters. They also pushed for studies of the conditions of women and children workers, as ammunition for child labor laws and other protective legislation. They initiated and helped compile the "Report on the Condition of Women and Child Workers" which I have used extensively for this study.

Finally, women were concerned about the nursing and education of those outside of their own homes. In the Civil War, women organized (and worked in) the Sanitary Commission to nurse their husbands and sons through the war. Women also took their husbands' places in the labor force when they went to war—for the country. Women worked to ensure the formal teaching of the young, especially of young women, who would soon be mothers. In both of these areas, social homemakers recruited other women to do this work, and in this process encouraged women's professional development. We will study this more in the next section.

Women, previously banned from the political sphere, were drawn into the movement to develop a welfare state by their homemaking vocation. Their feminine morality—a concern that the needs of particular individuals be filled—was a perfect complement to capitalism's masculinity. Capitalism gave all men a chance to compete; the existence of low-wage and unemployed workers was simply part of the game. Social homemakers, progressives, and eventually the welfare state charitably "mothered" the losers; they did not try to change the game. Social homemaking was an integral part of capitalism rather than a revolutionary movement.

Homemaking Develops Woman

The emergence of the homemaking vocation demanded the development of woman. The more woman's vocation was exalted and its importance recognized, the more woman herself was revealed to be shockingly unprepared for her task. The push for women's education in the nineteenth century, much of it undertaken by social homemakers and scientific homemakers, was a logical outgrowth of the cult of domesticity's recognition of the social content and importance of homemaking, especially mothering. Once women's work in the home was recognized as a social activity rather than a natural, instinctive one, women's need for formal training became evident. As early as the late eighteenth century, Benjamin Rush had begun to argue for female education as a necessary adjunct to the development of men's property rights and political freedoms. Wives had to be able to assist as "stewards and guardians of their husbands' property," to educate their children because their husbands' businesses now took them away from the home, and to "concur in instructing their sons in the principles of liberty and government."[54]

Nineteenth-century advocates of female education developed a clear set of arguments, and eventually triumphed. Primary, of course, was woman's mothering vocation: as Charles McIver put it, "The cheapest, easiest, and surest road to universal education is to educate those who are to be mothers and teachers of future generations . . . the proper training of women is the strategic point in the education of the race . . . educate a man and you have educated one person—educate a mother and you have educated a whole family."[55] As Emma Willard, a teacher and successful advocate of women's education, wrote to the Governor of New York, arguing for the establishment of "a grade of schools for women, higher than any heretofore known":

> As evidence that this statement does not exaggerate the female influence in society, our sex need only be considered in the single relation of mothers. In this character, we have the charge of the whole mass of individuals, who are to compose the succeeding generation; during that period of youth, when the pliant mind takes any direction, to which it is steadily guided by a forming hand. How important a power is given by this charge! yet, little do too many of my sex know how, either to appreciate or improve it. Unprovided with the means of acquiring that knowledge which flows liberally to the other sex—having our time of education devoted to frivolous acquirements, how should we understand

the nature of the mind, so as to be aware of the importance of those early impressions which we make upon the minds of our children? or how should we be able to form enlarged and correct views, either of the character to which we ought to mould them, or of the means most proper to form them aright?[56]

Another important reason given was that women needed "an education as shall make them fit wives for well educated men"; to be good companions and advisers to their husbands, women needed to be as educated as they were.[57] A final justification for women's education was its usefulness when a woman was suddenly left to provide for herself. The cult of domesticity thus led to the recognition and development of women's mental capacities. Society's firm belief in women's "natural" advantage in child-bearing and -rearing overpowered the eighteenth-century conception of women as physically unfit for education. Women were sent to school and colleges, while social scientists anxiously checked them for signs of illness or decreased fertility.[58]

Many of the early female seminaries and colleges were formed, at least in part, to train women to be teachers. The complicated connection between vocational homemaking and professional teaching brought the development of women who chose careers other than homemaking, but careers that were considered, nonetheless, to be feminine. Teaching as a profession for woman was a logical product of the vocational homemaking of the cult of domesticity. The argument that women, as mothers, were the educators of the young and hence should be educated was simply extended. First, the formal teaching of the young in schools was professional mothering; women were best suited for it. As Emma Willard argued, "That nature designed our sex for the care of children, she has made manifest, by mental as well as physical indications. She has given us, in a greater degree than men, the gentle arts of insinuation, to soften their minds, and fit them to receive impressions; a greater quickness of invention to vary modes of teaching to different dispositions; and more patience to make repeated efforts." According to Catherine Beecher, "Our Creator designed woman to be the chief educator of our race and the prime minister of our family state, and our aim [in female seminaries] is to train her to this holy calling and give her every possible advantage for the performance of its many and difficult duties." Furthermore, as a kind of mothering, the teaching profession would prepare women for their future mothering in their own families. It could employ middle-class women in the period before their marriages; Beecher envisioned her seminaries to train "young ladies scarcely out of their teens, whose souls are burning for some channel into which they can pour their benevolence, and who will teach two, three, or four years and then marry and become firm pillars to hold up their successors." This would be an efficient use of social resources, argued Willard, for it would "probably place the business of teaching children, in hands now nearly useless to society; and take it from those [men], whose services the state wants in many other ways." Indeed, the universalization of education with the common school movement meant a rapidly growing demand for teachers, a demand which could not be filled by educated men, given their many alternatives. The recruitment of men into the Civil War effort speeded this transformation of formal elementary and secondary school teaching from a man's to a woman's profession.[59]

Teaching was constructed as social homemaking and was seen as such by women. It had an almost missionary quality—the bringing of literacy and knowledge to the young. The modest pay of such work—Thomas Woody described it in his *History of Women's Education in the United States* as one of the most lowly, lonely, and unattractive means to earn a living—was an essential aspect of its self-sacrificial character. He wrote, "The states made out of the Northwest Territory became the missionary field for numerous advocates of higher education of women who had studied at schools . . . and had become teachers." Many felt, with Catherine Beecher, that the West had to be saved; and in her *True Remedy* and an essay entitled "American Women, Will You Save Your Country?" she made it clear that this salvation was to come chiefly through education, and that women's part in education was more important than men's. As one of her disciples, teaching out of a small log house in the West, wrote to Catherine Beecher, "When I came here, I intended to stay only one term; but the people urged me so much to remain, and have done so much in building me a schoolhouse, that I concluded to stay longer. I did not leave my home to seek pleasure, wealth, or fame, and I do believe my heavenly Father will bless my labors here, even if I never see the fruit." Another, teaching in a poor and newly established community, wrote, "There is so much to do, and, where all are so ignorant, so much instruction to give, one can not but feel anxious to know what will be most profitable. I long, and hope, to see things wear a more cheerful aspect, and for this would labor untiringly. 'Hope on, and hope ever,' I would take as my motto."[60]

The missionary, social homemaking sentiments of female educators were passed on to new generations of women in the female seminaries and later in colleges, especially the women's colleges. While the higher education of women had been pursued in order to train women for their domestic role, it also had the effect of turning young women toward social homemaking, as a Smith college student of the 1880s described:

> We were talking last night about what the girls were going to do who were to be home next year. Of course they would not settle down to a mere hum-drum existence after our busy systematic work here. They would get restless and discontented as so many do. We have been discussing temperance, hospitals, and all sorts of training schools and industrial and charitable works in which we could interest ourselves. And there are so many things of that sort that I never heard of which need women who are dedicated and know how to plan and carry out such ideas.[61]

The Settlement House Movement, a movement of college graduates, was the heritage of earlier generations of women who, as social homemakers, had taken up teaching. While many of the graduates did volunteer social homemaking, a large percentage became teachers. Indeed, a large number of early college graduates were so dedicated to social homemaking and/or to women's professions that they never married. Of Mount Holyoke's 2,341 recorded graduates between 1837 and 1877, 1,690 taught, 807 for over 5 years, and only 1,391, or 59%, married.[62] This dedication to social homemaking professions rather than homemaking was not peculiar to Mount Holyoke: a 1900 *Statistical Study of Women College Graduates* found that only about half of the graduates had married by the age of 50.[63]

So the cult of domesticity brought the development of women's professions. Although Catherine Beecher was not a feminist, her belief in and dedication to the development and elevation of woman's domestic vocation led her to fight for the professional development of woman, a development that brought women out of the home, into seminaries, high schools, and colleges, and into paid vocations, particularly teaching. At the same time, nursing emerged as another women's profession. The American Women's Education Association in 1852 called the "care of the human body in infancy and sickness" part of the appropriate profession of woman and supported the development of nursing schools to professionalize what had previously been a part of untrained domestic service. When their husbands and children were injured in the Civil War, women formed the Sanitary Commission, organized nursing efforts, and helped professionalize nursing. Social homemaking led, then, to efforts by women to form paid professions for women, professions whose service to others made them "feminine" in the eyes of these reformers. Thus the activities of social homemakers insured that the rise in women's education and in women's participation in the professions of teaching and nursing went hand in hand. The teaching profession was one of many roads to professional social homemaking.

While teaching and nursing were understood as woman's duty, as caretaker and homemaker for society at large, and were entered into with a "missionary" spirit, a spirit of self-sacrifice, they nevertheless allowed for the development of woman as an independent, self-supporting yet feminine being; they gave women for the first time in American history a profession other than homemaking which was respected, a profession clearly distinct from the nurturing of children, which had formed the core of women's work. The social homemakers were themselves largely single women who had chosen social homemaking as a life vocation or as a preparation for private homemaking. The efforts of social homemakers led to the constitution of social homemaking professions as *alternatives* to private homemaking. Susan B. Anthony, Frances Willard, Mary Lyons, M. Carey Thomas, and Catherine Beecher—famous social homemakers—were all single. Social homemaking hence provided a life path for women which did not include marriage and a vocation for the woman who found no acceptable suitor. It transformed the life of the spinster from one of dependence and misery to one of independent social service. Social homemakers had this in mind during their push for the feminization of teaching; in public, however, they stressed the needs of the children. "Inasmuch, then, as popular education was the topic which was every day rising in interest and importance, it seemed to me that, to fall into this current, and organize our sex, as women, to secure the proper education of the destitute children of our land was the better form of presenting the object, rather than to start it as an effort for the elevation of woman," wrote Catherine Beecher, knowing full well that the latter would result.[64]

The difficulty of getting husbands (quite pronounced in the East due to a scarcity of men) and the possibility of a single spinster life must have encouraged women to develop themselves and go to college. In her 1858 book, *A Woman's Thoughts about Women*, Dinah Mulock gave advice to the single woman, "We must help ourselves . . . marriage is apparently ceasing to become the common lot, and a happy marriage the most uncommon lot of all." On this basis, she called for the education of woman, which would be of more value to women than "any blind clamour for ill-defined 'rights.' "[65] Once women began to think for themselves and plan out their lives, the dependence of their homemaking futures upon the proposal of a man made them work to better the single state, through which all passed and in which some would stay. On the other hand, once women had begun to develop the "single option," they were less willing to settle for marriage with an "unsuitable" suitor. In this way, the growth of social homemaking professions was not only a result but probably also a cause of the low marriage rates of those born in the second half of the nineteenth century.[66]

So teaching and nursing, and later librarianship and social work, constructed as inherently "women's professions," became acceptable women's careers, alternatives to homemaking. Furthermore, as women's social welfare work was institutionalized, many of the social homemakers who had fought for these programs were put at their heads. Although many women pursued careers only briefly, until marriage, some of the early graduates of female seminaries were so imbued with the social homemaking spirit that they took on women's professions as life-time vocations. Again, such behavior represented something revolutionary and new in woman's work life—yet something which, as a logical expression of the ideas of the cult of domesticity, could not be stopped.

Social homemaking also led women into the political sphere. When women began to take up social homemaking, their lack of political and property rights constrained their ability to do their social homemaking. Lacking property rights, women organizers and volunteer workers could not sign checks to disburse funds. Arguing the cause of the enslaved, women such as the famous Grimke sisters found they were not allowed to speak in public; as a result they and others added the fight for suffrage to their fight for abolition. The nineteenth-century feminist movement was based largely on the claim that woman's special homemaking abilities should be allowed expression in the public sphere. Women fought for the vote as a means to use their special moral abilities to better society, to balance the participation of self-seeking impersonal men in the government; indeed, Frances Willard first asked that women be able to vote on the specific issue of Temperance, given their special knowledge of the damage alcohol wreaked on their homes.[67]

The separation of spheres brought by the development of capitalism let loose two powerful forces: masculine self-seeking in the labor force and among capitalists, and feminine self-seeking in homemaking. Masculine self-seeking meant competition in the economy with other men for advancement and wealth. Feminine self-seeking meant seeking ways to fill the needs of the members of one's family.

Family life began to emerge as distinctive when commodity production left the home. Yet family life was undeveloped; the requirements of mothering and of healthy family life were not known. Given the attachment of woman to homemaking and, in particular, to child-rearing as her "natural vocation," it was woman who inherited the responsibility for defining the needs of the family. It was this process, of both delineating the needs of the family and of filling them, that constituted feminine self-seeking under the cult of domesticity. Women transformed family life by controlling family size, by determining family commodity consumption, and even by influencing the morals of their husbands. But in this process of defining and filling the needs of their families, homemakers ran up against larger social institutions which threatened the health and happiness of their homes. For this reason, some women interpreted their vocation as demanding public and even political activity, and they entered into the world in which their husbands worked and from which their commodity products came.

The active self-seeking activity which the cult of domesticity unleashed in women led them to apply their feminine morality and vocation, not only to their own homes, but to capitalism at large, to treat the world, as Carl Degler has put it, as a "large home." This process actually took women out of the domestic sphere to which the cult of domesticity supposedly confined them. It is in the first instance a puzzle to understand why men accepted women's active entrance into and criticism of their sphere. After all, in the colonial economy homemakers had led a private, disenfranchised existence. Why did nineteenth-century society tolerate, even accept and submit to, women's entrance into and transformation of the public sphere? The natural connection of women to homemaking had produced a contradictory result. Given that the women were seen as "naturally" able to fulfill the social vocation of homemaking, men were naturally unable to judge women's performance. If women claimed that the needs of women and family life called them into the large public sphere, men were hard pressed to disagree. When women defined certain professions outside of the home which resembled homemaking as inherently feminine, their efforts were successful.

The social homemaking movement was a middle-class movement. But it aspired to define and protect *the* homemaking vocation, the vocation of *all* women, not simply that of the middle or privileged classes. Hence an important aspect of social homemaking was the struggle to better the conditions of the most disenfranchised families, first through charity, and later through pressures on economic and political institutions. Given the inequalities between men inherent in capitalism, the realization of a common standard of homemaking across classes was impossible. Yet the conception of womanhood as a natural condition shared by the female sex, and of homemaking as a specific social profession, necessarily brought attempts by government and social homemakers to impose their "ideal" upon the families at the bottom. So, for example, middle-class homemakers fought to prevent their poorer "sisters" from sending their children into the factories.

As the twentieth century advanced, homemakers indeed became more and more homogeneous. Rising living standards extended to more and more homemakers the use of new consumer goods. As commodities began to reduce drudgery work in the home, the use of servants by the wealthy became less common, allowing the wealthy home to emerge as a more personal place and reducing its difference from the poorer home. At the same time, compulsory elementary and eventually high school education, along with child-labor laws, brought in by the social homemaking efforts of wealthy homemakers, enforced the adoption of this personalized conception of family life in the poorer families. Child labor disappeared from poor homes, and servants from the rich homes. In most families, the homemaker began to realize the domestic ideal of home and motherhood first articulated by the cult of domesticity in the nineteenth century. As Theodore Caplow wrote in *The Sociology of Work:*

With the passage of time, housewives have come to be the only large group in the population engaged in the same activity, and their work and working conditions have become ever more the same with urbanization and with the diffusion of middle-class values. On the technical side, the transfer of household industries to outside agencies, the reduction of the home-making arts to a few essential technics, the distribution of identical household machinery everywhere in the country, and above all, the development of the communications network focused on the housewife as consumer and principle domestic purchaser, all these have created an occupational culture of remarkable uniformity in which not only the technics but the values are effectively standardized. This identity of metier transcends class lines and regional boundaries.[68]

The social homemaking movement was bound to lose momentum as the century advanced, in the very process of achieving its goals. Homemakers helped convince their society of the necessity for public institutions and regulations to humanize capitalism; once they had done so, their social mission was transferred to the growing government sector, to the emerging welfare state. The movement virtually collapsed after the winning of suffrage assured each homemaker her voice in the determination of the public sphere. Privileged homemakers could now concentrate on their own homes. Homemaking was to become increasingly private and personal as the twentieth century advanced.

However, the dynamism initiated by the cult of domesticity's socialization of homemaking was not at an end. It was to be carried on in the individual conflicts embodied in each woman's search to accomplish her homemaking vocation. These conflicts made the twentieth century as important a century for women as the nineteenth century—and eventually led to the rebirth of feminism. We will discuss these developments in Part III. But first we must discuss a final aspect of the sexual division of labor under nineteenth-century capitalism—the sex-typed job structure.

9

The Development of Sex-typed Jobs

In the family economy, most employment was either self-employment within one's family or servile employment, and most worked within agriculture. In the nineteenth century, agriculture became increasingly productive, freeing its labor force to manufacturing and service work: farm workers were 70% of the labor force in 1830, 50% in 1880, and 30% in 1910, and only 2% in 1960.[1] The form of employment was changing as well as its sector. As we have seen, in their struggle for self-advancement, successful petty producers grew into capitalists employing wage labor, while those who failed were driven into the proletariat. As the century advanced, more and more employment took the form of wage labor: from about 60% of those employed outside of agriculture in 1860, to 76% in 1900, to 89% in 1960.[2] As time passed, the American labor force was increasingly composed of urban wage laborers.

Because these jobs were created within the sexually differentiated social climate which we have examined in the previous chapters, the sexual division of labor was built into their very content: jobs were developed as masculine or feminine jobs, as men's work or women's work. This chapter will analyze the development of sex-typed jobs in capitalism: after developing a theoretical explanation of capitalism's sex-typed job structure, it will illustrate the working out of these principles by analyzing the sex-typing of different kinds of paid work.[3]

The Existence of Sex-typed Jobs

We have examined the particular way in which females as women entered into the labor force, the masculine sphere, under the cult of domesticity. This labor-force participation was not in any way a rejection of womanhood. The labor-force participation of a female was

187

either the subordination of her self to the needs of her family as a daughter or homemaker, or the subordination of her self to the needs of the society in a "women's profession." These women, then, entered the labor force, the sphere of masculine competition, as part of their self-constitution as women. They did not become masculine self-seeking property owners. They did not, could not, leave their femininity behind and merge into a sexless mass of laborers.

The masculine/feminine difference was expressed in the labor force in the sex-typing of jobs. Jobs in industrial capitalism were constructed as either men's jobs or women's jobs: most women in the labor force have worked at women's jobs, most men in the labor force have worked at men's jobs. This sex-typing of jobs is the subject of this chapter.

Studies of the sex-typing of jobs have suffered from an over-empirical focus. Many study the sex-typing of jobs by simply detailing the particular jobs of women and men over time. Given the continual process of technological change caused by the dynamics of capitalist production, plus the multiplicity of different jobs that are continually being divided between the sexes, such a description can occupy a whole volume.[4] But in the end one has made little progress toward an understanding of the laws determining the sex-typing of jobs. One is left either making simple superficial correlations between empty categories—males and females appear to have biologically determined propensities for particular physical/technical processes—or broad tautological generalizations—women universally earn lower wages than men and hence must be worth less.

In fact, on an empirical level, it is often hard to find the sex-typing of jobs. Social scientists have pointed to the fact that women are employed in almost all industries as some crude measure of their freedom and equality with man. And indeed, occupational statistics indicate that men and women often share occupations. One must know enough to push into more detailed occupational categories if one is to uncover the sex-typing of jobs. Let us examine, for example, the occupational statistics for 1900 presented in Table 9-1. At the general occupational level, we detect a concentration of women in the services, and of men in farm work. Moving to major occupational groupings, managers and proprietors, skilled craftsmen, laborers, and farmers emerge as predominantly male, while private household workers are female. Other occupations are not yet sex-typed. For example, professional and sales jobs appear to lack sex-typing. But if we look more closely, we find nurses were almost exclusively women, and lawyers, stock and bond salesmen, and motor vehicle salesmen were almost exclusively men. It would also seem that operatives were not sex segregated, but if we divide operatives into their industries, we find some sex-typing; for example, construction, railroads, and coal and petroleum operatives were almost all men. But the jobs of operatives in the boot and shoe industry and in the cotton textile industry were not sex-typed. To uncover the sex-typing of jobs here we must go beyond the occupational data into special factory reports. At the very detailed occupational level we find, in both industries, some very strict sex-typing of jobs. In boots and shoes, finishing and cutting were men's work, and upper stitching was women's work. In the cotton mills, loom fixers were men and drawers-in, women. Sometimes it is necessary to differentiate between factories to uncover the sex-typing of jobs: one factory will type a job masculine, and another, feminine. Drawing frame tenders were 91% female in one northeast factory, and 100% male in a Southern factory.[5] To find the sexual division of jobs one has to look for it, knowing that it must be there.

But then a good empiricist will bring up the exceptions, uncommon but definitely real, of women who have done men's work. Does this not destroy the notion then that men's work and women's work exist as meaningful categories? We cannot move beyond this cul-de-sac with further statistics. To retain the notion of the sex-typing of jobs in the face of such conflicting evidence we must recognize the social content of the categories of men, women, and labor. This means distinguishing men and women from biological males and females, and differentiating labor from a mere technical process. Then the presence of a female in men's work leads us to question not the sexual division of labor, but rather the femininity of the female. A person who enters the employment of the opposite sex is somehow deviating from the ideal of manhoood or womanhood after which males and females strive, respectively, or is caught in exceptional circumstances.

In certain situations, the demands of womanhood drove females, as women, into men's work. As we have seen in Chapter 3, women in the family economy occasionally entered into men's work of petty commodity production. But such women were not destroying the sexual division of labor, or even challenging it; as widows, daughters, or sisters, they were fulfilling their womanly obligation of replacing an absent or deceased male family member at the helm of a family

Table 9–1: The Sex-typing of Jobs, 1900

	% male or female									
	m	f	m	f	m	f	m	f	m	f
Total Labor Force	82	18								
White-collar										
Professional, technical and kindred			81	19	65	35				
Professional nurses*							6	94		
Lawyers*							99	1		
Managers, officials, proprietors					97	3				
Clerical and kindred workers					76	24				
Salesworkers					83	17				
Stock and bond salesmen*							94	6		
Salesmen of motor vehicles, retail*							97	3		
Manual workers			86	14						
Craftsmen, foremen, and kindred workers					97	3				
Laborers, except farm and mine					96	4				
Operatives and kindred workers					66	34				

Operatives and workers in construction, railroads, coal, and petroleum*	99	1
Boot and shoemakers and repairers*	81	19
Finishers†	97	3
Cutters†	99	1
Upper stitchers†	1	99
Cotton textile workers‡	45	55
Loom fixers‡	100	0
Drawers-in‡	0	100
Service workers	28	72
Private household workers only	3	97
Farm workers	91	9
Farmers and farm managers only	95	5

SOURCES:

U.S. Department of Commerce, Bureau of the Census, *Historical Statistics of the U.S.: Colonial to 1970*, p. 139.

*U.S. Department of Commerce, Bureau of the Census, *Twelfth Census of the U.S., 1900: Special Report: Occupations*, p. cxxvi.

†Statistics on 30 factories in Connecticut, Maine, Massachusetts, Missouri, New York, New Jersey, Ohio, and Pennsylvania in 1897 from the U.S. Bureau of Labor's *Eleventh Annual Report of the Commissioner of Labor 1895–96: Work and Wages of Men, Women and Children* (1897), pp. 73–91.

‡Statistics on Northeast and Southern cotton mills from U.S. Department of Commerce, Bureau of the Census, *Twelfth Census of the U.S., 1900: Special Report: Employees and Wages*, pp. xxxii, 786–806.

business. In such cases, it was within their duties as women to enter into men's work, and their actions were understood as such. Women continued to enter into men's work for such family reasons into the twentieth century. A 1929 article on "Women in Odd and Unusual Fields of Work"—that is, men's work—found that "an exceptionally large number are widows who stepped into their husband's jobs."[6] With the development of industrial capitalism, family-owned and -managed businesses gave way to impersonal corporations, and the wives of owners of managers were no longer called upon to take over in case of family emergencies. For this reason, there have been fewer such "exceptions" to the sex-typing of jobs.

On the other hand, the female who entered men's work on her own account did so as a man. The defining of jobs as men's or women's was so strong under the cult of domesticity that some females who wanted to do men's jobs became men. Only if they acted as men was their presence in such jobs acceptable. A female who called herself Charles Warner described her story in the 1860s:

> When I was about 20 I decided that I was almost at the end of my rope. I had no money and a woman's wages were not enough to keep me alive. I looked around and saw men getting more money and more work, and more money for the same kind of work. I decided to become a man. It was simple. I just put on men's clothing and applied for a man's job. I got it and got good money for those times, so I stuck to it.[7]

"Passing" as a man, as historians have called this phenomenon, was not easy for one brought up as a woman. First one had to learn masculine mannerisms: one female "took great pains to observe carefully the ways of masculinity in general and even has taken lessons in manly deportment from an actor under the pretext of turning to the stage."[8] Wearing men's clothes was illegal for females in many states, as was, of course, voting; if such females were discovered they would lose their freedom. Nevertheless, some females passed as men very successfully. For example, Murray Hall, a female man, became a prominent New York politician in the late nineteenth century and exercised the privilege of voting. "Passing women" often married women and lived accepted and undetected as men and husbands for years. Numbers of them fought in the Civil War. Indeed, we know of some of them only because their illness or death brought a medical examination during which their physical sex was inadvertently discovered. The shock of such a revelation was often great enough as to bring newspaper headlines, from which historians have gathered most of these accounts.[9]

While it was certainly rare for females to act as men, the experience of these female men forcefully illustrates our central point: man and woman are indeed social, rather than natural, categories. The sexual division of labor and personality creates and differentiates men and women. Society's equation of male with man, and female with woman, has served to channel unquestioning males and females into manhood and womanhood, respectively. However, the female who chose to reject this equation and to be a man could do so by doing men's work, developing a masculine personality, and marrying a woman. Society would accept her/him as a man and, furthermore, deduce from her/his manhood that she/he was a male.

The existence of a sex-typed job structure was, as we will show, an integral part of the nineteenth-century separation of sexual spheres. It is not, however, simply a thing of the past. The following discussion of the reasons for sex-typed jobs is largely applicable to the labor force through the present. It has only recently begun to be eroded, as we shall see in Part III.

The Roots of Sex-typed Jobs

We will start our investigation of the sex-typing of jobs, then, not with an empirical study, nor with the biological differences between the sexes. The sex-typing of jobs was created by the interaction, in capitalist society, of family and economic life. Hence we will begin with the conceptions of man and woman under the cult of domesticity which we have developed above, and with the laws of capitalist production. It is our task here to show how the sex-typing of jobs has been produced and reproduced within the United States economy.

We have noted, in our introduction, that the sexual division of labor has been historically and culturally universal. Its categorization of activities as either men's work or women's work and concomitant exclusion of males from women's work and females from men's work have been part of all social life we have known. On the most general level, the sex-typing of jobs under capitalism was just another form of this sexual division of labor, a new version of this ancient principle. A basic force behind the sex-typing of jobs was the workers' desires to assert and reaffirm their manhood or womanhood, and hence their difference from the opposite sex—the same force that underlay the general sexual division of labor.

Employment in a clearly masculine job, doing a job done by other men, fortified a man's sense of manhood; competition with these men to do the job well, or unification with them against the "big man," the employer, actively expressed and measured his manhood. However, doing a job that women also performed expressed a man's similarity with the opposite sex, showed him to be womanly and feminine. Competition against women for advancement, rather than proving a man's manhood, would devalue him, since the rule of the cult of domesticity was that men protected and dominated women as distinct and weaker beings. If a man won a competition against a woman, it proved him not to be a man but to be a sissy, a man unfit for competition against men. If a man lost a competition with a woman, if a woman performed better at his job, a man's masculinity was destroyed; he was clearly proven to be at a woman's level. The mere threat of losing such a contest made men unwilling to accept jobs with women. Men strenuously resisted being employed with women in the same job; once their job was sex-typed, they fought against any attempts by women to enter into their jobs. Such resistance ranged from the overt opposition of unions to the membership of women, to the ridicule and sabotage of women who might make it into such a position.[10] These tactics quite successfully kept many jobs masculine in the face of employers' attempts to integrate them.

Likewise, women wished to work in jobs done by women. A woman's femininity was already threatened by her presence in the labor force, the masculine sphere. This was one reason that women sought employment within the feminine home sphere, either in their own homes or in the homes of others. If a woman was forced to seek wages outside of the home, she would seek jobs which were clearly women's work, which employed only or predominantly women. Employment in a job that also included men would constitute her as masculine; bettering a man in the labor force would undermine her femininity, as well as his masculinity. So although the sex-typing of jobs brought men the more interesting, higher-paid jobs, women rarely tried to cross over the sex-type barrier and enter into men's jobs. The desires of the sexes to assert their sexual identities by undertaking work reserved for their sex alone was a powerful force underlying the sex-typing of jobs, especially within a particular firm or region.

However, the sex-typing of jobs also resulted from the general differentiation of the sexes in society. Capitalists took the social differentiation of the sexes into account in their hiring; they therefore created jobs appropriate either for men or for women workers, masculine and feminine jobs. We have studied the social differentiation of the sexes from the standpoint of the marital relationship: the placement of man, as husband/provider, in the labor force competition, and of his wife, as homemaker, in the private service of her family. We have seen how young women sometimes left women's domestic sphere to aid their parents as daughters or to serve society as social homemakers, until they married. To investigate the manner in which capitalism built the sexual division into the job structure, we must simply look at these social practices from the point of view of the hiring firm. Men and women entered into the wage contract with the capitalist as beings with different personalities and capabilities who sought different things. Men were competitive, aggressive, rational, and self-concerned; women were servile, family-oriented, self-effacing. A man sought through his labor-force participation the means to constitute himself as a man; he actively took on the work identity given him by his employer and sought its advancement. A woman sought through her labor-force participation the means to fill the needs of others—of her family members or, if she worked as a social homemaker, of society at large. So whereas men's identities were centered in their jobs, women's were centered in their relationships to their families, as wives, mothers, or daughters. Whereas men needed to participate in the labor force to be men, women only entered the labor force if their families' needs so dictated.

Men were both more demanding of their jobs than women were and more willing to subordinate themselves unilaterally to the requirements of their jobs. Men were seeking advancement and power and self-hood in the labor force; they dedicated their lives to this endeavor. They demanded for their services at least a family wage, a wage that would allow them to provide for a family and a homebound homemaker. Men were best utilized by capitalists in jobs that demanded the development of a work self, and the competition of this self with others; the fact that capitalism did not have enough of these jobs for all men made the masculine struggle all the more competitive. Women were both less demanding of their jobs and of income, and less willing to dedicate themselves to their jobs. Most striking was the partial commitment a woman made to the labor force. A woman usually worked only part of her life—before she was a home-maker, if her husband was unable to support the family, or if she lost her husband/provider. When she did enter the labor force, she often worked either part time or part year only. Women were reticent to leave their homes to earn income; a very high percentage of "gain-fully employed women" were engaged in home-based work, such as putting-out or taking in boarders and lodgers. Due to the polarization of adult men and women in the marital relationship, family responsi-bilities pushed a man to dedicate his life to his job, whereas they prevented a woman from gaining any independent job identity.

These differences between masculine and feminine labor were built into the job structure in specific ways. Jobs ladders including mone-tary rewards for training were constructed, developing man workers' dedication to self-aggrandizement while harnessing it to the service of the firm.[11] Men would give themselves to their jobs only in exchange for advancement, forcing firms that employed skilled men to con-struct for them ways to advance and allowing firms to benefit from a man's jobs experience. Firms could also induce men to acquire train-ing at their own expense by rewarding such training with higher wages, for masculine self-seeking meant following whatever course brought the best rewards, in terms of either earnings or advance-ment. Job ladders could not, however, engage the heart of the woman worker, could not induce her to put her job's demands before those of her family. Indeed, a job's characteristics and future pros-pects would have little effect on whether she stayed on the job; her labor-force presence was determined by her position in the life cycle and the success of her husband in the labor force. Except for the few unusual women who planned lifetime vocations in the labor force as social homemakers (and these did so to help others, not simply for self-advancement), women would not undertake special training for jobs in the labor force, for their life plan was to be homemakers. Women's jobs did not need to be enriched as did men's, nor could they demand such dedication. A suitable job for a woman was one that required little job-specific training or special job experience. This did not mean that women's jobs could never require developed skills. Middle- and upper-class women who undertook the general training necessary for good homemaking certainly increased their productivity on the job. Unlike job-oriented men, however, these women would acquire such homemaking training regardless of whether or not it increased their returns in the labor force. Therefore, women's jobs could require a high school or college education without rewarding it with a wage premium.

In this section we have argued that the workers' needs for a sex-typed job structure, as well as their differentiation by sex in marriage, lay at the root of the sex-typing of jobs. Now we will go on to study the creation of sex-typed jobs in different sectors of the economy. First, note that we will not be discussing simply the external labeling of a job as masculine or feminine. Rather, we will show how the sexual differentiation of individuals was built into the very *content* of jobs. Capitalist firms hired wage laborers to cooperate in the production of commodities to fill needs of firms (producer or capital goods) and consumers (consumer goods). Yet neither the needs that the firms were to fill with their products nor the set of jobs they created to harness wage laborers to this production nor the wages attached to these jobs were natural givens. All were *socially* determined; all, as a result, reflected the social differentiation of the sexes and changed through history as capitalist society developed in complexity and wealth.[12]

We cannot discuss in full the articulation of a particular set of jobs and its transformation through history with the development of the economy. Instead, we will focus on the creation of sex-typed jobs in four different areas: consumer services, the professions, blue-collar work, and office work. We will show how the work in each of these areas was organized into sex-typed jobs, and how, in most cases, its sex-typing has persisted through 1960. While we are unable to examine the totality of the job structure, these studies will exemplify the different ways in which the sexual difference was built into the job structure. Then we will go on to examine further divisions within feminine jobs—by race, ethnicity, and class. We will conclude the chapter with an examination of the mutual reinforcement of the sexual division in economy and family life.

Feminine and Masculine Service: Domestic and Protective Service

In this section we will examine two very different kinds of service work: the feminine work of domestic service, and the masculine protective and political services. They are the expression, in capitalism's labor force, of traditionally feminine and masculine ways of serving others.

In the family economy, much work was done within the home by non-family members, "domestic servants" or slaves. These workers aided the household in its production, in return for room and board, and in some cases a money wage. In the nineteenth century, commodity production moved out of the household, and laboring for others began to change into wage labor, labor which allowed the worker a home of his own, and freedom in consumption. Meanwhile, the house was developed into a private, familial sphere, the home, and became the work space of the homemaker. However, these developments did not eliminate all drudgery work from the home, and hence did not end the practice of domestic service. Although scientific homemakers agreed that the ideal home would be freed of all non-family members, they also accepted that as long as homemaking involved impersonal time-consuming work, it was logical for wealthy homemakers to employ domestics.

Domestic work was clearly a feminine job. It was employment at women's work supervised by a woman. As home and shop became separate, the home became woman's domain and the work within it, clearly women's work. The domestic was hired to help the homemaker with her work; the homemaker's need for help was expressed as a need for a woman. The domestic worked to fill the needs of the family, only in her case, the family served was not her own. Such work was ideally suited for single, divorced, or widowed women without children who needed the means to live and lacked families of their own; it provided them with "a living" in their traditional sphere, a home, and a family to care for. Young women saw domestic work as a way to develop their homemaking skills, as an apprenticeship to an older, more accomplished homemaker. Indeed, the mistress–servant relationship commonly developed qualities of the mother–daughter relationship.[13] In the words of one domestic interviewed by Lucy Salmon for her 1911 book, Domestic Service: "I choose housework as my regular employment for the simple reason that young women look forward to the time when they will have housework of their own to do. I consider that I or anyone in domestic employment will make a better housekeeper than any young woman who works in a factory." Another explained her choice of work in this way: "I like it best, was used to it at home, and it seems more natural like."[14] Some immigrant groups preferred domestic service as employment for their young girls, for it gave them basic training in American language and culture, which was invaluable to the immigrant homemaker.[15] In 1900, homemaking for strangers in their homes provided about one-fifth of the employment opportunities of women (see Table 9-2).

On the other hand, domestic work was clearly inadequate for a man. While the mistress–servant relationship was relatively comfortable between two women, it was not so with a man servant. A young man could not be trained for manhood by serving a woman as a son; for a boy, adulthood meant breaking away from his mother and her world into the masculine sphere of property owners and competition. Working as a domestic would not only keep him in the feminine, home sphere, but, as servile labor, keep his identity submerged in that of another, in this case his employer. While for a woman such merging was "natural," for a man it was "unnatural" and childish, antithetical to manhood. Rather than establishing his position among men as more or less successful, his energies would only brand him as inferior to another, and worse still, to a woman. So while in the family economy, domestic service had occupied both sexes, the development of wage labor and of equality of rights between men, combined with the increasing femininity of the home, drove men out of servile labor, transforming the servant into a domestic, a woman. Even the most destitute of men began to shun domestic service; by 1900, fewer than 2% of employed men worked as servants.[16] Half of these men were blacks, schooled in servility by slavery, and furthermore excluded from white men's jobs.[17]

Another form of personal service was homemaking for others, for strangers, but within the confines of one's own home. Prominent here was the taking in of boarders and lodgers, common in nineteenth and early twentieth century cities, as we discussed in Chapter 6. As a simple extension of homemaking, this was clearly women's work. Others employed in this manner were laundresses and dressmakers and seamstresses. In 1900, about 40% of the women working for income were doing homemaking for others in their own homes (see Table 9-2).

We cannot leave the area of women's homemaking for income without mentioning a "time-honored" form of homemaking for non-family members, prostitution. Given its illegal character, we do not know much about prostitution, and it is generally ignored. Yet it is often referred to jokingly as "the oldest profession," and it has been a common, if not a major source of employment for women, especially unmarried, young women. Prostitution varied from being put up by one's lover as an almost wife to working in a whore house; further-

Table 9–2: The Femininity of Personal Service, 1900, 1960

Occupation	% women in occupation (no. women in occupation ÷ total no. in occupation)	% of all employed women	% women in occupation (including prostitution and taking in boarders and lodgers)	% of all employed women (including prostitutes and taking in boarders and lodgers)
1900				
In Employer's Home:	95.6	25.3	95.6	17.2
Domestic servants and housekeepers	96.1	23.5		15.9
Midwives*	100.0	0.1		0.1
Practical nurses*[a]	88.9	1.7		1.2
In Own Home:	98.1	14.1	99.6	42.0
Laundresses[b]	99.3	5.2		3.5
Taking in boarders and lodgers[c]			100.0	31.5
Boarding and lodging housekeepers[c]	83.4	1.1		0.8
Prostitutes[d]			100.0	1.0
Dressmakers and seamstresses[e]	99.9	7.8		5.2
1960				
In Employer's Home	96.4	8.5	96.4	8.0
Domestic servants	95.9	5.4		5.1
Housekeepers	98.3	0.7		0.6

Laundresses	100.0	00.001		0.001
Babysitters	97.6	1.5		1.4
Practical nurses[f]	96.0	0.9		0.9
In Own Home				
Laundresses	95.9	0.9	99.6	7.3
Laundresses	97.9	0.2		0.2
Taking in boarders and lodgers[g]			100.0	5.7
Boarding and lodging house-keepers	88.7	0.1		0.1
Prostitutes[h]			100.0	
Dressmakers and seamstresses	96.9	0.6		0.8
				0.5

SOURCES:

U.S. Department of Commerce, Bureau of the Census, *Occupational Trends in the U.S. 1900–1950*, Working Paper No. 5; pp. 10–15, 22–27; idem, *Census of Population: 1960, 1900, Occupational Characteristics* (for persons 14 years and over), pp. 11–20.

*U.S. Department of Commerce, Bureau of the Census, *Special Reports: Occupations at the Twelfth Census, 1900* (for persons 10 years and older), p. 7.

a. Includes those who worked in medical institutions and who did not specify training.

b. Includes those who worked in employers homes.

c. The figure for "taking in boarders and lodgers" is a crude but conservative estimate based on the reports of the Immigration Commission: U.S. Senate, *Immigrants in Industries* (1910), p. 128; *Immigrants in Cities* (1911), Vol. I, p. 136. "Boarding and lodging housekeepers" includes only those who declared themselves to be running boarding and lodging houses professionally.

d. This is a crude but very conservative estimate based on William Sanger, *The History of Prostitution* (New York: Arno Press, 1972: original 1859), pp. 575–85; George J. Kneeland, *Commercialized Prostitution in New York City* (New York: The Century Co., 1913), p. 100.

e. Includes the impersonal service of putting-out for capitalist merchants.

f. Includes those working in medical institutions.

g. This is a crude estimate.

h. This is a crude but conservative estimate based on Gail Sheehy, "Cleaning up Hell's Bedroom," in *New York*, November 13, 1972, pp. 58–66.

more, prostitutes of different "classes" existed to serve the differentiated needs and budgets of men. Prostitution was a creation of the particular sexual needs of men; in the nineteenth century, the insistence of many wives on abstinence, along with the conception of man's sexuality as limitless, uncontrollable, and impersonal, sustained a lively prostitution trade.[18] As the service of the sexual needs of heterosexual men, prostitution was very much "women's work," although it lacked social acceptance. Early stories of the horrors of city prostitution stressed the manner in which girls were enticed into it by promises of marriage; prostitution was also made attractive by the relatively high wages and glamour it offered young women, attributes absent from women's other jobs. In the West, some women were able to move from prostitution to ownership and management of a brothel, earning wealth and occasionally even respectability.[19]

Personal service, as the subordination of one's activities to the needs of particular individuals in a home, was an inherently feminine activity: over 95% of all workers employed in such pursuits were women; furthermore, a majority of employed women worked in such home-based jobs. In 1900, private household work (in one's own home or in the home of the employer) provided income to almost 60% of all gainfully employed women (see Table 9-2). Capitalism drew women, especially girls, into the labor force; however, they remained more attached to the home than their male counterparts. Into the twentieth century, most wage-earning women had not yet experienced the independence and freedom involved in wage work outside of the home. They voluntarily concentrated themselves in those jobs which were most similar to woman's true vocation, homemaking.

Private household employment—in one's home or in that of the employer—represented a vestige of the family economy within capitalism. With the advance of the twentieth century, such employment has decreased. As labor-saving consumer goods became available to homemakers, the latter substituted such goods for domestic servants, allowing the home to become more private. The number of female servants per thousand households fell from 111 in 1870 to 95 in 1900 to 55 in 1920 to 33 in 1960; fewer and fewer of these domestics are asked to "live in" the home of their employers.[20] The development of restaurants, hotels, and motels has provided homeless individuals with homemaking-like services and reduced their need to seek room and board in private homes. Laundromats, washing machines, and ready-made clothes have reduced the demand for laundresses and seamstresses. Opportunities for private household employment have shrunk; between 1900 and 1960, the percentage of employed women working in homes declined from about 60% to about 15% (see Table 9-2). Women were increasingly forced to leave their feminine, familial sphere and enter into more impersonal work relationships when they needed to earn income for themselves and their families.

While personal service clearly excluded men, another kind of "service" was intrinsically masculine. The social differentiation of the sexes placed men in the political sphere as the representatives and protectors of their households. As jobs developed that embodied these masculine services, they were defined as masculine from the start. Political jobs, both elected and appointed, were, of course, masculine. Politics were men's responsibility; women's right to vote was not even recognized until after World War I. Military service, both volunteer and drafted, was inherently masculine; it was part of man's duty to protect his family and country against invaders. On the other hand, the prevalence of violent relationships between countries or blocks of countries—"national defense"—has reflected the domination of states by masculine, competitive principles. War has been the ultimate competition between men, and participation in a war, a life-or-death competition, the quintessential proof of masculinity. Women, whose ultimate concern has been the fulfillment of individual needs, have not only been excluded from such "work" but often opposed it for its destruction of life. Protective service workers of another sort—policemen, firemen, and guards—were also necessarily masculine. While such jobs did not employ a high percentage of men, they were overwhelmingly populated by men (see Table 9-3).

The Creation of Sex-typed Professions

Sociologist William Goode argues that professions have two central characteristics: a basic body of abstract knowledge, and the ideal of service to society.[21] Yet given these two shared qualities, the professions differ greatly. Indeed, it is easy to divide them into at least two groups—the great, "person professions," and the feminine professions. Historically, the great professions emerged first, and were masculine; the feminine professions are of more recent origin, and differ qualitatively from the first group.

The original professions were the ministry, medicine, law, and uni-

Table 9–3: Masculine Services, 1900, 1960

Occupation	% males employed in occupation (no. males in occptn. ÷ tot. no. in occptn.)	% of employed males (no. males in occptn. ÷ no. males employed in labor force)
1900		
Armed forces	100.00	.537
Watchmen, policemen, and detectives	99.2	.483
Firemen (fire protection)	100.00	.061
Elected govt. officials (includes federal and state as of Jan. 1901)	100.00	
Total		1.08
1960		
Policemen and detectives	97.2	.564
Firemen, fire protection	99.7	.316
Guards, watchmen, and doorkeepers	97.1	.541
Marshals and constables	96.7	.015
Sheriffs and bailiffs	94.8	.053
Watchmen, crossing and bridge tenders	55.8	.031
Armed services	98.3	
Elected govt. officials[a]	96.5	
Total		1.52

SOURCES: U.S. Department of Commerce, Bureau of the Census, *Special Reports: Occupations at the Twelfth Census*, Table 1 (for persons 10 years and older); idem, *Census of the Population: 1960, Occupational Characteristics*, Table 21 (for persons 14 years and older); U.S. Bureau of Labor Statistics, *Occupational Outlook Handbook*, Bulletin #1450 (1966–67); Harry Hansen, ed., *The World Almanac and Book of Facts: 1960* (New York: New York World-Telegram, 1960), p. 66; idem, *The World Almanac and Book of Facts: 1961* (New York: New York World-Telegram, 1961), pp. 132–6.
a. Includes 100.0% of the Governors, 97.4% of the Lieutenant-Governors (only 39 states), 88.0% of the Secretaries of State governments, 99.0% of the U.S. Senators, and 96.3% of the U.S. Representatives of the House.

versity teaching; they emerged in pre-capitalist Europe out of theology.[22] The clergy taught at the early universities; medicine was merged with religious principles; law was originally God's. As capitalism began to emerge and the church was separated from the state and from natural science, these professions were distinguished and individually developed; with colonization, the English system was transplanted to the North American colonies. These great professions were masculine, originating among Catholic theologians, who were, by God's law, exclusively men; they continued as "brotherhoods" after their separation from the church. While a few social homemakers attempted, in the nineteenth century, to gain entrance into them, particularly into medicine, their attempts were, for the most part, failures. The masculine typing of these professions had been clearly established, discouraging most women from even considering them. The lengthy periods of formal training that these professions began to require excluded all but the most dedicated social homemaker, while the latter's efforts were easily thwarted due to the resolve of professional organizations to prevent the entry of the "weaker sex" into their midst. The successful efforts of a minority of women to enter medicine in the late nineteenth century are the exception which proves the rule. These women were confronted by "multiple lines of conservative defense. If one were scaled, the opposition re-formed in the rear. If women could get into schools, the hospitals were still closed; and if the latter were finally opened, internships and residencies were still denied them. When doctoring ladies appeared, physicians refused to consult with them and prevented their entrance into medical societies."[23] Table 9-4 shows the masculinity of the four great professions both in 1900 and in 1960.

Table 9-4 also lists feminine professions, professions dominated by women both in 1900 and in 1960. Rather than entering the established masculine professions, women in the nineteenth and early twentieth century participated in the development of a new set of professions—secondary school teaching, social work, nursing, and library work. As we saw in Chapter 8, women sought to serve society at large as social homemakers; this process led many to seek entrance into teaching or to work to professionalize their helping work of nursing and social work. Nineteenth-century women worked hard to transform nursing from unskilled, low-paid domestic work to a respected profession. Nursing had originally been a kind of homemaking for money—the 1900 Census listed "Nurses and Midwives" under

Table 9–4: Sex-typing of Selected Professions, 1900, 1960

	1900		1960	
	% males employed in occptn.[a]	% females employed in occptn.	% males employed in occptn.	% females employed in occptn.
Old Masculine Professions				
Physicians and surgeons	94.4	5.6	93.3	6.7
Professors in colleges and universities	93.6	6.4	78.5	21.5
Lawyers and judges	99.6	0.4	96.6	3.4
Clergymen	97.0	3.0	97.8	2.2
Feminine Professions				
Nurses	6.4	93.6	2.4	97.6
Librarians	27.5	72.5	14.2	85.8
Teachers	25.4	74.6	28.4	71.6
Social workers	25.0[b]	75.0[b]	36.3	63.7
New Masculine Professions				
Accountants and auditors	93.4	6.7	83.5	16.5
Dentists	97.3	2.7	97.9	2.1
Veterinary surgeons	99.8	0.2	98.2	1.8
Architects	99.1	0.9	97.9	2.1
Surveyors	99.98	0.02	96.2	3.8
Engineers	99.8	0.2	99.6	0.6
Designers and draftsmen	94.8	5.2	93.9	6.1

SOURCES: U.S. Department of Commerce, Bureau of the Census, *Special Reports: Occupations at the Twelfth Census,* Table 1 (for persons 10 years and older); idem, *Census of the Population: 1960, Occupational Characteristics,* Table 21 (for persons 14 years and older); U.S. Bureau of Labor Statistics, *Occupational Outlook Handbook,* Bulletin #1450, (1966–67); U.S. Department of Commerce, Bureau of the Census, *Occupational Trends in the U.S. 1900–1950,* Working Paper #5, pp. 10–15, 22–27.
a. % men (women) employed in occupation is the number of men (women) in the occupation divided by the total number in the occupation.
b. These are estimates made by Elizabeth Kemper Adams in *Women Professional Workers* (New York: The Macmillan Co., 1921), p. 173.

the category of "Domestic and Personal Service." Professional nursing developed as a complement to the medical profession; the unskilled nurse of the nineteenth century was "professionalized" into the doctor's helper. Yet nurses never attained the professional status and independence of doctors: doctors held the monopoly over health knowledge, while the essential requirement of a nurse was a willingness to serve, rather than knowledge gained through an extended training program. Nursing was an inherently feminine profession; the nurse both mothered the patients and occupied the feminine position of personal helper or assistant to the male doctor.

While women were able to transform nursing into a woman's profession, they were not as successful in trying to professionalize midwifery, for it was not clearly outside of and complementary to the masculine sphere of medicine. In colonial times, both male doctors and female midwives delivered children. Women were considered fit for midwifery if they had themselves given birth to a child, or even if they had simply seen another women give birth. Whereas masculine doctoring was a profession developed through formal training or an apprenticeship to another practicioner, midwifery grew directly out of woman's own experiences of childbirth. As medicine began to formally organize itself in the nineteenth century, obstetricians fought against the unscientific character of midwifery. However, they did not try to upgrade midwifery by bringing it under their umbrella and accepting women into apprenticeships and schools; as Dr. Channing, Professor of Obstetrics at Harvard, wrote, "It is obvious that we cannot instruct women as we do men in the science of medicine."[24] Rather, they simply fought, successfully, to eliminate midwifery with public education about the dangers of childbirth and the resultant need for the formally trained obstetrician.[25]

In colonial times, rural schoolhouses had employed both men and women; generally, single women taught the young children in the summer, while young men taught the older children during the remainder of the year. Women had also started their own "dame schools" for girls. As the nineteenth century advanced, schooling became more organized, particularly in the urban, "graded" school, where students were separated according to age, and teaching material was strictly determined by school superintendents. Elementary school teaching became increasingly feminized. Women such as Catherine Beecher fought to convince the public that professionalized teaching was properly women's work, and claimed as women's work not simply the education of the very young, so clearly similar to mothering, but also all elementary and secondary training, and indeed the college education of women. Educated women were anxious to serve society in this motherly role, while educated men were drawn away by higher-paid, higher-status jobs. Since teaching so resembled mothering, yet at the same time required formal training of different degrees, it was not clear whether it was inherently masculine or feminine. However, society needed to have a sex-typing for teaching (as for all jobs); the push of social homemakers in the late nineteenth century, and the many preferable options for their educated male counterparts, claimed lower-level teaching for single women.[26] Some men teachers remained, concentrated in the upper grades and in administration and college teaching; women were virtually excluded from administration and college teaching, except in certain subjects or institutions, such as women's colleges.[27]

Women, as social homemakers, actively undertook the care of the poor and needy in the nineteenth century; their volunteer work was often the backbone of local charitable organizations. As these social welfare institutions became established, women entered into the new profession of social work. This profession was not totally monopolized by women; men occupied the executive and administrative positions, as well as the community organizing work. Women concentrated in those jobs that involved helping needy individuals, such as case work. Librarianship also developed in the late nineteenth and early twentieth centuries as a feminine profession, one dedicated to the service of the needs of others. As Elizabeth Kemper Adams pointed out in 1921 in her book on *Women Professional Workers*, "like teaching also, it is actually or practically a form of public service, since libraries are democratic institutions serving disinterestedly and impartially all elements in the community."[28]

Although both served the public, the new feminine professions differed qualitatively from the older, masculine professions. Indeed, social scientists sometimes refer to them specifically as the "semi-professions" or the "sub-professions," describing them as less professional than men's.[29] Why? Nineteenth-century men professionals worked to advance themselves through their professional lives; they concentrated their efforts on developing formal training programs that would both restrict their numbers and increase their knowledge and power. On the other hand, women professionals, as social homemakers, had as their first priority the filling of the needs of others. The nurse or social worker subordinated herself to her client's needs; special knowledge was less necessary for her work, nor did she seek it out as a means to establish her autonomy and power. Although men professionals also served the public, they used their special knowledge to define the needs of their clients, and hence to place themselves above, rather than in a servile relationship to, the latter.[30] In keeping with their focus on the needs of clients, the feminine professions have not participated in the development of knowledge as much as in the communication and application of it. And whereas the masculine professions used special knowledge to claim autonomy from hierarchical authorities, the feminine professions did not seek autonomy, nor have the special knowledge to substantiate such a claim. Feminine professionals have been easily integrated into administrative hierarchies and placed under the power of superviors or of men professionals.[31]

In these ways, the social differentiation of the sexes was built into the development of the professions. This process was somewhat different for blue-collar work, as we will see in the next section.

The Sex-typing of Blue-collar Work

The blue-collar work of industrial production was also sex-typed. Capitalism inherited the masculine craft system and the predominantly feminine putting-out system. Although it continually broke down masculine skilled work as well as feminine putting-out work, replacing both with unskilled laborers plus machinery, it did not eliminate the sex-typing of blue-collar work.

THE MASCULINITY OF THE CRAFTS

Craft production, the production of manufactures for exchange, had been men's work in the colonial economy. The development of capitalism and of the factory system undermined the masculine craft system by developing technologies that replaced skilled craft work with machinery tended by unskilled labor. Men craftsmen themselves aided this process by the subdivision of their crafts and the introduction of unskilled or putting-out labor to aid and expand their scale of production.[32] At the same time, this mechanization did not eliminate all craft work. Men were able to take over new, skilled blue-collar jobs as the old were eliminated, to organize themselves into craft unions, and to formalize restrictive apprenticeship programs. (While some skilled and paraprofessional *feminine* jobs also fit apprenticeable criteria, the women working in them did not similarly upgrade them into crafts.)[33] The crafts employed 16% of men in 1900, and 18% in 1960. In 1900, in 50% of the crafts, over 99% of the workers were men; in 97.1% of them, over 90% of the workers were men. In only 2.9% of the crafts were less than 90% of the workers men. In 1960 these percentages were 42.9%, 83.7%, and 16.3%, respectively.[34]

Some feminist historians have stressed the fact that craftsmen worked to exclude women from their ranks.[35] Craftsmen did so out of a desire to work with men, which we have analyzed above, and as part of their general strategy of eliminating competitors who would depress the wage. But, furthermore, few women were anxious to enter into the crafts, given their masculine character. First, women did not want to enter a job that was, and had been for years, typed as men's work. Second, the strict apprenticeship requirements of the crafts discouraged women; in the labor force as present or future homemakers, they were not interested in dedicating years to acquiring skills through apprenticeship. They needed money immediately, and they did not expect to remain in the labor force.

"The invasion of the crafts by women has been developing for years amid irritation and injury to the workman," wrote union man Edward O'Donnell in an article for the *American Federationist* in 1897 entitled, "Women as Breadwinners—The Error of the Age."[36] Women did not, however, invade the crafts by forcing themselves into apprenticeship programs; rather, their "invasion" was part of the replacement of skilled craft work with machinery and unskilled labor. Unskilled labor did not, as did the crafts, require formal apprenticeship programs; unskilled laborers were, furthermore, difficult to organize, since they were usually in abundant supply. Yet these jobs were nevertheless sex-typed, as we shall see. But first let us look at another kind of work inherited from the family economy—industrial homework.

THE FEMININITY OF INDUSTRIAL WORK IN THE HOME

Industrial work in the home was wage work done for firms through the putting-out system. We met this brand of work in the colonial economy, and noted its femininity. In the nineteenth century, such work continued to be attractive to women, especially to married women who needed extra income but wished to remain in their homes, homemaking. The subjective private quality of such work made it desirable to women; a woman could do it in her own home, at her own pace. It could be combined with homemaking and childcare, the children could even be enlisted to help. This same private and flexible quality made putting-out work undesirable to men, who sought a publicly recognized laboring existence and a consistent, objectively defined job outside of the home. Hence putting-out work continued to be the province of women and children. Needy married women, willing to do such work for almost any wage, bid down wages to make putting-out even less suitable for men. In a 1915 study of putting-out workers in Massachusetts, over half of the individual home workers employed for more than nine months earned less than $100 yearly (the average annual earnings of a domestic in 1900 were $240!). The study concluded that "only in the rarest cases does home work bring in a living wage." The same study revealed that only 6% of the 2,410 home workers studied were men over the age of sixteen: 69% were women, and 25% were children. The few men employed were mostly factory hands helping with home work at night; home work was an occupation "which the ordinary man undertakes only in a desultory way to fill his evenings, or as a last resort when disabled or incapacitated by age."[37]

But putting-out work was only an intermediate form. While it allowed a more developed division of labor than craft production, such home production lacked the objective determination and collective laboring with machinery which could be achieved in a factory setting. Hence it was increasingly replaced in the course of the nineteenth and twentieth centuries by factory work. These factories hired unskilled wage workers to tend their machines.

THE SEX-TYPING OF UNSKILLED JOBS

The replacement of industrial home work and craft work with unskilled work did not eliminate the sex-typing of jobs. The new, unskilled jobs were also sex-typed, due to the differences between men and women workers and these workers' needs to work in a sex-typed job structure. Helen Sumner's 1910 study of women in industry, which closely examined women's occupations in unskilled areas, found almost universal sex-typing of unskilled work.[38] Looking at one particular industry—boots and shoes—an examination of the Commissioner of Labor's report on the employment of men and women shows that of 650 jobs in 31 factories, less than 1% were not sex-typed. Of the 3,964 employees listed, 99% worked in jobs with only their own sex; 10 women were employed in men's jobs, 7 men in women's jobs, and 39 people in jobs that were not sex-typed.[39]

What determined how these jobs were sex-typed? Asking the employers or workers helps little: both employers and employees tended to view unskilled factory jobs as inherently suitable only for one or the other sex. When factory managers were asked in an 1896 study why they employed women instead of men in particular jobs, the most common response was that women were "better adapted"—the most common reason for not employing women was that "women could be employed only in certain occupations" (see Table 9-5). It would seem than that there were qualities inherent in different types of unskilled work that made them suitable only for one or the other sex. Commonly cited were the requirement of strength (men's jobs) and the requirement of dexterity (women's jobs). However, explanations that thus reduce the masculine/feminine difference to a biological one are immediately suspect as after-the-fact rationalizations. Their falseness is revealed by the fact that, while unskilled jobs were almost always sex-typed, they were not always typed similarly in different factories or different localities. It was not uncommon for a job typed women work's in one factory to be men's work in another. Helen Sumner found an interesting example of this in the manufacture of nuts, bolts, and screws:

> It is difficult, however, to speak with any certainty of the division of work between the sexes, since it varies so much in different plants. Of three bolt, nut, and screw factories visited in Pennsylvania, one employed no women, the manager stating emphatically that he did not consider such work suitable for them, while the other two employed women numerously in all the lighter, unskilled work. In Ohio all four of the factories visited employed women, but in one they did nothing beyond sorting and packing, they operated a few light machines; and in the other two they were numerously employed in machine work as well as in the few hand operations required.[40]

Again, we cannot account for the sex-typing of unskilled jobs simply by referring to the natural differences between the sexes. Indeed, remembering our study of the slave economy, size, strength, and

Table 9–5: Reasons for Employing
Women instead of Men for Unskilled
Factory Jobs, 1890s

Better adapted	795
Cheaper	329
More reliable	110
More easily controlled	99
Neater, cleaner	97
More rapid	64
More industrious	62
More careful	18
More easily procured	17
Less liable to strike	11
More temperate	10
More patient, content, quiet	9
Learn more rapidly	7
Don't wish to learn trade	5
More skillful or competent	3
More polite	3
Good effect on men	3
More pleasing	1

SOURCE: Compiled from U.S. Bureau of Labor, *Eleventh Annual Report of the Commissioner of Labor 1895–6. Work and Wages of Men, Women and Children (1897)*, pp. 583–610.

health are more important than sex in determining one's ability to do unskilled industrial or agricultural work.

Most unskilled jobs did not, by their physical requirements, exclude either males or females. Neither did they exclude women or men: unlike jobs in domestic service, they lacked servile or inherently feminine qualities that would exclude men; unlike the crafts and the masculine professions, they did not require a job commitment that women would not make. Their impersonal content further stripped such work of sexual content. Yet they were nevertheless sex-typed. Since workers wished to work in sex-typed jobs, such jobs were sex-typed, at least on the factory level.

To determine how employers chose between women and men workers for their jobs (when they did not just accept the sex-typing of a job as given from the past), we must examine the difference in the ways in which the sexes acted with their employer. The wage contract between the employer and the laborer determined the rate at which labor power would be exchanged for income. The employer and the laborer confronted each other as two individuals with opposing interests: the employer wanting to extract as much labor power as possible for a given pay, the laborer wanting to procure the highest pay for his or her labor power. The actual terms of the exchange were set not only in the wage bargain but on the job by the speed at which the laborer worked. In unskilled jobs the laborer's bargaining power was limited by the ease of replacement: his or her labor power held no special value to the employer as long as other workers were available. However, a laborer could refuse to accept a job and/or threaten to quit if the wage rate was inadequate; unskilled laborers could also unite in unions and use their collective power to bargain with the employer.

Men and women entered the labor force differently; a man seeking to establish himself as a successful man and head of household, a woman as a daughter or homemaker seeking money to aid her family. The two acted differently in the wage bargain which determined the exchange between worker and employer. A man actively confronted his employer as a distinct and opposed individual: he asserted his individuality by thus opposing himself to his employer. A woman did not seek to establish herself as an individual and did not in the same way oppose herself to her employer. The same lack of an active job identity that made women unsuitable for high-level or skilled jobs made them good candidates for unskilled jobs. Their feminine training, which taught them to please others without demanding recognition and valuation for their efforts, was, to profit-minded employers, an invitation to exploitation.

As a result, men were able to procure better wages for their unskilled labor than women were. Ironically, the fact that women were in the labor force only for the wage made them unable to extract a decent wage from their employers, for women, wanting only money, were willing to work for almost any quantity of money offered to them. If they worked as supplementary workers for their families, as daughters or homemakers, they were willing to accept very low, supplementary wages. Employers of working girls claimed that the latter would accept almost any wage, would "generally take what we offer," and, once employed, "don't ask for a raise."[41] If women sought work as heads of households, because they lacked the support of a husband or family, they were desperate for money, and without a reason (such as manly pride) to say no to any wage; furthermore, their demands were undercut by the majority of women workers who sought only low, supplementary wages. Men, on the other hand, were in the labor force to establish themselves as men—as important and valuable individuals, and as husbands who could support their families. A man's whole sense of self, his pride, was at stake in the wage bargain; therefore he demanded, not only money, but a certain amount of money, his "worth." A man would not work, even as an unskilled laborer, for wages below his worth; in particular, as a present or future head of household, a man demanded from his employer a "family wage," a wage sufficient to support his wife and children, as well as himself. The American Federation of Labor member who claimed in 1910, "We believe that the man should be provided with a fair wage in order to keep his female relatives from going to work. The man is the provider and should receive enough for his labor to give his family a respectable living," voiced the shared conception of man's duty under the cult of domesticity.[42] As a result, in unskilled jobs, men received considerably higher wages than women. In 1900, females in all manufacturing jobs, semiskilled and unskilled, earned, on the average, only 76% of the hourly wage of the unskilled males.[43] This percentage would, of course, be even lower if work of equal skill level were compared. Women provided cheap labor and were attractive to cost-cutting employers for this reason. In the survey of reasons for which employers hired women instead of men, the second most popular reason, after "better adapted," was that women were cheaper (see Table 9-5).

The difference in the stances that men and women took with their employers was also expressed in different behavior on the job. A man laborer, once he had agreed to a certain wage, gave to the employer only what he had agreed to give; he saw pressure to do more work as an opportunity to demand a higher wage. He constantly fought the employer on the job, as the employer tried to extract more labor from his labor power. Since there was little opportunity for individual self-advancement in unskilled labor, he united with his fellow (male) workers and fought to establish unions. Within these unions, men workers fought for better job conditions and established seniority systems which allowed them to advance themselves over time.[44] Men's unions also fought to exclude the low-wage competition of women. Women laborers, because they were not as aware of themselves as individuals with interests opposed to those of the employer, were less combative on the job. Many were pliant, even pleasing on the job, responding to demands for more work by their employers without insisting on recognition, through higher wages, of this alteration of the wage contract. For example, women piece workers commonly cleaned up the factory after work without demanding extra pay.[45] An investigator of unskilled women workers in New York City in 1914 claimed, "The girl of this class accepts in a matter-of-fact way conditions of work that impress the outsider as very hard. Sometimes she tells of having cried with weariness when she started. But complaints of the long day, the meager reward, and the monotony are few. She has not thought out the general aspects of the factory."[46] Women were not actively *in* the labor force; working girls' most common subject of conversation was boyfriends, not their job prospects; as a result, they rarely defended themselves as workers.[47] This does not mean that women never fought back: on the contrary, the job experience of women, in particular the extremely inhumane conditions under which they often worked, sometimes incited them to strike. They had difficulty following through in these efforts, however, and their more unionized brothers rarely helped, and often hindered, their efforts.[48] In the 1897 survey, employers praised women workers over men for unskilled factory work as "more reliable, more easily controlled, neater, more rapid, more industrious, more careful, less liable to strike, more temperate, learn more rapidly, don't wish to learn trade, more content and more patient, more skillful, more pleasing, and more polite" (see Table 9-5).

Therefore, firms with unskilled jobs had real reason to seek out female labor for them: women were cheaper, more docile, more pliable—perfect for unskilled jobs. If they were available, the job would by typed as feminine and a low wage rate set. However, it was not always easy for a firm to hire female workers: there were simply not enough of them to fill all unskilled jobs. In 1900, for example, only one-third of factory operatives were women.[49] When asked why they did not employ women for unskilled factory labor, managers commonly answered that it was hard to find women to fill the jobs.[50]

Helen Sumner found in her extensive survey of women in industry of 1910 that variations in the sex-typing of work were often linked to labor supply differences between localities. For example, she discovered that "dippers helpers" in the pottery industry were men in New Jersey and women in Ohio. She attributed the difference to the hegemony of the pottery industry in East Liverpool, Ohio: women in East Liverpool had few other industrial employments open to them, whereas in Trenton a variety of industries competed for their labor.[51]

If it could not procure enough women to totally fill a certain job, a firm had difficulty hiring both men and women for the same job while maintaining lower wages for the women. This was not only because women would protest such blatant inequality of treatment. The real opponents to such inequality were the men. Once men were hired for a job, they correctly saw the employment of women in their jobs at lower wages as a threat to their wages and their jobs, as well as to their masculinity. Men workers worked formally and informally to meet the threat of displacement by women. They attempted to limit the entry of women into men's work by excluding them from the unions. If they were unable to exclude women, men workers demanded that women be paid equally with men and even helped them unionize, thus eliminating both the competition and attractiveness of women's labor. As Helen Sumner described in her *History of Women in Trade Unions* of 1911: "Where women were just beginning to enter the various trades in competition with men, they met the open opposition of the men; but when women were once established as permanent factors in any given trade, the men encouraged them to organize to prevent the lowering of wage standards."[52] The result was often that unskilled work was men's work in organized factories and industries, whereas it was women's work in unorganized shops.[53] This difference between men and women laborers has, through time, resulted in the concentration of men in the more powerful, monopolized firms or industries (such as automotive and steel), leaving women industrial workers in the less concentrated and less profitable industries such as textiles.[54]

While men laborers fought for advancement through unions, women workers were "protected" by special legislation. Women workers were, relative to men, less able to defend themselves against employers. Their superexploitation brought efforts to "protect" them by both social homemakers and male unions. The unions worked to limit women's labor-force participation because her low wage competition was ruining the working man: "She in a measure stands in the way of the male when attempting to raise his prices or equalize his labor; and her efforts to sustain herself and family, are actually the same as tying a stone around the neck of her natural protector, man, and destroying him with the weight she has brought to his assistance."[55] Furthermore, as social homemakers argued, since women could not protect themselves from exploitation by their employers, they worked in inferior laboring conditions, which threatened their homes and their motherly abilities. State laws were passed that protected women workers by a variety of measures: minimum wages (lower than men's going wages), weekly or daily hours limitations, night-work prohibitions, required labor conditions, prohibitions against work in certain jobs, and prohibitions against employment before and after childbirth.[56] In exchange for protective legislation, whereby the state took responsibility for her well-being, the woman worker lost her contractual rights, in particular her ability to offer her labor for many of the more lucrative jobs.[57] The restrictions placed on women's employment by protective legislation worked to reduce the special attractiveness of their labor to employers.

The sex-typing of an originally "neuter" job became an integral part of the job and remained attached to it over time, only to be unseated by major disturbances. Most often the sexual composition of an occupation was altered only with a major technological change that introduced a new set of jobs; extreme changes in labor supply, as caused in wartime, have also resulted in changing the sex-typing of unskilled jobs.[58]

The Sexual Division of Labor in the Office

We have discussed the development of sex-typed professions, the persistence of masculine craft work, and the sex-typing of unskilled jobs. We have yet to analyze white-collar jobs. In early capitalism, the firm was small and simple; the owner, the capitalist, was also the firm's head or manager. He enlisted the aid of blue-collar foremen and of a male clerk or two. The early managers were, then, capitalists, successful petty producers. But as firms grew in size and complexity, management began to separate itself from ownership, and the job of directing the firm became the province of the office employees.

As the office developed in size and complexity, it was transformed from a masculine preserve to a distinctly sex-divided sphere, where men and women parodied in many ways their familial sex roles. The new office employed managerial and technical as well as clerical staff.

THE CREATION OF MASCULINE, SELF-DEVELOPING JOBS

As firms developed, and ownership was separated from control, a new set of workers was employed to personify the firm, to actively pursue its interests. These workers were men. As we have discussed briefly above, men were willing to dedicate their lives to their jobs if such dedication would gain them advancement and power. In blue-collar jobs, where the content of work was determined by the employer, and job advancement limited, men workers fought against their employers to restrict the labor supply and to build the process of advancement into their jobs through seniority systems and apprenticeship programs. But as firms developed, they were also able to offer, to an elite of men, jobs that promised them real power and individual self-expression—managerial and salaried professional jobs.

Corporations harnessed and developed men's desires for self-advancement by creating managerial/professional pyramids. Job ladders were constructed in which lower-level jobs trained for upper-level ones, which were higher paid, higher status, and in control of those below. Unlike in the craft or blue-collar hierarchies, however, all employees did not advance with experience. Only the best employees moved up through the hierarchy; the losers stayed put or were fired. By making advancement an issue of comparative rather than absolute abilities, the managerial job structure caused employees to compete with each other for advancement. Rather than uniting against their employers to bring their collective advancement, employees fought against each other to more perfectly obey the wishes of the firm. Striving to do more than their competitors, they continually intensified their commitment to their jobs. In times of heightened competition, this could mean planning years ahead, undergoing years of education, working long hours, being willing to move geographically to suit the needs of the corporation, even enlisting the energies of one's wife in the service of the corporation. These prerequisites, of course, gave men of privileged family background a better chance to reach the top. The willingness of men to do virtually anything to win in job competition created a set of elite, masculine jobs which, indeed, took everything from these men; jobs which ruled over their lives and those of their families.[59] Table 9-6 lists such masculine jobs, and shows their monopolization by men.

When their competitive desires were thus harnessed by firms through job ladders, men became the perfect embodiments of the firms' struggles for expansion: such men would, as a rule, do anything in exchange for self-advancement, playing the game to win without challenging its ethical content. At the same time, the competition between firms was driven by the competition between these men; in order to provide continual opportunities for advancement in power and position to its managers, a firm had to keep growing. While men vied with each other over such jobs, women were not only unqualified but also uninterested. The demands that such jobs made for educational preparation, for commitment of time, energy, and self, which men embraced as the means to self-advancement, were, to a woman with feminine goals, only burdens that would interfere with her life work of caring for her family. The success, power, recognition, and self which they would give to her were not what she sought—they were masculine by definition. On the other hand, feminine office jobs had developed simultaneously with the development of the managerial/technical staff—clerical jobs.

THE FEMINIZATION OF CLERICAL JOBS

Clerical jobs were developed for women in offices in the late nineteenth century; with the advance of the twentieth century, these jobs not only proliferated but also became more feminized.

The early office, as we have seen, did not employ women. Its clerical workers were clerks, men. Harry Braverman describes early clerical work as a craft:

> Although the tools of the craft consisted only of pen, ink, or other desk appurtenances, and writing paper, envelopes, and ledgers, it represented a total occupation, the object of which was to keep current the records of the financial and operating condition of the enterprise, as well as its relations with the external world. Master craftsmen, such as bookkeepers or chief clerks, maintained control over the process in its totality, and apprentices or journeymen craftsmen—ordinary clerks, copying clerks, office boys—learned their crafts in office apprenticeships, and in the ordinary course of events advanced through the levels by promotion.[60]

Table 9–6: The Sex-typing of Office Work, 1900, 1960

	1900	1960
Masculine Office Jobs	% men employed in occupation	
Farm managers and farm foremen	91.2	97.7
Officials, government	91.2	80.7
Bank and finance officials	98.1	86.7
Other managers, officials, and proprietors	98.5	87.0
% of all employed men[a]	1.01	7.6
Feminine Office Jobs	% women employed in occupation	
Secretaries		97.2
Stenographers	76.2	95.6
Typists	79.8	95.2
Receptionists		97.6
Doctor's and dentist's office attendants		97.4
% of all employed women[a]	3.2	11.8

SOURCES: U.S. Department of Commerce, Bureau of the Census, *Special Reports: Occupations at the Twelfth Census,* Table 1 (for persons 10 years and older); idem, *Census of Population: 1960, Occupational Characteristics,* Table 21 (for persons 14 years and older).

a. % of all employed men (women) is the number of men (women) in the occupation divided by the number of men (women) workers in the civilian labor force.

Since clerks often rose into management positions, owners often filled clerical positions with (male) family members.

As the office developed in complexity and size, clerical work was mechanized. It required special skills, especially the abilities to operate a typewriter and take stenography; these skills differed increasingly from those required of managers. Women were introduced into offices to work with the new office machinery. Firms took advantage of the supply of middle-class, high school or college-educated women who would work for lower wages than men of comparable education.

Women were attracted to such jobs by their wages, which were higher than those offered to women in factory and service work, and by the higher status these white-collar "business" jobs offered.[61]

The introduction of women into the office, however, meant the entry of women into a previously masculine sphere. Clerking had been a man's job, and society was at first hard pressed to believe women fit to do it. In 1900, the *Ladies Home Journal* counseled women to shun employment in the office:

> Although the statement may seem a hard one, and will unquestionably be controverted, it nevertheless is a plain, simple fact that women have shown themselves naturally incompetent to fill a great many of the business positions which they have sought to occupy. . . . The fact is that no one woman in a hundred can stand the physical strain of the keen pace which competition has forced upon every line of business today.[62]

Indeed, women were not qualified for clerical work as it had been constituted; however, as women were drawn into clerical work, the jobs' contents changed. The previously masculine job of clerk, an apprentice who moved up the ladder of management with experience, was transformed into a permanently subordinate, and hence feminine job. For the secretary, job advancement meant simply subordination to a more advanced man. The interaction of the sexes in the office further differentiated the jobs according to sex: the secretary took on the role of wife and mother to her male superior, as well as that of servant of the consumer. Such interaction reaffirmed the femininity of the clerical workers and the masculinity of their bosses. As clerical work acquired these qualities, it increasingly excluded men, who entered the office on an altogether separate track. Even though the mechanization of the office and the redivision of clerical jobs in the twentieth century have reduced such opportunity for personal contact, as well as the kinds of skills demanded, the branding of clerical work as feminine, along with its low wage, have kept men out (see Table 9-6).

The relationship between the personal secretary and her boss is an archetypal example of the reflection of the sexual division in marriage into the labor force. Managers with considerable power and work identity have demanded personal secretaries to serve their particular needs. The manager directly defines the work of his secretary: it can include anything from communicating for him by letters or telephone to other firms, to making him personally comfortable with coffee or an attractive apperance, to buying his wife's birthday present. Although the personal secretary works for the firm, she also works for her boss; she is his aide, his working wife—identified with him, yet in permanent subordination. In 1935, *Fortune* magazine wrote the following of the male employer:

> What he wanted in the office was something as much like the vanished wife of his father's generation as could be arranged—someone to balance his checkbook, buy his railroad tickets, check his baggage, get him seats in the fourth row, take his daughter to the dentist, listen to his side of the story, give him a courageous look when things were the blackest, and generally know all, understand all . . . it is the male employer who is chiefly responsible for the female secretary.[63]

The man at the top had so much of a business identity that he needed a helper, a subordinate—but not a man, who would be competing with him for advancement. He needed someone he could trust to have his best interests at heart, someone who would seek his advancement rather than her own. Who else but a woman, a feminine being, a secretary?

The social differentiation of the sexes was built into the very content of office jobs and, indeed, into the masculine identity of the modern corporation. Managerial positions were intrinsically masculine, developing and giving expression to masculine competition for self-advancement. Clerical positions were permanently subordinated, dead-end positions, which allowed women to keep their femininity but did not give them pay commensurate with their skills.

The Typing of Feminine Jobs According to Marital Status, Race, Ethnicity, and Class

We have focused on the sex-typing of jobs as the reflection of the masculine/feminine difference in the labor force. But women were also differentiated from each other by marital status, race and ethnicity, and class. These differences were also reflected in the occupational distribution.

MARITAL STATUS

Given that a woman's life was governed importantly by her marital status, it is not surprising to find that many feminine jobs were typed by marital status. Jobs incompatible with active homemaking were almost exclusively reserved for single women: in 1900, these included teaching, the professions, clerical work, and domestic service (except for black women). As an extension of homemaking, home work, in particular laundering, putting-out, and taking in boarders, was the province of married or widowed women. And although they were only 17.7% of the female labor force, widows formed the great majority of female farmers, planters, and overseers (73.4% of them)—as in the colonial economy, the best way for a woman to become a farmer was to inherit a farm from her husband.[64]

RACE AND ETHNICITY

We can study the concentration of racial or ethnic groups in particular occupations by comparing their representation with that which would have prevailed with equal representation of groups in occupations. Tables 9-7 and 9-8 show the relative concentrations of women of different ethnic and racial groups in different occupations. A number of 100 suggests that a group's participation in an occupation was the same as its overall participation in the labor force; a relative concentration of 200 means that the group was twice as prevalent in the particular occupation as it was in the overall labor force.

Table 9-7 shows a great deal of occupational concentration of women according to race and general nativity. Black women were twice as likely as expected to be in agriculture or laundering; they were virtually excluded from the mills, from clerical work, and from retail sales. Asian-Americans were concentrated in agriculture, peddling, and in seamstress work. Stenography and typing and teaching were more or less reserved for native whites, excluding black, Asian, and white immigrant women. The latter were overrepresented in mill work, as seamstresses, and as hucksters and peddlers, and were virtually absent from agriculture. As Table 9-8 shows, white immigrant women were further segregated according to ethnicity. Mill work was the province of Italians, English and Welsh, and Irish. Tobacco and cigar factories were monopolized by Bohemians, Russians, and Italians. And the female huckster or peddler was Italian, Russian, Bohemian, or German. These statistics only show that a woman's ethnicity and race were significantly correlated with her occupation; we cannot here examine the particular combination of factors that underlay the particular work experiences of each group. One of the main factors other than the obvious ones of cultural differences and racism, however, was the economic status of their fathers and husbands: those of immigrant and black women tended to be poor and without substantial property or education.

CLASS DIFFERENCES

The sex-typed job structure provided work for women of different classes. Female professionals, three-quarters of whom were teachers, represented the upper- and middle-class employment, the province of social homemakers, or, at least, of educated and independent-minded women. The expanding field of clerical work provided a new work opportunity for the middle-class girl. Factory work was somewhat less respected, while domestic service (other than nursing) was at the bottom of the hierarchy in both wages and status, monopolized by blacks and immigrants.

The structure of men's jobs also differentiated them. Managerial and professional jobs had the highest status, pay, and freedom. Craft workers were the privileged portion of the working class, unionized factory workers its middle. At the bottom of men's job hierarchy was unskilled service work and non-unionized factory work, work in which poor immigrants and blacks were concentrated.

Wives and daughters were constrained to work in jobs suitable to their family background, corresponding roughly to the class of their husband or father. A wife could not be "above" her husband without his ego suffering: this, however, was unlikely given the much lower wages received by women workers at all levels. Neither could a daughter or wife properly work too far below the status of her husband. However, if a privileged homebound wife or daughter lost her husband or father, and his wealth, her former class position was not insured; on her own, she was often reduced to the most menial of work.

Capitalism did not, then, create a homogeneous labor force. It not only sex-typed jobs but also distributed them unequally according to race, ethnicity, and marital status. Racial and ethnic minorities were segregated into low-status and low-wage jobs. Furthermore, because the job structure was pyramidal, it limited the number of workers who could become part of the elite, perpetuating inequality.

Table 9–7: Relative Concentrations[a] of Women in Selected Occupations, by General Nativity and Race, 1900 (age 10 and over)

	% of all employed women in occupation	Native-born white	Foreign-born white	Black	Asian[b]
As % of all women in labor force		58.4	16.5	24.7	.4
Agriculture	18.4	61	26	240	208
Laborers	12.5	38	5	310	165
Farmers, planters, and overseers	5.8	110	69	94	244
Professional	8.1	155	37	15	18
Teachers and professors	6.2	155	32	17	19
Domestic and Personal	39.4	77	135	132	67
Servants and waitresses	24.1	81	157	109	45
Laundresses	6.3	37	78	263	80
Nurses and midwives	2.0	100	149	69	32
Trade and Trans-	9.4	148	75	3	7

Occupation					
Hucksters and peddlers	0.1	31	387	70	145
Stenographers and typists	1.6	159	42	1	2
Saleswomen	2.8	150	73	1	4
Manufacture and Mechanical	24.7	129	130	10	111
Dressmakers	6.5	137	105	15	9
Seamstresses	2.7	126	112	32	90
Tailoresses	1.3	105	232	2	56
Cotton mill operatives	2.3	105	231	1	1
Woolen mill operatives	1.0	116	194	1	0
Tobacco and cigar mill operatives	1.0	108	153	48	2

SOURCE: U.S. Department of Commerce, Bureau of the Census, *Special Reports, Occupations at the Twelfth Census*, (Washington: Government Printing Office, 1904) pp. 10–15.

a. The relative concentration of women workers of a particular race or nativity in a given occupation is obtained by computing the proportion of women of this race or nativity among all women workers in the given occupation, and then stating this proportion as a percentage of the proportion of women of this race or nativity among all employed women. The relative concentration figure of 100 for native-born white women in nursing and midwifery means that native-born white women were found in the same proportion among nurses and midwives as among all employed women, that is, 58.4%. Those numbers over 100 indicate overrepresentation in an occupation and those under 100, underrepresentation.

b. Chinese, Japanese, or Indian.

Table 9–8: Relative Concentrations[a] of White Women in Selected Occupations, by Ethnic Background, 1900 (age 10 and over)

	Native white of native parentage[b]	Foreign born						% of all employed white women in occptn.
		Irish	Italian	German	Bohemian	Russian	English and Welsh	
As % of all white women in labor force	48.0	6.2	0.5	4.1	0.3	0.9	1.6	
Agriculture								
Laborers	187	2	86	23	86	22	6	3.9
Farmers, planters, overseers	160	46	10	135	115	15	81	5.9
Professional								
Teachers and professors	138	19	5	26	9	5	39	7.9
Domestic and Personal								
Servants and waitresses	78	230	39	155	170	59	93	23.5
Laundresses	77	222	85	216	103	36	107	2.9
Nurses and midwives	101	113	38	144	58	43	247	2.3

Trade and Transport

Hucksters and peddlers	30	69	1434	231	252	1480	51	0.1
Stenographers and typists	111	16	5	20	11	38	77	2.2
Saleswomen	87	33	43	62	47	155	70	3.7
Manufacture								
Dressmakers	96	57	106	78	63	95	101	8.3
Seamstresses	70	48	186	92	117	420	65	3.4
Tailoresses	46	36	1289	159	702	977	50	1.7
Cotton mill operatives	87	112	327	22	7	20	236	3.0
Woolen mill operatives	54	130	336	70	84	37	281	1.0
Tobacco and cigar factory operatives	82	18	476	103	2058	535	44	1.0

SOURCE: E. P. Hutchinson, *Immigrants and Their Children: 1850–1950* (New York: John Wiley and Sons, Inc. 1956), pp. 182–85.

a. The relative concentration of white women workers of a particular ethnic background or nativity in a given occupation is obtained by computing the proportion of women of this background among all white women workers in the given occupation, and then stating this proportion as a percentage of the proportion of women of that background among all employed white women. As in Table 9–7, those numbers over 100 indicate overrepresentation in an occupation and those under 100, underrepresentation.

b. Calculated from U.S. Department of Commerce, Bureau of the Census, *Special Reports, Occupations at the Twelfth Census*, pp. 10–15.

Women's Labor-force Participation and the Sexual Separation of Spheres

The creation of sex-typed jobs not only reflected but also reinforced the sexual separation of spheres. It became an integral part of the social differentiation of the sexes, contributing to the prevailing conceptions of man and woman, masculine and feminine. The existence of sex-typed jobs appeared as just another manifestation of the natural differences between men and women. The concentration of women in the inferior jobs, and in jobs resembling homemaking, seemed proof of the male's natural superiority in the economic sphere of self-seeking and of the female sex's natural predisposition for homemaking. The fact that the wages a woman could earn were usually inadequate to support an adult female, much less an entire family, "proved" her innate dependence on "her natural protector," man. Inferior working conditions, low wages and monotonous work discouraged working girls from considering continued employment and encouraged them to find husbands/providers. In her 1909 study *Women and the Trades*, Elizabeth Beardsley Butler noted how feminine jobs both reflected and reinforced woman's vocation of homemaking:

> Cause and effect in their case work in a circle. Expectation of marriage, as a customary means of support, stunts professional ambition among women. This lack of ambition can have no other effect than to limit efficiency, and restricts them to subsidiary, uninteresting, and monotonous occupations. The very character of their work in turn lessens their interest in it. Without interest, they least of all feel themselves integral parts of the industry and in consequence assume no responsibility, affect no loyalty. They do not care to learn; opportunity to learn is not given them; both are causes and both are effects. Women see only a fight for place, and a very uncertain advantage if they gain it; wages are low, again both cause and effect of their dependence on others for their support. They shift around on lower levels of industry from packing room to metal work, from metal work to laundry work; a very few, through unwonted good fortune, unwonted determination, break through the circle and rise.[65]

While the existence of sex-typed jobs reinforced the sexual division of labor in many ways, the participation of women in the labor force nevertheless represented a departure from the "separation of sexual spheres" put forward by the cult of domesticity. The participation of women in the labor force represented a movement away from home-bound homemaking and toward the sphere of men. The virtual absence of married women from the labor force prevented this contradiction from undermining the sexual division of labor. But women's labor-force participation did subtly change their status and set the stage for the radical changes of the twentieth century.

First, women's labor-force participation helped gain property rights for married women. In the family economy, a woman's public existence had been entirely submerged into that of her husband; as we have seen, early factories sometimes used the family wage system, employing an entire family through a contract with its "head," the man. Well into the nineteenth century husbands had the right to take the wages of their legal wife, even if the two were not living together; while a woman was employed as an individual, she was still "working" for her husband or father. Harriet Robinson, in *Loom and Spindle*, an account of her experience as a worker in the early Lowell mills, wrote:

> The laws relating to women were such, that a husband could claim his wife wherever he found her. . . . I have seen more than one poor woman skulk behind her loom or her frame when visitors were approaching the end of the aisle where she worked. Some of these were known under assumed names, to prevent their husbands from trusteeing their wages. It was a very common thing for a male person of a certain kind to do this, thus depriving his wife of *all* her wages, perhaps, month after month.[66]

However, such laws were out of rhythm with the nature of the wage contract. As a contract between a firm or capitalist and a worker, the wage bargain required no approval or notification of family members. Furthermore, the physical separation of the home and workplace made it difficult for husbands to enforce their right over their wives' wages. As the century advanced, and women's participation in the labor force as individuals became common, women's right to own property, whether or not she was married, became established.

The entrance into wage contracts also spurred women into organized economic and political activity. A small number of women workers were active in union organizing—some of the earliest militant unionists were women textile workers. Women workers, organized into associations or unions, sometimes developed women's rights platforms and fought against the cult-of-domesticity doctrine of separate spheres by demanding equal participation of woman in economic and political life. One example of this was an 1836 workers' "turnout" (an unorganized work walkout) in the early mills; the female operatives paraded around the town of Lowell and one of them, standing in the public square, gaven an ardent speech for women's rights.[67] The act itself was a stand for women's rights: according to the report, this was the first time a woman had given a public speech in Lowell!! Another example is this statement by the Female Labor Reform Association, an organization of women textile workers, which challenged the separation of spheres in 1846:

> We feel that if there is a place in the wide universe where true liberty and freedom should be enjoyed—where the press should be untrammeled—and where woman should take her proper place and standing in society, as a rational intelligent being—a fit *companion* and *friend* of man, not a *slave*—it is in the United States of America! . . . Too long has she been considered an inferior being; merely capacitated to bask in the sunshine of fashion and prosperity contributing to the happiness of those around her, by offices of kindness and labors of love. Her mind and intellect suffered to dwindle, through lack of cultivation and improvement—her sphere of action, being exclusively domestic, she rarely presumed to think or act independently or clearly on any subject. Those days thank heaven have passed and a new era in the life of women has dawned upon her hitherto prescribed and limited sphere of action.[68]

The political claims of these working women flew in the face of the prevailing conception of womanhood, and as such did not draw a vast following. We have already seen, however, how the cult of domesticity's insistence on the social import of homemaking led social homemakers to seek to transform the public sphere. This movement brought two important departures from the doctrine of separate spheres. First, it inspired women to organize themselves politically to achieve their social homemaking goals, including the mounting of a successful fight for suffrage; women became recognized outside of the domestic sphere, as citizens in their own right. Second, it led some women to reject the homemaking career for careers in the labor force—social homemaking. Although she acted in a wholly feminine manner, the professional social homemaker broke the automatic equation between mothering and successful womanhood and hence began to undermine the sexual division of labor.

So while the participation of women in the labor force in the nineteenth century did not challenge the sexual division of labor, it began to extend womanhood in a way that would become increasingly contradictory in the twentieth century. We will examine the gradual breakdown of the sexual division of labor which resulted in Part III.

Part III

THE BREAKDOWN OF THE
SEXUAL DIVISION OF LABOR

10

The Entrance of Homemakers into the Labor Force as Homemakers

The Development of a System of Commodity Needs

In the first half of the twentieth century, capitalist production began to bear fruit, creating in America a wealthy society. Wealthy society meant a dynamic, consumption-oriented society—a society in which new needs were always being created and families continually strove for increased consumption.

Through the end of the nineteenth century, capitalist productive efforts had centered on the development of basic infrastructure and heavy industry; commodity production had barely commenced to focus itself on consumer needs, other than the essentials of food, fuel, and fabric for clothing. Capitalist production of consumer goods remained at an undeveloped stage: this was expressed by the fact that wealthy families spent their income on hiring others as domestic servants rather than on commodities. Poor families did not need a complicated set of commodities, for such commodities had not been developed. Homemaking, the filling of the needs of the family, still had a self-sufficient character; it involved much drudgery work.

By the onset of the twentieth century, American capitalism had matured. In their competition for growth and profits, entrepreneurs had initiated cost-cutting technological change, increasing labor's productivity in agriculture and heavy industry, freeing up labor for the production of consumer goods and services, and increasing the general standard of living. At the same time, industries were becoming increasingly concentrated, that is, occupied by fewer and fewer firms. This concentration reduced price competition between firms, securing their profit margins, and setting a new limit to their growth, the growth of the market. Firms began to work to expand their markets both by universalizing the needs for their products, and by creating new products to fill new needs. At the same time, rising real wages were allowing consumers to purchase these new commodities, completing the process of wealth-creation. This dynamic expansion of needs and of wealth, and its effects on homemaking and homemakers, are the subject of this chapter.

In their search for new salable products, firms were aided by the scientific homemaking movement. Wealthy homemakers actively sought out superior methods of homemaking, methods that would purge the home of drudgery work, free it from the need for domestic servants, and improve the quality of home life. Firms, sensing this generalized need, gave it form by developing a set of commodities suitable for the family. Hence, specific needs for these commodity products did not preexist in the minds of homemakers, but rather were articulated by firms to fill the homemakers' more general need to care for their families. We studied this process in detail in Chapter 8, noting its initiation by privileged homemakers.

Between 1880 and 1930, the following new commodities appeared on the market in most towns and were introduced into American life: electricity, furnaces, running water, running hot water, plumbing, electric appliances (toasters, irons, vacuum cleaners, washing machines), telephones, refrigerators, movies, automobiles, phonographs, radios, and more. Before 1880, these commodities had not been available, even for the rich; they could not even be imagined, much less needed. When companies created new commodities they had to advertise about them—to inform consumers about what the commodity could be used for, thus cultivating in consumers the need for the new commodity. Since companies invented products by anticipating potential needs of consumers, most new products produced "love at first sight"; it was simply necessary to let consumers know what a product was and did. Advertising expenditures, in newspapers and periodicals alone, expanded by a factor of 10 between 1867 and 1900, and again between 1900 and 1925, from $9.6 million to $95.8 million to $923 million![1]

To launch a new product successfully, a firm had to convince homemakers that it was essential to acceptable family or home life. As the Lynds described in *Middletown,* "Advertising is concentrating increasingly upon a type of copy aiming to make the reader emotionally uneasy, to bludgeon him [her?] with the fact that decent people don't live the way *he* does; *decent* people ride on balloon tires, have a second bathroom, and so on." For example, the electrical industry instituted a nationwide essay contest among school children on home lighting. "In this campaign 1,500 Middletown children submitted essays on how the lighting of their homes could be improved, and upwards of 1,500 families were made immediately aware of the inadequacies of their homes as regards library table lamps, porch lights, piano lamps, and convenient floor sockets. As one of the winning local essays said: 'I and all my family have learned a great deal that we did not know before, and we intend improving the lighting in our own home.' "[2]

When new commodities were introduced, homemakers whose families were at the top of the income pyramid were the first to buy them; poorer homemakers simply could not afford them. As one of the wealthy scientific homemakers, Christine Frederick, wrote;

> Another reason why the tool is not so important as more efficient working methods is that while some women can afford a vacuum cleaner or an electric motor, or other excellent tools, thousands of women cannot afford these devices, even though they wish to use them. But any one of these women can reduce the drudgery of her work by better planning and more intelligent systematization and by observation and experiment with her work. . . . Some will say it is useless to reduce dishwashing to a science, because there are mechanical dish-washers which will eventually replace all hand washing. But how many families can afford such a device?[3]

When Frederick wrote, she was keenly aware of the wealthy homemakers' monopoly on such goods. But firms soon found that the secret to their expansion was not simply the creation of new commodities for the rich, but the diffusion of these commodities across income groups. This process was surprisingly simple. The mass production of a consumer good decreased the unit costs for firms; this allowed firms to lower their prices, making mass marketing feasible. While for most firms, this process was not consciously planned out, Henry Ford actively sought wealth and expansion of automobile production by just this strategy: he cut the price of his cars, from $950 in 1909–10 to $290 in 1924, transforming his product from an extravagant luxury for the rich to an increasingly affordable necessity for the middle class. Meanwhile, the resulting jump in sales allowed him to introduce more and more efficient production techniques, drastically reducing unit costs and bringing hefty profits.[4]

So although the new commodities developed by firms were, when first introduced, luxuries affordable only to the wealthy, as time passed, they became necessities for all classes. Firms were able to rationalize the production of these consumer goods, cheapen them, and bring them within reach of lower-income families. With time, more and more commodities were introduced into the household and diffused gradually from the upper class to poor families, transforming homemaking in this process. A study of homemaking from 1900 to 1930, describes the introduction of commodities into the household as follows:

> First utilities and services—gas, electricity, water and sewage, garbage removal, and central heating; second, consumer durables—irons, vacuum cleaners, washing machines, refrigerators, and stoves; third, the semi- or non-durables—canned and packaged food and ready-made clothing. . . . By 1930 most of the new products for the home were in widespread use in all classes.[5]

The commodities listed have now become such an integral and seemingly necessary part of American life that it is hard to believe that they were once considered to be luxuries. Tables 10–1, 10–2, and 10–3 show the diffusion of the consumption of these new commodities across families, their rapid transmutation from luxuries to necessities.

An integral part of the development of the consumer goods industry was, of course, the rise in the average "real wage" available to the worker. Increases in money wages and decreases in commodity prices brought a rising real wage, which allowed families to purchase these new consumer goods. Average real earnings of non-farm employees grew at an accelerating rate in the late nineteenth and early twentieth centuries: they increased by one-fourth from 1869 to 1900, almost doubled between 1900 and 1940, and almost doubled again in the next twenty years, from 1940 to 1960.[6] Rising money incomes, as well as falling commodity prices, allowed families to purchase more commodities, to fill more of their needs, and to fill newly developed needs through the marketplace rather than through home production. Siegfried Giedion called this process the mechanization of the household and described it in detail in his book, *Mechanization Takes Command*.[7]

This combined process of the articulation of the new commodities and new needs and the universalization of the consumption of these commodities across classes created a powerful dynamic. An industry

Table 10–1: Percentage of Households with Selected Household Appliances, 1908–1979

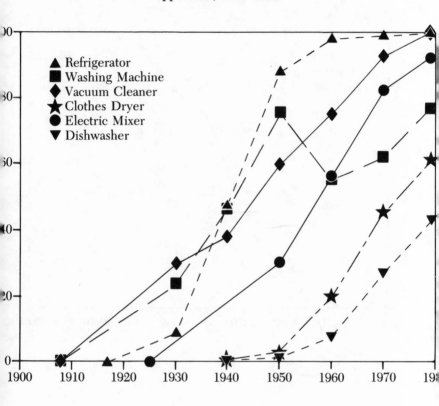

▲ Refrigerator
■ Washing Machine
◆ Vacuum Cleaner
★ Clothes Dryer
● Electric Mixer
▼ Dishwasher

SOURCES: James F. Dewhurst, *America's Needs and Resources: A New Survey* (New York: Twentieth Century Fund, 1955), pp. 200, 240–42, 1041; *Information Please Almanac: 1980* (New York: Simon & Schuster, 1979), p. 63; U.S. Department of Commerce, Bureau of the Census, *Historical Statistics of the United States, Colonial Times to 1970*, Part 2, p. 646; idem, *Statistical Abstract of the United States: 1980*, p. 796.

Table 10–2: Percentage of Households with Electricity and Telephones, 1880–1977

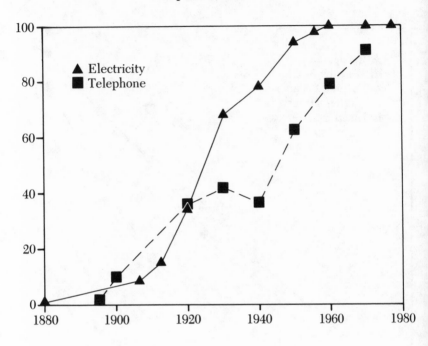

SOURCES: U.S. Department of Commerce, Bureau of the Census, *Historical Statistics of the United States, Colonial Times to 1970* (1975), Part 2, pp. 783, 827; idem, *Statistical Abstract of the United States: 1979*, p. 583.

Table 10–3: Percentage of Households with Automobiles, Radios, and Televisions, 1900–1979[a]

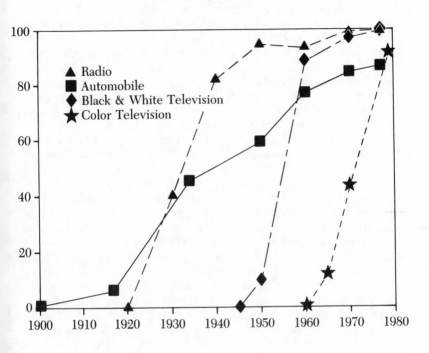

SOURCES: U.S. Department of Commerce, Bureau of the Census, *Historical Statistics of the United States, Colonial Times to 1970* (1975), Part 2, pp. 646, 716–17, 796; idem, *Statistical Abstract of the United States: 1980*, pp. 653, 796; U.S. Department of Labor, *How American Buying Habits Change* (1959), pp. 64, 185.
a. For 1917–1934, number of registered automobiles divided by number of households.

created a new commodity and advertised about it to all consumers through the mass media. The result was, at first, the consumption of the commodity by wealthy homemakers, and the cultivation of a need for it in poorer homemakers which could not be filled. However, mass production and marketing eventually brought the commodity within the reach of the working-class family. At the same time, new commodities were being introduced and purchased by the wealthy, recreating neediness in the poor. Universalization of needs and differentiation in family purchasing power were enmeshed in a competitive hierarchy of consumption and situated within a dynamic process of economic growth and a rising overall standard of living.

This was a process peculiar to capitalism. In previous societies, differences in consumption between families had expressed fixed differences in status. For example, under slavery, masters and slaves had lived at two very different levels; their different levels and kinds of consumption represented and reproduced a given difference in social position between the master as property owner and the slave as property. In feudalism, peasants and lords had lived standards of living so different and fixed that peasants did not even aspire, except in fancy, to the life styles of the lords. In capitalism, however, all men began as property owners and competed on the basis of this right for advancement in the labor-force hierarchy. The development of the sphere of consumption built on and reinforced this competition.

In the first instance, the development of a world of commodities to fill needs allowed for the expression of personality, both the personality of a family, and that of each individual within it. The family, in particular the homemaker, chose from among the world of commodities those which complemented and developed the particular personalities of the family members. The family's particular consumption pattern allowed it to distinguish itself from other families, to individuate itself and its members.[8] But this freedom of choice of commodities did not simply bring the horizontal differentiation of families, for it was set within a hierarchy of consumption. It was this hierarchy that made the family's striving to fill its needs an inherently endless search, and that made needs infinitely expandable.[9]

As the process of the creation of new commodities and the extension of their consumption across classes became generalized, consumption expenditures began to symbolize a family's relative wealthiness. Advertising informed all consumers of the existence of the new commodity, producing a universalized need for it. Differences in commodity ownership between families represented not only differences in tastes but also differences in families abilities to fill a common set of social needs. Consumption levels soon became a sign of the family's relative wealthiness; those with the most and newest commodities were shown to be the wealthiest. As wealth was largely earned through the competitive struggle of husband/providers in the labor force, consumption became a symbol for the success of a man and his family. Consumer wealth represented success in the labor force, and the striving for advancement was at the same time the striving after a higher relative standard of living. The Lynds' famous study of Middletown, done in 1929, noted this universalization of needs in the following manner:

> In 1890 Middletown appears to have lived on a series of plateaus as regards standard of living; old citizens say there was more contentment with relative arrival; it was a common thing to hear a remark that so and so "is pretty good for people of our circumstances." Today the edges of the plateaus have been shaved off, and everyone lives on a slope from any point of which desirable things belonging to people all the way to the top are in view.[10]

Once a hierarchy of consumption was established and gained this meaning, a particular family's sense of wealthiness or neediness was determined by its position within the system of families as a whole, relative to that system as a whole. Wealth was no longer an absolute phenomenon, a particular standard of living; wealth became having the most commodities, having commodities that others did not own. Poverty was no longer an absolute phenomenon either; it meant having less than the majority of Americans, rather than the absence of some fixed set of necessities.

The elite of super-wealthy families did not feel needy. The high incomes of these families came from their ownership of wealth, money which acted as capital and brought in income. The ownership of capital, of income-producing wealth, is very concentrated in the United States: in 1962, for example, the top 1% of families owned over half of America's capital.[11] These families are not preoccupied with finding income to fill their needs. Their energies have had to be devoted, indeed, to finding unique and special ways to fill needs, ways which would set them apart, which would express not just their wealth, but their superior command of wealth. At the turn of the century, Thorstein Veblen wrote insightfully about their "problem" in

The Theory of the Leisure Class. One way to signal one's wealthiness was conspicuous waste, finding objects of consumption whose very ownership signified a superfluity of money. Thus the leisure class shuns machine-produced goods which "fall short under the test of honorific waste. Hand labour is a more wasteful method of production; hence the goods turned out by this method are more serviceable for the purpose of pecuniary reputability."[12] The wealthy also expressed their income superiority by purchasing commodities which were inherently limited in quantity, which could not be reproduced, such as artwork and antique furniture. The need that such products filled was the need to express being the wealthiest. Homemakers in this group have continued to employ retinues of servants to look after their many residences. Much of their attention has been spent on making themselves and their houses into unique objects. The taking over of social homemaking by the government in the twentieth century has cut many of them off from their more socially constructive charity work.

While wealthy families have competed in consumption within each other to show who is the wealthiest (a competition that is different from the labor-force competition, for it is financed by inherited wealth), families who have not been at the top of the income hierarchy have been kept in a continual state of neediness. "Consumption is a constant struggle between what people want and what they have, between standards of living and levels of living."[13] Unless a family had a virtually unlimited income from capital ownership, they were bound to have unfilled needs, if only for more of a certain commodity, or for a better quality commodity. As soon as one need was satisfied, another less pressing one was there to fill its place. By the time a family had achieved a particular standard of living, that standard had been upped to include new commodities.

The relativity of neediness has insured its continual perpetuation. In capitalist society, poverty can never be eradicated by the expansion of wealth, for neediness is the product of the inequality of income, not its absolute level. While the laborer's family in the 1920s was better provided for than the wealthiest families of earlier centuries, it felt needy and deprived next to its wealthier neighbors.[14] So, as Carolyn Shaw Bell noted in her study of consumer choice, "The luxuries of one generation become the necessities of the next."[15] By integrating consumption into the struggle for competitive self-advancement, capitalism has simultaneously produced both wealth and scarcity.[16] Growth is able to sustain itself because as competing firms increase labor productivity and per capita wealth, consumer needs can be continually expanded, providing a market for the increased product and stimulating workers to continue to work hard in spite of increasing real wages.[17]

A family's consumption goals, both specific and general, related to their place in the hierarchy of consumption and wealth. Among the non-wealthy, needy families, the poorest strove to establish that they were "average," that they had the average standard of living; those in the middle class strove to establish themselves as above average. The goals of a family were also affected by its occupational grouping. For example, craft workers earned about as much as clerks and salesmen, but the former were more satisfied with their incomes than the latter. This is because craft workers saw themselves at the top of their blue-collar hierarchy, whereas clerks and salesman saw themselves as the bottom of their white-collar hierarchy.[18] The particular needs felt by a family also differed according to ethnic background, geographical location, and the occupation of the husband/provider. For example, in families of equal income, professionals focused their consumption on education, while craft workers purchased boats and color television sets. Homemakers in the working class valued appliances and home furnishings, whereas those in the middle class cared more about the external appearance and beauty of their homes.[19] Some "loser" families planned their upward mobility through their children, and invested in their education, while others, expecting their children to repeat their life patterns, concentrated on present consumption as a sign of wealth and freedom. This is not the place to investigate all of the differences in needs between families, but to note the involvement of all families in a process of identifying themselves within a complex hierarchy of consumption. Now we must move on to consider the effects of the development of consumption on the homemaker, the professional consumer.

Homemakers Enter the Labor Force

The development of an expanding system of commodity needs and the creation of constant neediness had a powerful effect on homemakers. Not only was the homemaker transformed from a home producer to a consumer of commodities, she was the family member most caught up in the process of competitive consumption, for it was her job to see that the family's needs were filled.

The development of capitalism linked the homemaker into the market in a new and powerful manner. The sexual division of labor that emerged in the nineteenth century had been centered in the separation of sexual spheres; it had been man's duty to compete for wealth in the economy, and woman's duty to fill family needs through work in the domestic sphere and through the consumption of commodities. Since the cornerstone of nineteenth-century womanhood was the domestic presence of the homemaker, the latter had essentially accepted her husband's income as the family's income, supplementing it, in cases of extreme neediness, with the earnings of her children, or with home work for income. The homemaker had defined her family's commodity needs according to her husband's income. As a result, homemakers had provided their families with a range of living standards, and their children with a variety of upbringings. The development of capitalism gradually changed this. Rising living standards, compulsory elementary and then high school education, and child labor laws allowed (and forced) poorer families to live out the cult of domesticity conception of childhood as a distinct and protected life stage. Furthermore, as consumer goods proliferated and standards of living were raised, homemakers and their families began to look to the market to fill their needs and to develop needs which far outstripped family resources. For in addition to filling the family's commodity needs, the system of commodity production was continually generating new ones. The more a household became tied into the consumption of commodities, the more its needs were expanded, and the more it became addicted to the consumption of more and newer commodities. Homemakers in all but the wealthiest families experienced their families' ties to commodity consumption as permanent, unrelenting neediness.

Given the accepted sexual division of labor, in particular the domestic ideal of womanhood, the "correct" behavior of the homemaker in this situation was to accept her husband's means and tailor her family's consumption accordingly. Her ingenuity would be applied to saving pennies or finding sales or purchasing the most durable products. As time passed, her family could add to its stock of consumer durables—first a house, then maybe a car, then the appliances. Studies of homemakers indeed showed such behavior, and the resulting differentiation of standards of living among families, according to their husbands' occupations and incomes. Yet in spite of the protection of a peer group of equally deprived homemakers and their families, families continued to experience their relative deprivation, and homemakers continued to feel conflicts with their lot, to feel that their incomes prevented them from adequately providing for their families' needs. As consumers, they were duty-bound to keep informed as to the world of commodities, yet this world taught them that they and their families were needy of more commodities.

The kind of family neediness experienced by homemakers differed between classes. Those families on the bottom of the income distribution felt particularly deprived for not providing their families with the "average" living standard. As Rainwater, Coleman, and Handel described in their 1959 study *Workingman's Wife:*

> It is not that they believe they are particularly disadvantaged compared to their neighbors and other average people; rather it is that they feel their incomes just are not large enough to cover the things they think they should buy, are entitled to have. They tend to think of themselves as people for whom ends meet, but not as comfortably as they should, and sometimes the ends are made to meet by a sacrifice in the mid-section.
>
> Thus the working class women have a strong psychic sense of money deprivation in spite of their relatively good incomes. In comments about their economic position, we find a persistent theme of not having enough to go around, yet we know that they have close to average incomes for their community and that they amass a respectable quantity of goods.[20]

This study compared the working-class homemaker's struggle with money with that of the middle-class woman, who also felt needy, but in a different way:

> Working class women, like most American women, are somewhat discontented with their financial status. However, they express more "absolute" discontent than do middle class women, whose discontent is more nearly "relative." The former do not admit that their dissatisfaction is rooted in human nature as do the latter; they do not blame their dissatisfaction on any human weakness to "want more no matter how much you already have." Working class housewives genuinely feel that their incomes are inadequate for participation in many of the normal activities of American life, like being in afternoon clubs, taking "nice" vacations every year, going "out on the town" in the evening now and then, or stocking their homes as well as they would like.[21]

Homemakers in lower-income families did not, then, simply adjust their needs to their husbands' incomes; most felt needy and dissatisfied with the standards of living they could afford. Even homemakers in "middle-class" families sensed pressing needs they were unable to fill. Once homemakers acknowledged the existence of family commodity needs that their husbands' incomes could not fill, they experienced a need for extra income. The family need that cried out most to be filled was the need for income, to fill those unfilled commodity needs.

Faced with this family need for income, some homemakers interpreted the dictates of vocational homemaking in a new and heretical manner. Rather than adjusting their families' needs to their husbands' incomes, or patiently waiting for their families' incomes to increase; these homemakers judged their husbands' incomes to be inadequate to their families' commodity needs and entered the labor force to remedy the situation. Such a homemaker gave priority to her own conception of the family's needs, rather than simply adjusting family needs to that which her husband's income could purchase. This was a perfectly logical extension of homemaking. Such women were simply living out their vocation of finding out what the family needed and then filling those needs.[22] The fact that many of these women had worked in the labor force before marriage facilitated this extension of homemaking into wage-earning: many homemakers were returning to the labor force, rather than entering it for the first time.

While working in the labor force was consistent with woman's vocation of filling family needs, the extension of homemaking to include labor-force participation was not without contradictions. First, while filling needs for commodities, it neglected the apparent need of children for a homebound mother. Further, the homemaker's labor-force participation was a direct threat to the masculinity of her husband, signaling, as it did, his inability to provide adequately. His work, as a man, was to provide income for his family; hers, to fill the needs of the family with the aid of this income. To assert his masculinity, a husband had to claim that his income was adequate to fill family needs. As Mirra Komarovsky wrote in her classic study, *Blue Collar Marriage*, "there are only one or two husbands who had urged their wives to work, for the men take too great a pride in their role of provider to demand such assistance."[23] As a homemaker told Lillian Rubin in an interview:

My husband says I don't have to work, but if I don't, we'll never get anywhere. I guess it's a matter of pride with him. It makes him feel bad, like he's not supporting us good enough. I understand how he feels, but I also know that, no matter what he says, if I stop working, when the taxes on the house have to be paid, there wouldn't be any money if we didn't have my salary.[24]

Or in the words of an interviewed man, "I feel the man could do the work, and he should bring home the money. And when he's over working, he should sit down and rest for the rest of the day."[25] Husbands resisted their wives' employment to protect their husband/provider roles, an essential part of manhood. A man's defensiveness was, of course, all the more pronounced if he was indeed a relative failure in the labor force, for in this case, his provider status was the only sign of his adequacy as a man.

The attachment of the man to his husband/provider role, and his resultant opposition to his wife's employment, was also expressed when he was unemployed. A study of unemployed men during the 1930s found them (1) emotionally devastated over the loss of their provider role and (2) adamantly opposed to the employment of their wives. "I would rather starve than let my wife work," and, "I would rather turn on the gas and put an end to the whole family than let my wife support me."[26] These cases show how much a man's masculinity was bound up with his ability to provide for the family. So although unemployment of the husband made the family especially needy of income, it did not always lead to the employment of the homemaker.

Disagreements over the homemaker's planned employment often centered in arguments over what the family really needed. She claims that pressing family needs cannot be met with his income. He disagrees; they have enough, and besides, what about his needs, and those of the children, for her presence at home? He has tradition on his side. She has her special vocational knowledge on her side; she, after all, is the homemaker, the professional consumer. As a twenty-six-year-old garage mechanic told Komarovsky:

I just as soon get along with what we have, but she wants a new living room. She isn't the kind who wants to keep up with the Joneses, she gets disgusted with the women who have to have anything they see in a friend's house. But she thinks we need a new living room. She is talking about taking a job before Christmas in the department store. She wants to make a bigger splash around Christmas time, but I am going to talk her out of it.[27]

Often the labor-force participation of the homemaker started with the national emergency of war. Both World War I and World War II "drafted" married women into the labor force to support the war effort; it was typically feminine to enter the labor force to help one's family as well as one's country. After having had this working experience, some women stayed. As one Middletown homemaker told the Lynds:

> I began to work during the war [World War I] when every one else did; we had to meet payments on our house and everything else was getting so high. The mister objected at first, but now he don't mind. I'd rather keep on working so my boys can play football and basketball and have spending money their father can't give them. We've built our own home, a nice brown and white bungalow, by a building and loan like every one else does. . . . No, I don't lose out with neighbors because I work; some of them have jobs and those who don't, envy us who do. . . . We have an electric washing machine, electric iron, and vacuum sweeper. . . . We own a $1200 Studebaker with a nice California top, semi-enclosed. Last summer we all spent our vacation going back to Pennsylvania—taking in Niagara Falls on the way. The two boys want to go to college, and I want them to. I graduated from high school myself, but I feel if I can't give my boys a little more all my work will have been useless.[28]

This enterprising woman expresses her upwardly mobile notions of her family's needs, particularly those of her children. War alone was not a reason for the wife's continued employment after the war. However, in the case where the homemaker had been feeling the pressure of unfilled family needs, but was unable to break out of her traditional domestic existence, the experience of working during the war, including the family's experience with a higher income, could facilitate her continuation in the labor force in peace time.

The Lynds' study of homemakers with children (and husbands) who had worked for income during the five years previous to their 1929 study found that twenty-four cited their husband's unemployment as the major reason, six cited money needed for their children's education, five mentioned debt, and four said they "always needed money." The Lynds noted a clear increase in the tendency for married women to work: "56% of the 124 working class wives interviewed had not worked for money during the five years 1920–24, while 75% of 102 of their mothers on whom data was secured had not worked for money during their entire married lives. These figures undoubtedly dwarf the extent of the shift, as the interviews took place in most cases during the day and therefore included few women continuously employed away from home at the time."[29]

The entrance of homemakers into the labor force to provide their families with needed commodities has been a gradually snow-balling phenomenon, its strength and continuity somewhat masked by the pull of the two wars and the push of the depression. World War I drew many homemakers into the labor force; the booming economy of the twenties absorbed many of them who wanted to stay. The depression of the thirties meant high unemployment, and public opinion adamantly opposed the employment of married women claiming it would "take jobs away from men who needed to support their families;" nevertheless; it brought an overall increase in the proportion of the homemakers in the labor force.[30] The participation of the United States in World War II brought the economy out of the depression and called married women to enter into the labor force, again for their countries. Postwar growth, particularly in the service sector, provided them with continued employment opportunities. But behind these cycles, the labor-force participation rate of working-class married women has risen steadily over the twentieth century (see Table 10-4). Although husbands' real incomes have risen sharply during most of this period, homemakers have cited economic necessity as the reason for their new entrance into the labor force. They are being pulled by their homemaking vocation, by their mandate to fill the family's expanding needs; they have been drawn into the economic competition, on the side of consumption. And as more homemakers enter into the labor force, moving their families up in the income hierarchy, they raise average consumption standards, putting pressure on their fellow homemakers who stayed at home.[31]

We have discussed the fact that such labor-force participation was already the experience of a significant percentage of black homemakers in 1900, one of the effects of the blacks' slave past combined with enduring racism. The impact of the development of consumption on black homemakers was not, then, as dramatic as it was on their homebound white counterparts. However, black families were not unaffected by the development of consumer needs, and black homemakers have been drawn into the labor force in the twentieth century

Table 10–4: Labor-force Participation Rates of Married Women, Husband Present, by Husband's Income Position, 1940, 1960, 1977[a]

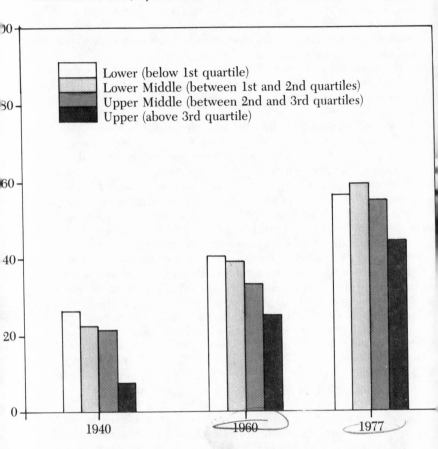

Lower (below 1st quartile)
Lower Middle (between 1st and 2nd quartiles)
Upper Middle (between 2nd and 3rd quartiles)
Upper (above 3rd quartile)

SOURCES: 1940: U.S. Department of Labor, Women's Bureau, *Handbook of Facts on Women Workers*, Bulletin 225, (1948), p. 11 (for married women whose husbands had no other means of support in cities of 1,000,000 or more); 1960, 1977: U.S. Department of Labor, Bureau of Labor Statistics, *Monthly Labor Review*, 102, (June 1979), Table 2, p. 41.
a. For 1940, estimate is not by quartile, but by averaging the labor-force participation rates of eight income groups.

along with whites. The labor-force participation rate of non-white women with husbands present has risen continually—from 27.3% in 1940, to 31.8% in 1950, to 40.5% in 1960, to 50% in 1970—and has consistently remained higher than that of whites.[32]

The entrance of homemakers into the labor force to fill family needs has also accelerated because the more it has happened, the more acceptable it has become. When the first white homemakers began to enter the labor force to "make ends meet," husbands and society argued that the labor force was no place for a white married woman or that children would suffer irreparable damage if their mothers worked in the labor force. These arguments have been heard (and are still being heard) since women first began to thus interpret their vocation. On the other hand, as more and more homemakers have entered the labor force, without any noticeable deterioration of their children, the wage-earning of the homemaker has become increasingly acceptable, even expected. The old demand that married women must be in the home has been altered to "married women must be home when the children are small," and recently even this has been weakening.[33]

While it may seem at first glance that this entrance of homemakers into the labor force, as homemakers, is simply the substitution of the wife's supplementary labor for the children's, or of the wife's efforts in the labor force for home work, it in fact represents a very important transformation of the sexual division of labor, which is, in some sense, a breakdown. First, the very entrance of a homemaker into the labor force represented her self-assertion as a homemaker: her insistence that the needs of the family were insufficiently filled by her husband's income, and her undertaking the responsibility to remedy the situation. Wage-earning home-makers were enlarging their freedom and responsibility, asserting independently their conceptions of the requirements of family life, rather than passively adjusting their work to their husbands' positions.

Second, once in the labor force, homemakers have gained a new sense of themselves, a new sense of pride, and an enjoyment in their work. Interviews with wage-earning homemakers show that labor-force participation, which started out as a mere means to make ends meet, soon became a source of pride in itself. Because such a homemaker was able to provide her family with tangible things, such as a car or a college education, she felt of clear value to her family (remember the pride of the Middletown mother). Besides the feeling of usefulness to her family, the employed homemaker gained an independent feeling of her own importance. As one beautician explained:

> In my work at the salon, it's really like an ego trip. It feels good when people won't come in if you're not there. If I go away for two weeks, my customers will wait to have their hair done until I come back. I'm not always very secure, but when I think about that, it always makes me feel good about myself, like I'm really okay.[34]

Homemakers also enjoyed being able to earn money; it gave them a sense of their own value, as well as some independence and power in their families. Women felt that they had some independent say about what to do with the money they earned; it could fill their needs, not just those of the family. One working homemaker told Komarovsky that "when I work and have my own money, I do as I please"; in her instance, doing as she pleased was entertaining the bridge club at her house, even if it added three or four dollars to the food bill.[35] So although these homemakers entered the labor force as part of their homemaking work, for the good of their families, many began to enjoy the experience in its own right and to continue working whether or not their families were in pressing need. When women working in non-elite jobs were asked in a 1970 study whether they would continue working if they could afford not to, about half said they would (see Table 10-5). Black women were more committed to remaining on the job in all occupational groups.[36]

Third, as the homemaker's work has been extended into the labor force, her side of the marriage relationship has been transformed. The traditional sexual division of labor in marriage has been changed, causing conflicts between husband and wife, and transforming domestic homemaking. We will examine the important changes this has engendered in Chapter 13.

So the expansion of consumer wealth in twentieth century America has, ironically, caused American to want more, and to work harder in order to get it. The pressure placed on families by competitive consumption has gradually caused homemakers to join their husbands in the labor force, as an extension of their work of homemaking—a movement facilitated by the acceptance of women in the labor force before marriage and by the recruitment of homemakers into the labor force during the two world wars. As the century advanced, an in-

Table 10–5: Percentage of Women Who Would
Work Even If They Received Enough Income to
Live without Working[a]

	Whites	Blacks
Professional/managerial	74	76
Clerical/sales	60	62
Blue-collar	45	59
Domestic service	40	66
Non-domestic service	56	74
Total/Average	59	67

SOURCE: U.S. Department of Labor, 1970, *Dual Careers: A Longitudinal Study of Labor Market Experience of Women*, Manpower Research Monograph No. 21, Vol. 1, pp. 21, 196.
a. 86% of whites, 67% of blacks, were married.

creasing proportion of American women joined American men in the struggle for more wealth, destroying the separation of sexual spheres, and weakening the sexual division of labor within marriage. The force of these transformations has been multiplied by a different development—the entrance of privileged, educated homemakers into the labor force and into men's jobs. These are the subject of the next two chapters.

11

The Career Girl and the Second-career Woman

Women's Education, Women's Professions, and the Emergence of the Career Girl

While the development of consumerism was drawing working- and middle-class homemakers out of the domestic sphere and into the labor force, another development was undermining domestic homemaking in a very different way—the emergence, among the most privileged and educated women, of the "career girl."

The nineteenth century saw the establishment of the privileged woman's right to higher education. The cult of domesticity idea of professional homemaking had let loose in women, particularly in privileged women, an active search for the homemaking vocation, the struggle to prepare themselves adequately for this vocation, and the extension of this vocation outside the purely domestic sphere to protect their own homes and children, as well as those of their less fortunate sisters. The social homemaking and feminist movements fought for women's higher education as a necessary preparation for their future profession of mothering; they also secured the femininity of the task of teaching women, along with children. Their rational arguments soon won over the strenuous opposition to women's higher education; as Inez Irwin wrote in *Angels and Amazons: A Hundred Years of American Women*, in 1933, "A scandal in 1833, a butt of ridicule in 1860, daring departure in 1880, a faint oddity in 1900, higher education has become in 1933 a commonplace—like literacy in general."[1] By 1900, both women's and coeducational colleges had been established, along with female seminaries and high schools. Women college graduates did not, as had been feared, develop illnesses from the strains of studying, neither did they prove lacking in mental capacities. The fight for women's higher education had been won, in principle. With the advance of the twentieth century, higher education for women was transformed from an unhealthy or unwomanly oddity occupying a minority of questionable young women to a desirable training for womanhood. The cost of an education, combined with the opportunity cost of college (the foregone wages) made it a luxury, the prerogative of the wealthy. Furthermore, as the sons of the wealthy were being educated, it became accepted that their wives and the mothers of their children should possess the same level of knowledge of the world. The penchant for college-educated daughters among the wealthy (and the professionals) made it all the more desirable by other families, as a sign of one's father's success, as well as a means to propel one's daughter to an upwardly mobile marriage. So while high school and college graduates represented a privileged minority of women through World War II, they were an increasing minority.[2] As the century advanced, high school and college educations were gradually diffused through the classes, much like the consumer goods we studied in the previous chapter. Women college graduates were no longer pioneers, and higher education became an expected part of training for motherhood among the very privileged.[3]

While the purpose of women's higher education was to prepare them for their vocation of homemaking, higher education also developed women's capacity for vocations other than homemaking. The combination of higher education and social homemaking led, as we have seen, to the emergence of feminine serving professions—teaching, social work, nursing, librarianship. Between 1890 and 1920, women's participation in the paid professions increased by 226%, and men's by only 78%.[4] Once these feminine professions were established, they became accepted *alternatives* to marriage and homemaking. Given that homemaking was considered a full-time profession, comparable to professions in the labor force, a feminine profession in the labor force was considered incompatible with marriage and homemaking. One could not simultaneously serve the needs of one's family and subordinate oneself to the demands of one's job. So whereas for men, marriage and family life were consistent with having a job or vocation—indeed they demanded it—the sexual division of labor in marriage made marriage and a labor force vocation incompatible for women. Because women accepted the traditional sexual differentiation lived out in marriage, they accepted the incompatibility of homemaking and other professions. At this time in history, this need to choose was experienced as a new freedom, rather than as an unfair sacrifice. Previously, homemaking had been the only accepted profession for a woman, and women who did not marry had been pitied and useless. Now, for the first time, a woman who never married could gain respectability, even social recognition, through a lifelong commitment to one of the feminine labor-force professions. Some women entered college with such a vocation in mind, seeing themselves as different, as not "cut out for" marriage. This choice was not restricted to daughters of the wealthy. Among those women who paid half or more of their tuition bill by working (17% of college graduates in one study), a large percentage (about 45%) did, indeed, become career women and never marry.[5] Ida Tarbell, an active social homemaker and sociologist in the early twentieth century, was one such woman. She wrote in her autobiography, "I could never marry. It would interfere with my plan; it would fetter my freedom." Tarbell prayed in her youth not to find a man to marry.[6]

There is evidence that some women pursued college and professional careers upon the urging of their parents. A social homemaking daughter could fulfill her parents' desires to help society. In her study of single academic women at Wellesley College from 1880 to 1920, Patricia Palmieri found that their fathers had often been active in temperance and abolition work, while their mothers had regretted their own inability to go to college. Such parents supported the career pursuits of their daughters. Emily Balch, Wellesley professor and recipient of the Nobel Peace Prize, received the following encouragment from her father: "It seems to me it would be a mistake to give up what you are doing unless it becomes very irksome. I believe you can do a great deal of good. You have a very sound mind on all social questions, a high order of ability, and a kindly and equable spirit . . . [you will be] a strong influence."[7] The stigma of being a nontraditional daughter was often lessened by the traditional domesticity of a sister, which reduced the familial obligations of the career-oriented daughter and made her parents appear more traditional.[8] So high schools, and especially colleges, were filling a dual function in the early twentieth century: training an elite of young women for their futures as homemakers, and preparing others for the practice of a feminine profession in the labor force.

Other women were led inadvertently by their college educations to reject homemaking for a career in the labor force. They had been sent to college to prepare themselves for lives of homemaking, but their educations, often at the hands of career women, opened up their minds and put them in contact with their potentials in the professional world. In this way, college instilled in many women the positive desire to pursue a labor-force profession. As Ida Tarbell wrote in 1912 in *The Business of Being A Woman:*

> In the process of preparing herself to discharge more adequately her task as a woman in the republic, her respect for the task has been weakened. In this process, which we call emancipation, she has in a sense lost sight of the purposes of emancipation. Interested in acquiring new tools, she has come to believe the tools more important than the thing for which she was to use them. She has found out that with education and freedom, pursuits of all sorts are open to her, and by following these pursuits she can preserve her personal liberty, avoid the grave responsibility, the almost inevitable sorrows and anxieties, which belong to family life.[9]

Few women thus tempted into paid professions made clear choices never to marry; however, once a woman had begun such a profession, marriage did become less pressing, less attractive, and less probable. Ernest Groves described this in an article for *Annals* in 1929: "Where the occupation builds up an intense interest in achievement or promises a financial advancement which the ambitious girl makes a goal for her efforts, attention is turned away from matrimony at least during the years when an attachment would most easily and naturally be made." When women were devoted to pursuing women's careers, their "chance for marriage as well as their desire for it [are] decreased."[10]

Hence women's college education, planned as preparation for homemaking, had the unforeseen effect of creating many women who never took up homemaking, but rather followed social homemaking careers in the labor force. Haverman and West's extensive survey of college graduates, done in 1947, contained a chapter entitled "The Ubiquitous Spinster." It noted that spinsterhood was much more common among college graduates than in the female population as a whole: 41% versus 25% when under 30 years of age, 22% versus 11% between the ages of 30 and 39, 26% versus 8% between 40 and 49, and 35% versus 8% when over 50. These authors explained the high percentage of women over 50 as a generational phenomenon: the early college graduates had been trailblazers, more overtly feminist, "a somewhat different breed from the current crop. . . . Careers for women, representing a relatively new idea, appeared much more exciting and glamorous. It seems only logical that what we now call the older generation of college women should have been much more doubtful about the advantage of marriages—and also been viewed with considerably more suspicion by male contemporaries who had not yet fully reconciled themselves to the thought of higher education for women."[11] But the authors' statistics show the phenomenon of "spinsterhood" continuing, if at a somewhat reduced rate.

While these women did not live in traditional heterosexual marriages, some of them experimented with alternative families, forming intimate emotional attachments with women. Jessie Taft, a twentieth-century sociologist, wrote in 1916 that women unwilling to "take on the restrictions of matrimony" were choosing an alternative home life:

> Everywhere we find the unmarried woman turning to other women, building up with them a real home, finding in them the sympathy and understanding, the bond of similar standards and values as well as the same aesthetic and intellectual interests, that are often difficult of realization in a husband. . . . One has only to know professional women to realize how common and how satisfactory is this substitute for marriage.[12]

In constructing relationships of love and intimacy with other women, these professionals were carrying on a tradition established in the nineteenth century by the early social homemakers.[13] For example, in a letter printed in *Good Housekeeping* in 1885, "Priscilla" pointed out to readers that it was quite possible for two independent women to live together quite contentedly, without worrying about "husband-hunting."[14] These untraditional career women were traditional enough to consider it impossible to live with men and pursue their selves in careers. Rather than leading them to unorthodox heterosexual marriages, their careerism turned them toward other career women.

While some college graduates were undertaking lifetime professions and remaining unmarried, they were not in the majority. Their rejection of homemaking, even if it was for a profession which served society in a womanly fashion, made them oddities. Their choice not to marry and have children was considered unnatural; they were seen as not quite women, and pitied as unable to catch husbands. If they had romantic relationships with women, they were condemned as perverted.[15] Most college women planned for careers as homemakers;

they saw their college years merely as preparation for their responsibilities as homemakers, particularly mothering. Freed from financial pressures by successful marriages, they could focus their lives on enlightened homemaking, reading the latest on child-rearing, and keeping up with the newest appliances and fashions.

However, a third option existed for women college graduates. They could combine career and family, not simultaneously, but as life stages: college, work in the labor force, and then marriage and homemaking. This option had the further attractions of preparing a girl for the possible threat of remaining a spinster and of giving her work experience which would be useful if she became a widow or divorcee later in life. We saw in Chapter 7 how Catherine Beecher, pioneer for women's education and profession of teaching, envisioned teaching as a premarriage vocation for women, rather than as a lifetime alternative to marriage. In the first quarter of the twentieth century it became increasingly acceptable for a young single women to undertake paid work, not simply as a daughter in order to help her parents "make ends meet," but as an individual in her own right, as a part of her self-development. Experience in the labor force, in the world at large, seemed, as did higher education, to be an important training ground for a woman's future of homemaking. One 1916 book, *Girl and Woman: A Book for Mothers and Daughters*, actually advised the middle-class girl to pursue "some kind of definite occupation before she marries and goes to a home of her own."[16] Another, *The Renaissance of Motherhood*, of 1914, suggested that women work before marriage and did not object to their employment after their children grew up. The participation of women in the labor force during World War I, for the good of the country, further allowed them to experience their abilities and gain confidence—even in men's jobs. Louis Dublin, the chief statistician of the Metropolitan Life Insurance Company wrote, in 1926:

> The whole aspect of a woman's life has been changed, and community life has been correspondingly transformed. A hundred years ago, women had only one career to look forward to, and that was home-making; today the average American girl thinks of many other fields for her activities. Home-making as a career is being relegated for the most part in the minds of young people to a secondary place. Even if most of the educated women still look forward to marriage as an ultimate goal, their first and immediate choice is very often along other lines.[17]

These vocations were seen as temporary commitments which would eventually give way to marriage and homemaking. According to the President of Smith College for Women in 1907:

> It is not the chief happiness or the chief end of woman, as a whole, to enter these new occupations [in the labor force] to pursue them through life. They enter many which they soon abandon; and that is good—particularly the abandonment. . . . The prime motive of the higher education of women should be recognized as the development in women of the capacities and powers which will fit them to make family life more productive in every sense, physically, mentally, and spiritually.[18]

This pattern proved to be a long-lasting one, incorporated easily into the middle- or upper-class woman's life cycle. By 1940, a survey of the middle-class readers of *Woman's Home Companion* found that although all but one saw marriage as their ultimate career, 75% of the high school girls wished to go on to college, and 98% wished to pursue a brief business or professional career before they married. The reasons they gave for working before marriage were the following:

> 1. I think a woman sets a better value on money if she has to earn it herself.
> 2. I want to satisfy myself that I am of some use in the economic world.
> 3. I want to be able to support myself and my children if anything happens to my husband.[19]

These were not career women: only 25% were "willing" to maintain their professions after marriage. Mirra Komarovsky reported in her 1951 study, *Women in the Modern World*, that 90% of the women undergraduates she surveyed "intended to hold a paid job between commencement and marriage," while "all but a handful" wanted to get married and have children.[20] Their desire for premarriage working experience had become generally accepted by society at large. Henry A. Bowman, in his 1942 book, *Marriage for Moderns*, wrote of the desirability of labor-force participation before marriage:

> Even though a young woman is definitely planning on home-making as her lifelong career, there are good reasons for her preparing herself for a vocation to be pursued between school and marriage. She proves to herself and to others that she can do something useful and remunerative. She may save money to be used in buying things for her home-to-be. She is

further educated by her contacts in the business or professional world. She learns the value of money. . . . Preparation for a vocation is a sort of insurance policy. The girl's fiancé may die or disappoint her, so that she will remain single. Her husband may die or become incapacitated, so that she will have to earn a living for herself, or for both of them. . . . She may get training and experience that will enrich her marriage.[21]

So whereas single women originally had entered the labor force in the service of others—their parents or society at large—by the twentieth century paid employment had become an accepted means to the middle-class woman's self-development, to be followed by a future of homemaking, of course.

It all seemed clear, simple, and positive. Rather than being constrained to homemaking alone, women now had a choice between the homemaking profession and women's professions in the labor force, as well as the option of having both, sequentially. But, in fact, the introduction of these new options into her life placed the woman college graduate in a contradictory position, in a dilemma for which there was no easy solution.

Marriage and Career: From Either/Or to Both/And

By the 1920s, women had already begun to find their new freedom upsetting, their new choices frustrating. Their labor-force careers had been undertaken to fill the interim between college and marriage. However, the practice of such careers was addictive; it gave a woman a position in the public sphere and recognition of her abilities, rewards absent from a homemaker's life. While her desire for marriage and homemaking was not directly affected, giving up her profession upon marriage now seemed to be a sacrifice. One young woman voiced this dilemma in a letter to the *Ladies Home Journal* in 1912: "I am a young school-teacher holding an enviable position and am thoroughly in love with my work." A man was in love with her and wanted to marry her, and she could not decide what to do. To the columnist, the answer was simple: marriage. "If you truly desire to influence the future generation what broader life could you have than to be the mother of boys and girls whom you could train daily in all good and upright ways? When I think of the power of a true mother to benefit her whole generation I marvel at the makeshifts that women adopt to stultify their ambitions."[22] However certain this columnist was of the superior appeals of homemaking, many women were finding this choice difficult. Jessie Taft, an early twentieth-century career woman and feminist, described the choice as being "between crippled life in the home, or an unfulfilled one out of it."[23] Louis Dublin, from whom we have heard above, diagnosed the problem in the following way. First, the college environment separated women from contact with homemaking and children, while impressing upon them the unmarried lives of their teachers. After they graduated, women wished to use their new abilities in labor-force careers. Once they had had the career experience, they were inevitably faced with a dilemma, for marriage and career could not be combined:

> From the point of view of the individual concerned, the pursuit of one of these alternatives [marriage or career] without the other, involved inevitably the impoverishment of life. Professional women generally miss the home-making activities of their married sisters and regret the incompleteness of their personal experiences. There is possibly just as much regret on the part of an ever increasing number of married women who find themselves on the shelf too soon, unable to participate in the many outside activities for which they find themselves amply prepared.[24]

Women had originally been sent to college to be trained for homemaking. Then, after college, some wished to have occupations for a period before marriage. The practice of these labor-force professions gave women the experience of self–expression in the economy, making their futures of full-time home-making seem incomplete and unfulfilling. Women's active participation in World War I, in men's jobs even, made them all the more bold in the economic sphere. By the twenties, the dilemma of the modern woman—between continuing on in a career or giving it up for marriage—was hotly discussed. In 1919, the *Smith College Weekly* wrote, "We cannot believe it is fixed in the nature of things that a woman must choose between a home and her work, when a man may have both. There must be a way out, and it is the problem of our generation to find the way."[25]

In 1929, feminist Edith Puffer Howes described the problem this way: society did not allow for "the natural and necessary development of woman's affectional life, along with the natural continuous development and exercise of her individual powers [in work]. The man demands of life that we have love, home, fatherhood and the special work which his particular brain combination fits. Shall the women demand less?"[26] Howes founded The Center for the Coordination of Women's Interests at Smith College to solve this dilemma. She wrote eloquently of the necessity of women to continue their paid professions after marriage:

> We see the psychological impossibility of denying development to youth that is eager to learn, to act, and, for the most part, to work, or that needs to work . . . (and) the psychological impossibility of restraining the exercise of a faculty which has once been developed, without danger of ill effects, even tragic ills. A hundred years ago, such a policy might have had some success, because women then did not as a class realize that their abilities were, broadly, equivalent to men's. But there is now no more chance of diverting those who thirst after knowledge and skill and the use of that skill, than of turning democracy permanently back to despotism.[27]

Elizabeth Kemper Adams wrote, as early as 1921, "The question for many women today is not so much a choice between a profession and marriage as the question of how they may combine a profession and marriage with justice and profit to all concerned."[28]

Yet it was not easy to combine homemaking with another career. Society was pervaded with the domestic ideal of homemaking and, in particular, with the belief that children needed full-time mothering. We have noted the opposition encountered by married women who entered the labor force as homemakers, for the good of their families. The career woman was even more of an outrage; she wished to leave the home sphere not for the good of her family but rather for her own self-development and fulfillment. She was, then, putting her own needs before those of her family, breaking the essential rule of womanly behavior. Her dual career life was made easier if family poverty legitimized her labor-force participation; indeed, Virginia Collier's 1926 study of married career women, *Marriage and Careers,* found that 52% of married career women cited financial necessity as a reason for their pursuit of careers.[29] Those who did not have such a typically feminine rationalization found their behavior stigmatized as selfish and uncaring, neglectful of their children and husbands. So while a few brave and motivated women retained their careers upon marriage, most gave them up and became full-time homemakers. In the first generation of women college students, interviewed in 1900, only 9.8% of those who married had jobs, although 74% of these had had careers before marriage.[30]

Until recently the majority of college-educated women have accepted the frustrating choice between a lifetime labor-force profession and a life of homemaking, preceded possibly by a stint in a labor-force career. As Mirra Komarovsky wrote in her pioneering study of the issue in 1951, *Women in the Modern World*, "Whatever the woman does, whether she is single or married, a homemaker or a career woman, childless or a mother—each design for living has its own pattern of frustrations."[31] The necessity to choose either marriage or career as one's major life work was already evident during a woman's college years; Komarovsky found that female undergraduates were torn between the desire to achieve in their classes and to be popular with college men. These two paths conflicted not only as demands on the female undergraduate's time, but also intrinsically. Most college men were not looking for smart girls; some 40% of those women Komarovsky interviewed admitted to "playing dumb" to resolve this problem.[32]

A substantial number of college women continued to define themselves as "career girls." The woman who, before or during college, decided to commit herself first and foremost to a career risked having no family life. She would have difficulty finding a husband willing to marry such a masculine woman; once married, her husband might demand that she quit her job—because he wanted children and wanted her to be with them, because he wished to move for job advancement, or because he wanted her total dedication as a homemaker. Komarovsky found few women undergraduates who were absolutely determined not to marry, but 20% were committed to careers whatever that would mean for their family lives.[33] More remained single than had planned for it: 31% of the 4,000 women college graduates studied in 1952, who had graduated from 1920 on, were still unmarried.[34] These career women were, hence, forced to give up "normal family life"—husbands and children. While we can assume that some of them had important unmarried intimate relationships, with either men or women, these did not have the recognition of society. And few dared to have children while in such an unorthodox position. Yet these women were able to achieve recognition for their career work; some even became the first women in the more prestigious men's jobs.

On the other side of the choice were the full-time homemakers. Fully 50% of the women undergraduates interviewed by Komarovsky wanted to be "full-time homemakers."[35] The Haverman and West survey found that the largest percentage of women college graduates fell into the category of full-time homemaker—an average of 42% of them.[36] Armed with their special high school or college preparation for their homemaking vocation, and perhaps with job experience to boot, women from the 1920s on into the 1950s set upon their calling—professional homemaking. They were educated, armed with an increasing array of appliances, and freed from the larger social obligations of social homemaking, which had now been shouldered by government institutions. They were aided by psychologists and social scientists who undertook the scientific study of the dimensions of good mothering.

Yet the homemaking profession brought them increasing frustration, frustration which sent them back out into the labor force. The frustrations of the college-educated full-time homemaker were noted by feminists as well as by social conservatives. Komarovsky's excellent study noted two sorts of discontent faced by college-educated homemakers: those relating to the transition from their labor-force career to the career of homemaking, and those stemming from frustrations with homemaking itself. Ten years later, Betty Friedan's *The Feminine Mystique* pointed out many of the same frustrations.[37] Komarovsky found the following problems with the transition from paid work to homemaking in her in-depth interviews with women in the early fifties: longing for the relinquished occupation, resentment and unhappiness at the loss of economic independence, discontent with the unstructured nature of homemaking compared to the previous occupation, loss of self-esteem given the clear social value of the previous job and the privacy and lack of recognition of homemaking, and a sense of injustice at having been forced to give up her career while her husband was able to continue on in his.[38] The labor-force experience of these women led them to compare homemaking with their previous professions; they found the former inferior on many counts. We have already noted the attachment of working homemakers in non-elite jobs to their work. Such attachment was stronger among women whose education had allowed them entry into more interesting and fulfilling jobs, making their disappointment upon leaving their jobs for homemaking all the more pronounced. In the course of the twentieth century, the path through college, career, and homemaking altered somewhat; working before marriage increasingly turned into working so that a couple could get married, and often into working temporarily after marriage to put one's husband through graduate or professional school. But these changes did not make the transition from a paid profession to homemaking any easier.

But even women who did not evince a desire to return to their previous occupations in the labor force expressed problems with homemaking brought on by their college and/or labor-force experiences. Many women expressed to Komarovsky the feeling of stagnating intellectually. College had developed their intellectual abilities; because homemaking did not utilize these abilities, homemakers found their lives unfulfilling. Furthermore, graduates could feel their intellectual abilities declining due to disuse. As a Phi Beta Kappa graduate confessed: "I have acquired such an inferiority complex that I am afraid to ask a question at a public lecture. And to think that in college I used to preside over a meeting of my college class." Another woman, a former high school teacher, complained, "I am turning into a vegetable."[39]

A second problem was that the college-educated woman, committed to performing her homemaking vocation in an enlightened, professional manner, often felt discontented with her results. If she focused on housework while her children were young and demanding, her lack of attention to her own mind would keep her from being intellectually stimulating to her adolescent children, or to her husband. Although women almost universally found mothering to be the most satisfying part of homemaking, they worried about their performance in this role. Prevailing wisdom gave them complete responsibility for the futures of their children, but the resultant feeling of power brought with it the fear of failure, guilt at being less than ideal. College women feared being overprotective, or that their discontent at having given up their careers would be sensed by their children. When Komarovsky asked 306 mothers to indicate the main sources of fatigue, worry, and friction in their lives, the majority answered each question with "child-rearing."[40]

Indeed, in the 1940s and 1950s, psychologists studying child development began to claim that vocational mothers were very bad mothers. Philip Wiley's *Generation of Vipers* blamed mothers for every problem known to man.[41] More scientific and rational monographs, such as the well known *Modern Woman: The Lost Sex*, by Ferdinand Lundberg and Marynia Farnham, were equally critical of the twentieth century homemaker's mothering abilities. "The spawning ground of most neurosis in Western civilization is the home. The basis for it is laid in childhood. . . . And as we have pointed out, the principal agent in laying the groundwork for it is the mother."[42] Their study claimed that only about half of America's mothers were healthy, "fully maternal mothers" who "merely loved their children." The other half were unhealthy—rejecting, overprotective, or dominating. They traced this problem to the desire of women to derive "ego-satisfaction" from their mothering, something which it could not, in fact, provide.

> Certainly the tasks of a woman in bearing and educating children as well as maintaining, as best she may, the inner intregrity of her home are capable of demanding all her time and best attention. However, she cannot obtain from them, so attentuated are their tasks now, the same sort of community approval and ego-satisfaction that she can from seemingly more challenging occupations which take her outside the home.[43]

The desire for ego-satisfaction to which they refer was promised by the cult of domesticity and developed by women's higher education. Homemaking, in particular mothering, was seen as a vocation for which women needed to be trained. Yet the selves that future mothers developed in college yearned for self-affirmation and self-expression.

Not only was ego-satisfaction difficult to derive from homemaking, but the woman seeking ego-satisfaction would be a bad mother:

> To a certain extent a woman can derive great ego satisfaction from playing a full feminine role, but there are dangers in it both to herself and to her children. Too many women today are forced to derive their entire ego-support from their children which they do at the expense of the children, to the danger of society. A child can never be a plaything and turn out well.[44]

Lundberg and Farnham cogently showed how women seeking their own self-fulfillment through vocational homemaking were, indeed, bad mothers. They could try to fulfill their own desires for careers by living through their children—the domineering mother. They could attempt to create permanent vocations for themselves by perpetuating their children's dependence upon them—the overprotective mother. Indeed, the good mother, who created healthy, independent individuals of her children, was, at the same time, depriving herself of her life vocation. One of the most painful parts of vocational mothering was this forced unemployment, which, since woman's life expectancy was increasing and family size falling, came at her prime.[45]

So a final problem with vocational homemaking, particularly for the college-educated woman, was the period of leisure coming after the maturity of her children. Women's former outlet—volunteer work—was less and less satisfying; after their college and labor-force experiences, homemakers desired a more professional experience. One woman, frustrated with a volunteer effort after having had a profession of her own, complained to Komarovsky, "For one thing, I am irritated by the inefficiency of amateur enterprises. Every time we undertake a project I can't help thinking that a professional person could do in a month what all of us well-intentioned but untrained women accomplish in a year. . . . I get impatient with the slow pace and the "tea party" flavor of club activities. Above all, for me this volunteer work is a demotion." The professionalization of social work exacerbated this problem by depriving volunteers of the most fulfilling parts of serving their communities. As an active civic volunteer worker told Komarovsky, "All this is not enough of a personal challenge to me. The really interesting work is done by the staff members, whether teachers, social workers, musicians or psychiatrists.[46]

The problem with homemaking as a life vocation was not that it was not a full-time, full life occupation; as the sustenance of family life, it was intrinsically without limit, expanding as Betty Friedan has noted, "to fill the time available."[47] Rather, there was a basic contradiction in middle- and upper-class homemaking. It required a person with a well-developed mind, with a sophisticated knowledge of the world outside of the home, of men's world. Therefore women were sent to college, where their minds were developed, their academic abilities recognized, and their potential for living in the professional world developed. Yet once a woman began her career as a homemaker, her knowledge of the public sphere was to be used only for the advancement of husband and children. Her abilities could be used only according to their needs and interests, in gaining recognition of their selves. The public self which higher education and work had developed in her was denied an existence of its own, forced to express itself indirectly through the members of her family. If she asserted this self strongly and actively tried to direct the lives of her husband and children, she was attacked as domineering; if she carefully nurtured their selves, she was "ideal," yet her own abilities remained hidden. The educated homemaker's life was fraught with these contradictions. Komarovsky noted them in the early fifties; Friedan described "the problem that has no name" so well in the early sixties that she shocked many privileged homemakers into self-consciousness.[48]

There was only one way for the educated woman to find direct expression of her abilities—in her own labor-force participation—and eventually more and more educated homemakers began to seek "second careers" in the labor force. Unlike the earlier career girls, these women embraced homemaking as their life vocation. They simply felt the need to supplement their homemaking with a second career, a career in the labor force which would allow them direct self-expression and would bring public recognition of their abilities. These women felt the need for *both* careers; they wished to marry and subordinate themselves to the needs of their families, but they also wished to express their own talents in the labor force.

At first the decision to follow a second career was an afterthought. Full-time homemakers, left idle when their children left home, sought to fill the void with a second labor-force career. Learning from their mothers' frustrations at homemaking and difficulties at reentering the labor force, succeeding generations of women are growing up expecting to undertake second careers after or even during their years of active mothering. They spend their years in college acquiring the training necessary for vocations in the labor force. The plan to combine two careers in their lifetimes has also led women to structure mothering around their second careers—having fewer children and having them all at once. The labor-force participation rate of married college-educated women has hence risen dramatically: from 9.8% in 1900, the early days of marriage or career, to 27% in 1952 to almost 59% in 1974.[49]

The entrance of these women into the labor force is a new and important development. These women are not entering the labor force as homemakers seeking to fill family needs. Nor are they choosing labor-force participation as an alternative to private homemaking and, hence, as a social homemaking profession. They are entering the labor force to find self-fulfillment, to use their minds and wills in a public manner. Since they work not to help their husbands or families (who often oppose such a decision) but for their own self-fulfillment, they behave differently from the woman workers or professionals of the past. "Second-career women" are seeking more from their jobs than simply money for their families or a way to serve society at large; they want self-development and self-expression in their jobs. This has led them to shun most women's jobs and to seek entrance into men's jobs. We will analyze these efforts in the next chapter.

At the same time, these women are or plan to be homemakers and are attached to the traditional conception of homemaking as woman's vocation. If the contradictions in vocational homemaking have pushed women into "second careers," the attempt to combine homemaking with a second vocation has not freed women from these contradictions. For homemaking is incompatible with the practice of a labor-force career: a woman cannot simultaneously determine her actions according to her family's needs and a career's demands. With the rise of the second career woman, the educated homemaker's "problem without a name" has been transformed to a more concrete and real one—a conflict between her career life and her homemaking life. This leads her to join her poorer, less-educated counterparts in questioning the sexual division of labor in her marriage, a process we will study in Chapter 13.

The Homebound Homemaker: From Ideal to "Just a Housewife"

Twentieth-century homemakers, in the living out of the demands of homemaking and of womanhood, have inadvertently upset the cornerstone of the cult of domesticity, the ideal of the homebound homemaker. While trying to perform their homemaking vocation, they have been led to reject the separation of sexual spheres which was the essence of the cult-of-domesticity marriage. Homemakers from poor or needy families have entered into the labor force in response to the expansion of their families' commodity needs; they have been joined by college-educated homemakers seeking second careers. Table 11-1 shows the dramatic increase in the percentage of married women in the labor force in the course of the twentieth century; Table 10-4 (p. 252) shows that this increase has taken place in all classes. The decline of the homebound homemaker has also occurred among all races: by March 1979, 46% of Hispanic, 49% of white, and 60% of black married women with husbands present were in the labor force.[50] By 1980 a majority of homemakers was in the labor force! And only 8% of women over sixteen had never been in the labor force.[51] When seventeen-year-old girls were asked, in 1974, what their first choice for a career was, only 3 percent of them se-

Table 11–1: Marital Status of Women in the Urban Labor Force, and Labor-force Participation Rates of Women by Marital Status, 1890–1980[a]

| | Percent distribution of female labor force | | | | Labor force participation rates | | | | |
| | | Married | | | | | Married | | |
	Single	Total	Husband present	Widowed or divorced	Total	Single	Total	Husband present	Widowed or divorced
1980	25.6	59.7	55.5	14.7	50.7	62.7	50.0	49.4	40.0
1970	22.5	62.3	57.1	15.0	41.6	50.9	40.2	39.6	36.8
1960	23.6	60.7	55.2	15.7	34.5	42.9	31.7	30.6	36.1
1950	31.9	52.2	46.5	16.0	29.0	46.3	23.0	21.6	32.7
1940	49.0	35.9	30.1	15.0	25.8	45.5	15.6	13.8	30.2
1930	53.9	28.9		17.2	24.8	50.3	11.7		34.4[b]
1920	77.0	23.0		[b]	23.7	46.4	9.0		
1910[c]	60.2	24.7		15.0	25.4	51.1	10.7		34.1
1900	66.2	15.4		18.4	20.6	43.5	5.6		32.5
1890	68.2	13.9		17.9	18.9	40.5	4.6		29.9

SOURCES: For 1890–1970, U.S. Department of Commerce, Bureau of the Census, *Historical Statistics of the United States: Colonial Times to 1970*, p. 133; for 1980, *Statistical Abstract of the U.S.*, 1980, p. 402.

a. Persons 15 years old and over, 1890–1930, 14 years old and over, 1940–1960, 16 years and over, thereafter. In 1980, figures are of the civilian labor force, rather than urban labor force.

b. Single includes widowed or divorced.

c. Data not comparable: census enumerators, encouraged to record "the occupation, if any, followed by a child of any age or a woman," included more women in labor force.

lected housewife, although all but 10 percent expected to have children![52]

The accelerating entrance of homemakers into the labor force has brought the increasing deprecation of the full-time homemaker. The latter has been transformed from a proud ideal of womanhood into an apologetic housewife, the onus of guilt shifted to her and away from the wage-earning homemaker. The old criticisms of the wage-earning homemaker are losing their force. Given the absence of apparent damage to their children, working mothers are less frequently accused of neglecting their children.[53] Moreover, the "double day" worked by the wage-earning homemaker earns her special praise for superior feminine dedication to her family's needs. The wage-earning homemaker is able to hold down a job and do her housework and child care. Without the demands of a job, "What does the home-bound homemaker do all day?" Answer: she's "just a housewife."

Equally central to the transformation of the homemaker from an ideal to "just a housewife" has been the entrance of privileged home-makers into the labor force. Without this, the labor-force participation of a married woman would have continued to represent the failure of her husband to provide for his family's needs: the home-bound homemaker would have continued to represent the ideal woman. However, the presence of upper-class women in the labor force has worked to erase the class smear on the working homemaker, removing one of the biggest blocks to the labor-force participation of homemakers. Now that the wives of the most successful men are often in the labor force, a homemaker's labor-force presence no longer clearly signifies the failure of her husband to provide. This has freed the wives of middle-class men to enter the labor force, seeking both extra family income and a degree of self-expression and independence. Furthermore, the decision of privileged women to pursue second careers in the labor force "for themselves" has brought recognition of the homemaker's need for self-expression, a need not satisfied by homemaking. These women had said, by their actions, that homemaking was not enough to fulfill them, that they possessed a professional self, a work self, which needed expression. This complaint gave validation to the middle-class homemaker's frustration with her career, creating much discontent among these homemakers. Middle-class homemakers who felt Betty Friedan's "problem that has no name" either joined the movement into the labor force or began to complain about the lack of self-fulfillment in homemaking.

Meanwhile, the same discontent with homemaking was surfacing, in a different manner, among less privileged women. They experienced this new kind of "self," not by entering labor-force professions, but by having their work rewarded with a paycheck. Their labor-force jobs gave homemakers public recognition as workers and specific valuation in the form of pay; working in the labor force developed in them the need for such recognition and pay. In the past, women had always asked what they could do for their families and accepted their families' dependence and success as adequate "payment" for their efforts. The more women combined homemaking with a paid job, the more they began to evaluate homemaking as a job, asking themselves what it gave them. When examined in this light, homemaking came out wanting. It is not paid; it must not be important. As one homemaker and typist put it: "If you don't bring home a paycheck, there's no gauge for whether you're a success or not a success. People pay you to work because you're doing something useful and you're good at it. But nobody pays a housewife because what difference does it make; nobody really cares."[54]

Homemakers who were not in the labor force compared themselves with those who were, and, again, felt devalued because they received no pay—none of the explicit social valuation that the wage-earning homemaker received. This lack of an income was even more salient in light of the homemaker's risk of losing the financial support of her husband because of his unemployment, illness, death, or desertion. In the 1970 Parnes study we cited earlier (see Table 10–5, p. 255), about 60% of women in the labor force claimed they would work even if they did not need the income. When asked why, over half gave as their reason discontent with being a homebound homemaker.[55]

The growing discontent among traditional homebound homemakers has brought a defensive rebirth of the cult of domesticity, a movement reaffirming that woman's vocation of homemaking is a God-given and exalted one. This literature blames homemakers for their discontent; in particular, it blames their development of "self." Ella May Miller, a radio talk-show host, wrote a book entitled *Happiness Is Homemaking*. She prefaces her book with the following: "It is popular for the modern woman to resent being a housewife, to feel it is a second-rate profession. This need not be the case. Homemaking can be enjoyable, when you join hands with God." She asks homemakers, "Aren't we focusing on wrong values—on purely selfish goals? Somehow we have failed to emphasize woman's role as helper to man (not his boss or competitor); woman's role as mother to man-kind (not mother of gadgets, and of dogs). . . . Real happiness comes in forgetting self. You forget self as you get interested in Jesus Christ. . . . He also helps you to see others and to find something to do for them." Giving up "self" includes giving up the desire for a career:

> The currently popular argument that only professional work enables a woman to find herself is not the answer. . . . Although many women claim that marriage and motherhood hinder them from finding themselves, basi-cally a girl's desire is to be married and to be a mother. Her body and her emotions are created for giving and receiving love . . . becoming one with the opposite sex. God designed her this way.
>
> Again, I come back to emphasize—the one who has already chosen wifehood and motherhood must give priority to adapting her life to meet her husband's and children's needs. When she has met these needs, then she can work toward other goals which do not conflict with her primary responsibility.[56]

What if the homemaker resents such self-sacrifice? In a chapter enti-tled "Overcome Housewife Resentment," she urges homemakers to face themselves and accept their role. Resentment of homemaking comes when a homemaker does not totally accept her position. As "Gloria" wrote her, "The day I accepted my job of wife and mother as a calling from the Lord, my chores turned into challenges. . . . God has shown me that to be a homemaker is one of the greatest tasks on earth."[57] In her best-seller, *Total Woman*, and in her Total Woman courses, Marabel Morgan gives essentially the same advice to un-happy homemakers: suppress your ego, your "self." "What causes most of the problems in your marriage? I find that the conflict be-tween two separate egos is usually the culprit—your viewpoint versus his viewpoint." She traces the problems of her own previously un-happy marriage to her habit of expressing her opinion about her husband's job and criticizing his ineptitude. "The Biblical remedy for marital conflict is stated, 'You wives must submit to your husbands' leadership in the same way you submit to the Lord.' . . . God origi-nally ordained marriage. He gave certain ground rules and if they are applied, a marriage will work." Being a total woman means suppress-ing self—"Self cries, 'Love me, meet my needs' "—and replacing it with love—"Love says, 'Allow me to meet your needs.' " In other words, women must return to traditional womanhood and become homemakers whose only desire is to fill the needs of others. "Behind every great man is a great woman, loving him and meeting his needs." If she has needs, she must not express them directly: "Fulfill him by giving him everything he wants, and he'll want to give back to you."[58]

History suggests that these homemakers will be unable to turn back the clock and reestablish the viability of the old ideal of woman as homemaker. Women's work selves, their public selves, have inadvertently been developed by the living out of the cult of this domesticity ideal of womanhood. Now, when judged on the basis of its rewards to self, homemaking, the subordination of self to others, is bound to appear inadequate. Yet domestic homemaking has defined womanhood and family life as we have known it. Its decline has brought into question the content of the marriage relationship and of family life—indeed, the very content of womanhood and manhood. The next two chapters will examine the pressures on the sexual division of labor in the labor force and in marriage resulting from these changes.

12

The Breakdown of the Sex-typing of Jobs

As we saw in Chapter 10, the twentieth century has been a period in which capitalist development dramatically increased the productivity of labor, and in doing so expanded commodity needs. These changes necessarily transformed the job structure. Agricultural labor was dramatically decreased, both as a percentage of total employment and in absolute numbers. Manufacturing employment has increased absolutely, but not as a percentage. The growing sector of employment has been the "service sector," which includes white-collar work in offices and in sales. Meanwhile, the labor force has grown not only with the growth of the population but also as a percentage of the population. Much of this is accounted for by the entrance of women into the labor force, which we have studied above. From 1900 to 1960, the male labor force grew by 38.2 million workers and the female labor force by 15.8 million.[1] Women increased from 18.1% of the total labor force in 1900 to 25.4% in 1940 and 32.7% in 1960.[2] This was mainly due to the entrance of married women into the labor force, as homemakers seeking extra family income or as second career women. Although women have been overrepresented among the unemployed, most of these new labor-force entrants have found jobs, bringing a tremendous increase in employment. The entrance of married women into the labor force and the movement of women's jobs out of the household sphere, which we noted in Chapter 9, have dramatically transformed the economy—from a sphere monopolized by men, in which women were simply peripheral and temporary participants, to a sphere shared by both sexes.

How have these developments affected the sex-typing of jobs? The sex-typing of jobs was both extended and attacked by these changes. As we have seen, homemakers have entered the labor force in two somewhat distinct manners: as homemakers, seeking income to fill family needs, and as career women, seeking self-expression and self-fulfillment. The first type of wage-earning homemakers offered feminine labor to their employers and accepted the sex-typing of jobs; the second type, on the other hand, has begun to seek entrance into men's jobs, challenging the sex-typing of jobs. In this chapter, we will examine these two phenomena and evaluate their consequences for the sex-typing of jobs.

Homemakers in the Labor Force as Consumers: The Extension of Feminine Jobs

As we have seen, a large percentage of the women who entered the labor force in the twentieth century were doing so in a typically feminine manner: they worked before marriage to aid their parents or future husbands, and they worked after marriage to obtain added family income to purchase needed commodities. Their goal in the labor force was to fill the needs of their families, not to advance themselves in the labor-force competition. Even those more middle-class homemakers who desired some financial independence along with a way to get outside of the home were entering the labor force in a feminine manner; their primary commitment remained with their families, and their personalities remained feminine.

The characteristics of this feminine labor were transformed, however, with the entrance of married women into the labor force; feminine labor has become more similar to masculine labor. The typical woman's life-cycle was altered—from working only until marriage; to working before marriage, before children, and after children; to leaving the labor force only when her children were very small; to virtually working through her adult life. The continuity of the typical woman's labor-force participation was dramaticaly increased. Table 12-1, which charts labor-force participation rates by age, shows the way in which "working girls" were joined by middle-aged homemakers and then by young homemakers as the century advanced. Women who worked before marriage are now returning to the labor force after marriage; some do not even leave the labor force upon marriage and childbirth. Hence, as the table shows, the average woman's lifetime pattern of labor-force participation profile is growing closer and closer to the "inverted U" of the average man.[3] Since women have increasingly

Table 12–1: Labor-force Participation Rates[a] by Age, of Women, 1900–1980, and of Men, 1980

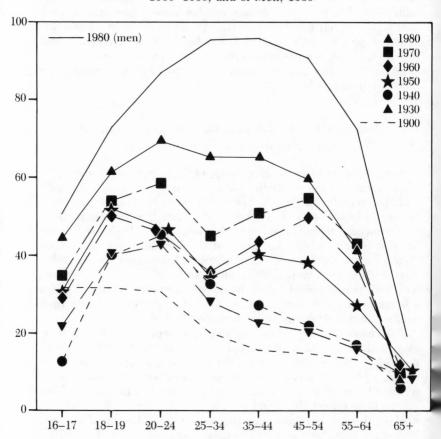

SOURCES: 1900–1940: U.S. Department of Commerce, *Statistical Abstract of the United States* (1950), p. 173, Table 208 (1900–1930 figures are as % of gainful workers), 1950–1970: U.S. Department of Labor, *Employment and Training Report of the President* (1978), p. 182, Table A–Z. 1980: U.S. Department of Labor, *Employment and Earnings* (Jan. 1981) pp. 166–7, Table 4.
a. In the civilian labor force.

expected to remain in the labor force for a major period of their lives, they have had more incentive to invest time and money into training themselves for higher paying jobs. As they have been more likely to remain in their jobs than before, superiors have been more likely to consider giving them on-the-job training and to hire them for jobs that require some regularity of employment. These developments have made women's labor more appropriate for the more skilled and on-the-job trained jobs. They may also make women more likely to unionize to fight for better job conditions, as these conditions will be with them for possibly a lifetime.

While women's labor is becoming more similar to men's, it remains distinct. Women and men are still differentiated in personalities and in motivations, in the ways we outlined in Chapter 9. Married women continue to define themselves as homemakers first; while this is less and less responsible for keeping them out of the labor force, it does reduce their labor-force commitment. For example, a higher proportion of women than men works only part time or part year. In 1980, 29.8% of married women with husband present worked part time, compared to 6% of married men, wives present: women were also more likely to work part year. As a result, the average work week of these women was 34.3 hours, compared to 42.9 hours for the men.[1]

Furthermore, these changes have not eliminated an essential reason for the sex-typing of jobs—the desires of men and women as workers to work in appropriately sex-typed jobs and the desires of customers for service from the appropriate sex. Women still have sought to maintain their femininity by undertaking women's jobs; entrance into a man's job would bring their femininity into question. Neither did these developments make men more willing to enter jobs that employed women; if anything, the attenuation of man's role as sole husband/provider has led him to attempt to more strongly assert his masculinity in the labor force by segregating himself in a masculine job and by struggling to be more successful. If women were beginning to monopolize a man's job, he would be motivated to change jobs so as to preserve his masculinity.

Married women entering the labor force as homemakers have sought feminine jobs, and, for the most part, there have been sufficient jobs to absorb them. First, although many of the former feminine jobs, such as domestic service, have declined with the advance of capitalism, the new feminine jobs, especially clerical work, have expanded. Second, the development of capitalism has continually created new unskilled and semiskilled jobs, which can be sex-typed either way. Finally, the transformation of woman's labor has qualified her for jobs that were previously inherently masculine. We will briefly examine these processes in turn.

First, there has been a decline in many of the old feminine jobs, especially those that included work in the home. Many fewer women are now employed by wealthy homemakers to perform homemaking tasks such as domestic service, home laundry work, or sewing. Homemakers, aided by labor-saving appliances, have had less need for domestics; at the same time, as women workers have gained continuity of participation and appreciation of the wage labor relationship, they have become less willing to do such servile labor. The number of female servants per one thousand families has fallen from 95.6 in 1900 to 33.3 in 1960.[5] Another type of feminine work that has declined is the taking in of boarders and lodgers. Not only has the immigrant population decreased, but also this service has been taken over by hotels and motels, drawing potential lodgers away. Furthermore, as households gained an awareness of themselves as private, family units, such boarding was less desirable. The decline of paid work in homes has meant that women in the twentieth century are not only entering the labor force in increasing percentages but are also leaving the home in greater percentages. As Table 12-2 shows, women have moved from domestic nonemployment, to domestic employment, to employment in the public labor force.[6]

The rapid, almost spectacular growth of the service sector—particularly of clerical and sales positions—has been central in the absorption of female labor. Indeed, it may have even encouraged the employment of married women, given that these growing occupations were white collar and more acceptable to middle-class women than the previous feminine jobs of domestic service or factory operatives.[7] Those entrepreneurs who sex-typed clerical work feminine at the beginning of the century had the good fortune to link this rapidly growing occupation with a fast growing part of the labor force. Between 1900 and 1960, the number of secretaries, stenographers, and typists grew by a factor of 20, absorbing over 2.1 million additional workers. All but 50,000 of these additional workers were women, changing these occupations from 77% female to over 96% female.[8] As Table 12-3 shows, by 1960 almost one of every three employed women worked in clerical jobs as opposed to one in a hundred in 1870.

Table 12–2: The Movement of Women out of the Domestic Sphere, 1900, 1960, 1980

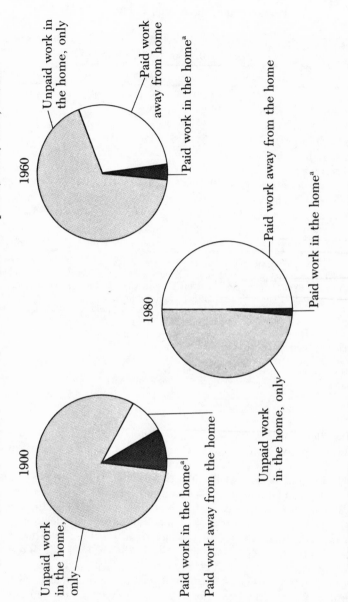

SOURCES: U.S. Department of Commerce, Bureau of the Census, *Occupational Trends in the United States 1900–1950*, pp. 22–27; idem, *Census of Population: 1960 Occupational Characteristics*, pp. 11–20; U.S. Department of Labor, Bureau of Labor Statistics, *Employment and Earnings* (Jan. 1981), pp. 163, 182.
a. This is an underestimate, for it does not include prostitutes or boarding and lodging house keepers.

Table 12–3: Percentage of Employed Women in Each Occupational Sector, 1870, 1900, 1930, 1960[a]

	1870	1900	1930	1960
Service	49.7	38.4	37.1	29.6
Private household	48.9	10.2	17.7	7.8
Personal service (excluding private household)	.81	28.2	19.4[b]	21.7[c]
Clerical/kindred	1.3[d]	8.6[d]	20.8	29.3
Crafts and Manufacture	19.4	25.4	18.9	19.3
Professional/Technical	5.6	11.2	14.2	12.8
Agriculture	21.6	15.9	8.4	3.7
⟨ Managerial/Official	.03	.2	.4	1.7
Totals[e]	97.6	99.7	99.8	96.4

SOURCES: U.S. Department of Commerce, Bureau of the Census, *Census of Population: 1870, Population and Social Statistics*, Table XXIX (persons 10 years and older); idem, *Special Reports: Occupations at the Twelfth Census*, Table 1 (persons 10 years and older); idem, *Census of Population: 1930, Occupations; by States*, Table 3 (for persons 10 years and older); idem, *Census of Population: 1960, Occupational Characteristics*, Table 21 (for persons 14 years and older).
a. Number of women employed in sector divided by total number of women employed.
b. Includes 7.85% salesworkers.
c. Includes 6.7% salesworkers.
d. Salesworkers are included as clerical in this year.
e. Errors due to rounding and occupations unreported.

Unskilled and semiskilled jobs do not by their content alone exclude either sex. In its history, capitalism has constantly transformed and rationalized the production process by breaking skilled labor up into steps and then replacing it with unskilled labor and machines—first in agriculture and manufacture, and recently in the service sector. In this process, it has turned masculine jobs into jobs that can be typed either way. Historically, when capitalism has destroyed the skilled crafts, masculine work, it had replaced them with unskilled work, and often typed it feminine. Furthermore, unskilled and semiskilled jobs can easily change their sex-typing according to relative supplies of the sexes; in Chapter 9 we noted regional and factory differences in the sex-typing of such jobs. Between 1900 and 1960, 3 million additional women were absorbed into such jobs.[9]

Finally, some jobs which had excluded women due to their expected lack of continuous work experience, and hence were previously typed masculine, were now within women's reach. The increasing longevity and stability of the average woman's labor-force experience made feminine labor more suitable for jobs that required formal or on-the-job training. Furthermore, not only has the general level of the education of women increased, but also women from the more educated middle class are more likely to spend a major part of their lives in the labor force. These factors have combined to increase the potential scope of feminine jobs. Women workers are now qualified for many skilled jobs in capitalism which previously would have had to be typed masculine. Their abilities are being discovered by employers, sometimes during the stress of war, which pulls women into men's jobs. Thus women have been hired for previously masculine jobs and are "taking over" some of them. In the financial world, women are becoming bank tellers; in the insurance industry, women are becoming insurance agents. The result has not been, however, the elimination of sex-typing in these jobs, but rather, the changing of these jobs from men's work to women's work.

Therefore, homemakers entering the labor force as homemakers have entered into feminine jobs—formerly masculine jobs, and also newly created jobs. Many of the new feminine jobs require more education or job commitment than previous feminine jobs, for these are now common among women workers. Thus, the job structure has developed in such a way as to be able to absorb the increased numbers of women entering the labor force within feminine jobs. Table 12-3 shows the changing distribution of women workers between occupational sectors.

The Entrance of Career Women into Masculine Jobs

While homemakers entering the labor force seeking extra family income did not challenge the sex-typing of jobs, the career girl and the second-career woman have not so easily accepted the sex-typing of jobs. Indeed, they have set in motion the attenuation and open questioning of the sex-typing of jobs. We have seen how, from the onset of women's higher education, women began to claim their need for and right to the practice of "careers," either temporarily or as lifetime alternatives to homemaking. These women, following in

the footsteps of the active social homemakers of the nineteenth century, entered largely into careers which their foremothers had
claimed or constructed as inherently feminine: elementary and high
school teaching, nursing, social work, librarianship, and teaching in
women's colleges. Their segregation in feminine careers made their
professional employment more palatable for them and for society at
large; indeed, women argued, as we have seen, that teaching and
nursing were inherently women's careers due to their resemblance
to homemaking.

Although many career women entered into women's professions,
other such women challenged the masculine typing of many jobs,
particularly of the professions. Women's attacks on the masculinity of
the professions took place in two waves. First, as an outgrowth of the
social homemaking and women's education movements, and then as
part of the dual-career family and the second feminist movement.

To begin, let us again examine those factors that have discouraged
even the attempt to enter into an occupation, once it has been sex-
typed the work of the opposite sex. One is the stigma against doing
the work of the opposite sex. This is quite strong, for doing the work
of the opposite sex, without extenuating circumstances such as being
the widow of a former entrepreneur, proves one to be deviant, odd,
not part of one's biological sex. Another is the belief that the source of
the sex-typing of jobs is natural differences between the sexes, which
make males unable or less able to perform women's jobs, and females
unable or less able to perform men's jobs. Accepting these ideas, a
woman would not believe herself capable of adequately performing a
man's job.

Nineteenth-century women were led to challenge both these prem-
ises. Individual women, acting as social homemakers, challenged the
masculinity of male-dominated professions. Some claimed that these
professions were properly an extension of homemaking and hence
women's work, freeing themselves from the stigma of doing men's
work. For example, Elizabeth Blackwell "believed that women, because of their role as mothers, could play a special part in improving
human health and welfare."[10] She fought, successfully, to become one
of the first women medical doctors. While social homemaking led
women to attempt entrance into some of the masculine professions,
the entrance of women into higher education, especially college and
coeducation, challenged another basis of their sex-typing—the supposed natural superiority of men for such work due to women's lim-

ited mental capacities. The higher education of women began to attenuate the eighteenth-century belief that women had smaller and hence less capable brains, as well as the nineteenth-century derivative that mental activity was harmful to females. The entrance of women into colleges and their education alongside men began to prove the sexes to be equally capable of intellectual activity. At the same time, intellectual training was the necessary prerequisite for entrance into many men's jobs, particularly the professions. It was unavoidable that some college trained women would, once their minds were developed, choose to pursue courses of study that were not traditionally feminine, particularly once they had begun to believe in their abilities. In the nineteenth century, Maria Mitchell became a well-known scientist, and Victoria Woodhull, a stockbroker. Women fought to gain admittance to the American Bar Association, and, by the early twentieth century, had succeeded. It was difficult for professional schools and employers which had standardized educational requirements automatically to reject a qualified student, even if she were a woman. By the end of the first half of the twentieth century, educated women had broken down most of the formal rules barring their education for or employment in men's professions.[11]

So a small number of exceptional women fought for and gained entrance into the masculine professions in the nineteenth and early twentieth centuries on the basis of their educational qualifications, their social homemaking callings, or both. But their lives were extremely difficult. First, women who had overcome their own inhibitions and had trained for men's jobs had difficulty finding employment. Employers, colleagues, and potential customers, believing in the natural basis of the sex-typing of jobs, considered them inherently unqualified. Male co-workers adamantly opposed hiring women for it placed their masculinity in jeopardy. Faced with such opposition, women without special connections or extraordinary abilities and confidence in them found entering men's professions virtually impossible. Ruth Weyand, who attempted to be a lawyer in the 1930s, found that family connections were necessary to the starting up of a practice: "There was no woman lawyer in any firm in Chicago at that time who had not come in as a wife, daughter, sister, or niece of a partner, as far as I could discover." She did not give up, however:

I canvassed all the lawyers in Chicago building by building, but they told me that their clients would not accept me, their wives would be jealous.

There were firms in Chicago in those days [the New Deal years] where even secretaries were all male and all the secretaries, both male and female, would walk out rather than take a dictation from a female lawyer. . . .

In desperation I finally went to Dean Bigelow [her dean at the University of Chicago Law School] and asked him to change all my records to R. Weyand and omit all items that would show my sex. I was going to move to another state and masquerade as a man in order to practice law. . . . I had a female relative on my father's side of the family who practiced medicine in the early 1800's by masquerading all her adult life as a man. Dean Bigelow made a few comments about my figure, my hands—I wouldn't get away with it. I insisted I would smoke a big black cigar and blow the smoke around so no one would ever get a good look at my hands or figure.

Her threat worked: within three weeks she had received offers from three top law firms. It took her thirty-five years of pushing, however, to achieve her original career goal—to be a lawyer on the staff of a union.[12]

If a woman did successfully enter a man's job, she faced stigmatization by her family, friends, and society at large. A woman in a man's occupation was seen as unnatural, her femaleness/femininity—equated in people's minds—questioned. Given that these women, like other early career women, took up their careers as alternatives to family and homemaking and remained unmarried, they proved themselves furthermore to be odd women. Rather than being admired as successful and important members of their sex and of society, they were often dismissed as failed homemakers, as women driven to work because they had been unable to "catch a husband," or as women whose biologies were somehow defective. The career woman who chose a woman's profession was ostracized, but not as much, for this choice expressed and maintained her femininity.

In spite of all of this discouragement, women made considerable inroads into most of the college-prepared masculine jobs during the first half of the twentieth century (see Table 12-4). All but five of the thirty-three masculine jobs in professions, management, and sales experienced an increase in the percentage of women workers between 1900 and 1960. Women's efforts were aided by the two World Wars, during which women were actively recruited for many men's jobs and encouraged to discard their stereotypes and stigmas. Although the policy at the close of the wars was to return these jobs to their previous

Table 12–4: Entrance of Women into Selected Masculine Jobs, 1900, 1960, 1980[a]

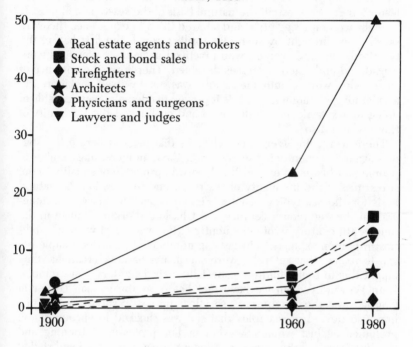

SOURCES: 1900: U.S. Department of Commerce, Bureau of the Census, *Occupational Trends in the United States 1900 to 1950*. Working Paper No. 5, (1958), Table 6b. 1960: Idem, *Census of the Population 1960. Subject Reports: Occupational Characteristics*. Final Report Pc (2)–7A (1964), Table 21. 1980: U.S. Department of Labor, *Employment and Earnings*, Jan. 1981, pp. 180–81.
a. The number in the occupation who are women divided by the total number in the occupation.

male inhabitants, the experience brought important changes. It showed women as well as employers that women could do such work, leading them to question the natural basis of the sex-typing of jobs. It brought women recognition and allowed them to experience the extra satisfactions brought by such jobs. Still, through the first half of the twentieth century, women who practiced in men's professions were considered odd, their successes devalued. Therefore, the entrance of such "odd" women into men's jobs was not by itself an inherently accelerating phenomenon; while it proved that females were capable of doing men's work, it also devalued and challenged the femininity of those who did so.

There were, however, other changes that began to erase the stigmas against women doing men's work. First, an increasing number of people had begun to extend the American principle of equality to the sexes, to see the inequality of sex roles, and to question the natural basis for the sex-typing of jobs. Feminists such as Mary Wollstonecraft in the eighteenth century and Charlotte Perkins Gilman in the nineteenth century wrote eloquently of the wasting of women's abilities in homemaking.[13] As increasing numbers of educated people began to realize that sex roles were social, not natural, creations, they taught this to their children, especially their daughters. For example, Ruth Weyand, whom we have met before as the woman lawyer in Chicago, was the daughter of a sociology professor; she was raised in a home so devoid of sex roles that she was shocked to encounter the prejudice against women lawyers in her professional training and practice. Many of the women's colleges were administered and staffed by women, teaching their students of women's capabilities. Since the sexual division of labor and the sex-typing of jobs were based on the unquestioning acceptance of the social differentiation of the sexes as either natural or God-given, they could be easily challenged by an understanding of their social origins, their injustice, or simply by knowledge of the ability of females to do men's work. In this way, education both motivated women to pursue careers in the labor force and provided them with a rationale for doing so.

The entrance of educated women into masculine jobs was further encouraged by another trend—the choice of increasing numbers of educated women to try to combine homemaking with a second, labor-force, career. This development contributed to the entrance of women into masculine jobs in two related ways. First, the more that a woman's labor-force career was followed *in addition to* the career of homemaking, the less need she had to affirm or prove her femininity by entering into one of the "women's professions." Her existence as a homemaker itself proved her femininity, for it showed her capable of performing the ultimate and exclusively feminine work, homemaking. Thus it inadvertently freed her from social stigma thrown at the unmarried woman who worked at a man's career. Second, the very fact that increasing numbers of women were entering careers in combination with homemaking—either before, during, or after homemaking—made them less committed to doing specifically feminine vocational work. Their primary motive for entering the labor force was not to serve others but to find self-fulfillment. Indeed, given the frustrations of vocational homemaking, many women sought something different, the opportunity to help themselves rather than to serve others. Given that they had done their essential womanly duty, many home-makers experienced no guilt at acting totally out of their own needs for self-development, power, recognition, wealth. This new stance toward a career, as something a privileged woman does for herself, has been passed from the second-career women to their daughters, who plan career and family simultaneously. Women college graduates now seek out the most lucrative careers, whereas a century ago their counterparts agonized over which vocations would best allow them to serve humanity.

The entrance of women into masculine careers and the rise of the second-career woman have reinforced each other, for the more interesting a woman's employment opportunities in the labor force were, the more her job could vie with homemaking for her interest. The option of pursuing a career in one of the limited number of women's professions was less attractive to the woman seeking self-expression and recognition than the possibility of pursuing any one of the elite of men's jobs. Furthermore, these men's professions were much more lucrative than the traditional women's professions. The addition of the second-career woman to the single-career "girl" also made the latter less stigmatized. One could no longer assume that a woman undertaking a man's job was unmarried, a non-homemaker; neither could one assume that the single career woman was a special breed, inherently different from all other women.

In the process of the twentieth century, then, increasing numbers of women have attempted to and succeeded in entering into the elite of men's jobs. Although these jobs remain, today, for the most part, dominated by men, the percentage of women in many of them has been rapidly increasing from insignificant amounts to a substantial portion of those employed. Between 1960 and 1980, women's representation increased significantly in all of the elite masculine occupations (see Table 12-4).[14]

The penetration of women into men's jobs in the twentieth century has been uneven, as would be expected. In some professions, women have taken over the more feminine subfields—family practice in medicine, family and divorce law, residential rather than industrial property in real estate. In others, women remain clustered in the lower ranks—middle rather than top management, lecturers and assistant professors, rather than full professors and Presidential advisors.[15] The sex-typing of jobs is simply reconstituting itself differently; masculine jobs are being splintered into masculine and feminine jobs. When we recall that the overwhelming majority of all such positions were monopolized by men at the beginning of the century, this fact represents a clear and steady progression of women into men's jobs. However, the redivision of masculine jobs expresses the strength of the sex-typing of jobs.

Thus larger and larger numbers of college educated women are seeking entrance into men's jobs. This opening up of their sights, which means ignoring the traditional stigma against women doing men's work, is itself a very significant phenomenon. Furthermore, the entrance of second-career women into masculine jobs has begun to erode the stigma against women doing men's work. Given the superior status and pay of men's work, it has become increasingly acceptable that women in the labor force seek to enter into men's jobs. This questioning of the sex-typing of jobs has been extended from the minority of privileged career women to all homemakers in the labor force. Married women entering the labor force to earn extra income for their families have begun to try to enter into the more lucrative, masculine jobs. In particular, they are qualified to enter many of the unskilled unionized jobs monopolized by men. Some have even attempted to gain entrance into the crafts, although progress there has been slow, given restrictive apprenticeship programs and the overt resistance of craft unions to bringing in women. (At the moment, it is unclear whether women are making net progress in the crafts. For example, between 1960 and 1979, while women's representation more than doubled in seven of the twenty-nine crafts listed in *Employment and Earnings*, it fell by more than half in six of them.[16]) While some progress is being made, those who choose "non-

traditional jobs" are still in a minority. The Parnes study of the occupational choices of women found that in 1968, 14% of the white and
10% of the black non-college women chose masculine occupations; in
1973, these figures had risen to 19% of the white and 13% of the
black non-college women.[17] When young college women were asked,
slightly more chose masculine jobs: 22% of blacks and 25% of whites
mentioned masculine jobs. However, those who listed men's jobs
limited their choices to a small number of such jobs.[18]

The choice of increasing percentages of working women to prepare
for and enter into men's jobs is not identical with their success in this
area, for these women are inadvertently confronting full force the
logic of the sex-typing of jobs.

Sex Discrimination and Sexual Harassment: The Trials of Women in Men's Jobs

Women who have sought entrance into men's jobs have, as their
foremothers had, faced hostility from employers and fellow employees, disbelief from customers, difficulty on the job, and conflicts at
home. All the reasons militating for the sex-typing of jobs work
against the woman seeking to succeed at an inherently masculine job,
and have hence confronted these new career women. At the same
time, as these women grow in numbers and become less defensive
about their femininity, they have attacked these impediments as discriminatory and unfair.[19]

We need only review our discussions of the sex-typing of jobs to
discover the problems faced by such women, which are now much
discussed in the literature. First, a woman is confronted with external
discrimination. Central is the fact that, given that society believes
that the sex-typing of jobs has a natural origin, employers, co-
workers, and customers will think that because she is a woman, this
worker will be unable to perform a man's job. They have all of history
to substantiate their claim: if women are capable of being presidents
of corporations, why have they never done so? The belief that
women, as females, are biologically incapable of doing a man's job
prevents employers from seeing her actual qualifications and hiring
her or from acknowledging her successful performance in such a job.
They "won't believe their eyes." This acceptance of the natural basis

of the sex-typing of jobs makes it difficult for a woman even to be hired for a man's job, regardless of her qualifications.

Men employees are also likely to block the hiring of a woman for their jobs. Why? Men find working with a woman in the same job to be demeaning and threatening to them, to say nothing of the insult involved if they must work with her as a superior. First, a woman's ability to perform a man's job devalues it in his eyes. Second, it is not manly for a man to compete with a woman, only to compete with men. Finally, if a man engages in on-the-job competition with a woman, he may actually be "beaten" by her, she may be proven his superior, an occurrence which would destroy many a man's sense of self. How can men employees block the hiring of women? They can directly pressure their employers with threats or complaints; strong unions, especially the craft unions, have been quite successful at this. If a woman is hired into a masculine job, her men co-workers can sabotage her work to prove her incompetent and get her fired, or make her work life so difficult that she voluntarily quits. Studies of the experiences of women in men's jobs are replete with stories of such opposition by men co-workers. If a woman succeeds in securing a supervisory or managerial job which gives her power over men, the men placed in such an emasculating position will be even more difficult to handle.[20] In white-collar jobs, men exclude women from their informal communication channels through which employees inform and advise each other, plot strategies for advancement, and even do business.[21] Men can sexually harass women and make them so uncomfortable that they quit. In blue-collar jobs, women report being openly harassed by male co-workers and giving help to male co-workers which is not reciprocated. Yet the only way they find to survive such opposition is to work hard, demonstrate determination, and "maintain a friendly and cooperative attitude despite taunts and harassments;" they have to grin and bear it, take their punishment, and show that it will not dissuade them from their purpose.

Even if her men co-workers do not consciously resist her employment in a masculine job, they will find interacting with her on the job difficult, making her work life difficult. How is a man supposed to act in such a situation? It is hard for him to ignore her sex, her femininity, yet if he treats her as feminine, he discriminates against her, acts differently toward her than toward his male co-workers. Since such women are still very much in the minority, their femininity comes even more to the fore. Yet a man's way of acting toward women—

flirting, fathering, or seeking mothering—fits poorly into the structure of these jobs. Rosabeth Moss Kantor noted four roles in which token women can be placed by their colleagues. "Mother," "seductress," and "pet" are roles which play off of her femininity. A woman's sex can not be ignored when it is the characteristic which differentiates her from the group; if she refuses to respond to sexual innuendo, she is viewed as the "iron maiden," seen as more militant than she really is, and denied help or support on this basis.[22] Whichever role she takes, a woman is prevented from participating equally with the men.

Women in masculine jobs have to walk a very fine line, as evidenced by the following quotes from their fellow employees: "I think she probably knows the job very well, but she doesn't act like it. She spent too many years as a secretary, and she still acts like a secretary. She seems to find it hard to assume behavior that is appropriate to her new staff role." But if she acts too competent: "Sometimes she comes on too strong, and this irritates the men. I don't think they would think anything about it if a man acted the same way, but when a girl does, they see it as smartass behavior and you can just see them bristle."[23] Women in masculine jobs have to combine masculine and feminine qualities to be accepted. The same study of women in white-collar men's jobs found that, to succeed, they had to "strike a balance between being assertive to command respect and yet not overly aggressive to be accepted. This adds up to 'good leadership' and is a combination of feminine and masculine qualities." One male worker described such a successful female co-worker in the following manner: "She really knows her stuff, but she's not a 'know it all.' The fellas would really resent a smarty girl in the group."[24]

A second major on-the-job problem for women attempting professional or service jobs has been the sex-typed ideas of their customers. If customers treat women in men's jobs as women, such sexual "discrimination"—that is, noting the person's sex—can impede her success. First, many customers will not believe that a woman doctor or lawyer is capable and will simply not engage her services (although the flip side occasionally occurs, and customers, aware of the social opposition put forward to the entrance of women into these jobs, believe that this women must be super-qualified). In addition, even if customers believe that women are not genetically disqualified for such work, many may simply feel uncomfortable relating with a woman in such an untraditional manner. Although customers or clients are comfortable with women workers who perform mothering-type services, they are not used to relating to women in positions of authority; men, in particular, are not used to taking orders from women. Studies abound to confirm the existence of such prejudice. For example, of the lawyers responding to a 1973 questionnaire for the American Bar Association, 90% of the men and 72% of the women said that clients discriminated by refusing to accept the services of female lawyers.[25] Furthermore, since not only professionals but also firms selling services to other firms, such as marketing firms, deal directly with customers, such attitudes are a major impediment to women trying to work in men's jobs. Potential discrimination by customers or clients gives employers a reason to discriminate against women in hiring for masculine jobs other than the simple belief that, as a female, she can not be qualified.

The above-mentioned obstacles face all women entering all men's jobs, regardless of their qualifications; they make success at a masculine job much more difficult for a woman to achieve than for a man. Only singularly motivated individuals are able to survive such opposition; yet most women seeking careers are themselves uncertain about their ability to do such jobs as well as in their commitment to succeeding in them. Hence many give up along the way, unable or unwilling to fight for and win acceptance in a masculine job. Their failure is cited as proof of women's inherent inability to do masculine jobs. However, the more women successfully break into masculine jobs and attenuate their sex-typing, the easier it becomes for their successors.

Further difficulties are faced by women who try for the most prestigious masculine jobs. These jobs involve women in a competition for self-advancement which is inherently masculine. Essential to performance in these jobs is masculine self-seeking, the search to better other men and to achieve recognition for it. Women are not prepared for this activity. They have grown up feminine and possess feminine personalities and motivation. Given their training, they are not equipped with the necessary informal training for masculine jobs. Furthermore, their training actually ill-equips them for such jobs. Whereas men are trained at competition and self-advancement from their early years by parents, sports coaches, and teachers, women are brought up to follow an opposite principle—to fill the needs of others, to repress their needs, to act dumb and self-effacing. Women are not brought up as competitors, they do not know the rules of competing, they do not know that competing is expected from those in masculine jobs. They do not know when they have been insulted and must defend their pride. They do not know how to be part of a "team" and still take credit for their own initiatives.[26]

Rather than entering into the competition as an equal, women relating to men within a job hierarchy are likely to try to interact with them in the typically feminine manner—not competing with them, but serving them. The feminine way of getting what one wants from a man is not to ask for it directly or demand it but rather to manipulate the man into providing what is wanted. Overtly expressing one's will is unfeminine. One kind of manipulation is flirting with or offering sexual favors to a man—pleasing him in hopes that he will reward her with a promotion. Sexual harassment has always been a part of the job structure. Men are given power over women, and they use this power to extract sex. However, the new desire of women for advancement within the masculine job hierarchies has led some of them to initiate such sexual bargaining, making sexual harassment into mutual exploitation, rather than simply the exploitation of women.[27] While such overtures to the men in power may and do indeed procure advancement for some women, such strategies are not only risky but also limited. Not only is there no guarantee of advancement, the woman's position is rendered dependent upon the whims of one particular man (or a series of them); she can be dismissed at any time with no good recourse; her advancement is circumscribed to areas within his control. And most important, her advancement does not represent her work achievements; she has reduced herself to a sexual being and earns resentment rather than respect from her colleagues, whether or not she was indeed qualified for the promotion. Indeed, if a woman is emotionally involved with her superior, the company will assume that she has earned her position on the basis of this involvement and deny her accomplishments. The recent resignation of Mary Cunningham from Bendix illustrates the subtle way in which a personal relationship with her superior can work against a qualified woman. Although all evidence indicates that she was qualified for her promotion, her friendship with her superior and the sexual innuendos surrounding it vitiated her achievements. Her superior's attempt to quell rumors—by announcing to the employees that their relationship was only a friendship—only fanned suspicions and employee resentment. The situation became untenable and she resigned.[28]

While some women mistakenly seek advancement through feminine behavior, others simply do not try to get to the top. Hennig and Jardim compare the typical woman and man in middle management, contemplating the move upward from supervisory responsibilities to broader, cross-departmental ones:

> Her great fear is to be cut off from what she knows, from the comforting familiarity of an area she has mastered in depth . . . only to confront new and quite different problems, new and quite different people, in a setting where she may now be the *only* woman. . . . His great fear is that he may be entering a backwater, cut off from the people who helped him. Can he put a team together? . . . Will his new boss be a man from whom he can learn—who has influence enough to help him advance?[29]

A 1978 study of a Fortune 500 Company sued for sex discrimination in promotion found that women were underrepresented in promotions because they had not exhibited "promotion-seeking behavior." Women were half as likely as men to request promotions; and while the same percentage of women and men were asked whether they were interested in promotion, only 43% of the women thus asked expressed interest as compared to 74% of the men.[30] Why? Moving up the ladder of masculine jobs requires acting like a man—subordinating one's life to one's job in a furious competition for self-advancement. Yet few woman enter such jobs with masculine motivations, with a desire to become men—to dedicate their lives to their jobs and to prove themselves through competition with men. Women have been led to enter masculine jobs by their developing desire for self-expression and recognition. They find much more and much less in masculine jobs: the opportunity to attain power and prestige, and the necessity of giving up other primary life commitments. And for women, the latter has a very different meaning than for a man. For a man, marriage and family life mean acquiring the aid of a homemaker in his struggle for success. For a woman, marriage and family have meant being a homemaker, subordinated to the needs of one's family—something which comes into direct conflict with the demands of a competitive job.

A woman seeking to combine homemaking with a competitive masculine job faces multiple conflicts. First, in order to compete successfully with men she must, as they do, place her job and its demands first; she must structure her family life around her job. This conflicts directly with the career of homemaking, which demands that the woman structure her life around the particular and changing needs of her family. Furthermore, homemaking requires a feminine personality from the woman, while her job requires masculinity. The attempt of a woman to combine an inherently masculine job with homemaking puts extreme pressure on her, and on both of her jobs. This conflict intensifies if her husband also works at one of the competitive men's jobs, and hence needs more direct assistance from her; yet the chances of this are great, given than few men would be willing to marry a woman positioned higher than them in the job hierarchy. A woman can resolve the conflict most simply by giving up one of her two conflicting careers—divorcing and giving up her children, or quitting her job. Or she can work to change either or both of these careers, so as to make them more compatible. She can settle for less advancement in her job, or work to get more flexibility in hours or location—certainly not an easy task, when the men competing with her are willing to commit their energies totally, along with the aid of their wives, to their jobs. She can try to change the sexual division of labor in her marriage and family, getting her husband and children to share the homemaking responsibilities, but this threatens not only his masculinity but also his own job, if it is a masculine job. Or she can do as many of her predecessors have done—not get married. All of these options are less than optimal; women are bound to feel ambivalent about whatever choice they make. This ambivalence is bound, in turn, to adversely affect women's performance on the job, giving employers yet another reason to discriminate against them.

So we see that the career woman who naively attempts to choose a man's job for her second career faces immense opposition, both from her potential colleagues on the job, from her husband or future husband, and from within her own self. Even if she has obtained and excelled in her professional training for the job, she is likely to fail at it. Little wonder that the world of masculine jobs seems to be mounting a conspiracy against the entrance of women, and that women faced with such opposition have begun to complain about discriminatory treatment.

The combination of discrimination by co-workers and customers with the problems posed by her feminine upbringing and goals make a woman indeed a bad risk for an employer, even if he (or she) does not believe that women are inherently disqualified for men's work by their female biologies. "Statistical discrimination" ensues: individual women are assumed to behave as the average woman and have problems in masculine jobs, and hence are discriminated against by employers.[31] Yet such de facto exclusion of the individual woman from men's jobs denies her the basic American "right" of equal opportunity. When women have begun to complain about the treatment they have received when applying for or working in men's jobs—and remember, many of these women are from the upper class and are used to having what they want—they have received sympathetic hearings. To those who reduce the sexual difference to a natural difference, the exclusion of a qualified woman from a man's job appears as overt and unfair discrimination. It seems unfair to assume that a woman will be more likely to give up her job, to be unsuccessful with customers, to not get along with fellow workers—if she indeed exhibits all of the formal requirements for the job. Hence, organized woman have succeeded in gaining political support for antidiscrimination legislation, and even for the principle that women should be equally represented in all jobs. The efforts of individual women to enter into masculine jobs have been transformed into a political struggle for sexual equality. We will discuss this movement in the conclusion.

13

The Breakdown of the Sexual Division of Labor in Marriage

The entrance of married women into the labor force is transforming the average family from a one-earner to a two-earner family. In March 1979, both husband and wife were in the labor force in over half of the husband–wife families (50.9%), while only 33.1% of families followed the traditional pattern of husband in the labor force, wife out of the labor force (see Table 13–1). The two-earner marriage has become the predominant form for both white and black marriages, comprising 50% of the former and 57% of the latter.[1] Those couples who choose to maintain the husband/provider, wife/homemaker roles can continue living out the traditional sexual division and can live out perfectly complementary marriages, although not without problems and pressures. As we discussed in Chapter 11, wives who remain in the domestic sphere can find homemaking a frustrating career, made more frustrating by comparison with "superwomen" who combine wage-earning and homemaking, and with the increased standards of living such families enjoy. Yet they are supported by tradition and religion and are able to avoid a different set of conflicts which, as we will see, arise from living as a two-earner family. Indeed, their claim to being the "correct" family form has been strengthened by the problems faced by the two-earner family.

The entrance of homemakers into the labor force, although an expression of womanhood, transforms the sexual division of labor in marriage. Although such women are not rejecting homemaking, they are extending it to include the provision of income to the family. This has immediate effects upon their husbands and their marriages.

Having a wage-earning wife attacks the masculinity of a man. Under the cult of domesticity, the husband's success as a man was expressed by the presence of his wife in his home, that is, her ab-

301

Table 13–1: Husband–Wife Families by Labor-force Status of Family
Members, March 1979

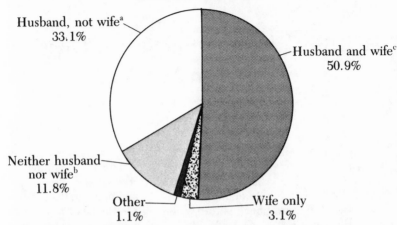

Husband, not wife[a]
33.1%

Husband and wife[c]
50.9%

Neither husband
nor wife[b]
11.8%

Other
1.1%

Wife only
3.1%

Source: U.S. Bureau of Labor Statistics, *Marital and Family Characteristics of the
Labor Force,* Special Labor Force Report 237 (Jan. 1981), p. 49.
a. This includes husband only and husband and other (not wife).
b. This includes no earners and other relative only.
c. May also include sons, daughters, or other family members.

sence from the labor force. Men who were unable to attain high
levels of earnings and status in the labor force based their claims to
masculinity on their ability to financially support their wives. When
working-class homemakers began to enter into the labor force to fill
family needs for commodities, they branded their husbands as less-
than-adequate husband/providers, as less manly. Although the
entrance of middle- and upper-class wives into the labor force for
self-expression has erased this stigma, a basic transformation has nevertheless occurred. Wives are sharing a position in the family which
the husband previously monopolized. The husband is no longer the
sole family provider; he is likely to feel defensive about his position as
head of the family, anxious to maintain his authority. His wife needs
his income-providing less than before—she needs him less. Furthermore, her active presence in the labor force, more and more a lifetime affair, puts her in the labor-force competition against him. The
possibility that she may earn more than her husband and be more

successful in the labor force than he, is a real one—and this is a threat to his masculinity.[2] With both of them in the labor force, it is no longer obvious to the outside world who is "wearing the pants in the family." Furthermore, their relationship's primacy is threatened; she has to serve other men, in the labor force, sometimes literally, as in secretarial or waitress jobs.[3] In these ways, the husband's masculinity is attacked by his wife's labor-force participation; as a result, husbands seem to be, on the average, significantly less happy the more their wives participate in the labor force.[4] The attenuation of the husband's masculinity is the other side of the attenuation of his wife's femininity. Although the homemaker enters into the labor force as a woman—either for the income to fill family needs or to express her womanly "self"—her femininity is lessened by this action. In particular, she is no longer so differentiated from her husband; she is no longer as dependent, no longer so helpless in the world of work. She is in the position of income provider, not just need filler.

The decreased differentiation between husband and wife brings decreased dependence, and more insecurity for the couple. The traditional sexual division of labor in marriage, by placing the wife in the home and the husband in the labor force, made the wife dependent upon her husband's earnings for her survival, and made the husband dependent upon his wife's homemaking for his. The wage-earning wife is less financially dependent upon her husband, and therefore he feels less responsible for her. Since they need each other less, each is likely to feel less sure of their marriage, or less bound to it.

The entry of the wife into the labor force destabilizes the sexual division of labor in marriage. One response to such unbalancing of the marriage has been to avoid the problem—to keep the homemaker out of the labor force, or take her out once these effects are felt—and maintain the old division of labor; about one-third of families now follow this path. However, at least half of the couples have chosen to be two-earner families and have hence transformed the sexual division of labor in their marriages. Families can respond to the resultant destabilization of the sexual division of labor in marriage in one of two ways: they can reassert the traditional sexual differences as much as possible, or they can follow the movement toward more similarity between the sexes.[5] If the husband and wife move in opposite ways, tension is produced, and separation or divorce can result. We will examine these alternatives in turn.

Reasserting the Sexual Division of Labor

One response of a couple to wage-earning by the wife is to work to reaffirm the differentiation of their positions as much as possible. This is the logical response of most men and women today, who automatically and uncritically accept society's conceptions of man and woman. However, some are especially likely to seek out and maintain a traditionally sex-divided two-earner family (or, indeed, a traditional family, without the wife in the labor force). Among men, those at the top and at the bottom of the job hierarchy are likely to want to maintain traditional marriage arrangements. Those at the top, in the competitive masculine jobs, actually need a dedicated wife's help to succeed in their jobs (corporations, in fact, often interview the wife of their potential executives before deciding on hiring). They will prefer a homebound wife, or a wage-earning wife whose job is clearly secondary to homemaking and her husband. Men at the bottom of the hierarchy are likely to seek a traditional wife for a different reason: their jobs do not demand her aid and dedication, but their relative lack of success in the labor force weakens their claim on masculinity and makes them more likely to want to be the "king" of their home. What kind of women are likely to agree to this pattern of work? Two, not necessarily mutually exclusive groups: women who enjoy mothering and homemaking and are unwilling to give it up; and women who lack interest in or preparation for those jobs which conflict with homemaking. Some women, however, may desire both to hold onto mothering and homemaking, and to have demanding careers in the labor force: they want to have two primary commitments; they plan on being "superwoman."

Such men and women find marriage partners and plan out marriage so as to maintain their sexual differentiation (or if they are choosing in midlife to send the homemaker into the labor force, they do so planning to maintain the same division of responsibilities at home). In these marriages, the husband will continue on, as before, dedicating his life to advancement on the job, expecting service and support at home. He may do less housework, to reassure himself and the outside world that he is a man—or if he is relatively secure, he may "help" his wife with the housework or child care when he wishes to. The wife will remain a homemaker, responsible for caring for their children and filling her husband's needs.

However, now the wife's living out of homemaking must change, for she has added a paid job to her unpaid housework. This added time commitment forces her to restructure her life and her homemaking, reducing both her leisure time and her time spent on housework. Although she is constrained by the responses she receives from her family, how she transforms homemaking will be largely up to her, for homemaking remains her turf, her vocation, her responsibility. A woman can reduce domestic homemaking's claims on her time in different ways. She may try to limit the size of her family in order to reduce her homemaking responsibilities. Unless she works the night shift, she will need to find others who can supervise her children (or leave them alone)—relatives, paid babysitters, or day-care centers. She can reduce her housework by reducing her standards, by hiring a domestic servant, and/or by buying labor-saving commodities and services—restaurants or precooked meals, clothes cleaning and mending services, dish washers, permanent-press shirts. Many women were drawn into the labor force to earn income to purchase commodities to fill new family needs—but their very entrance into the labor force further accelerates this trend. Now not only the husband's life, but also a large portion of that of the homemaker is being dedicated to the struggle to attain more and better commodities.

Looking at the transformation of homemaking only in terms of time, however, is insufficient. The homemaker's personality and her relationship to her homemaking work are changed by having a job. Although one might suppose that a wage-earning homemaker would substitute commodities for her own home time when possible, she may, if she feels guilty about abandoning her family, insist instead on performing tasks whose time-intensiveness will signal her commitment to her family. Her sense of importance on her job may reduce her need to feel needed by her family; she may cultivate in them, particularly in her children, more independence, more participation in their own care or amusement. Presuming that she sought a job out of frustrations with homebound homemaking—either her inability to purchase needed commodities or her lack of fulfillment in the home—taking on a job may make her a happier and less neurotic homemaker. The response of a homemaker to undertaking a job will vary widely, then, according to her personality, her job, and her husband. All that is certain is that the time she spends in domestic homemaking must decrease, that the content of her homemaking is bound to change, and that her homemaking will remain a private activity determined by her particular conception of the requisites of family life, by her own need to constitute her femininity, and by her husband's need to assert his masculinity.

The other side of this woman's life, her job, is clearly affected by her maintenance of her homemaking priority. She must put home-making first, job second. Traditionally feminine jobs are most suited to her, for they allow her to maintain a low job commitment. A homemaker can also restrict her labor-force participation to part-time or part-year. In 1974, only 42.6% of employed married woman worked full time, full year; the rest have limited their time commit-ment in some way.[6] If she attempts a career, she will try to find one with a flexible schedule. She will leave her job if her family's needs call—if her husband needs to relocate for his job advancement, if her children are ill. Interested in maintaining her femininity, she will seek to work in a clearly feminine job; neither will she be driven by a desire for advancement or higher pay to work to upgrade her job or to move into a masculine job. She will not only not attack the sex-typing of jobs but will be hostile to such attempts by other women. Finally, rather than demanding more power and voice in the marriage com-mensurate with her increased financial contribution, such a woman will play down the importance of her earnings in the family budget.[7]

In 1980, this kind of two-earner family was still the most common. Most working homemakers are found to maintain prime responsibility for the care of the family.[8] A study done by Walker and Woods in the late sixties found that employed homemakers spent 34% less time in housework than the unemployed homemaker.[9] However, studies show little or no significant difference in the housework time of hus-bands with employed and unemployed wives.[10] Hence wage-earning wives are overloaded: the Walker and Woods study showed that the average employed homemaker's working day was 10.1 hours, com-pared to 9.2 hours for the husband.[11] Yet wage-earning wives do not, for the most part, express dissatisfaction with their husbands' low level of participation.[12] Indeed, some studies have shown that women defend their homemaking territory; one quoted a high-status career woman as saying, "As far as the womanly chores . . . these are things I like doing my way and try to do them myself."[13] In 1970, 47% of a sample of women did not agree that "men should share the work around the house with women, such as doing dishes, cleaning, and so forth."[14] There is evidence, however, that wage-earning homemakers have been able to reduce their "role overload," by further reducing their time spent in housework; one study found a 20% decrease in woman's housework time, for both employed and unemployed home-makers, between 1965 and 1975.[15] And while women seem to be holding onto their household work, they are also holding onto their feminine jobs, without much evidence of dissatisfaction; indeed, the percentage of employed wives doing part-time work increased from 26% in 1965 to 29% in 1976.[16]

Such a two-earner marriage can be a stable one—if both husband and wife continue to desire complementary behavior from the other and to follow it themselves. In many ways, such a marriage is more stable than the traditional, one-earner one. Extra commodities can be obtained with the homemaker's earnings; she now can be assured that she is doing her most to fill family needs. The homemaker who was frustrated with the isolation of homemaking, or who was plagued by the "empty nest syndrome," can ease these problems with a job without altering her traditional conception of marriage or giving up her monopoly on homemaking and child-rearing. There are, however, contradictions within this pattern which may upset the compromise. Feeling overburdened by their "double day" and aware of their role in bringing in income to the family, women may resent the fact that their husbands have more leisure. They may ask for more help from their husbands than the husbands will give. And the "super-woman" career woman will probably be forced to choose between career or family or to pressure her husband to take his share of housework. These problems can destabilize the sexual division of labor in marriage and cause conflict between husband and wife.

Movement in Two Different Directions: The War Between the Sexes

A woman's entrance into the labor force makes her more similar to men; it gives her a public self and a degree of financial independence. The experience of being in the labor force can make a woman less willing to unilaterally subordinate herself to the family's needs, less willing to accept her husband as the unquestioned head of the household. If, however, her husband wishes to maintain his position as household head and her subordination to his needs as homemaker, conflict will result. Each cannot be who they wish to be without the cooperation of the other. A man cannot be a man—truly masculine—within his marriage unless his wife subordinates her life to him; a woman cannot grow out of her femininity unless she can find a husband who will share homemaking with her.

Who is most likely to fall into this pattern of discord? Those who begin their marriages with unrealistic expectations of themselves and/or each other. Wives who planned on being superwomen—painlessly combining demanding masculine jobs with impeccable homemaking—yet find their home responsibilities continually conflicting with their jobs. Men who are most insecure about their masculinity, or those with demanding masculine careers as well as an attraction to career women. Indeed, although most two-earner couples plan to live out their lives in peace, as in pattern one, many are likely to find contradictions in that kind of marriage leading them to discord.

The presence of the homemaker in the labor force can bring conflict between husband and wife. First, her mere presence in the labor force may threaten her husband; as we have seen, the two-earner family destabilizes the traditional sexual division. If, rather than playing down this change, the homemaker revels in it—enjoys it, talks about it, begins to claim some of the power her husband has monopolized as the family provider—she is attenuating the masculinity of her husband and starting a fight. Lillian Rubin's study of working-class families found that in over one-third of the families where wives were in the labor force, husbands complained that their wives were "getting too independent." As one thirty-three-year-old repairman told her:

> She just doesn't know how to be a real wife, you know, feminine and really womanly. She doesn't know how to give respect because she's too independent. She feels that she's a working woman and she puts in almost as many hours as I do and brings home a paycheck, so there's no one person above the other. She doesn't want there to be a king in this household. . . . She needs to be more feminine. . . . I believe every woman has the right to be an individual, but I just don't believe in it when it comes between two people. A man needs a feminine woman. When it comes to two people living together, a man is supposed to be a man and a woman is supposed to be a woman. I'd like to feel like I wear the pants in the family. Once my decision is made, it should be made, and that's it. She should just carry it out. But it doesn't work that way around here. Because she's working and making money, she thinks she can argue back whenever she feels like it.[17]

This man is speaking of very subtle changes which occurred when his wife entered the labor force. She did not refuse to do her homemaking work, she did not openly attack him; however, she felt more powerful and independent and able to express her own opinions, and this alone was enough to shake his masculinity and upset their marriage. The threat is even greater to the man who is unemployed or clearly at the bottom of the hierarchy. The segregation of black men into the most menial and low-status jobs, as well as their higher risk of unemployment, combined with the developing individuality of the black woman in the labor force, has certainly contributed to the instability of the black family and the dramatic increase in number of female-headed households among blacks: in 1978, 45% of black families were female-headed.[18] Similarly, the career woman who is successful in her career may inadvertently upset the ego of her husband. In her study of college men Komarovsky found "even equality in achievement of husband and wife is interpreted as a defeat for the man."[19]

Contradictory expectations have led many couples who planned marriage without disagreement to end up with problems. Studies of the family in the 1970s have found that "while changes in women's [traditional] occupational behaviors are increasingly preferred, changes in men's and women's [traditional] household behaviors are comparatively less strongly preferred by both sexes."[20] But such expectations are unrealistic: women's position in the labor force cannot improve unless the sexual division of labor at home is altered. Hence couples are setting themselves up for conflict. Many women now believe that they can easily combine success in the labor force with traditional homemaking—and they marry with the expectation of serving their husbands in the traditional manner. Once they become involved in their careers, however, they may find themselves forced to make demands upon their husbands which neither of them had foreseen, bringing a potential for conflict. Mirra Komarovsky found that "neither the [male] seniors nor the female national sample, including non-college women, explicitly perceived that their advocacy of sex equality in the public spheres was undermined by continued adherence to sex-role segregation within the family. This is the case of the great majority of women who wish or need to combine familial and economic roles."[21] Likewise, liberal husbands who entered marriage with the plan to share housework equally are led, by the demands of their jobs and personalities, to revert to the old pattern.[22] Some men marry "career women" because they are more interesting and alive than housewives, yet expect such women to always put their husbands' careers first.[23] If either partner is ambivalent—uncertain of what he or she wishes to do, or wishes from his or her partner—the problems are even more complex and impenetrable.

Hence, while a couple may enter into a relationship expecting to continue the traditional polarization in roles, the pressures of the wife's career can lead her to push for "reforms." It is one thing for a homebound homemaker to serve her husband when he returns from a long day's work; but when they both return from a long day's work, and she is expected to start dinner while he watches television, the arrangement begins to appear inequitable. Its injustice is further emphasized when she is forced continually to sacrifice her job advancement to support his. However, if she asks for, or demands help, he may respond defensively. Essential to a husband's masculinity is the attentions of his wife in his home, and his lack of responsibility for her particular needs and those of his children. Responding to her requests or demands not only violates this rule, but also places him under her direction, reversing the traditional authority relationship between them. If he gives in to her demands, he is "weak," set up for ridicule by his peers. If he has not been successful in the labor force, he will be even more resistant. While men with successful and demanding careers may be less defensive of their masculinity, and more willing to help, they will insist on placing their jobs first. The stage is set for conflict within the marriage over the husband's participation in the work of homemaking, a conflict added to that occasioned by the wife's labor-force participation itself. A man who refuses to lift a finger at home will face the resentment of his spouse; so will the woman who forces a reluctant husband to do housework.

The expansion of woman's sphere to include work in the labor force has thus unleashed a plethora of possibilities for discord and misunderstanding in marriage.[24] If men and women come to marriage with different conceptions of their respective roles, or, in the living out of their marriage, begin to find that their conceptions diverge, their marriage relationship will become full of conflict. Neither can be fulfilled unless a common ground is established. One way out of the impasse is, of course, the threatened divorce and remarriage to another, more compatible spouse. And for the two-earner family, divorce is less difficult. Woman's increasing financial independence not only makes her more willing to divorce her husband, it also makes her husband more willing to divorce her. Many men have been held into their marriages by their very responsibility to provide for their wives' livelihoods, that is, by their wives' financial dependence upon them. Unhappy couples who previously would have stayed together now divorce and seek other partners. Hence the rise of the two-earner family has contributed to the recent dramatic increase in the divorce rate. Between 1965 and 1980 the divorce rate in the United States increased from 2.5 per thousand to over 5.0; in 1972 it was the highest in the world.[25] It is estimated that 30 to 40% of marriages contracted will end in divorce.[26] Rising divorce rates have contributed to the dramatic increase in the numbers of the female-headed households—woman living alone with their children.[27] These high divorce rates are accompanied by very high remarriage rates—four of every five divorced persons eventually remarry.[28] People are dissatisfied with their particular marriage partners, unafraid of leaving them, and willing to try again.

At the same time, there has been an increase in the number of unmarried adults, some of which is certainly due to dissatisfaction with marriage or inability to find a compatible spouse. Some women who seek careers are, like their foremothers, remaining unmarried: the percentage of women who remain single is high among women who have graduated from college (10% in 1960 and 8% in 1970), and even higher among those who have graduate training (24% single in 1960 and 19% in 1970).[29] There has been a rapid increase in the number of people living alone or with "unrelated individuals." The number of unmarried couples who were living together increased dramatically in the 1960s and 1970s;[30] many individuals now wish to "try out" their relationships before committing themselves to marriage. Given these changes, the proportion of people living in married-couple households has fallen from 85% in 1960 to 75% in 1978.[31]

The departure of women from their previous, complementary relationships with men, inadvertent or not, has unleashed a certain amount of hostility between the sexes. Conflicts over respective roles bring out a tension latent in the sexual division of labor, that between human beings who live out their lives according to diametrically opposed principles—subordination of oneself to the service of others, and advancement of oneself through domination of others. This oppositeness, while the basis of the traditional attraction between the sexes, is at the same time a reason for their alienation from and dislike for one another. This difference and antagonism, quiescent when the sexes complement each other in their traditional roles, becomes apparent when one or the other moves out of their place, jeopardizing the position of the other. In particular, the attempts of women to move out of their service of the needs of their husbands, causing the latter to more strongly assert their domination, have made women aware of men's lack of concern with their needs. On the other hand, some men who wish to move out of their polarized position and express more weakness and dependence find themselves attacked by women seeking to maintain their femininity. Wives are battered by husbands seeking to assert their masculinity; then the former let out their frustrations upon their children.[32]

Individuals or couples can try to resolve the conflicts caused by a movement away from womanhood by returning to the traditional sexual division in marriage—reducing the wife's job commitment or bringing her out of the labor force altogether. There is, however, a different way to resolve this discord without moving back to the old pattern—giving up the sexual polarization in marriage and establishing a "symmetrical marriage."

Similar and Equal: The Symmetrical Marriage

Contradictions in womanhood and homemaking have led women to move out of womanhood, to expand it to include activities previously defined as masculine, and to reduce the sexual difference within marriage. When this is a one-sided development, it upsets the stability of the marriage, necessitating a reassertion of the sexual difference, or bringing discord within the couple. However, the movement out of womanhood does bring the possibility of men moving out of manhood—and of replacing marriage based on difference and inequality with marriage based on similarity and equality.

There are contradictions in masculinity which are activated by woman's growth out of feminity, contradictions which lead some men to increase their involvement in family life and reduce their difference from their wives. In the nineteenth century, the economy offered men the chance for self-advancement, a new opportunity to determine themselves apart from their inherited status. This new freedom excited men and incited them to dedicate their energies, their lives, to the struggle for self-advancement. However, as time passed, their struggle became increasingly contradictory.

In the family economy and in the nineteenth century, men sought wealth as petty producers, self-employed farmers, craftsmen, or retailers. However, competition for profits and growth brought the development of larger and larger firms with whom petty producers could not effectively compete; the latter were driven into wage or salaried employment in the labor force, deprived of their independence. Increasingly, men's fight for self-advancement has necessitated that they subordinate themselves to others, within large organizations.

Craft and blue-collar workers could achieve self-advancement only through unionization and the creation of seniority systems. However, such organizing worsened the problem of alienation already engendered by the mechanization and de-skilling of blue-collar work. First, by clearly separating workers from management and setting up an opposition between the two, it put clear limits on worker's advancement, depriving them of the dream of really "making it." Second, by relying on seniority as the criterion of job advancement, unions made increases in worth simply a function of years on the job, rather than of the individual worker's performance. This, combined with explicit limitations on the work process (instituted to avoid speed-up), deprived men blue-collar workers of the opportunity to self-seek individually on their jobs. Finally, the hierarchical structure of their unions discouraged the workers' active involvement in collective bargaining. Thus men working in skilled and semiskilled blue-collar work have had to seek opportunities for self-expression and competition elsewhere.[33]

Meanwhile the management of the firm has passed from the hands of capitalists to a staff of hired managers. While these men are offered, even demanded, to develop their selves, their freedom is severely restricted: they must please their superiors. The requirements for success include not only much servile and petty behavior (such as staying in the office until the boss leaves, whether or not there is work to be done), but also immoral or antisocial behavior (undermining one's opposition, illegal bribes or price fixing, lying to the consumer, destroying the environment). A man is forced to put aside his own personal beliefs, to compromise his integrity, in order to advance. By the age of forty, most men have realized that they will not reach the top ranks, but must continue plodding along nevertheless. Those who reach the top cannot rest on their laurels, for competitors are always threatening; indeed, the need for corporations to provide continual opportunity for advancement is leading them to dismiss older corporate heads even if they are still performing well.[34]

The frustrations men face in the economy have been exacerbated by the shrinking of other opportunities for masculine self-expression, in particular sports and war. As sports have become more formalized and professionalized, men, since they are so concerned with winning, are less and less willing to participate on anything but the professional level: they are forced to compete vicariously, watching professional sports or pushing their sons into school sports or "Little League." War has provided men with another major arena for proof of masculinity; however, the increasing importance of war machinery, the failure in Vietnam, and the development of nuclear armaments have reduced the possibility for individual heroics while depriving war of its moral justification.[35]

The entrance of women into the labor force, and the desire of some of these to involve their husbands more actively in family life, provides an opportunity for men to escape some of the frustrations involved in contemporary masculinity. First, a wife's participation in the labor force relieves her husband of the sole financial responsibility for the family. This reduces his employer's leverage over him, allowing him to refuse to put up with certain practices, or even to leave his job to take another one which pays less, but is more fulfilling. Second, her willingness to let him share in housework offers him an new opportunity for creativity and self-fulfillment, particularly in the primary care of the children. Finally, a more symmetrical marriage offers a man more companionship and understanding from his wife, on the basis of their shared experiences; the acceptance, respect, advice, and love of a person who is herself a participant in the masculine world of work is much more meaningful than that of a person whose life is spent at home.[36]

Many men become open to such changes in their forties when, as social scientists have noted, many realize that their jobs will not bring them success or fulfillment. Other men are shocked into realizing the emptiness of the masculine ideal when their wives threaten to leave them.[37] As sons learn from their fathers' frustrations, just as daughters have learned from their mothers', they begin to reexamine and question the traditional expectations of men. Increasingly, they are entering into marriage with the wish to share home and work responsibilities with their wives. A CBS News–*New York Times* National Survey in October 1977 found that 46% of men said they believed that a marriage where both spouses worked in the labor force, did housework, and took care of the children was more satisfying than one where the husband provided for the family and the wife took care of the house and children.

So some wives have asserted their right to enter the labor force and have pressured their husbands to "help" with the housework. Instead of defensively shoring up their masculinity, some men have taken this as an opportunity to grow out of their own restrictive roles by sharing with their wives the responsibility of bread-winning as well as home-making. This, in turn, forces their wives to change, to be more stable in their labor-force commitments. And, most important, wives are asked to *share* the responsibility for the care of the family with their husbands, rather than simply asking them for "help." Giving up their monopoly on parenting represents a threat to women equal to or per-haps greater than the threat men face when giving up their husband/provider role. For women, segregated at present into the least paid, least status jobs, and absent from positions of political power, mother-ing has represented the only claim to special excellence and power. Yet sharing mothering with their husbands also allows women to have equal marriages, lives which can combine fulfillment in the home with a commitment to and pride in a job. American women are showing increasing willingness to give up their monopoly on homemaking and mothering in favor of more equal marriages. In one study, the percent-age of married women who believed that their husbands should not help around the house after he returned from work fell from 54% in 1962 to 38% in 1977; and while in 1962, 44.5% of the women had agreed that "there is some work that is men's and some that is women's, and they shouldn't be doing each other's," in 1977, this percentage had fallen to 32.6%.[38] A different study found a sharp in-crease in the numbers of married women who endorsed sharing cook-ing, cleaning, and other household tasks with their husbands between 1970 and 1974.[39] The CBS–*New York Times* National Survey cited above found 50% of women endorsing a family where both husband and wife had jobs, did housework and took care of the children.

A new conception of marriage and family life is clearly emerging among both men and woman; the conception of the "symmetrical marriage," in which spouses, instead of specializing in family or eco-nomic life, each participate actively in both spheres.[40] While the CBS poll found 48% of all those questioned endorsing the symmetrical marriage, resistance was concentrated among the elderly. Only 29% of those over sixty-five endorsed the symmetrical marriage, compared to 67% of those from eighteen to twenty-nine years of age. Indeed, the younger the respondents were, the more they believed in the symmetrical marriage, signaling a clear historical trend. Table 13–2 shows that support for this new kind of marriage exists in all income groups and races and is more pronounced the more educated the individual. Ideas change more rapidly than actions; it is much more difficult to live out the symmetrical marriage than people suspect. Nevertheless, studies show that many couples are trying. Remember that in 1980, half of married women were in the labor force! Furthermore, a 1980 survey of married individuals found substantial percentages of husbands actively participating in homemaking work: doing the dishes (44%), cooking (44%), caring for the children (38%), vacuuming (31%), doing the laundry (30%), mopping floors (25%), cleaning the bathroom (23%), cleaning the stove (23%), ironing (12%).[41]

The rise of the symmetrical marriage is connected with the rise of the gay movement in an important if complicated manner. The symmetrical marriage is not built on the difference and complementarity of the spouses, and thus does not sustain the masculine/feminine difference; homosexual relationships are based on the sexual similarity of the spouses. Both repudiate the basis of the sexual division of labor—the belief that marriage is a naturally defined and complementary relationship based in the sexual differentiation of the spouses, and parenting the physical creation and mothering of offspring. While not all gay relationships attempt to eliminate masculine and feminine sex roles, some individuals have chosen spouses of their own sex as a way to free themselves from traditional sex role expectations, as a way to achieve symmetrical marriages.[42] The gay movement's demand that committed gay relationships be acknowledged as marriages has forced society to reexamine its definition of marriage. While most still balk at the idea, the rise of the symmetrical marriage is indeed freeing marriage from the necessity of sexual difference, freeing individuals to choose their marriage partners from those of both sexes. And by recognizing that men as well as women can "mother," it is separating parenting from the physical conception and extending the possibility of parenting to homosexual as well as heterosexual couples.

The symmetrical marriage does not sustain the sexes as complementary and different; it does not produce men and women. In working to establish symmetrical marriages, neither males not females are consciously looking to eliminate their manhood or womanhood, respectively; yet the changes we have described do, in fact, have this

Table 13–2: Complementary versus Symmetrical Marriage

Question: Now I'd like to ask about your preferences—what kind of marriage is the more satisfying way of life—one where the husband provides for the family and the wife takes care of the house and children [complementary], or one where the husband and wife both have jobs, both do housework, and both take care of the children [symmetrical]?

	Complementary	Symmetrical	Other[a]
Sex			
Male	47	46	9
Female	41	50	10
Education			
Less than high school	52	38	11
High school	42	50	8
Some college	38	56	5
College graduate	31	58	11
Age			
18–29	27	67	6
30–44	44	50	7
45–64	53	36	11
Over 65	58	29	13
Race			
White	45	46	9
Black	34	57	8
Other	27	60	13
Family income			
Less than $8,000/yr	49	43	8
$8–12,000	44	49	7
$12–20,000	45	48	7
Over $20,000	38	53	8
Religion			
Protestant	45	46	9
Catholic	40	51	9
Jewish	32	57	11
Other	50	46	4
None	41	56	3

SOURCE: CBS News–*New York Times* National Survey, Oct. 1977; sample of 1,603 respondents.
a. Both, neither, don't know, not applicable.

ultimate result. Just as the traditional marriage, centered in a sexual division of labor, constituted the sexes as socially differentiated and complementary, so the symmetrical marriage will begin to construct the sexes as similar and equal. By leading husbands to share in women's work of homemaking, and wives to share in men's work of providing, it is breaking down the differentiation of the sexes within marriage.

Furthermore, and perhaps most important, the increasingly symmetrical marriage will not raise children impressed from infancy with the social difference of the sexes. Children are growing up with increasingly similar parents. First, many of them have both parents in the labor force. In 1979, 39.3% of mothers with children under three years of age were in the labor force; 43.2% of those with children under six; and 59.1% of those with children between the ages of six and seventeen.[43] Children of all racial groups are growing up with both parents in the labor force: 50.7% of white children under eighteen had mothers in the labor force in 1979, 56.2% of black children, and 41.6% of hispanic children.[44] Second, many children are being actively parented by both parents, both sexes. Studies show that husbands are beginning to take a primary role in child-care. A 1975–76 time-use study showed men doing about one-fourth of all family work and about one-fifth of all child-care (differences between men with or without employed wives were not large).[45] Behavioral change lags behind attitude change: a 1976 Gallup survey found that half the males interviewed believed that husbands should do *as much* housework and child care as their wives, if their wives were employed.[46] As Jessie Bernard told a congressional subcommittee in 1973, "The trend of the times is in the direction of greater sharing of the child-rearing function by both parents."[47] One index of this trend is the increasing rate at which divorcing men are gaining custody of their children: 15% in 1976, as opposed to 10% in 1969.[48]

This trend toward equal parenting is significant since an essential force behind the reproduction of the sexual division of labor has been infants' and children's early experiences of the difference between their parents. In the traditional marriage, only mothers participate in the early nurturant relationship with the infant; only fathers provide children with a reflection of the world of work and politics. Raised in such a family, both sexes could not avoid being imprinted at an unconscious as well as conscious level with an ingrained sense of difference between the sexes—of women as self-sacrificing providers of warmth and nurturance, of men as distant, public-identified beings who embody authority and power. Further, when parented by individuals also imbued with these notions of sexual difference, children "naturally" identified themselves with one or the other, according to their physical sex, and conceived of the opposite sex as the appropriate marriage partner.

Feminist theorists have used psychoanalytic theory to point out the manner in which these arrangements contribute to inequality between the sexes and hostility toward women. Being parented by a woman engenders in men an unconscious fear of and wish to dominate women.[49] A man needs a woman to provide him with the intimacy and nurturance he experienced as an infant, yet he fears women who, as mothers, exercised absolute power over him (and all men) in infancy. Men seek to redress this power imbalance by deprecating women and by seeking to dominate them. Men have further problems in establishing their masculinity, for their first images of humanity were learned in their infant relationships with their mothers, feminine beings. This difficulty is exacerbated since the development of capitalism also removed fathers from the everyday life of children. This has made men develop a weak sense of masculinity, a weak internalized authority, and a readiness to define masculinity in negative terms, simply as not feminine.[50]

The emergent symmetrical family does not produce the same dynamic. Both sexes participate in primary parenting or "mothering," in the first, intimate relationship between parent and infant.[51] The feared and sought-after motherer is actually parents of both sexes; the fear of that early helplessness no longer attaches itself to the female sex. Boys are no longer deprived of a parent of their own sex to identify with. At the same time, children do not learn of man and woman as different and polarized beings, since in the child's experience both sexes "mother" and both participate actively in the public sphere. The two parents with which the children identify are not opposites and different; there is no reason for the child to identify only with the parent of his or her sex. Indeed, as we have seen, parents do not even need to be of physically opposite sexes; they each need only to be full human beings. Hence, the symmetrical family does not provide the children with any real basis for the construction of polarized, masculine *or* feminine personalities, nor provide any necessity for heterosexual love.

As marriage becomes symmetrical, then, it begins to undermine the unconscious underpinnings of the sexual division of labor. Males and females feel less and less necessity to differentiate themselves from the opposite sex, to prove their manhood or womanhood by participating in sex-segregated activities. However, the social differentiation of the sexes lives on in the shape of masculine and feminine jobs. Hence the development of the symmetrical marriage has created pressure for changes in the job structure; we will discuss this final aspect of the breakdown of the sexual division of labor in the conclusion.

Conclusion:
The Breakdown of the Sexual Division
of Labor

In the process of American history, the sexual division of labor has begun to break down, undermined by transformations in women's work of homemaking. As economic and family life grew separate, women's "natural" work emerged as a distinct and recognized sphere of social life, and womanhood developed for the first time an independent determination of its own. Instead of simply responding to the changing needs of her husband and family, as in the colonial economy, the homemaker gained an important social vocation to pursue, the maintenance of the new home sphere, the care of her husband, and, most important, the nurturance of her children. The development of woman's individuality and freedom, as a home-maker, was the other side of the development of man's individuality and freedom as a competitor in the economy—woman living through the active subordination of herself to the needs of her family, man through the active quest to advance himself (and subordinate other selves) in the economy.

The pursuit of this new vocation led women to move outside of the domestic sphere and to develop their capacities as individuals in their own right. In the nineteenth century, the efforts of families to keep their homemakers out of the masculine sphere of the labor force led to the labor-force employment of women as daughters, before marriage. Privileged daughters went to school and college to prepare themselves for mothering, and/or participated in the social homemaking movement; some of these ended up pursuing lifelong careers in social homemaking. In response to the expansion of needs in the twentieth century, some middle- and working-class homemakers entered the labor force seeking income to fill what they interpreted as pressing family needs. Meanwhile, women whose college educations had developed their labor-force capacities rebelled against the forced choice between labor-force and homemaking careers and began to seek "second careers" in the labor force, even in masculine jobs. By 1970, it was no longer clear what womanhood was: the nineteenth-century ideal—the full-time homemaker—had been joined by the wage-earning homemaker and the second-career woman.

The development of manhood has not brought such expansion; indeed, masculine competition for economic advancement has gradually transferred economic activity from the hands of self-employed individuals to large impersonal corporations; the development of these organizations, and the counter-organization of workers in unions, has strictly delimited the manner in which men may work for self-advancement, robbing most of them of the opportunity for individual creativity or real self-development. To this crisis in masculinity was added the extra threat of women's entry into masculine jobs and their challenge to the sexual division of labor in marriage. While many men have responded defensively to women's "invasion" of men's sphere and worked to reassert their difference from women by opposing these changes or by intensifying the sexual division of labor in their homes, more and more men are interpreting women's development as an opportunity to free themselves from subordination to the requirements for advancement at work. Moreover, they have begun to enter into women's work of primary parenting—a logical extension of the cult of domesticity's establishment of mothering as a social rather than natural activity which nevertheless violates another basic premise of the sexual division of labor, the attachment of women, and only women, to infant care. Finally, the participation of men in child-care combined with that of women in paid employment means that children are being brought up with less and less awareness of the opposition of the sexes, and hence feel less need to abstain from the activities of the other sex.

These developments have violated an essential part of the sexual division of labor—the exclusion of females and males from the work of the opposite sex. They have hence shocked our society into a reconsideration of the beliefs upon which the sexual division of labor has rested, in particular the belief that a natural inability (or lesser ability) to perform the work of the opposite sex is at the root of the sexual division of labor. Women have sought entry into men's jobs on the basis of their qualifications, directly challenging this old principle. Their successful violation of the natural conception of the sexual division of labor has spurred study of the actual physiological differences between the sexes as well as comparison of their performances in different activities. Although findings and their meaning are still debated, studies have established the fact that some females are perfectly qualified for elite men's jobs and that males are capable of "maternal" care.

In this way, the rationale for the sexual division of labor has been undermined. Those interested in crossing over the line, predominantly women, have been able to convince policy makers that opposition to the employment of an individual solely on the basis of sex is unfair, contrary as it is to the principles of free choice and equal opportunity. The result: anti-sex-discrimination measures, even affirmative action, since discrimination is so difficult to detect and punish. In the last ten or so years, the contention that sexes are naturally different and opposed in their abilities, once an unquestioned basis of social life, has been rejected, its proponents accused of unfair and illegal discrimination. Indeed, today the attitudes of men employers are often blamed for the sex-typing of jobs as a whole; the merging of natural and social, of female and woman, has blinded society to the fact that females have actively excluded themselves from men's jobs, and sought out the less demanding women's jobs, as part of their living out of womanhood.[1] At the same time, the increasing freedom of movement of males and females into women's and men's work, respectively, has begun to reduce the social differentiation of the sexes, making "man" and "woman" come more and more to mean "male" and "female": in other words, it has begun to reduce the sexual difference to simply a biological difference.

In this first stage of the breakdown of the sexual division of labor, individuals have been freed to take up the work of the opposite sex. Many of them, especially second-career women and their husbands, are trying to straddle the masculine world of the economy and the feminine world of the family, trying to combine active participation in the family with the struggle for job advancement. This is by no means easy. As we have seen, these two spheres of social life have been structured as the mutually exclusive vocations of women and men, respectively. A female (or male) can succeed in the masculine job world by giving up her commitment to the family, and dedicating her life to job advancement: by acting like a man. A male (or female) can be a successful, active parent if he refuses to sacrifice the needs of his family for his job. But success in both spheres is virtually impossible: individuals seeking to excel are usually forced to focus on one or the other sphere or to accept mediocrity in both. Nevertheless, more and more individuals are beginning to lead schizophrenic existences, combining the masculine struggle to subordinate others with the feminine activity of serving their families.

This expansion of individuals into the realm of the "opposite" sex has not been a balanced one. As we saw in Part III, the impetus for this rejection of the natural basis for the sexual division of labor has come from women. Furthermore, since women's work of parenting is unpaid, low-status work, whereas men's offers opportunities for power, prestige, and money, more females are taking advantage of this new freedom than males. The feminist movement is thus commonly called "the women's liberation movement" and is still conceived of and fought predominantly as a woman's struggle. The onesidedness of the breakdown of the sexual division of labor has meant more masculinity, females joining males in the struggle for economic self-advancement.

As a result, the marriage tie has become increasingly fragile, engendering widespread social concern about the demise of the family. Marriage has already been undermined, as we have seen, by women's growing economic independence and shaken by disagreements over respective duties. The increased masculinity of women has brought further instability in marriage ties: women are becoming less and less willing to sacrifice themselves to keep their families together, while most men are unwilling to take up the slack. Two beings dedicated above all to their own economic self-advancement cannot sustain a marriage relationship with children: both need to be given to, served, and supported; neither can commit him- or herself to thus supporting a spouse, much less to actively parenting children. As both sexes become captivated by the public sphere's promises of wealth and consumption, their relationships with each other and with their children have begun to suffer.[2] Conservatives, in the so-called Moral Majority, clamor for a return to the former sexual division of labor as the only possible solution. And indeed, it did create an ordered society in which marriage, childbearing and -rearing, and wage work were taken up without question. However, even though the new freedom of the sexes seems only to produce chaos and to undermine the generational reproduction of society, to restrict this freedom and force women back into the home would violate the essential principle of capitalism, freedom of choice and contract. While it is inconceivable that society can thus turn back history, it is also unlikely that we will remain in this state of chaos. The struggles of the sexes to combine masculine and feminine activities are leading them to transform the content of both and, in the process, to transform their own personalities. The first stage of the breakdown of the sexual division of labor, which freed the sexes to do the work of the other, is bringing on a second stage, during which masculinity and femininity are being eradicated both from personality and from social institutions.

We have already discussed the way in which marriage is being transformed from a complementary relationship, based on masculinity and femininity, to a symmetrical one, based on a new kind of personhood. Yet, since participation in a symmetrical marriage means combining economic self-seeking with familial care for others, the full development of symmetrical marriage comes into conflict with the job structure and leads individuals to work to transform their jobs.

Since feminine jobs are becoming less and less acceptable to individuals, these jobs are being forced to change. As women's commitment to their jobs grows, they are becoming dissatisfied with the low wages, lack of advancement, and servility required in most women's jobs. Secretaries are refusing to do personal favors for their bosses and beginning to flock to organizations such as "9 to 5" and "Working Women" to learn organizing strategies; nurses' associations are fighting for less self-sacrificial working conditions. Meanwhile, the now-perceived inferiority of such jobs when compared to masculine jobs requiring comparable education training is discouraging women and men from even entering such jobs, creating shortages which strengthen the hand of the workers. Teaching, previously a feminine job, has drawn more and more men and, through unionization, has been upgraded. As men have become airline stewardesses, the job title has been changed to "flight attendant" and no longer requires a sexy, unmarried woman who will flirt with the male passengers. Live-in domestic servants are becoming impossible to find except among recent immigrant populations or foreigners; American women are less and less willing to do such work, given its servility and lack of independence. Eventually housework will be done by firms, as the production of prepared foods, as the cleaning of houses by the hour, or as day care for children in

centers. Feminine jobs are, then, being upgraded to bring the employees better wages, less servile working conditions, and more opportunities for self-development and advancement.

Individuals are also pressing for changes in competitive masculine
jobs, for workers are finding that these jobs conflict with full participation in family life. First, participation in more and more symmetrical marriages forces individuals to give time and emotional support to
their spouses (as well as receiving it from them) and to take the career
needs of their spouses into consideration, as well as their own. This
makes total subordination of their lives to their jobs impossible. Individuals are simply unable to find the time and energy needed for both
job and family; occasionally, job demands conflict overtly with family
ones, as in the case of geographical transfers or extensive travel
requirements.[3] At the same time, participation in symmetrical marriages, by lightening the financial burdens on individuals, allows
them to dare to experience and express discontent on the job and to
begin to question the employment practices that have made their
work so inhuman. Meanwhile, dissatisfaction with job content is
bound to increase. As women, who are still brought up to be more
sensitive to others, more able to express their feelings, and less ob-
sessed with self-advancement than men, enter these jobs, they bring
less competitive, more cooperative working styles. And as men begin
to explore the feminine sides of themselves, caring for others in the
family and becoming more aware of their feelings, they may begin to
find the cut-throat competition with other employees and the need to
ignore one's ethnics in the drive for profits less and less acceptable.

In Chapter 13 we discussed the problems men have been experiencing in their unskilled and semiskilled jobs; but much of their
white-collar work is becoming just as routine and alienating. As men
begin to participate actively in family life and learn to acknowledge
the needs and feelings of others as well as their own, they should
become more aware of these oppressive aspects of their jobs. Men
have put up with the dehumanization and emptiness of this work
under the pressure to provide livings for their families and with the
reward of full service at home. Again, participation in symmetrical
marriages will give these men (or women) less reason to accept such
inhuman work conditions, as well as less ability to do so.

The attempts of individuals to combine masculine and feminine
activities are not only leading to changes in the contents of jobs; they
are also bringing about qualitative changes in personality. Masculinity

and femininity are difficult to combine, as they embody in their es-
sences opposing principles: the seeking of self through the subordination of other selves, and the seeking of self through subordination to
other selves, respectively. The attempts to combine them can be
expected to lead to a qualitatively different kind of self—one which
combines, and yet transcends, masculinity and femininity; one which
seeks self-development and that of one's loved ones, without desiring
to place others above or below oneself; one which denies neither
one's own needs nor those of others; one which is able to care for
others and nuture children, as well as develop an independent self.
Women are learning from men that it is unhealthy to live through
one's children, to see them as one's whole life, and to deny oneself a
separate identity; they are discovering their individual abilities and
learning how to develop them in their jobs; they are learning how to
fight to protect themselves. Men are learning from women that competition with others is self-destructive and unproductive; they are
learning to care for themselves, rather than depending completely on
the support of their wives; they are learning to form intimate friend-
ships with other men; they are learning to become aware of their own
feelings and to refuse to put them aside when at work. In this way, a
new kind of personhood is emerging.

This second stage of the breakdown of the sexual division of labor is
bringing new insight into social life. As they begin to come across
constraints in the present structuring of jobs, individuals begin to
realize that free choice among existing options is not enough, is not
real freedom. They are hard pressed to find, within the present job
structure, a job that is compatible with symmetrical marriage as well
as allows self-development. They realize that the existing job structure forces them into masculine or feminine behavior, prevents them
from growing into full human beings. Similarly, the traditional conception of homemaking and mothering does not allow the individual
to develop an independent, public self; it sustains the traditional,
"selfless" woman. Social institutions, in particular family and work,
have produced and reproduced the social differentiation of the sexes,
and "human nature"; if the emergent individual is to achieve fulfil-
ment, these institutions must be transformed.

Individuals working to humanize the economy can be expected to
add a new side to the present political discourse. Today, our society's
economic options are grasped either as laissez-faire, maintaining rewards for individual self-seeking and paying the price of inequality

and poverty, or as government charity for the poor financed through taxes, depriving the poor of self-respect and dulling individual initiative. Neither really solve the problem of inequality: both limit the options to masculine and feminine ethics, competitions, and/or charity. However, a new option is emerging with the breakdown of masculinity and femininity: one of eliminating hierarchy and competition as the motors of our economy. The rise of symmetrical marriage is already breaking down inequality between the sexes. And, as we have discussed, the combining of masculinity and femininity is leading to a new self which seeks neither subordination to others or subordination of others. This offers society the possibility of dispensing with hierarchy and competition altogether, replacing them with egalitarian, cooperative structures that more directly tap the individual's desire for social importance and recognition.[4] By eliminating the seeking of inequality from the center of our economic and political life, this change would go far in eliminating the connected problems of racism, violence, and war.

Similarly, family policy has ranged between imposing and rewarding the traditional family, and supporting individual freedom to choose; the first strives to maintain the stability of the family at the price of individual freedom, while the second supports individual freedom, yet offers no solution to today's fragile family. As we have seen, a new option is emerging: that of supporting the emergence of a new, more egalitarian family, centered in the symmetrical marriage. This means recognizing that family life—including marriage and active parenting—is a vital part of social life which should be made compatible with full participation in economic and political life. Social institutions would then be transformed so as to make this a reality, so that individuals would no longer be penalized in the economy for having active commitments to their families.

With such changes, family and economic life would no longer be constituted as different, mutually exclusive vocations, masculinity and femininity would be transcended, and women and men would evolve into equal, similar, and fully human beings. History has brought us within sight of such a breakthrough; the rest is up to us.

Notes

INTRODUCTION

1. For some early women's studies writings, see Vivan A. Gornick and Barbara K. Moran, eds. *Women in Sexist Society: Studies in Power and Powerlessness* (New York: Basic Books, 1971), Robin Morgan, ed., *Sisterhood Is Powerful,* (New York: Random House, 1970), Betty Roszak and Theodore Roszak, eds., *Masculine/Feminine: Readings in Sexual Mythology and the Liberation of Women* (New York: Harper & Row, 1969). Women's studies journals were created: *Feminist Studies* (1972); *Women's Studies: An Interdisciplinary Journal* (1973); *Quest* (1974); *Signs* (1975); and *Frontiers* (1976), among others. For a contemporary, interdisciplinary collection of women's studies scholarship, see Jo Freeman, ed., *Women: A Feminist Perspective* (Palo Alto, Calif.: Mayfield Publishing Co., 1975). For a collection of feminist critiques of the social sciences, see Julia A. Sherman and Evelyn B. Beck, eds., *The Prism of Sex: Essays in the Sociology of Knowledge: Proceeding of a Symposium* (Madison: University of Wisconsin Press, 1979).

2. Overall analyses of the effects of capitalist development on women's work from which my work here has greatly benefited are: Edith Abbott, *Women in Industry. A Study in American Economic History* (New York: D. Appleton & Co, 1910); Helen Sumner, *History of Women in Industry,* vol. 9 of U.S. Senate Document No. 645, 61st Congress, 2d session, *Report on the Condition of Women and Child Wage-Earners in the United States* (Washington, D.C.: Government Printing Office, 1910); Ann Oakley, *Woman's Work: The Housewife, Past and Present* (New York: Pantheon, 1974); Mary P. Ryan, *Womanhood in America, from Colonial Times to the Present* (New York: New Viewpoints, 1975); Eli Zaretsky, *Capitalism, the Family, and Personal Life* (New York: Harper & Row, 1976); Joan Scott and Louise Tilly, "Women's Work and the Family in Nineteenth Century Europe," *Comparative Studies in Society and History* (Jan. 1975) and in Charles Rosenberg, ed., *The Family in History* (Philadelphia: University of Pennsylvania Press, 1975), and their more recent book, *Women, Work, and Family* (New York: Holt, Rinehart & Winston, 1978).

3. While capitalist development is not synonymous with industrialization, and refers specifically to Western Europe, North America, and Australia, some of the processes studied here have been experienced somewhat similarly in the industrialization of Third World countries and the Soviet Union.

4. Contemporary social theory, particularly in economics, tends to claim the opposite—that is, that the selfish, self-seeking individual is naturally so, and that history is the increasing adjustment of society to this fact. See for example, Frederick von Hayek, *The Road to Serfdom.* (Chicago: University of Chicago Press, 1944). Marx's criticism of this view is relevant: ". . . the period in which this view of the isolated individual becomes prevalent is the very one in which the interrelations of society have

reached the highest state of development. Man is, in the most literal sense of the word . . . not only a social animal, but an animal which can develop into an individual only in society." "Contribution to a Critique of Political Economy," quoted in Adam Schaff, *Marxism and the Human Individual* (New York: McGraw-Hill, 1970), pp. 61–2. George Herbert Mead's *Mind, Self, and Society* (Chicago: University of Chicago Press, 1934) contains an excellent treatment of the manner in which ideas, as expressed in language, form the substance of the mind and self of the individual.

5. Sociobiologists, of course, disagree.

6. Many social scientists discuss this difference as that between "sex" and "gender," seeing sex as the natural and gender as the social. See, for example, Ann Oakley, *Sex, Gender, and Society* (San Francisco: Harper & Row, 1972), and Carolyn Shaw Bell, "Economics, Sex, and Gender," *Social Science Quarterly* (Winter 1974).

7. For this reason, we will pay special attention to thoughts and writings on what womanhood should be. These are not idle wishes, but attempts to clarify and develop society's concept of woman which, as such, both reflect and influence the concrete life experiences of women.

8. This argument is made by Jessie Bernard in *The Female World* (New York: The Free Press, 1981).

9. See David P. Levine and Lynn S. Levine, *Personality Structure and the Family* (University of Denver: unpublished book, 1980), for an excellent and much fuller discussion of the relationship between natural differences and social life. The analysis in this part has benefited greatly from their work and discussions with them both. See also Anna Yeatman, "Gender Ascription and the Conditions of Its Breakdown" (Flinders University, South Australia, unpublished paper, 1978), for a somewhat different formulation of the same issue.

10. Orthodox or "neoclassical" economic theory would have us believe that the division of labor was the result of the choices of individuals faced with scarcity to maximize their consumption, choices informed by a scientific understanding of the work implications of the biological differences between the sexes; see, for example, Isabelle Sawhill, "Economic Perspectives on Women," *Daedalus* (Spring 1977). However, societies before ours have not had a scientific understanding of natural laws, nor an overriding goal of efficiency. Early social life was not marked by a meeting of human animals who decided to maximize utility and possessed a developed knowledge of natural science. Even today, few couples question the essence of the sexual division of labor—that family life must be the marriage of males and females.

11. This perspective is put forward by radical feminists, following the lead of Shulamith Firestone, *The Dialectic of Sex: The Case for a Feminist Revolution* (New York: Morrow, 1970), prominent among which is Mary Daly, *GYN/ECOLOGY: The Metaethics of Radical Feminism* (Boston: Beacon Press, 1978). Sally Gearhart's radical feminist novel, *The Wanderground: Stories of the Hill Women* (Watertown, Mass.: Persephone Press, 1979), epitomizes the radical feminist conception of women's liberation as a struggle against men. Many Marxist-feminists conceive of "patriarchy" as a struggle between the sexes similar in nature to "capitalism's" struggle between the classes: see Heidi Hartmann, "Capitalism, Patriarchy, and Job Segregation by Sex," in the collection *Capitalist Patriarchy and the Case for Socialist Feminism* (New York: Monthly Review Press, 1979), edited by Zillah R. Eisenstein, and the latter's essay, "Developing a Theory of Capitalist Patriarchy and Socialist Feminism." See also Roisin McDonough and Rachel Harrison, "Patriarchy and Relations of Production" in *Feminism and*

Materialism, edited by Annette Kuhn and Ann Marie Wolpe (London: Routledge & Kegan Paul, 1978).

12. See, for example, the study of early women college graduates, *Statistical Study of Women College Graduates* (Bryn Mawr, 1917), for exhaustive tables on the health and fertility of college graduates compared with their sisters.

13. Indeed, Claude Levi-Strauss, a prominent anthropologist, has claimed that it was the adoption of the conception of the sexual division of labor, combined with the incest taboo, which constituted the origins of social life, the transition into social life. If the individual social member is subordinated to these two social rules, society is capable of perpetuating and reproducing itself as society. See his essay, "The Family" in Arlene Skolnick and Jerome Skolnick, eds., *The Family in Transition*, (Boston: Little Brown, 1971).

14. See Michelle Zimbalist Rosaldo, "Women, Culture, and Society: A Theoretical Overview," in Rosaldo and Louise Lamphere, eds., *Woman, Culture, and Society* (Stanford: Stanford University Press, 1974).

15. This is the argument made by Sherry B. Ortner in "Is Female to Male as Nature Is to Culture?" *Feminist Studies* 2 (Fall 1972), also in *Woman, Culture, and Society*. However, Ortner herself confuses nature or biology with society's view of what is "natural," therefore succumbing to society's view that woman's work of child-rearing is, indeed, more natural. In fact, child-rearing is *the* ultimate social activity, being, as it is, the raising of the animal-like infant into a civilized, social being. Interestingly, primitive societies, which saw themselves as dominated by nature, accorded more social status to women, as peculiarly tied to nature.

1. THE FAMILY ECONOMY

1. For an excellent discussion of the relationship of individual to society in feudalism see Walter Ullman, *The Individual and Society in the Middle Ages* (Baltimore, Md.: Johns Hopkins Press, 1966).

2. Marc Bloch presents an excellent analysis of these feudal relationships in *Feudal Society*, translated by L. A. Manyon (Chicago: University of Chicago Press, 1961), Part IV. See also Karl Marx, *Precapitalist Economic Formations*, edited by E. J. Hobsbawn (New York: International Publishers, 1965).

3. Bloch, *Feudal Society*, Part III.

4. J. Hodgson, *History of Northumberland* (Newcastle, 1840), Part II, Vol. iii, 1500–1800 (New York: Harper & Row, 1977), p. 143.

5. J. J. Bagley, *Life in Medieval England* (New York: G. P. Putman's Sons, 1960).

6. See Maurice Dobb, *Studies in the Development of Capitalism* (New York: International, 1963), Chap. 2.

7. For an excellent Marxist analysis of the transition from feudalism to capitalism see Dobb; also, Eric Hobsbawm, "The Crisis of the Seventeenth Century," in *Crises in Europe 1560–1600*, edited by T. Aston (New York: Doubleday Anchor Books, 1967). A debate as to the actual causes of these transformations can be found in Paul M. Sweezy, ed., *The Transition from Feudalism to Capitalism; A Symposium* (New York: Science and Society, 1954).

8. See Christopher Hill, *Society and Puritanism in Pre-Revolutionary England* (New York: Charles Scribner's Sons, 1965), Chapters 1–3. Max Weber connected

Protestantism and capitalist development in his book, *The Protestant Ethic and the Spirit of Capitalism,* translated by Talcott Parsons (New York: Charles Scribner's Sons, 1958).

9. Marxian economics calls this economic system, "petty commodity production." I use the term *family economy* instead, to emphasize the fact that the nuclear family and its household acted as the commodity-producing unit, merging economic and family relationships. Joan Scott and Louise Tilly use the term *family economy* in a similar manner in their excellent study of women's work and family life in Europe, *Women, Work and Family* (New York: Holt, Rinehart & Winston, 1978). See its first part for an analysis of women's work in preindustrial Europe; their findings corroborate those I present in Chapters 1–3.

10. The understanding that self-seeking within a system of property owners will result in a wealthy expanding economy was first grasped by Adam Smith and his notion of the invisible hand. See *An Investigation into the Nature and Causes of the Wealth of Nations,* 5th edition (New York: The Modern Library, 1937), Book V, Chap. II. David P. Levine has developed these ideas and those of Marx and Hegel in his work: see Chap. 1 of Levine, *Economic Theory,* Vol. 1 (Boston: Routledge & Kegan Paul, 1978).

11. *A Relation of the Island of England,* Camden Society, 1847, XXXVII, pp. 24–25, quoted in Lawrence Stone, *Family, Sex, and Marriage, in England 1500–1800* (New York: Harper & Row, 1977), p. 107, and Phillip Aries, *Centuries of Childhood: A Social History of Family Life* (New York: Alfred A. Knopf, 1962). Both of these books include excellent discussions of the development of childhood during this period.

12. See Peter Laslett, *The World We Have Lost: England Before the Industrial Age* (New York: Charles Scribner's Sons, 1971), Chap. 1; see also Aries and Stone.

13. There is some debate on the extent of individuation achieved in the colonial economy. James Lemon, in *The Best Poor Man's Country: A Geographical Study of Early Southeastern Pennsylvania* (Baltimore: The Johns Hopkins Press, 1972), describes these colonists as "individualists" who "planned for themselves much more than they did for their communities" (p. xv). In "Families and Farms: Mentalité in Pre-Industrial America," *William and Mary Quarterly,* 3rd Series, 35:1 (Jan. 1978), James Henretta criticizes this view, claiming that the household head was constrained by his parents, and by his need to insure adequate subsistence as well as sufficient property for his children in the face of partible inheritance. Both are right: "individualism" existed, but emerged first as the freedom of the family and its lineage (parents and children) to determine themselves, rather than as the freedom of single adult men or nuclear families.

14. Stone, *Family, Sex, and Marriage,* p. 158.

15. Christopher Middleton, "The Sexual Division of Labor in Feudal England," *New Left Review,* 113–114 (Jan.–April, 1979), p. 162.

16. Aries, *Childhood,* p. 386. Aries is excellent on the absence of a conception of childhood in medieval times. He points out that children were dressed as little adults as soon as they could walk and that pictures showed children participating in the adult world.

17. See Alice Clark, *The Working Life of Women in the Seventeenth Century* (New York: Harcourt, Brace & Howe, 1920), Chapters 2–4; and Laslett, *The World We Have Lost,* Chapters 1–3.

18. Aries, *Childhood,* pp. 366–67. For more on master–servant relationships, see the treatises describing the "relative duties" of family members: for example, Rector

W. Fleetwood, *Relative Duties of Parents, Husbands, Masters and Children, Wives, Servants* (London: Charles Harper, 1705); and William Gouge, *Of Domestical Duties, Eight Treatises* (London: George Miller, 1634).

19. William B. Weeden, *Economic and Social History of New England 1620–1789*, Vol. 1 (New York: Houghton Mifflin Co., 1891), p. 19.

20. This is not to say that there were no differences between colonial America and Britain. It has been argued that the colonies not only reproduced but further and deeper extended the principles of capitalism developing in the mother country; in particular, the colonists started with a clean slate, less constrained by the remnants of aristocratic privilege and feudal institutions than Britain or the other countries of Western Europe. This allowed American society to realize more completely the new principle of individualism and prevented the perpetuation of rigid class divisions. Others have argued that the high sex ratio (men per women) in the early colonies strengthened the position of women. See, on this latter point, Roger Thompson, *Women in Stuart England and America: A Comparative Study* (Boston: Routledge & Kegan Paul, 1974). Also, life in the colonies was obviously more primitive than in Britain, with more self-sufficient production. William N. Parker's "American Capitalism: The Differentiation from European Origins" (New Haven: unpublished paper, 1981) provides an insightful analysis of this process.

21. Judah Champion, *A Brief View of the Distresses, Hardships and Dangers Our Ancestors Encounter'd, in Settling New England—The Privilages We Enjoy, and Our Obligations Thence Arising; With Moral Reflections Thereupon* (Hartford: Green & Watson, 1770), p. 11.

22. See Frederick Engels, *The Origins of the Family, Private Property and the State in Light of the Researches of Lewis H. Morgan* (New York: International Publishers, 1972).

23. See for example, Francis Rawle, *Ways and Means for the Inhabitants of Delaware to Become Rich* (Philadelphia: Keimer, 1725).

24. Robert Beverley, *History and Present State of Virginia in Four Parts—By a Native and Inhabitant of the Place* (London: R. Parker, 1705), p. 295.

25. In *Democracy in the Connecticut Frontier Town of Kent* (New York: Columbia University Press, 1961), p. 101, Charles S. Grant shows how the property of one family, the Fullers, diminished through three generations; for a discussion of the importance of patterns of inheritance and the age stratification it brought, see Henretta, "Mentalité," pp. 6–8. Some families arranged kin marriages or marriages with one particular family to avoid the break-up of family capital; see Peter Dobkin Hall, "Marital Selection and Business in Massachusetts Merchant Families, 1700–1900," in Michael Gordon, ed., *The American Family in Social-Historical Perspective* (New York: St. Martin's Press, 1973).

26. Henretta, pp. 12–13; this is his revision of Grant's estimate of 40 of 103 or 39%.

27. John Winthrop, *History of New England 1630–1649*, edited by J. K. Hosmer, Original Narrative of Early American History Series (New York: C. Scribner's Sons, 1908), p. 31, quoted in Rolla M. Tryon, *Household Manufactures in the United States 1640–1860; A Study of Industrial History* (Chicago: University of Chicago Press, 1917), p. 44.

28. Lois G. Carr and Lorena S. Walsh, "The Planter's Wife: The Experience of White Women in Seventeenth Century Maryland," *William and Mary Quarterly*, 3rd. Ser., 34 (1977), and in Nancy F. Cott and Elizabeth H. Pleck, eds., *A Heritage of Her*

Own: Toward a New Social History of American Women (New York: Simon & Schuster, 1979), pp. 41–42.

29. There is a good discussion of this subject in Tryon, *Household Manufactures,* Chap. 2, "Factors Affecting Household Manufactures in the Colonies."

30. The entrepreneurial view is shared by Grant, *Democracy in Kent;* Richard Hofstadter, "The Myth of the Happy Yeoman," *American Heritage,* 7 (April 1956); Lemon, *Best Poor Man's Country;* and Clarence H. Danhoff, *Change in Agriculture: The Northern United States 1829–1870* (Cambridge, Mass.: Harvard University Press, 1969). The last writes of the early nineteenth century, "The rural sector shared with the larger American society the belief that any man could and should constantly seek to improve his position" (p. 15). This view has been challenged by Henretta's thought-provoking article, "Mentalité in Pre-Industrial America." In Marxist circles, the issue is debated as to whether the dominant mode of production was capitalist, petty commodity, or independent: see Bob Sherry, "Comments on O'Connor's Review of *The Twisted Dream, Monthly Review* 28:1 (May 1976), and James O'Connor, "Reply to Sherry," in the same issue.

31. Danhoff, *Change in Agriculture,* pp. 15–18. According to Danhoff, this semisubsistence strategy slowed the economic success of family farmers when growing and stable markets developed in the nineteenth century.

32. Henretta quotes this farmer in the course of his argument against the existence of an entrepreneurial spirit; "Mentalité," p. 13.

33. For evidence of the increasing concentration of wealth ownership in the colonies, see Percy W. Bidwell and John I. Falconer, *History of Agriculture in the Northern United States 1620–1860* (Washington: Carnegie Institution, 1925), pp. 54–55, and Henretta, p. 8.

34. Obediah Macy, *The History of Nantucket, Being a Compendious Account of the First Settlement of the Island by the English* (Boston: Hilliard, Gray, & Co., 1835), p. 110, quoted in Tryon, *Household Manufactures,* p. 60. See Mary Beth Norton, *Liberty's Daughters: The Revolutionary Experience of American Women, 1750–1800* (Boston: Little, Brown, 1980), for discussion of women and their work in the Revolutionary period.

35. Alice Clark, *Working Life,* and Elisabeth Dexter, *Colonial Women of Affairs: A Study of Women in Business and the Professions in America Before 1776* (New York: Houghton Mifflin Co., 1924); Alice M. Earle, *Colonial Dames and Goodwives* (New York: Houghton Mifflin Co., 1895).

36. Edith Abbott, *Women in Industry, a Study in American Economic History* (New York: D. Appleton & Co., 1910); Robert W. Smuts, *Women and Work in America* (New York: Schocken Books, 1971).

37. See, for example, Mary P. Ryan, *Womanhood in America, from Colonial Times to the Present,* 2nd ed. (New York: New Viewpoints, 1979).

38. Nancy Folbre has an excellent discussion of the power of fathers over sons in New England due to the issue of inheritance in "Patriarchy in Colonial New England," *Review of Radical Political Economics* 12:2 (Summer 1980), pp. 6–8. See also Philip J. Greven, "Family Structure in Seventeenth-Century Andover, Massachusetts," *William and Mary Quarterly* 23 (1966), and in Michael Gordon, ed., *The American Family in Social-Historical Perspective* (New York: St. Martin's Press, 1973), pp. 20–35; Daniel Scott Smith, "Parental Power and Marriage Patterns: an Analysis of Historical Trends

in Hingham, Massachusetts," *Journal of Marriage and the Family* 35:3 (August 1973); and R. Gross, *The Minutemen and Their World* (New York: Hill & Wang, 1976).

39. Cotton Mather, *Ornaments to the Daughters of Zion*, 3rd ed. (Boston: Kneeland & Green, 1741), p. 89. For England, see Stone, Ch 5.3; for early American ministerial sermons, see Laurel Thetcher Ulrich, "Vertuous Women Found, New England Ministerial Literature 1668–1735," *American Quarterly* 28 (Spring 1976); see also Arthur Schlesinger, *Learning How to Behave, A Historical Study of American Etiquette Books* (New York: Macmillan, 1946).

40. The exception to this was women's active, if secondary, participation in the church. Since Puritans believed that women had souls, they recognized woman's individuality, her independent existence. And this recognition caused religious women such as Ann Hutchinson to reject the patriarchal character of the church on the basis of its own teachings. See Lyle W. Koehler, "The Case of the American Jezebels: Anne Hutchinson and Female Agitation During the Years of the Antinomian Turmoil, 1636–1640," in Esther Katz and Anita Rapone, eds., *Women's Experience in America: A Historical Anthology* (New Brunswick, N.J.: Translation Books, 1980).

41. Cotton Mather, *Bethiah*, p. 34 quoted in Laurel Thetcher Ulrich, "Vertuous Women Found."

42. Alice Earle gives some interesting accounts of the attempts of husbands to convince their wives to come to the colonies in *Colonial Dames*, pp. 1–20.

43. See, especially, Joan M. Jensen, "Cloth, Butter and Boarders: Women's Household Production for the Market," *Review of Radical Political Economics*, 12:2 (Summer 1980).

44. The degree of participation of women in the fields during periods of labor shortage varied between areas. Among German settlers in New York and Pennsylvania, and in the southern colonies, women's field work was much more common than in New England. See Bidwell and Falconer, *Agriculture in the Northern United States*, p. 116 and Carr and Walsh, "The Planter's Wife," pp. 28–9.

45. Cotton Mather, *Ornaments*, p. 93.

46. William Secker, *A Wedding Ring Fit for the Finger: Or, The Salve of Divinity on the Sore of Humanity. With Directions to Those Men That Want Wives, How to Choose Them; and to Those Women That Have Husbands, How to Use Them* (Boston: J. Draper, 1750). This English pamphlet was reprinted in Boston in 1690, 1705, 1750 and 1773; the quote is from p. 18 of the 1750 edition.

47. Bidwell and Falconer, *Agriculture in the Northern United States*, p. 82.

48. John M. Faragher, *Women and Men on the Overland Trail* (New Haven: Yale University Press, 1979), Chapt. 3; quote from p. 75. This is an excellent study of the concrete living out of the sexual division of labor.

49. Mary Beth Norton, "Eighteenth-Century American Women in Peace and War: The Case of the Loyalists," in Cott and Pleck, *Heritage*.

50. Nancy F. Cott, "Eighteenth-Century Family and Social Life Revealed in Massachusetts Divorce Records," *Journal of Social History* 10 (Fall 76) and in Cott and Pleck, *Heritage*. Cott writes, "Petioners' and deponents' statements repeatedly made it clear that marriage was seen as a relationship in which the husband agreed to provide food, clothing, and shelter for his wife, and she agreed to return frugal management and obedient service" (p. 120).

51. Faragher, *Overland Trail*, p. 88.

2. HOMEMAKING: THE WORK OF THE MARRIED WOMAN

1. William Duance, ed., *Extracts for the Diary of Christopher Marshall Kept in Philadelphia and Lancaster During the American Revolution, 1774–1781* (Albany: Joel Munsell, 1887), pp. 157–58.

2. Ibid., p. 158.

3. Wilson H. Grabill, Clyde V. Kiser, and Pascal K. Whelpton, *The Fertility of American Women* (New York: John Wiley & Sons, 1958), pp. 10–11.

4. John Demos, "Infancy and Childhood in the Plymouth Colony," in Michael Gordon, ed., *American Family in Social-Historical Perspective* (New York: St. Martin's Press, 1973), p. 157.

5. Lawrence Stone, *The Family, Sex, and Marriage in England 1500–1800* (New York: Harper & Row, 1977), pp. 426–32.

6. Quoted by Claire E. Fox, cited in Edward Shorter, *The Making of the Modern Family* (New York: Basic Books, 1975), p. 176. Lorena S. Walsh found evidence of wet-nursing in seventeenth-century Maryland; see her " 'Till Death Us Do Part': Marriage and Family in Seventeenth-Century Maryland," in Thad W. Tate and David L. Ammerman, *The Chesapeake in the Seventeenth Century: Essays in Anglo-American Society* (Chapel Hill: University of North Carolina Press, 1979), pp. 141–42.

7. Cotton Mather, *Ornaments to the Daughters of Zion*, 3rd edition (Boston: Kneeland & Green, 1741), p. 105.

8. Fithian's diary, quoted in Philip Greven, *The Protestant Temperament: Patterns of Child-rearing, Religious Experience, and the Self in Early America* (New York: Alfred A. Knopf, 1977), p. 275.

9. Demos, "Infancy and Childhood," in Gordon, *American Family*, p. 161.

10. See Philip Greven, *The Protestant Temperament*, for an excellent discussion of the different kinds of parenting in the family economy: the evangelicals, the moderates, and the genteel; see also Edmund S. Morgan's fine discussion of the particularities of the parent–child relationship among early Puritan colonists in *The Puritan Family: Religion and Domestic Relations in Seventeenth Century New England* (New York: Harper & Row, 1944).

11. Mary Beth Norton writes the following ". . . formal child-rearing literature as was available to eighteenth-century Americans—most of it published in England—was addressed solely to fathers. . . . As befitted their dominant position in the family, fathers assumed a highly paternalistic, instructive stance with respect to all their off-spring, while mothers, at least until the last years of the century, confined themselves to advising their daughters. Fathers interested themselves in many aspects of their children's lives, peppering sons and daughters with advice about everything from posture to hairstyles to relations with the opposite sex and the selection of friends." *Liberty's Daughters: The Revolutionary Experience of American Women, 1750–1800* (Boston: Little, Brown and Company, 1980), pp. 95, 97.

12. Carole Shammas, "The Domestic Environment in Early Modern England and America," *Journal of Social History* 14:1 (Fall 1980), p. 10.

13. Arthur W. Calhoun, *A Social History of the American Family*, 1 (Cleveland: Arthur H. Clark Company), pp. 112–13.

14. John Demos, *A Little Commonwealth: Family Life in Plymouth Colony* (New York: Oxford University Press, 1970), pp. 41–42, and Shammas, "Domestic Environment."

15. See Thomas Woody, *A History of Women's Education in the United States* (New York: The Science Press, 1929), Vol. 1, p. 159.

16. Susannah Carter, *The Frugal Housewife or Complete Woman Cook* (Boston: Edes & Gill, 1772), title page.

17. J. C. Wylie, "Mrs. Washington's Book of Cookery," *The Pennsylvania Magazine of History and Biography*, 27 (1903), pp. 436–37.

18. For a more detailed examination of cookbooks, see Alice Messing, "American Foodways, The First Hundred Years of Domestic Cookery" (unpublished paper, University of Pennsylvania, 1979).

19. Carl Holliday, *Women's Life in Colonial Days* (Williamstown, Mass.: Corner House Publishers, 1922), p. 108.

20. Eliza Smith, *The Compleat Housewife or the Accomplished Gentlewoman's Companion* (Williamsburg, Pa: William Parks, 1742), p. 19.

21. Charles M. Andrews, *Colonial Folkways—A Chronical of American Life in the Reign of the Georges* (New Haven: Yale University Press, 1919), pp. 101–102.

22. "The wife of a large farmer, who must supply hearty meals for fifteen or twenty persons at least three times a day, passes a life of hopeless drudgery," wrote *The Genesee Farmer* XIX, p. 16, in 1858; quoted in David E. Schob, *Hired Hands and Plowboys: Farm Labor in the Midwest, 1815–1860* (Chicago: University of Illinois Press, 1975), p. 228.

23. See Joan Jensen, "Cloth, Butter and Boarders: Women's Household Production for the Market," *Review of Radical Political Economics*, 12:2 (Summer 1980). Little is known yet about the exact importance of such cash earning by women in the colonial economy; in her study of the nineteenth century, Jensen estimates that in some areas butter and egg money brought in up to 40% of a farm's income, although it is not clear that this was all the work of women (p. 17). John M. Faragher writes of the family farms in the early nineteenth century in *Women and Men on the Overland Trail* (New Haven: Yale University Press, 1979), pp. 62–3, "powder, glass, dyes, crockery, coffee, tea, store cloth, metal utensils, and sugar were bought on credit from the local merchant; butter, cheese, eggs, vegetables, homespun, and whiskey were the main items offered in trade to pay the tab." Both of these authors acknowledge that the earning of income by homemakers was distinct from that of men; Jensen describes the farm as a "dual economy—the women and children providing for living expenses and keeping these expenses on a cash basis while the men handled the field crops, using the income to pay for mortgages and the new machinery" (p. 18).

24. Rolla M. Tryon, *Household Manufactures in the United States 1640–1800* (Chicago: University of Chicago Press, 1917), pp. 190–216; and Alice M. Earle, *Home Life in Colonial Days* (New York: Macmillan Co., 1898).

25. Again, historians have not yet been able to ascertain the prevalence of yarn or cloth or clothing production by homemakers for the market; Nancy Folbre, in "Patriarchy in Colonial New England" (p. 9) argues that this was rare, while Joan Jensen, "Cloth, Butter and Boarders" (p. 16) claims it was more important. Both articles include references to relevant case studies and are published in *Review of Radical Political Economics*, 12:2 (Summer 1980).

26. A study of 109 rural household inventories for Suffolk County, Massachusetts, between 1675 and 1775 gives us a rough idea of the prevalence of home spinning and weaving. Spinning wheels along with carding equipment were present in 70% of the rural household inventories; looms were in less than 4%. Home spinning was not,

then, universal even in rural areas and was certainly even less common in the cities, where exchange was more prevalent; home-weaving was rare. Abbott L. Cummings, ed., *Rural Household Inventories Establishing the Names, Uses and Furnishings of Rooms in the Colonial New England Home, 1675–1775* (Portland, Maine: Anthoensen Press, 1964). For a detailed discussion of the prevalence of household textile production see Tryon, *Household Manufactures*.

27. The different types of needlework were listed in an advertisement in the *Boston Newsletter* of August 20–27, 1716: "Feather-Work, Filegre and Painting on Glass, Embroidering in a new way, Turkey-Work for Handkerchiefs two ways, fine new Fashion Purses, flourishing and plain Work. . . . Brocaded-Work for Handkerchiefs and short Aprons upon Muslin, artificial Flowers work'd with a Needle."

28. Edward Eggleston, *The Transit of Civilization* (New York: D. Appleton & Company, 1901), Chap. 2.

29. Smith, *Compleat Housewife*, Title Page.

30. Ibid., p. 197.

31. Wylie, "Cookery," pp. 438, 440.

32. Ibid.

33. Mather, *Ornaments*, p. 94.

34. William Secker, *A Wedding Ring Fit for the Finger: Or, The Salve of Divinity on the Sore of Humanity. With Directions to Those Men That Want Wives, How to Choose Them; And to Those Women That Have Husbands, How to Use Them* (Boston: J. Draper, 1750), p. 18.

3. HUSBANDLESS WOMEN IN THE COLONIAL ECONOMY: WOMEN WORKING FOR INCOME

1. Cotton Mather, *Ornaments to the Daughters of Zion*, 3rd edition (Boston: Kneeland & Green, 1741), p. 112.

2. Ibid., pp. 112–13.

3. Lois G. Carr and Lorena S. Walsh, "The Planter's Wife: The Experience of White Women in Seventeenth Century Maryland," in Nancy F. Cott and Elizabeth H. Pleck, eds., *A Heritage of Her Own: Toward a New Social History of American Women* (New York: Simon & Schuster, 1979); Alexander Keyssar, "Widowhood in Eighteenth-Century Massachusetts: A Problem in the History of the Family," in Esther Katz and Anita Rapone, eds., *Women's Experience in America: An Historical Anthology* (New Brunswick, N.J.: Transaction Books, 1980).

4. While precise statistics on the extent of widowhood in colonial times are not available, Mather's quote above suggests that such poor widows were not uncommon. Alexander Keyssar suggests that the extent of remarriage of widows has been exaggerated by historians. His study of Woburn, Massachusetts, in the eighteenth century showed considerable numbers of women who remained widowed for years. See Keyssar "Widowhood," pp. 52–53.

5. Mather, *Ornaments*, p. 112.

6. *Pennsylvania Packet*, Sept. 23, 1780, quoted in Alice M. Earle, *Home Life in Colonial Days* (New York: Macmillan Company, 1898), pp. 152–53.

7. W. Elliot Brownlee and Mary M. Brownlee, *Women in the American Economy:*

A Documentary History, 1675 to 1929 (New Haven: Yale University Press, 1976), pp. 76–77.

8. Samuel Sewall, "Diary," Vol. I, p. 385, quoted in Edmund S. Morgan, *The Puritan Family: Religion and Domestic Relations in Seventeenth Century New England* (New York: Harper & Row, 1944), pp. 37–38.

9. John Hammond, "Leah and Rachel, or, the Two Fruitfull Sisters Virginia and Mary-land," 1656, in *Narratives of Early Maryland 1633–1684*, edited by Clayton C. Hall (New York: Charles Scribner's Sons, 1910), pp. 290–91. Carr and Walsh suggest that such reports underemphasized the female servant's participation in agricultural work, so as to encourage indenturing. Carr and Walsh, "Planter's Wife," in Cott and Pleck, *Heritage*.

10. William Eddis, *Letters from America, Historical and Descriptive; Comprising Occurences from 1769–1777, Inclusive* (London: Printed for the author, 1792), p. 70.

11. Thomas Woody, *A History of Women's Education in the United States*, Vol. 1 (New York: The Science Press, 1929), p. 265.

12. Phillip A. Bruce, *Economic History of Virginia in the Seventeenth Century*, Vol. 2 (New York: Macmillan & Co., 1895), p. 51.

13. Eben Cook, "The Sot-Weed Factor: Or, a Voyage to Maryland. A Satyr, in which is described the Laws, Government, Courts and Constitutions of the Country, and also the Buildings, Feasts, Frolicks, Entertainments, and Drunken Humours of the Inhabitants of that Part of America," 1708, in *Early Southern Tracts*, edited by John D. G. Shea (Baltimore, Md., 1865), p. 21.

14. Ibid., pp. 6–7.

15. Alice M. Earle, *Colonial Dames and Goodwives* (New York: Houghton Mifflin Co., 1895), p. 11.

16. *The Providence Gazette*, March 9, 1765, quoted in Elisabeth Dexter, *Colonial Women of Affairs: A Study of Women in Business and the Professions in America before 1776* (New York: Houghton Mifflin Co., 1924), pp. 14–15. Dexter combed through colonial newspapers to find evidence of "colonial women of affairs." Her excellent research is still the best work on the subject; the remainder of this chapter relies heavily on it.

17. Quoted in Ibid., pp. 91–92.

18. *Boston Evening Post*, Feb. 1, 1748, quoted in Dexter, *Women of Affairs*, p. 93.

19. *The New York Gazette or the Weekly Post-Boy*, Feb. 29, 1768.

20. *The Pennsylvania Gazette*, Dec. 31, 1761, quoted in Dexter, *Women of Affairs*, p. 46.

21. *The Pennsylvania Gazette*, May 24, 1770, quoted in Dexter, *Women of Affairs*, p. 48.

22. Ibid., p. 68.

23. *Boston Evening Post*, March 28, 1748, quoted in Dexter, *Women of Affairs*, p. 72.

24. *The Pennsylvania Gazette*, Feb. 21, 1765, quoted in Dexter, *Women of Affairs*, p. 71.

25. *The New York Journal*, March 29, 1736, quoted in Dexter, *Women of Affairs*, p. 71.

26. Edward Eggleston, *The Transit of Civilization* (New York: D. Appleton & Company, 1901), p. 78.

27. Barbara Ehrenreich and Deirdre English, *Witches, Midwives and Nurses: A*

History of Women Healers (Old Westbury, N.Y.: The Feminist Press, 1973), and Eggleston, *Civilization*, pp. 20–22.

28. *History of the Town of Dorchester, Massachusetts*, By a Committee of the Dorcester Antiquarian and Historical Society (Boston: E. Clapp, Jr., 1859), p. 281.

29. *The Boston Newsletter*, March 27, 1729, quoted in Dexter, *Women of Affairs*, p. 41.

30. *The New York Journal and Weekly Register*, May 4, 1786.

31. *The Pennsylvania Packet and Gazette*, quoted in William R. Bagnall, *The Textile Industries of the U.S. Including Sketches and Notices of Cotton, Woolen, Silk and Linen Manufacture in the Colonial Period*, Vol. 1 (Cambridge, Mass.: Riverside Press, 1893), pp. 70–71.

32. *The New York Gazette or the Weekly Post-Boy*, Dec. 31, 1767.

33. *The Compact Version of the Oxford English Dictionary*, Vol. II (Oxford: Oxford University Press, 1971), p. 611.

34. Edith Abbott, *Women in Industry, A Study in American Economic History* (New York: D. Appleton & Co., 1910), pp. 40–41.

35. It is difficult to estimate the prevalence of putting-out manufacture in the colonies and in the nineteenth century; due perhaps to the private nature of such work, data are extremely scattered and sketchy. We emphasize putting-out here because, as work in the home for income, it was an important employment of women in need of income. There are some good studies of women in putting-out. Edith Abbott, in *Women in Industry*, provides the most comprehensive and well-documented treatment of the various forms of putting-out which employed women in the colonial times. See also Rolla M. Tryon, *Household Manufactures in the United States 1640–1860; A Study of Industrial History* (Chicago: University of Chicago Press, 1917), pp. 161–87, and Secretary of the Treasury Gallatin's "Report on Manufactures, 1810," in *American States Papers Finance*, Vol. II, pp. 427–39.

36. Dexter, *Women of Affairs*.

37. *The Pennsylvania Gazette*, Dec. 22, 1763, quoted in Ibid., p. 45.

38. Dexter, *Women of Affairs*, p. 47.

39. Ibid., p. 48.

40. Ibid., p. 50–51.

41. *The New York Journal*, Jan. 21, 1733, quoted in Ibid., p. 18.

42. Earle, *Colonial Dames*, pp. 71–73.

43. Dexter, *Women of Affairs*, pp. 37–38.

44. Ibid., pp. 166–79.

45. *The Annapolis Gazette*, April 1767, quoted in Ibid., p. 175.

46. See Mary P. Ryan, *Womanhood in America, from Colonial Times to the Present*, 2nd. ed. (New York: New Viewpoints, 1975), Chap. 1.

47. U.S. Department of Commerce, Bureau of the Census, *Statistics of Women at Work, 1900* (1908), p. 126.

48. Harriott H. Ravenel, *Eliza Pinckney* (New York: Charles Scribner's Sons, 1896). The following description of Eliza's life is based upon Ravenel's reconstruction using her letter-book.

49. Letter to Mr. and Mrs. Boddicott, May 2, probably 1740, quoted in Ravenel, *Pinckney*, p. 177.

50. Quoted in Ravenel, *Pinckney*, p. 100.

51. Letter of Sept. 25, 1758, quoted in Ravenel, *Pinckney*, p. 177.

52. *The New York Journal,* Jan. 21, 1733, quoted in Dexter, *Women of Affairs,* p. 18.

53. Earle, *Colonial Dames,* pp. 45–49.

54. Ibid., p. 49.

55. Quoted in Ibid., p. 48.

4. WOMEN'S WORK AND THE SEXUAL DIVISION OF LABOR UNDER SLAVERY

1. Eric Williams, *Capitalism and Slavery* (Chapel Hill: University of North Carolina Press, 1944), chap. 1. The colonists in Australia, faced with this same problem, encouraged the development of wage labor by buying up agricultural lands, thereby preventing wage laborers from transforming themselves into petty producers. See Karl Marx, *Capital,* Vol. 1 (New York: International Publishers, 1967), Chap. XXXIII.

2. Kenneth Stampp, *The Peculiar Institution: Slavery in the Ante-bellum South* (New York: Alfred A. Knopf, 1956), p. 22. See also Edmund S. Morgan, *American Slavery, American Freedom: The Ordeal of Colonial Virginia,* 1st edition (New York: Norton, 1975).

3. Early analyses of slavery totally ignored the persistence of parts of African culture through slavery; today, however, such elements are recognized as important. See Melville J. Herskovits, *The Myth of the Negro Past* (Gloucester: Peter Smith, 1970) originally published in 1941; Herbert Gutman, *The Black Family in Slavery and Freedom, 1750–1925* (New York: Pantheon Books, 1976); John Blassingame, *The Slave Community: Plantation Life in the Old South* (New York: Oxford University Press, 1972); and Eugene Genovese, *Roll, Jordan, Roll: The World the Slaves Made* (New York: Random House, 1972).

4. The most comprehensive of these is Robert W. Fogel and Stanley L. Engerman's *Time on the Cross: The Economics of American Negro Slavery* (Boston: Little, Brown and Company, 1974).

5. See Paul A. David, Herbert G. Gutman, Richard Sutch, Peter Temin, and Gavin Wright, *Reckoning with Slavery: A Critical Study on the Quantitative History of American Negro Slavery* (New York: Oxford University Press, 1976).

6. One early nineteenth-century slave preacher in Florida taught his congregation that slavery was evil and that it was wrong to contribute to it in any way, causing the slave women to try to avoid giving birth. See Leslie Owens, *This Species of Property: Slave Life and Culture in the Old South* (New York: Oxford University Press, 1976), p. 158. Earlier quotes are in Stampp: p. 144, (from *The Southern Cultivator, 1860*), and p. 146.

7. Quoted in Ann F. Scott, *The Southern Lady; From Pedestal to Politics 1830–1930* (Chicago: University of Chicago Press, 1970), pp. 50–51.

8. See Gerda Lerner, *The Grimke Sisters* (Boston: Houghton Mifflin, 1967), pp. 21 ff.

9. See E. Franklin Frazier, *The Negro Family in the United States* (Chicago: University of Chicago Press, 1939), pp. 81–85. This, of course, was little known between the mistress of the plantation and a male slave, for in this case the wife was not slave but master.

10. See especially Stampp, *Peculiar Institution*, Chap. 3; Paul Escott, *Slavery Remembered: A Record of Twentieth-century Slave Narratives* (Chapel Hill: University of North Carolina Press, 1979), Chap. 3; and Leslie Owens, *This Species of Property*, Chap. 4. See also Blassingame, *Slave Community*, for discussion of slave resistance and the punishment it brought.

11. F. L. Olmsted, *Journey in the Back Country* (New York: Mason Brothers, 1860), p. 183.

12. Fogel and Engerman correctly point out the use of these incentives in *Time on the Cross*; however, they neglect to bring out the contradictions inherent in the training of the slave.

13. Quoted in Frazier, *The Negro Family*, p. 40, from J. W. C. Pennington, *The Fugitive Blacksmith*, 1850.

14. Quoted in Genovese, *Roll, Jordan, Roll*, p. 393.

15. Alexis de Tocqueville, quoted in John Cairnes, *The Slave Power: Its Character, Career, and Probable Designs: Being an Attempt to Explain the Real Issues Involved in the American Contest*, 2nd. edition (New York: Harper & Row, 1969), pp. 116–17—first published in 1862.

16. See Stampp, *Peculiar Institution*, p. 32.

17. See Ester Boserup, *Women's Role in Economic Development* (London: Allen & Unwin, 1970), Chaps. 1–3; Hermann Baumann, "The Division of Work According to Sex in African Hoe Culture," *Africa*, 1 (1928); and C. S. Lancaster, "Women, Horticulture, and Society in Sub-Saharan Africa," *American Anthropologist*, 78 (1976).

18. See Gutman, *Black Family*, Part I.

19. Some historians traced the origin of this difference to the lower profitability of the southern plantation crops. While the profitability of breeding slaves was well below that of sugar, making breeding unattractive in much of the West Indies, the difference in rate of return was less in the South; indeed, for many of the small plantations, breeding was a major source of wealth. David Weiman brought this point to my attention. See James Henretta, *The Evolution of American Society 1700–1815* (Lexington, Mass.: Heath, 1973).

20. See Escott, *Slavery Remembered*, pp. 44–50.

21. Olmsted, *Back Country*, pp. 74–75.

22. Quoted in Genovese, *Roll, Jordan, Roll*, p. 489.

23. Quoted in Ibid.

24. Olmstead, *Back Country*, p. 76.

25. Jones, *The Religious Instruction of the Negro* (Princeton: O'Harte and Company, 1842), p. 241, quoted in Owens, *Property*, p. 53.

26. Genovese, *Roll, Jordan, Roll*, p. 319.

27. See Blassingame's *Slave Community* for the best discussion of such practices.

28. See Gutman, *Black Family*, especially Chap. 5, "Aunts and Uncles and Swap-Dog Kin."

29. Quoted in Frazier, *Negro Family*, p. 59.

30. Quoted in Genovese, *Roll, Jordan, Roll*, p. 421.

31. Moses Grandy, *Narrative in the Life of Moses Grandy*, quoted in Blassingame, *Slave Community*, p. 165.

32. Escott, *Slavery Remembered*, pp. 50–51.

33. Quoted in Olmsted, *Back Country*, p. 48.

34. Gutman, *Black Family*, p. 21.

35. Blassingame, *Slave Community*, p. 361.

36. Escott, *Slavery Remembered*, p. 48.

37. Fogel and Engerman, *Time on the Cross*, p. 39. As Gutman and Sutch argue, Fogel and Engerman probably overstated the percentage of men employed in skilled and "managerial" work, to make their argument about work promotion as a form of incentive. Using Fogel and Engerman's sources, they show that 88.5% of men were field hands, 3.3% drivers and assistant drivers, and 8% artisans and non-field workers. See their article "Were Slaves Imbued with the Protestant Work Ethic?" in David, et al., *Reckoning with Slavery*.

38. See Jacqueline Jones, "My Mother Was Much of A Woman: Black Women, Work, and the Family Under Slavery" (Wellesley: unpublished paper, 1980), p. 8, and *Feminist Studies*, forthcoming.

39. A. Steward, *Twenty-two Years a Slave and Forty Years a Freeman* (New York: Negro Universities Press, 1968; originally 1856), p. 14.

40. Olmsted, *Journey in the Seaboard Slave States*, (New York: Dix & Edwards, 1856), pp. 386–87.

41. Quoted in Jones, "Black Women," p. 10, from the *Texas Narratives*.

42. Olmsted, *Back Country*, p. 81.

43. Henry Baker, in John Blassingame, *Slave Testimony: Two Centuries of Letters, Speeches, Interviews, & Autobiographies* (Baton Rouge: Louisiana State University Press, 1977), p. 656. Fogel and Engerman, however, claim that it was "uncommon" for women to plow (p. 141).

44. Mary Frances Webb, quoted in Jones, "Black Women," p. 11.

45. Emily Burke, quoted in Lewis C. Gray, *History of Agriculture in the Southern United States*, Vol. I (Washington, D.C.: Carnegie Institution, 1933), p. 251.

46. Fanny Kemble, *Journal of Residence on a Georgian Plantation in 1838–1839* (London: Longman, Green, 1863), pp. 29–30.

47. From Andrew Flinn, *Plantation Book, 1840*, Rule 15, quoted in Owens, *Property*, p. 40.

48. Robert Starobin, *Industrial Slavery in the Old South* (New York: Oxford University Press, 1970) p. 167.

49. Quoted in Scott, *The Southern Lady*, p. 30, from the David Garvin Diary, 31 May, 1865.

50. See Rolla M. Tryon, *Household Manufactures in the United States 1640–1860; A Study of Industrial History* (Chicago: University of Chicago Press, 1917), p. 121–22 and 137–38.

51. See Peter Wood, *Black Majority: Negroes in Colonial South Carolina from 1670 Through the Stone Rebellion* (New York: Alfred A. Knopf, 1974), p. 198 ff.

52. Julia Spruill, *Women's Life and Work in the Southern Colonies*, (New York: W. W. Norton & Co., 1972), pp. 64–65.

53. Wood, *Black Majority*, p. 197.

54. Quoted in Scott, p. 30, from *A Southern Country Minister*, Old Pine Farm, 1860.

55. Claudia Goldin, *Urban Slavery in the American South 1820–1860* (Chicago: University of Chicago Press, 1976), p. 43.

56. Genovese, *Roll, Jordan, Roll*, p. 394.

57. Goldin, *Urban Slavery*, p. 43.

58. Blassingame, *Slave Testimony*, pp. 564–65.

59. Blassingame, *Slave Testimony*, p. 540.

60. Quoted in Jones, "Black Women," p. 13.

61. Blassingame, *Slave Testimony*, p. 656.

62. James Curry, in Blassingame, *Slave Testimony*, pp. 132–33.

63. Quoted in Jones, "Black Women," p. 11.

64. Quoted in Jones, "Black Women," p. 43, from Moses Grandy, *Narrative*.

65. Quoted in Frazier, *Negro Family*, p. 53.

66. Quoted in Frazier, *Negro Family*, p. 54.

67. Quoted in Genovese, *Roll, Jordan, Roll*, p. 499.

68. This point is made by Angela Davis in "The Black Woman's Role in the Community of Slaves," *Black Scholar*, 3, (Dec. 1971).

5. THE DEVELOPMENT OF SEPARATE SEXUAL SPHERES OF ACTIVITY AND OF MASCULINE AND FEMININE SELF-SEEKING

1. Marx' discussion of the development of industrial capitalism remains one of the best; he divides this process into two stages. In manufacturing, workers are brought under one roof, into the factory, and paid a wage, yet retain their control over the production process in the form of their craft skills. In the second stage, modern industry, machinery is introduced which contains within itself the design of the product; the worker, deskilled, is robbed of any control over the final product. See *Capital*, Vol. 1 (New York: International Publishers, 1967), Part IV.

2. Alfred Chandler's work on this transition is excellent; see especially, *The Visible Hand: The Managerial Revolution in American Business* (Cambridge, Mass.: Harvard University Press, 1977).

3. Although Afro-Americans were formally freed from slavery with the Civil War, their equality of rights was not recognized by white men in the nineteenth century and is still being fought for in the present.

4. See especially "Estranged Labor," in Karl Marx, *Economic and Philosophical Manuscripts of 1844*, edited and with an Introduction by Dirk J. Struik, translated by Martin Milligan (New York: International Publishers, 1964), pp. 106–19.

5. The freeing of sons from the control of their fathers in the nineteenth century is stressed in G. J. Barker-Benfield's *The Horrors of the Half-known Life: Male Attitudes Toward Women and Sexuality in Nineteenth-Century America* (New York: Harper & Row, 1977), Chapter 4, "Democratic Fathers and Democratic Sons," its psychoanalytic consequences forming the basis for the rest of his thought-provoking study of male attitudes toward women. David Levine points out the same rise of individuation in his study of demographic change in England: the rise of wage labor combined with the availability of job opportunities freed sons from the necessity to postpone marriage until they had inherited their positions from their fathers, bringing an earlier age at marriage and an increase in the birth rate. *Family Formation in an Age of Nascent Capitalism* (New York: Academic Press, 1977).

6. Quoted in Eric Foner, *Free Soil, Free Labor, Free Men: The Ideology of the Republican Party before the Civil War* (New York: Oxford University Press, 1970), pp. 14–15. Foner's discussion of the prevalence of the desire for self-advancement in Chap. 1, "Free Labor: The Republicans and Northern Society," is excellent.

7. Quoted from Ida C. Murray, "Small Things That Won My Success," *Ladies' Home Journal*, 24 (1907), in Irvin G. Wyllie, *The Self-made Man in America: The Myth of Rags to Riches* (New Brunswick, N.J.: Rutgers University Press, 1954).

There is still much debate over the extent to which upward mobility was actually experienced in the nineteenth century. Irvin Wyllie's 1954 study of the ideology of the self-made man in America was subtitled "The Myth of Rags to Riches." Recent scholarship has shown that mobility was not limited to the few "stars" that have received so much attention. Studies of four different American cities throughout the nineteenth century have shown that about one-fifth of all the men who entered the labor market as manual workers ended their careers in a middle-class calling; see Stephan Thernstrom, *The Other Bostonians: Poverty and Progress in the American Metropolis 1880–1970* (Cambridge, Mass.: Harvard University Press, 1973), p. 234. In his study of Patterson, N.J., Herbert Gutman wrote, "So many successful manufacturers who had begun as workers walked the streets of that city then that it is not hard to believe that others less successful or just starting out on the lower rungs of the occupational mobility ladder could be convinced by personal knowledge that 'hard work' resulted in spectacular material and social improvement." "The Reality of the Rags-to-Riches 'Myth': The Case of the Patterson, New Jersey, Locomotive, Iron, and Machinery Manufacturers, 1830–1880," in *Nineteenth-Century Cities: Essays in the New Urban History*, edited by Stephan Thernstrom and Richard Sennett (New Haven: Yale University Press, 1969). Whatever the exact prevalence of advancement "from rags to riches," it is clear that the possibility for such movement was a reality in the minds of Americans, as it had not been in the precapitalist, colonial economy.

8. David Montgomery, *Beyond Equality, Labor and the Radical Republicans 1862–1872* (New York: Knopf, 1967), pp. 26–27.

9. Foner, *Free Soil*, p. 25.

10. See especially Joe I. Dubbert, *A Man's Place: Masculinity in Transition* (Englewood Cliffs, N.J.: Prentice-Hall, 1979), Chap. 2. Dubert writes, "Above everything else, the guidebooks stressed that manliness assumed material and/or professional success . . . manly success in America came to be closely associated with highly competitive occupational and business achievement" (pp. 27–28). See also Wyllie, *Self-made Man,* and John G. Cawelti, *Apostles of the Self-made Man* (Chicago: University of Chicago Press, 1965).

11. David P. Levine, *Economic Theory*, Vol. II, Chap. 8, "The Social Purpose of the Market" (Boston: Routledge & Kegan Paul, forthcoming). See also Lynn Levine, "Masculinity" (New Haven: unpublished paper, 1980), for an excellent analysis of competition and the masculine personality.

12. See Christopher Lasch, *The Culture of Narcissism: American Life in an Age of Diminishing Expectations* (New York: Norton, 1978).

13. Philip Aries was the first to stress this important change in *Centuries of Childhood: A Social History of Family Life* (New York: Alfred A. Knopf, 1962). There is an enlightening discussion of the changing attitude toward the infant in Edward Shorter's *The Making of the Modern Family* (New York: Basic Books, 1975). See also Lawrence Stone, *The Family, Sex, and Marriage in England 1500–1800* (New York: Harper & Row, 1977).

14. Anonymous, *Woman's Influence and Woman's Mission* (Philadelphia: Willis P. Hayward, 1854), pp. 42–43. Here we can only discuss the most basic transformations in childhood and parenting. For a more detailed discussion see Bernard Wishy, *The*

Child and the Republic: The Dawn of Modern American Child Nurture (Philadelphia: University of Pennsylvania Press, 1968).

15. Harriet Beecher Stowe, *House and Home Papers* (Boston: Tichnor & Fields, 1865), pp. 60–61.

16. Quoted in Barker-Benfield, *Horrors*, p. 13, from the novel by Ik Marvel, 1859.

17. See Barbara Welter's seminal article, "The Cult of True Womanhood, 1820–60." *American Quarterly*, 18 (1966).

18. J. C. Abbott, *Mother at Home* (New York: American Tract Society, 1833), pp. 12–13.

19. Margaret Coxe, *Claims of the Country on American Females* (Columbus, Ohio: Isaac N. Whiting, 1842) p. 6.

20. See Lynn Levine, "Masculinity" and "Feminine Personality and Feminine Process" (New Haven: unpublished papers, 1980), for a more complete development of this argument, as well as an analysis of the internal contradictions of femininity.

21. Hubbard Winslow, *Woman as She Should Be* (Boston: T. H. Carter, 1838) pp. 18–19.

22. Mrs. Ellet, *The Practical Housekeeper: A Cyclopaedia of Domestic Economy* (New York: Stringent & Townsend, 1857) p. 18.

23. Winslow, *Woman*, p. 12.

24. Mrs. Lydia Howard Sigourney, *Letters to Young Ladies* (New York: Harper & Brothers, 1838) p. 232.

25. George W. Burnap, *The Sphere and Duties of Woman and Other Subjects* (Baltimore: John Murphy, 1841) pp. 45–48.

26. In the last fifteen years there has been considerable debate among historians as to whether or not woman's position relative to man's improved with the cult of domesticity. In the sixties and early seventies, feminist historians argued that woman's situation deteriorated in the nineteenth century. "The glorification of the Jacksonian go-getter businessman, the intrepid pioneer, the log-cabin-born President, coincided with the decline in women's status and the increasing restriction of middle-class women to domestic and ornamental functions," wrote Aileen Kraditor in *Up from the Pedestal: Selected Writings in the History of American Feminism* (Chicago: Quadrangle Books, 1968), p. 10. William O'Neil took a similar position, describing the cult of domesticity as follows: "The Victorians had attempted, moreover, to compensate women for their increased domestic and pedagogic responsibilities by enveloping them in a mystique which asserted their higher status while at the same time guaranteeing their actual inferiority," *Everyone Was Brave: The Rise and Fall of Feminism in America* (Chicago: Quadrangle Books, 1969), p. 5. O'Neil portrays nineteenth-century feminism as a reaction to this increased oppression (*Everyone Was Brave*, and *The Woman Movement: Feminism in the United States and England* [Chicago: Quadrangle Books, 1971]); a similar analysis was later presented by Carroll Smith Rosenberg in her analysis of moral reform societies, "Beauty, the Beast, and the Militant Woman; A Case Study in Sex Roles and Social Stress in Jacksonian America," *American Quarterly*, 23 (1971). However, the rebellious activities cited by both authors were efforts of women to protect homes and children, clear extensions of the cult of domesticity's conception of homemaking, rather than reactions against it. Alice Rossi, in *The Feminist Papers: from Adams to de Beauvior* (New York: Columbia University Press, 1973), argues that "while the colonial woman shared many of the same grounds for the cultivation of sense of self-worth as a man, such as pride in family and the possession and exercise of

productive work skills, the woman in the expanding era of Jacksonian democracy had a far less adequate basis for self-satisfaction than her brothers had" (p. 251). Rossi's judgment rests on a faulty understanding of woman's position in the colonial economy, the "equal partners" myth which we have dismissed (see Chapter 1, p. 29)—as well as a lack of appreciation of the transformation of the home in the nineteenth century. Daniel Scott Smith was the first to challenge the claim that the cult of domesticity was only a ploy to mask the deterioration of woman's position; in "Family Limitation and Domestic Feminism," *Feminist Studies*, 1 (Winter–Spring 1973), he dismisses claims of sexual equality in the colonial economy and argues convincingly that women gained autonomy within the family in the nineteenth century. This position has gained acceptance. Nancy Cott's *The Bonds of Womanhood: Woman's Sphere in New England 1780–1835* (New Haven: Yale University Press, 1977) claims that women were both more restricted to the domestic sphere and given more status for their activities there, while Carl N. Degler argues in his recent book that the nineteenth century was a time when women gained increasing control over their own lives; see *At Odds: Women and the Family in America from the Revolution to the Present* (New York: Oxford University Press, 1980). I am less interested in arriving at a transhistorical, quantitative measure of women's status than I am in explaining the forces behind the twentieth-century deterioration of the sexual division of labor; in Part 3, I will argue that the cult of domesticity was central to this twentieth-century change, for the idea of womanhood which it involved, and which, I would argue, women took seriously, was an inherently contradictory one.

27. Reverend Edward Scofield, A.B., *True Connubial Love: or Important Considerations for the Single and Married* (Cincinnati: J.A. & U.P. James, 1848), p. 15. See also James Foster, D.D., *The Married State: Its Obligations and Duties* (Hartford: S. Andrus & Son, 1843).

28. Stowe, *House and Home Papers*, 1865, p. 57. Carl Degler traces the emergence of romantic love in the nineteenth century in *At Odds*, Chap. 2.

29. Christopher Lasch, *Haven in a Heartless World: The Family Besieged* (New York: Basic Books, 1977). Unfortunately, Lasch is unable to conceive of another social system that could preserve such compassion, and in defending the family against the onslaught of capitalism, he ends up defending what is in fact a very distorted form of family life. We will discuss these issues more in Part III. Lasch also discusses the development of self-seeking, unfortunately without much reference to its differentiation into distinctively masculine and feminine modes, in his excellent book, *The Culture of Narcissism: American Life in an Age of Diminishing Expectations* (New York: Norton, 1978).

30. Reverend G. S. Weaver, *Aims and Aids for Girls and Young Women on the Various Duties of Life* (New York: Samuel R. Wells, 1875), p. 145.

6. HOMEMAKING UNDER THE CULT OF DOMESTICITY: UNITY AND DIVERSITY

1. The cult of domesticity appears to have been weaker in Western Europe, and the participation of married women in the labor force more common. See Louise Tilly and Joan Scott, *Women, Work & Family* (New York: Holt, Rinehart & Winston, 1978), pp. 123–36.

2. U.S. Department of Commerce, Bureau of the Census, *Women in Gainful Occupations 1870–1920* (1929), pp. 76, 84.

3. U.S. Department of Commerce, Bureau of the Census, *Statistics of Women at Work 1900* (1908), p. 15.

4. U.S. Department of Commerce, Bureau of the Census, *Population (General Report and Analysis)*, Vol. II, p. 387 and *Occupations*, Vol IV, p. 695; and *Statistics of Women at Work 1900*, p. 15.

5. *Statistics of Women at Work 1900*, pp. 15–16. For those who distrust Census statistics, the same numbers are found in many other studies. The U.S. Senate Report of the Immigration Commission, *Immigrants in Cities 1911*, Vol. I, p. 139, which focused on the poorest urban families, found only 17.7% of wives in the labor force. The Massachusetts Bureau of Statistics of Labor's *Sixth Annual Report* (1875), found 3% of wives earning income, providing only 0.8% of family income (pp. 368–69). For an excellent discussion of working-class woman's exclusion from the labor force in the early twentieth century, see Leslie Woodcock Tentler, *Wage-earning Women: Industrial Work and Family Life in the United States, 1900–1930* (New York: Oxford University Press, 1979), Chap. VI.

6. For a discussion of the prevalence of nonsupport as a reason for divorce suits, as well as examples of husbands deserting wives for whom they could not provide, see Elaine Tyler May, *Great Expectations: Marriage and Divorce in Post-Victorian America* (Chicago: University of Chicago Press, 1980), especially pp. 122–33, 147–48.

7. In spite of incontrovertible evidence of the absence of white homemakers of *all* classes from the labor force, many continue to claim that domestic womanhood was a privilege enjoyed only by middle-class women and that working-class wives have always been in the labor force. I believe that the difficulty in accepting the domesticity of the poor homemaker comes from the prevailing conception of ideas as "ideology" which, rather than determining women's lives, mask their true content. Such an interpretation reduces social life to a struggle for material well-being, and hence cannot fathom the reasons for poor homemakers to refrain from gainful employment. In fact, the maintenance of a sexual division within marriage was central to the "well-being" of the poor family in the nineteenth century, whereas struggle for more material goods had not yet become essential, as we shall see in Chapter 10.

On the other hand, once such thinkers accept the absence of poor wives from the labor force, they insist on explaining it as materially motivated: poor women had too much work to do in the home, or suitable jobs were not available. Orthodox economists have formalized this conception: they portray the sexual division of labor as a "rational choice," aimed at the maximization of utility. Housework, including child-rearing, creates "utility," and it is efficient, given their different productivities, for men and women to choose to specialize in wage and house work, respectively. See W. E. Brownlee, "Household Values, Women's Work, and Economic Growth 1800–1930," *Journal of Economic History*, 39 (March 1979). There is no place in their model for life actions that are not self-consciously chosen, actions that are the essence of the sexual division of labor.

8. See George S. Whitey, ed., *Memoires of Samuel Slater* (Philadelphia: No. 45 Carpenter Street, 1836), p. 127. Such family labor systems persisted into the twentieth century; see Tamara Hareven, "Family Time and Industrial Time," *Journal of Urban History*, 1 (May 1975), pp. 365–89, for her study of French Canadian immigrant families employed in textiles in Manchester, New Hampshire, 1900–1920.

9. See Mary Blewett, "From Their Kitchens to the Shops: The Role of Women in the Growth and Mechanization of the New England Shoe Industry, 1800–1865," in *New Work: Essays in Women's Industrial Employment in the Nineteenth Century* (Lincoln, Mass.: Penman Press, forthcoming).

10. Leila Houghteling, *The Income and Standard of Living of Unskilled Laborers in Chicago* (Chicago: University of Chicago Press, 1927), p. 8.

11. John Modell and Tamara K. Hareven stress the changes in the family's expenditure structure through the life cycle in their excellent article, "Urbanization and the Malleable Family," in Tamara K. Hareven, ed., *Family and Kin in Urban Communities, 1700–1930* (New York: New Viewpoints, 1977). Using an 1890 study of standards of living among working-class families, they found that family expenses, for families of nuclear composition, varied over $200 over the life cycle (a tremendous amount given that the mean income of all fathers was about $450). The mean incomes of fathers did not keep up, creating estimated deficits that increased through the family's life cycle from $4 to $249 (pp. 177–79).

12. See early twentieth-century family budget studies, e.g., Robert C. Chapin, *The Standard of Living among Workingmen's Families in New York City* (New York: Russell Sage Foundation, 1909), and Houghteling, *Income and Standard*. See also Massachusetts Bureau of Statistics of Labor's *Sixth Annual Report* for some detailed family budgets.

13. "Urbanization and the Malleable Household: An Examination of Boarding and Lodging in American Families," in Tamara K. Hareven, ed., *Family and Kin*.

14. Louise Bolard More, *Wage Earner's Budgets: A Study of Standards and Cost of Living in New York City* (New York: Henry Holt & Company, 1907), pp. 84–85, and Chapin, *Standard of Living* p. 64.

15. For an example of middle-class concern over boarding and lodging, see Lawrence Veiller, "Room Overcrowding and the Lodger Evil," in *Housing Problems in America: Proceedings of the Second National Conference on Housing* (Philadelphia: 1912).

16. Massachusetts Bureau of Statistics of Labor, *Sixth Annual Report*, p. 47.

17. *Immigrants in Cities*, Vol. I, p. 39; Vol. II, pp. 547–48.

18. U.S. Women's Bureau, *The Share of Wage-Earning Women in Family Support, 1923*, p. 74.

19. *Statistics of Women at Work 1900*, p. 16.

20. More, *Wage Earner's Budgets*, pp. 86–87.

21. Gwendolyn S. Hughes, *Mothers in Industry: Wage Earning by Mothers in Philadelphia* (New York: New Republic, 1925), p. 22.

22. Caroline Manning, *The Immigrant Woman and Her Job* (New York: Arno Press, reprint of 1930 edition, 1970), p. 45.

23. Manning, *Immigrant Woman*, pp. 50–1.

24. U.S. Department of Labor, Women's Bureau, *Married Women in Industry* (1924) by Mary Winslow, p. 4.

25. U.S. Department of Labor, Women's Bureau, *Share of the Wage-earning Women*, p. 84.

26. *Statistics of Women at Work 1900*, pp. 15–16.

27. *Immigrants in Cities*, Vol. 1, p. 139. The same pattern has been found in other data from the late nineteenth, early twentieth centuries: see Elizabeth Pleck, "A Mother's Wages," in Nancy Cott and Elizabeth Pleck, *A Heritage of Her Own* (New

York: Simon & Schuster, 1979), p. 372, and Claudia Goldin, "Female Labor Force Participation: The Origins of Black and White Differences 1870 and 1880," *Journal of Economic History* (March 1977).

28. U.S. Department of Commerce, *The Negro Population in the United States 1790–1915*, pp. 504–06.

29. *Immigrants in Cities*, Vol. I, p. 139; Vol. II, p. 552.

30. Goldin, "Female Labor Force Participation"; William G. Bowen and Aldrich Finegan, *The Economics of Labor Force Participation* (Princeton: Princeton University Press, 1969); Glen G. Cain, *Married Women in the Labor Force: An Economic Analysis* (Chicago: University of Chicago Press, 1966); James A. Sweet, *Women in the Labor Force* (New York: Seminar Press, 1973); and Duran Bell, "Why Participation Rates of Black and White Wives Differ," *Journal of Human Resources*, 9 (Fall 1974).

31. Gerda Lerner, *Black Women in White America: A Documentary History* (New York: Vintage Books, 1973), p. 292.

32. Elizabeth Pleck presents evidence of this in "A Mother's Wages," pp. 385–86.

33. Ibid., "A Mother's Wages," p. 379.

34. Noted by Goldin, in "Female Labor Force Participation," for seven southern cities in 1870 and 1880.

35. *Statistics of Women at Work 1900*, pp. 15–16.

36. *Women in Gainful Occupations*, pp. 135, 84.

37. Hughes, *Mothers in Industry*, p. 22.

38. Horace Greeley, editorial, *New York Daily Tribune*, October 14, 1845.

39. Matthew Carey, *An Appeal to the Wealthy of the Land, Ladies as well as Gentlemen, on Character, Conduct, Situation and Prospects of Those Whose Sole Dependence for Subsistence is the Labour of Their Hands* (Philadelphia: L. Johnson, 1833), pp. 18, 17.

40. U.S. Department of Commerce, Bureau of the Census, *Historical Statistics, from Colonial Times to 1970*, p. 133.

41. *Statistics of Women at Work 1900*, p. 15.

42. Ibid., p. 14.

43. Arthur P. Miles, *An Introduction to Public Welfare* (Boston: D. C. Heath & Company, 1949), pp. 202–05.

7. THE WORKING GIRL

1. U.S. Department of Labor, Women's Bureau, *1975 Handbook on Women Workers*, p. 11.

2. Louise A. Tilly and Joan W. Scott have an excellent analysis of the emergence of the working girl in Europe in *Women, Work & Family* (New York: Holt, Rinehart & Winston, 1978), Chap. 6.

3. U.S. Bureau of Labor, *Working Women in Large Cities, 1888;* Massachusetts Bureau of Statistics of Labor, *The Working Girls of Boston*, 1889.

4. U.S. Department of Commerce, Bureau of the Census, *Statistics of Women at Work 1900*, (1908), p. 14.

5. U.S. Department of Commerce, Bureau of the Census. *Historical Statistics of the United States from Colonial Times to 1970*, p. 133.

6. Robert C. Chapin, *The Standard of Living Among Workingmen's Families in New York City* (New York: Russell Sage Foundation, 1909), p. 58.

7. For example, see D. D. Scoresby, *American Factories and Their Female Operatives, with an Appeal on Behalf of the British Factory Population and Suggestions for the Improvement of Their Conditions* (Boston: William Tichnor & Co., 1845); Henry A. Miles, *Lowell as It Was and as It Is* (Lowell: Powers & Bagley, 1845).

8. "Visit to Lowell," *New York Daily Tribune*, August 16, 1845.

9. *The Voice of Industry*, September 18, 1845.

10. Ibid. See Philip S. Foner, *The Factory Girls* (Chicago: University of Illinois Press, 1977) for a collection of historical documents on the mill girls, with a good introductory essay.

11. "Leisure Hours of the Mill Girls," *The Lowell Offering*, Vol. 2 (1842) p. 73.

12. Massachusetts Bureau of Statistics of Labor, Carroll D. Wright, *Working Girls of Boston* (Boston: Wright & Potter, 1889), pp. 110–11.

13. Hazel G. Ormsbee, *The Young Employed Girl* (New York: The Woman's Press, 1927), pp. 50, 60–64.

14. Louise Bolard More, *Wage Earner's Budgets: A Study of Standards and Cost of Living in New York City*, (New York: Henry Holt & Co., 1907), pp. 84–85.

15. Chapin, *Standard of Living*, p. 67; Leila Houghteling, *The Income and Standard of Living of Unskilled Laborers in Chicago* (Chicago: University of Chicago Press, 1927), p. 65.

16. Day Monroe, *Chicago Families: A Study of Unpublished Census Data* (Chicago: University of Chicago Press, 1932), pp. 173–74, cited in Leslie Woodcock Tentler, *Wage-earning Women: Industrial Work and Family Life in the United States, 1900–1930* (New York: Oxford University Press, 1979), p. 85.

17. Claudia Goldin, "Household and Market Production of Families in a Late Nineteenth Century American City," *Explorations in Economic History*, 16 (1979), p. 124. Michael Haines reached the same conclusion in "Industrial Work and the Family Life Cycle, 1889–1890" in Paul Uselding, ed., *Research in Economic History* (New York: Academe Press, 1979), p. 309.

18. Tentler, *Wage-earning Women*, p. 108.

19. *The Lowell Offering*, Vol. 4, p. 23.

20. Harriet J. Robinson, *Loom and Spindle: Or Life among the Early Mill Girls* (New York: T. Y. Crowell & Co., 1898), p. 77.

21. Quoted in Tentler, *Wage-earning Women*, p. 103 from Mary Van Kleek, *Artificial Flower Makers*.

22. Anonymous, *Woman's Influence and Woman's Mission* (Philadelphia: Willis P. Hazard, 1854), pp. 51–52.

23. Lucy Larcom, *An Idyll of Work* (Boston: James R. Osgood & Co., 1875), p. 21.

24. Hannah Josephson, *The Golden Threads: New England Mill Girls and Magnates* (New York: Duell, Sloan & Pearce, 1949), p. 81.

25. U.S. Department of Commerce, Bureau of the Census, *Women in Gainful Occupations 1870–1920*, (1929), p. 74.

26. U.S. Senate Document No. 645, 61st Congress, 2d session, *Report on the Condition of Women and Child Wage-earners in the United States*, Vol. 9, *History of Women in Industry*, by Helen Sumner (1910), p. 31.

27. See Tentler, *Wage-earning Women*, pp. 93–104. She claims that the development and feminization of clerical work, which required a high school education,

brought more tangible returns to the education of a daughter and convinced many working-class families to keep their daughters in school.

28. Lucy Eaves, *A Legacy to Wage Earning Women: A Survey of the Gainfully Employed Women of Brattleboro, Vermont* (Boston: Women's Educational & Industrial Trust Union, 1925), pp. 75–77.

29. Ibid., p. 77.

30. Horace Greeley, "Employment for Women," *New York Daily Tribune*, June 18, 1853.

31. "The Affections Illustrated in Factory Life: The Betrothed," *The Lowell Offering*, Vol. 4, pp. 109–15.

32. Quoted in Thomas Dublin, *Women at Work: The Transformation of Work and Community in Lowell, Massachusetts, 1826–1860* (New York: Columbia University Press, 1979), pp. 37–38.

33. Dublin, *Women at Work*. From this evidence of the independence acquired by some mill girls Dublin draws the false conclusion that the mill girls were not, on the whole, working to help their parents financially. Given the nineteenth-century conception of womanhood, and of children, it is indeed difficult to understand why young women would suddenly seek independence and self-advancement in the labor force.

34. See Tentler, *Wage-earning Women*, pp. 109–114.

35. Elyce Rotella in *From Home to Office* (Ann Arbor: U.M.I. Research Press, 1981), pp. 48, 58, found that unmarried women's labor-force participation decisions became, over time, less responsive to the earnings of their fathers.

8. THE DEVELOPMENT OF THE HOMEMAKING PROFESSION, AND OF WOMEN AS HOMEMAKERS

1. Heidi Hartmann has examined these changes in a much more detailed manner than I do here in her thesis, "Capitalism and Women's Work in the Home, 1900–1930" (Ph.D. dissertation: Yale University, 1974), which has been helpful to my research here.

2. Ida Tarbell, "The Cost of Living and Household Management," *Annals of the Academy of Political and Social Science*, 48, p. 130.

3. Catherine Beecher, *A Treatise on Domestic Economy* (New York: Schocken Books, 1977). For a superb study of the way in which Catherine Beecher developed the ideals of the cult of domesticity, see Kathryn K. Sklar, *Catherine Beecher: A Study in American Domesticity* (New Haven: Yale University Press, 1973).

4. Clarence W. Taber, *The Business of the Household* (Philadelphia: J. B. Lippincott Co., 1918), p. 1.

5. Ibid., p. 2.

6. Mrs. Frank A. Pattison, "Scientific Management in Home-Making," *Annals*, 48 (July 1913), p. 96.

7. The Editors, "Christine Fredrick: The New House-Keeping," *The Ladies Home Journal* (Dec. 1912), p. 16.

8. Christine Fredrick, "The New House-Keeping," *The Ladies Home Journal* (Sept. 1912), p. 70.

9. Christine Fredrick, "The New House-Keeping," *The Ladies Home Journal* (Nov. 1912), p. 20.

10. Christine Fredrick, "The New House-Keeping," *The Ladies Home Journal* (Oct. 1912), p. 100.

11. Pattison, "Scientific Management," p. 98.

12. Abba G. Woolson, *Women in Modern Society* (Boston: Roberts Brothers, 1873), p. 258.

13. Anna Richardson, "The Woman Administrator in the Modern Home," *Annals*, 143 (May 1929), p. 32.

14. See Hartmann, "Capitalism and Woman's Work," Chap. 6, "Laundry: A Case Study of Home Versus Market Production."

15. Nevertheless, one feminist, Charlotte Perkins Gilman, argued in *1898*, that society would be benefited by the removal of production—including kitchens—from the home. This claim was accompanied by a thorough critique of woman's vocation of homemaking. The book in question remains thought-provoking today, and was republished in 1966; see *Women and Economics: The Economic Factor between Men and Women as a Factor in Social Evolution*, edited by Carl N. Degler (New York: Harper & Row, 1966).

16. Bertha June Richardson, *The Woman Who Spends: A Study of Her Economic Function* (Boston: Whitcomb & Barrows, 1904), pp. 35, 36, 38.

17. Mrs. Julian Heath, "The Work of the Housewives League," *Annals*, 48 (July 1913), p. 121.

18. Heath, "The Work," pp. 121, 123.

19. Benjamin Andrews, "The Home Woman as Buyer and Controller of Consumption," *Annals*, 143 (1929).

20. Ibid., p. 41.

21. In the 1960s, orthodox economists rediscovered such analysis and used it to extend their theory of choice and optimization into the home. They have come to the same conclusion: the specialization of woman in the home production of utility has been a utility-maximizing choice of the family, a choice which implies no important inequality between the sexes. See Gary Becker's "A Theory of the Allocation of Time," *Economic Journal*, 75 (Sept. 1965), also reprinted in Alice H. Amsden, *The Economics of Women and Work* (New York: St. Martin's Press, 1980). For a compilation of orthodox economic analyses of the family, see Theodore Schultz, ed., *The Economics of the Family: Marriage, Children, and Human Capital* (Chicago: University of Chicago Press, 1974).

22. Richardson, "The Woman Administrator," p. 32.

23. Hazel Kyrk, *Economic Problems of the Family* (New York: Harper & Brothers, 1933), p. 99.

24. Ibid., p. 100.

25. Kathryn Walker, "Home-Making Still Takes Time," *Journal of Home Economics*, 61:8 (Oct. 1969).

26. Anonymous, *Women's Influence and Women's Mission* (Philadelphia: Willis P. Hazard, 1854), pp. 57–58.

27. Lucy Salmon, *Progress in the Household* (Cambridge, Mass.: Houghton, Mifflin & Co., 1906), pp. 113–14.

28. Carl N. Degler, *At Odds: Women and the Family in America from the Revolution to the Present* (New York: Oxford University Press, 1980), p. 181.

29. Studies of this "demographic transition" are myriad; all connect it to industrialization. I am not proposing a new theory here; rather, I am pointing out the important

role women as mothers took in limiting the size of their families and the connection of this behavior to the new cult of domesticity conception of childhood and mothering.

30. Quoted in Degler, *At Odds*, p. 281. The following section draws heavily upon Degler's excellent discussion of the demographic transition in Chaps. 8–12 of *At Odds*. Degler sees the control of fertility and family size by women as the product of the development of woman's individuality, of her struggle to gain control over her life. Daniel Scott Smith made a similar argument in an earlier study, "Family Limitation, Sexual Control, and Domestic Feminism in Victorian America," *Feminist Studies*, 1 (Winter-Spring 1973); also in Nancy Cott and Elizabeth Pleck, eds., *Heritage of Her Own: Toward a New Social History of American Women* (New York: Simon & Schuster, 1979). Unfortunately, they do not clearly articulate the particularity of womanly individuality versus manly individuality, but rather reduces the issue to questions of having power and autonomy.

31. Quoted in Degler, *At Odds*, p. 201.

32. This argument is advanced by Linda Gordon in *Woman's Body, Woman's Right* (New York: Grossman, 1976), Chap. 5, "Voluntary Motherhood."

33. Degler, *At Odds*, Chap. IX.

34. Quoted by Mary Ryan, *Womanhood in America*, 2nd. edition (New York: New Viewpoints, 1979), p. 100, from Herman Humphrey's *Domestic Education*, 1840.

35. Ibid., p. 91.

36. Nancy Cott, *The Bonds of Womanhood: "Women's Sphere" in New England, 1780–1835* (New Haven: Yale University Press, 1977), pp. 149–51.

37. Richardson, "The Woman Administrator," p. 31.

38. Cott, *Bonds*, pp. 152–53.

39. Quoted in Phillida Bunkle, "Sentimental Womanhood and Domestic Education, 1830–1870," *History of Education Quarterly*, 14 (Spring 1974), p. 23.

40. By 1860, women initiated two-thirds of divorces. See Degler, *At Odds*, Chap. II, "Wives and Husbands," and Chap. VII, "Women Challenge the Family," especially pp. 167–68.

41. Richardson, "The Woman Administrator," p. 24.

42. Ida Tarbell, *The Business of Being a Woman*, pp. 88–89.

43. See Ryan, *Womanhood*, pp. 75–76.

44. Different terms have been used to describe the movement of middle-class women out of the home into reform in the nineteenth century, each with a somewhat different emphasis. William O'Neil, *Everyone Was Brave: The Rise and Fall of Feminism in America* (Chicago: Quadrangle Books, 1969), calls this movement "social feminism" and sees it as a response to the increased oppression of women due to their restriction to the home. Daniel Scott Smith, "Family Limitation, Sexual Control, and Domestic Feminism," *Feminist Studies*, 1 (Winter–Spring 1973), coined the term "domestic feminism," claiming that this movement was an *extension* of women's home responsibilities rather than a reaction against increased oppression. Implying a similar dynamic, Mary P. Ryan, *Womanhood in America: From Colonial Times to the Present* (New York: New Viewpoints, 1975), called these efforts "social housekeeping." While in agreement with these last two as to the general motivation behind the phenomenon in question, I have chosen to term it "social homemaking," signifying the extension into society at large of woman's vocation of homemaking.

45. See Gerda Lerner, *The Majority Finds Its Past* (New York: Oxford University Press, 1979), Chap. 6, "The Community Work of Black Club Women."

46. Quoted in Degler, *At Odds*, p. 281.

47. Lois Waisbrooker, quoted in Gordon, *Women's Body*, p. 113.

48. Cott, *Bonds*, pp. 133–57.

49. See Ryan, *Womanhood*, pp. 137, 140.

50. Heath, "The Work," p. 123.

51. Ibid.

52. See Ryan, *Womanhood*, pp. 105–07.

53. See Eleanor Flexner, *Century of Struggle* (New York: Atheneum, 1974), pp. 209–10.

54. Quoted in Thomas Woody, *A History of Women's Education in the United States* (New York: The Science Press, 1929), Vol. 1, p. 303; written in 1787.

55. Quoted in Woody, *Women's Education*, Vol. 1, p. 403.

56. Willard, 1818, quoted in Woody, *Women's Education*, Vol. I, p. 308, from Barnard, *Memoirs of Teachers, Educators, and Promoters of Education*.

57. Aide at meeting to open a public school (high school) for girls in Boston, 1825, quoted in Woody, *Women's Education*, Vol. 1, p. 525.

58. *Statistical Study of Women College Graduates*, completed in 1917, devoted 72 of 181 pages to analysis of the change in students' health during their college years, as the product of "intellectual overwork," "worry and social dissipation," physical accident, and sanitary conditions. They examined the students' health during menstrual periods, as well as the change in their degree of nervousness over their college years. The health of the graduates was also carefully compared with that of non-college educated sisters. It was found that a woman's health was not adversely affected by college education. *Statistical Study of Women College Graduates* (Bryn Mawr, 1917), pp. 45–117.

59. Woody, *Women's Education*, Vol. I, pp. 311, 323, 321, 311, 462.

60. Ibid., Vol. I, pp. 489, 363, 487–88.

61. Quoted in Ryan, *Womanhood*, pp. 138–39.

62. Woody, *Women's Education*, Vol. I, p. 361.

63. *Statistical Study*, p. 121.

64. Woody, *Women's Education*, Vol. I., p. 465.

65. Quoted in Degler, *At Odds*, p. 163.

66. While among those women born between 1835 and 1855, the proportion unmarried ranged from 7.1 to 8.0%, among those born between 1860 and 1880, the proportion unmarried ranged between 10 and 11.1%. Less than 5% of those born after 1915 have remained unmarried. See Daniel Scott Smith, "Family Limitation," p. 224.

67. See Flexner, *Century*, and William O'Neil, *Everyone Was Brave*, for good discussions of the nineteenth-century women's rights movement.

68. See Theodore Caplow, *The Sociology of Work* (Minneapolis: University of Minnesota Press, 1954), p. 266.

9. THE DEVELOPMENT OF SEX–TYPED JOBS

1. U.S. Department of Commerce, Bureau of the Census. *Occupational Trends in the United States, 1900–1950*, p. 9, and *1960 Census of Occupations*, pp. 277, 282.

2. David Montgomery, *Beyond Equality*, (New York: Random House, 1972) pp. 26–27; Stanley Lebergott, *Manpower in Economic Growth: The American Record Since 1800* (New York: McGraw-Hill, 1964), p. 513.

3. The analysis in this chapter builds on labor market segmentation studies, as well as on Marxist and feminist studies of occupational segregation and women's jobs. Labor market segmentation studies distinguish between primary and secondary jobs: the former allow advancement through mobility chains and earn high wages, whereas the latter are dead-end, high turnover, and provide little return to education. See for example Peter Doeringer and Michael Piore, *Internal Labor Markets and Manpower Analysis* (Lexington, Mass.: D.C. Heath, Lexington Books, 1971) and Richard Edwards, *Contested Terrain* (New York: Basic Books, 1979). However, this analysis does not deal explicitly with sexual differentiation and therefore is unable to grasp fully the dynamic behind this segmentation of the labor market—for example, Edwards reduces it to an issue of capitalist control over the worker and calls for a separate analysis for women and blacks (pp. 194–95). Other studies have focused on understanding women's jobs, or the sex-labeling of jobs. Heidi Hartmann has pointed to the ways in which men workers have been able to exclude women from their jobs ("Capitalism, Patriarchy, and Job Segregation by Sex," *Signs*, 3, Part 2, Spring 1976). Alice Kessler-Harris focuses on the manner in which women's primary commitment to the home was exploited by employers ("Stratifying by Sex: Understanding the History of Working Women" in *Labor Market Segmentation*, edited by Richard Edwards, Michael Reich, and David Gordon [Lexington, Ma: D. C. Heath and Company, 1975]). Valerie Kincade Oppenheimer has pointed out that the different attributes of men and women workers have made them appropriate for different jobs, bringing about the "sex-labeling" of jobs in her excellent book (*The Female Labor Force in the United States: Demographic and Economic Factors Governing Its Growth and Changing Composition*, Population Monograph Series No. 5 [Berkeley: University of California, 1970]). These are only a few of the many studies which have contributed to our understanding of the sexual segregation of the labor force. However, existing scholarship tends to take the structure of jobs, or at least of men's jobs, as a given, and look for the manner in which women have been excluded from men's jobs and shunted into a set of inferior ones. As such they ignore two central facts: that women and men have embraced the sex-typing of jobs, in fact, sought after it, and that the social differentiation of the sexes has shaped the content of all jobs, both men's and women's. Rather than simply labeling a job men's or women's work, the social differentiation of the sexes has been built into the core of the capitalist economy's job structure.

4. Elizabeth Baker, in *Technology and Woman's Work* (New York: Columbia University Press, 1964), has tried, with some success, to detail the concrete changes in woman's work in this period.

5. Francine Blau, in a study of the sex-typing of clerical work, has found the same phenomenon. Clerical jobs are most clearly sex-typed on the firm level; Blau calls this intra-occupational segregation. See her "Sex Segregation of Workers by Enterprise in Clerical Occupations," in Richard Edwards et al., *Labor Market Segmentation*.

6. Miriam S. Leuck, "Women in Odd and Unusual Fields of Work," *Annals of the Academy of Political and Social Science*, 232 (May 1929), p. 179.

7. Alan Berube, "Lesbian Masquerade," *Gay Community News*, Nov. 17, 1979.

8. Ibid.

9. See Jonathan Katz, *Gay American History* (New York: Thomas Y. Crowell Co., 1976), Chapter III, "Passing Women 1782–1920."

10. See U.S. Department of Commerce, Bureau of the Census. *Report on the Condition of Women and Child Wage-earners in the United States* (1915), Vol. 10:

History of Women in the Trade Unions, by Helen Sumner (1911), for some of this history.

11. Dual or segmented labor market theories provide excellent analyses of such job ladders. See Doeringer and Piore, *Internal Labor Markets.*

12. As we have seen, Marxist segmented labor market analysis has taken this position, arguing that job structures reflect capitalists' need for control over the worker. See especially Edwards, *Contested Terrain.* Recently, others have pointed out that this approach is one-sided. In "Structured Labor Markets, Worker Organization, and Low Pay," *Cambridge Journal of Economics,* 2:1 (March 1978), Jill Rubery points out that relationships between workers—in particular, workers' efforts to strengthen their labor force position by excluding competitors—have contributed to labor market segmentation. A 1979 symposium on the labor process in the same journal argued that the labor process is affected by (1) relationships between capitalists and laborers, (2) relationships between capitalists, and (3) relationships between groups of workers. See Bernard Elbaum, William Lazonick, Frank Wilkinson, and Jonathan Zeitlin, "The Labor Process, Market Structure, and Marxist Theory," *Cambridge Journal of Economics,* 3:3 (September 1979). I would add that the content of a job is also affected, in service work, by the relationship between worker and customer. Here I will show how the sexual division of labor contributed to the construction of jobs by affecting these different relationships.

13. David M. Katzman discusses in detail the mistress–servant relationship and its particular, personal character in Chapters 4 and 5 of *Seven Days a Week: Women and Domestic Service in Industrializing America* (New York: Oxford University Press, 1978).

14. Lucy M. Salmon, *Domestic Service* (New York: Macmillan Co., 1911), p. 137.

15. Mary Ryan, *Womanhood in America,* 2nd edition (New York: New Viewpoints, 1979), p. 109.

16. Included in this calculation are boarding, laundering, seamstresses, dressmakers, housekeepers or stewards, servants, and "other domestic and personal" workers. Compiled from U.S. Department of Commerce, Bureau of the Census, *Special Reports: Occupations at the Twelfth Census,* pp. cxxv–cxxvii, and idem, *Statistics of Women at Work in 1900* (1908), p. 40.

17. *Statistics of Women at Work,* pp. 40–41.

18. See John S. Haller and Robin M. Haller, *The Physician and Sexuality in Victorian America* (New York: W. W. Norton & Co., Inc., 1977), Chap. VI.

19. Paula Petrik, Montana State University, "Capitalists with Rooms: Prostitution in Helena, Montana, 1865–1900" (paper presented at 1981 Meetings of the Social Science History Association).

20. Calculated from U.S. Department of Commerce, Bureau of the Census. *Population and Social Statistics, Ninth Census,* Vol. 1, 1872, p. 704; *Occupational Trends in the United States: 1900 to 1950,* p. 26; *Historical Statistics of the United States, Colonial Times to 1970,* Vol. I, pp. 41, 140.

21. William Goode, "The Theoretical Limits of Professionalization," in Amitai Etzioni, ed., *The Semi-professions and Their Organization: Teachers, Nurses, Social Workers* (New York: The Free Press, 1969), pp. 276–80.

22. *Encyclopedia of the Social Sciences,* Vol. 12, p. 541.

23. Richard Shyrock, "Women in American Medicine," *Journal of the American Medical Women's Association,* 5, No. 9 (Sept. 1950), reprinted in his *Medicine in America: Historical Essays* (Baltimore: Johns Hopkins Press, 1966), p. 189.

24. Quoted in Mary Roth Walsh, "*Doctors Wanted: No Women Need Apply.*" *Sexual Barriers in the Medical Profession, 1835–1975* (New Haven: Yale University Press, 1977), p. 8. Chapter 1 has an excellent discussion of the sexual division of labor in colonial medicine and of the elimination of midwifery.

25. See G. J. Barker-Benfield, *The Horrors of the Half-Known Life* (New York: Harper & Row, 1977), Chap. 7, for a discussion of medicine's campaign against midwifery from 1900 to 1930. See also Barbara Ehrenreich and Deirdre English, *Witches, Midwives and Nurses: A History of Women Healers* (Old Westbury, N.Y.: The Feminist Press, 1973).

26. In 1900, 92.2% of women teachers were single, and another 3.3% were divorced or widowed. *Statistics of Women at Work in 1900*, p. 118.

27. U.S. Department of Commerce, Bureau of the Census. *Occupations*, p. cxxxv; Marion O. Hawthorne, "The Position of Women in Public Schools," *Annals*, 232 (May 1929), pp. 156–57. Myra Strober and David B. Tyack trace out in much detail the tipping of teaching from a mixed to a feminine job in the nineteenth century, as well as the reentry of men in the later twentieth century in "Jobs and Gender: A History of the Structuring of Educational Employment by Sex" in Patricia Schmuck and W.W. Charters, eds., *Educational Policy and Management: Sex Differentials* (San Diego: Academic Press, 1981).

28. Elizabeth Kemper Adams, *Women Professional Workers* (New York: Macmillan Company, 1921), p. 357.

29. See Amitai Etzioni, ed., *The Semi-professions*, for excellent analyses of women's professions. James W. Grimm analyzes the lesser professionalization of feminine professions in his article, "Women in the Female-Dominated Professions," in *Women Working: Theories and Facts in Perspective*, edited by Ann H. Stromberg and Shirley Harkness (Palo Alto, Calif.: Mayfield Publishing Company, 1978).

30. As William Goode pointed out in "The Theoretical Limits of Professionalization," "It is the practitioner who decides upon the client's needs, and the occupation will be classified as less professional if the client imposes his own judgment," *The Semi-professions*, p. 278.

31. An analysis of the conflict between administrative and professional authority is developed in Etzioni, *The Semi-professions*, p. x.

32. See Edith Abbott, *Women in Industry: A Study in American Economic History* (New York: D. Appleton and Co., 1910), and Harry Braverman, *Labor and Monopoly Capital: The Degradation of Work in the Twentieth Century* (New York: Monthly Review Press, 1974).

33. A study of apprenticeship programs concluded, "there appeared to be large numbers of skilled and paraprofessional jobs that fit apprenticeable criteria equally well [as those masculine crafts with apprenticeships], most of which fell into the 'traditional female' employment areas that had been overlooked." Norma Briggs, *Women in Apprenticeship—Why Not?* Manpower Research Monograph No. 33 (1974), quoted in Sally Hillsman Baker, "Women in Blue-Collar and Service Occupations," in Stromberg and Harkness, *Women Working*.

34. U.S. Department of Commerce, Bureau of the Census, *Occupations, 1900* Table 1 (for persons 10 years and older) and idem, *Census of Population: 1960 Special Reports: Occupational Characteristics*, Table 21 (for persons 14 years and older).

35. See, for example, Heidi Hartmann, "Capitalism, Patriarchy, and Job Segregation

by Sex," in Zillah Eisenstein, ed., *Capitalist Patriarchy and the Case for Socialist Feminism* (New York: Monthly Review Press, 1979).

36. Edward O'Donnell, "Women as Breadwinners—The Error of the Age," *American Federationist,* 48 (Oct., 1897), pp. 167–68, quoted in Rosalyn Baxandall, Linda Gordon, and Susan Reverly, *America's Working Women* (New York: Random House, 1976).

37. Amy Hewes and Massachusetts Bureau of Statistics of Labor, *Industrial Home Work in Massachusetts* (1915), pp. 39, 40, 31.

38. U.S. Bureau of Labor, *Report on the Condition of Women and Child Wage-earners in the United States* (1915) Vol. 9: *Women in Industry* (1910), by Helen Sumner.

39. U.S. Bureau of Labor, *Eleventh Annual Report of the Commissioner of Labor 1895–6. Work and Wages of Men, Women, and Children,* (1897), pp. 515–16.

40. Sumner, *Women in Industry,* pp. 232–33.

41. Leslie Woodcock Tentler, *Wage-earning Women: Industrial Work and Family Life in the United States, 1900–1930* (New York: Oxford University Press, 1979), pp. 16–21, 77.

42. William Gilthorpe, "Advancement," *American Federationist,* 9 (November 1910), quoted in Alice Kessler-Harris, "Where Are the Organized Women Workers," *Feminist Studies,* 3 (Fall 1975), and in Nancy Cott and Elizabeth Pleck, *A Heritage of Her Own* (New York: Simon & Schuster, 1979), p. 349.

43. U.S. Department of Commerce, Bureau of the Census. *Historical Statistics from Colonial Times to 1970,* p. 167.

44. In segmented labor market terminology, they worked to transform their jobs from secondary to primary jobs.

45. Tentler, *Wage-earning Women,* pp. 51–52.

46. Ruth True, quoted in Ibid., p. 77.

47. Tentler has an excellent discussion of the way in which women brought to their jobs their central concern for their prospective husbands and families; *Wage-earning Women,* Chapter III, "The Work Community."

48. See Eleanor Flexner, *Century of Struggle* (New York: Atheneum, 1974), Chaps. IX, XIV, XVIII, and Alice Kessler-Harris, "Where Are the Organized Women Workers?" for an analysis of women's unionizing attempts. See Philip Foner, *Women and the American Labor Movement* (New York: The Free Press, 1979) for a detailed history of them.

49. U.S. Department of Commerce, Bureau of the Census. *Historical Statistics,* p. 139.

50. U.S. Bureau of Labor, *Work and Wages,* pp. 30–31.

51. Sumner, *Women in Industry,* pp. 269–70.

52. Sumner, *History of Women in Trade Unions,* pp. 45–46.

53. See, for example, the discussions of the histories of the cigar and printing industries in Edith Abbott, *Women in Industry.*

54. Such an analysis coincides with that of dual or segmented labor theorists; they see this differentiation of industries between monopolized and competitive as the source of the difference between primary jobs and secondary jobs. Why, though, are men working in the concentrated industries? Only such industries are able to withstand strong unions, for they have monopoly power over their price and can increase it in response to union demands. See James O'Connor, *Fiscal Crisis of the State* (New York:

St. Martin's Press, 1973), Chap. 1. Since price-competitive industries cannot coexist with strong unions, women and minority workers are most suited to them.

55. *National Laborer*, November 12, 1836, in John R. Commons and Helen Sumner, *A Documentary History of American Industrial Society*, Vol. 6: *The Labor Movement 1820–40* (Cleveland, Ohio: Arthur H. Clark Co., 1910), p. 284.

56. For more detail see U.S. Department of Labor, Women's Bureau, *History of Labor Legislation in the United States* (1932).

57. When this limitation of her rights was challenged in *Muller v. The State of Oregon*, the Supreme Court ruled that women merited special protection "from the greed as well as the passion of man" because of her natural weakness and dependency upon man, and because of her child-rearing responsibilities. "By abundant testimony of the medical fraternity [sic] continuance for a long time on her feet at work, repeating this from day to day, tends to bring injurious effects upon the body, and as healthy mothers are essential to vigorous offspring, the physical well-being of woman becomes an object of public interest and care in order to preserve the strength and vigor of the race. . . . The limitations which this statute [an hours limitation] places upon her contractual powers, upon her right to agree with her employer as to the time she shall labor, are not imposed solely for her benefit, but also largely for the benefit of all." Josephine Goldmark, *Fatigue and Efficiency: A Study in Industry* (New York: Harper & Brothers, 1912), pp. 324–25 (the case is reprinted in this book).

58. Baker's *Technology and Woman's Work* has an example of this: a job typed men's work before World War II because "it required strength" was filled with women during the war years. After the war, women stayed in the job (unlike most other such situations) and the job became women's work. From then on it was described as women's work because it required dexterity.

59. Dual labor market theorists have done concrete studies of these job ladders; Richard Edwards' analysis in *Contested Terrain*, Chapters 9 and 10, is the most sophisticated, for it differentiates between these managerial hierarchies (independent primary jobs) and unionized blue-collar hierarchies (subordinate primary). However, because he ignores many of the distinctions between jobs which we have developed here, and in particular, neglects to examine seriously the social differentiation of the sexes, he ends up placing secretaries, nurses, and craftsmen into the same category, "independent primary," as managers and doctors!

60. Harry Braverman, *Labor and Monopoly Capital*, pp. 298–99.

61. Adams' *Women Professional Workers*, written in 1921, lists clerical positions. See Margery Davies, "Woman's Place Is at the Typewriter: The Feminization of the Clerical Labor Force," in Edwards et al., *Labor Market Segmentation*, and Elyce Rotella, "The Transformation of the American Office: Employment and Technical Change," *Journal of Economic History*, 51 (March 1981) for more detailed discussions of the feminization of clerical work.

62. Quoted in Davies, "Woman's Place," pp. 228–29.

63. Quoted in Davies, "Woman's Place," p. 291.

64. *Statistics of Women at Work 1900*, p. 38.

65. Cited in Tentler, *Wage-earning Women*, opening page.

66. Harriet Robinson, *Loom and Spindle: Or Life among the Early Mill Girls* (New York: T.Y. Crowell and Co., 1898), p. 41.

67. Massachusetts Bureau of Statistics of Labor, *14th Annual Report, 1883*, p. 391.

68. "Female Department," *The Voice of Industry*, March 6, 1846.

10. THE ENTRANCE OF HOMEMAKERS INTO THE
LABOR FORCE AS HOMEMAKERS

1. Frank Presbrey, *The History and Development of Advertising* (Garden City: Doubleday, Doran & Co., 1929), p. 601. For a Marxist analysis of the development of advertising see Stuart Ewen, *Captains of Consciousness: Advertising and the Social Roots of Consumer Culture* (New York: McGraw-Hill, 1976).

2. Robert S. Lynd and Helen Merrell Lynd, *Middletown: A Study in American Culture* (New York: Harcourt, Brace & Co., 1929), p. 82.

3. Christine Frederick, "The New Housekeeping," *The Ladies Home Journal* (Sept., 1912), p. 71.

4. Frederick Lewis Allen, *The Big Change: America Transforms Itself 1900–1950* (New York: Harper & Brothers, 1952), p. 112.

5. Heidi Hartmann, "Capitalism and Woman's Work in the Home 1900–1930" (Yale Ph.D. Dissertation, 1974), pp. 147–48.

6. Stanley Lebergott, *Manpower in Economic Growth: The American Record Since 1800* (New York: McGraw-Hill, 1964), pp. 524, 528.

7. Siegfried Giedion, *Mechanization Takes Command* (New York: Oxford University Press, 1948).

8. David P. Levine has an excellent discussion of consumption as the arena of the individual freedom in capitalism in *Economic Theory* (Boston: Routledge & Kegan Paul, 1978), Vol. I, Chap. I. "The Objects of Economic Science," and Vol. II, Chap. 7, "The Social Purposes of the Market."

9. Neoclassical economic theory simply assumes that the needs of the individual are infinite; it therefore tends to ignore the fact that the economy generates needs as well as fills them. In *The Affluent Society* (New York: Houghton Mifflin Company, 1958), John Kenneth Galbraith criticized this view, noting that, through advertising, firms expand consumer needs, and then use these expanded needs to justify increased production. Paul Baran and Paul Sweezy were the first to build the idea of expanded needs into the Marxist framework: in *Monopoly Capital* (New York: Monthly Review Press, 1966), they analyzed advertising as a way for corporations to increase their markets in the face of surplus profits which, if not spent, would cause stagnation. Other Marxists have followed their tradition, criticizing capitalism for creating false needs; they have, however, tended to ignore the real freedoms that the individual enjoys in consumption, particularly the freedom to express his or her particular personality. David Levine's *Economic Theory* and C. B. MacPherson's *Democratic Theory: Essays in Retrieval* (Oxford: Clarendon Press, 1973) are exceptions.

10. Lynd and Lynd, *Middleton*, pp. 82–83.

11. Frank Ackerman and Andrew Zimbalist, "Capitalism and Inequality in the United States," in *The Capitalist System: A Radical Analysis of American Society* (Englewood Cliffs, N.J.: Prentice-Hall, Inc., 1978), 300.

12. Thorstein Veblen, *The Theory of the Leisure Class: An Economic Study of Institutions* (London: George Allen & Unwin, Ltd., 1899), p. 159.

13. Joseph A. Kahl, *The American Class Structure* (New York: Rinehart & Co., 1957), p. 108.

14. There is excellent documentation of the development of neediness in the 1920s and 1930s in Winnifred D. Wandersee's, *Women's Work and Family Values, 1920–1940* (Cambridge, Mass.: Harvard University Press, 1981), Chap. 1.

15. Carolyn Shaw Bell, *Consumer Choice in the American Economy* (New York: Random House, 1967), pp. 46–47. See also James S. Dusenberry, *Income, Saving and the Theory of Consumer Behavior* (Cambridge, Mass.: Harvard University Press, 1949).

16. Marshall Sahlins, an anthropologist, has noted that the fixity of needs in early societies made them affluent, in spite of their limited consumption—for all their needs were filled. He argues, convincingly, that capitalism produced scarcity and wealth simultaneously. See "The Original Affluent Society," Chap. 1 of his book *Stone-age Economics* (Chicago: Aldine, 1974). However, Sahlins fails to point out that it is the fact that consumption is part of competitive self-seeking that allows, and indeed drives, needs to be continually expanded.

17. In *Democratic Theory*, MacPherson points out that this consumerism was useful in our economic development due to the way in which it stimulated work effort; the problem is that now that we have actually become a wealthy society, we have been unable to change gears and begin to fulfill other human needs, such as that for self-fulfillment through the development of human potential. Neoclassical economists have conceived of this phenomenon as the "relative income" effect, that the happiness one derives from consumption is a function not of the absolute level of income, but of its level relative to others—see J. S. Dusenberry, *Income, Saving, and the Theory of Consumer Behavior* (Cambridge, Mass.: Harvard University Press, 1952). While this phenomenon has led some of them to question whether economic growth indeed brings well-being—see, for example, Richard Easterlin, "Does Economic Growth Improve the Human Lot," in Paul A. David and Melvin W. Reder, eds., *Nations and Households in Economic Growth* (New York: Academic Press, 1974)—it has not led them to discard their theory, which holds that the role of the economy is to fill, rather than generate, needs, nor to criticize the income hierarchy and competition in consumption which are essential to capitalism.

18. Kahl, *Class Structure*, p. 113.

19. Lee Rainwater, Richard P. Coleman, Gerald Handel, *Workingman's Wife: Her Personality, World and Life Style* (New York: Oceana Publications, 1959), p. 176. On differences between blue-collar and white-collar consumption patterns, see also James M. Patterson, "Marketing and the Working-Class Family," in Arthur B. Shostak and William Gomberg, eds., *Blue-collar World* (New York: Prentice-Hall, 1964), and Kahl, *Class Structure*, Chap. IV.

20. Rainwater et al., *Workingman's Wife*, pp. 145–46.

21. Ibid., p. 145.

22. Wandersee makes a similar argument in *Women's Work and Family Values*, Chap. 4.

23. Mirra Komarovsky, *Blue-Collar Marriage* (New York: Random House, 1967), p. 70.

24. Lillian Breslow Rubin, *Worlds of Pain: Life in the Working-class Family* (New York: Basic Books, 1976), p. 173.

25. Ibid., p. 177.

26. Mirra Komarovsky, *The Unemployed Man and His Family: The Effect of Unemployment upon the Status of the Man in Fifty-nine Families* (New York: Dryden Press, 1940), p. 76.

27. Komarovsky, *Blue-Collar Marriage*, p. 71.

28. Lynd and Lynd, *Middletown*, p. 29.

29. Ibid.

30. See Wandersee, *Women's Work and Family Values*, Chap. 5.

31. Neoclassical economists have explained the paradox of increased married women's labor-force participation accompanying rising real incomes for men as follows: women's real wages have also been rising, increasing the "opportunity cost" of staying at home, and hence drawing women into the labor force. See Jacob Mincer's seminal article, "The Labor Force Participation of Married Women: A Study of Labor Supply," in *Aspects of Labor Economics, A Report of the National Bureau of Economic Research* (Princeton: Princeton University Press, 1962). Neoclassical theory takes for granted that needs have always been infinite. Therefore their analysis must ignore the fact that capitalist production is at the root of the creation of insatiable consumers, and at the heart of homemakers' entrance into the labor force.

32. U.S. Department of Commerce, Bureau of the Census. 1970. *Special Report: Employment Statistics and Work Experience*.

33. For discussion of early polls regarding a wife's labor force participation, see Valerie K. Oppenheimer, *The Female Labor Force: Its Changing Growth and Composition* (Westport, Conn.: Greenwood Press, 1970), pp. 40–55.

34. Rubin, *Pain*, p. 175.

35. Komarovsky, *Blue-Collar Marriage*, p. 68.

36. U.S. Department of Labor, 1970, *Dual Careers: A Longitudinal Study of Labor Market Experience of Women*, Manpower Research Monograph No. 21, Vol. 1, pp. 21, 196.

11. THE CAREER GIRL AND THE SECOND-CAREER WOMAN

1. Inez Haynes Irwin, *Angels and Amazons: A Hundred Years of American Women* (Garden City, N.Y.: Doubleday Doran, 1934), p. 279.

2. In 1900, not even 7% of seventeen-year-olds graduated high school, and in 1908, probably about 7 to 10% of high-school-age children in urban areas were in school; this percentage increased dramatically in the 1920s. See Carl N. Degler, *At Odds: Women and the Family in America from the Revolution to the Present* (New York: Oxford University Press, 1980), p. 156, and Leslie W. Tentler, *Wage-earning Women: Industrial Work and Family Life in the United States, 1900–1930* (New York: Oxford University Press, 1979), pp. 94–95.

3. In 1950, only 22.6% of women over twenty-five had graduated from high school, 5% from college; in 1960, 31.6% and 6.7%, respectively; and in 1970, 37.5% and 8.2%, respectively. U.S. Department of Commerce, Bureau of the Census. See *Historical Statistics from Colonial Times to the Present*, Vol. 1, p. 380.

4. Thomas Woody, *A History of Women's Education in America*, Vol. II (New York: The Science Press, 1929), p. 381.

5. Ernest Haverman and Patricia Salter West, *They Went to College* (New York: Harcourt, Brace & Company, 1952), pp. 19, 57.

6. See Degler, *At Odds*, p. 164.

7. Quoted in Patricia A. Palmieri, "Patterns of Achievement of Single Academic Women at Wellesley College, 1880–1920," *Frontiers: A Journal of Women Studies*, 5:1 (Spring 1980), p. 64, from an 1896 letter.

8. Ibid., pp. 64–65.

9. Ida Tarbell, *The Business of Being a Woman* (New York: Macmillan & Co.,

1912), p. 77. Tarbell was clearly torn, a bundle of contradictions. Although she was herself a successful and unmarried career woman, she wrote against the phenomenon of single professionals, calling the antagonism of society against them "a right saving impulse to prevent perversion of the qualities and powers of women which are most needed in the world, those qualities and powers which differentiate her from man" (*The Business*, pp. 46–47).

10. Ernest R. Groves, "The Personality Results of the Wage Employment of Women outside the Home and their Social Consequences" *Annals* 163 (May 1929), p. 341.

11. Haverman and West, *To College*, p. 62.

12. Quoted in Degler, *At Odds*, p. 165.

13. Carol Smith Rosenberg, "The Female World of Love and Ritual: Relations Between Women in Nineteenth-Century America," *Signs* 1 (Autumn 1975), and Nancy Cott and Elizabeth Pleck, *A Heritage of Her Own* (New York: Simon & Schuster, 1979), was the first historian to draw attention to such relationships; Carl Degler has added to her work in his Chapter VII, "Women Challenge the Family," in *At Odds*. The first monograph on the subject is Lillian Federman's *Surpassing the Love of Men: Romantic Friendship and Love between Women from the Renaissance to the Present* (New York: William Morrow & Company, Inc. 1981).

14. Quoted in Degler, *At Odds*, p. 163.

15. In *Surpassing the Love of Man*, Federman argues that love between women, accepted as an adjunct to marriage in the nineteenth century, grew illicit in the twentieth century when the romantic ideal of marriage, in which love and sex were one, became firmly established. In "From Sexual Inversion to Homosexuality: The Instrumentality of the Perverse, 1880–1930" in Ann Snitrow, Christine Stansell, and Sharon Thompson, eds., *The Politics of Sexuality* (New York: Monthly Review Press, forthcoming), George Chauncey points out that the medical profession's attack on love between women was part of an overall conservative reaction to women's movement into the masculine sphere. There was, however, another reason for the growing ostracism of love between women: it had begun to replace, rather than supplement, heterosexual marriage, particularly in the life of the career woman, and as such was challenging the basic premise of the sexual division of labor—the idea of marriage as a relationship between sexually different beings.

16. Caroline Latimer, *Girls and Woman: A Book for Mothers and Daughters* (New York, 1916), p. 263, quoted in Mary Ryan, *Womanhood in America*, 2nd edition (New York: New Viewpoints, 1979), p. 184.

17. Quoted in O. Latham Hatcher, ed., *Occupations for Women* (Richmond: Southern Women's Educational Alliance, 1927), p. xiv.

18. President Eliot, quoted in E. P. Howes, "The Meaning of Progress in the Women's Movement," *Annals*, 143 (May 1929), p. 18.

19. *Woman's Home Companion*, March 1940.

20. Mirra Komarovsky, *Women in the Modern World* (Boston: Little, Brown & Co., 1953), p. 92.

21. Henry A. Bowman, *Marriage for Moderns* (New York: Whittlesey House, 1942), p. 68.

22. *Ladies Home Journal*, Dec. 1912, p. 102.

23. Quoted in Degler, *At Odds*, p. 411.

24. Dublin, quoted in Hatcher, *Occupations*, p. xv.

25. Quoted in Peter G. Filene, *Him/Her/Self*, (New York: Signet, 1975), p. 141.

26. E. P. Howes, "The Meaning of Progress in the Women's Movement," *Annals*, 143 (May 1929), p. 18.

27. Ibid.

28. Elizabeth Kemper Adams, *Women Professional Workers* (New York: The Macmillan Co., 1921), p. 31. See also Elaine Showalter, ed., *These Modern Women* (Old Westbury, N.Y.: The Feminist Press, 1978), for more of such discussion, and a good introductory essay.

29. Virginia M. Collier, *Marriage and Careers* (New York: The Channel Bookshop, 1926).

30. *Statistical Study of Women College Graduates* (Bryn Mawr, 1917), p. 172.

31. Komarovsky, *Modern World*, p. 49.

32. Ibid., p. 77.

33. Ibid., p. 94.

34. Haverman and West, *College*, p. 44.

35. Komarovsky, *Modern World*, p. 93.

36. Haverman and West, *College*, p. 70.

37. Betty Friedan, *The Feminine Mystique* (New York: Norton, 1963).

38. Komarovsky, *Modern World*, pp. 127–46.

39. Ibid., pp. 113–14.

40. Ibid., p. 125.

41. Philip Wylie, *Generation of Vipers* (New York: Farrar & Rinehart, Inc., 1942).

42. Ferdinand Lundberg and Marynia Farnham, *Modern Woman: The Lost Sex* (New York: Harper & Brothers, 1947), p. 303.

43. Ibid., p. 233.

44. Ibid., p. 304.

45. Ibid., Chap. XII, "Mother and Child: The Slaughter of the Innocents." Contemporary psychologists call this "the empty nest syndrome"; see Pauline B. Bart, "Depression in Middle-Aged Women," in Judith Bardwick, ed., *Reading in the Psychology of Women* (New York: Harper & Row, 1972).

46. Komarovsky, *Modern World*, p. 156–57.

47. Friedan, *Feminine Mystique*, Chap. X.

48. Ibid., Chap. I.

49. U.S. Department of Labor, Women's Bureau, *1975 Handbook on Women Workers*, p. 23, and Havermann and West, *College*.

50. U.S. Department of Labor, Bureau of Labor Statistics, "Marital and Family Characteristics of the Labor Force." Special Labor Force Report 237 (January 1981), p. 50.

51. Calculated from U.S. Department of Labor, Bureau of Labor Statistics, *Employment and Earnings*, Jan. 1981, pp. 26, 66.

52. National Assessment of Educational Progress survey, cited in Kristin A. Moore and Sandra L. Hofferth, "Women and Their Children," in *The Subtle Revolution: Women at Work*, edited by Ralph E. Smith (Washington, D.C.: The Urban Institute, 1979).

53. A *Time* magazine poll taken in 1978 found that only 33% of those polled "believed completely" that "children suffer when the mother goes to work," and 31% no longer believed it at all. A General Mills American Family Report from polls in 1978–79 found that 61% agreed that "working mothers take as good care of their children's health as mothers who stay home." *Today's American Woman: How the Public Sees*

Her, prepared for The President's Advisory Committee for Women by the Public Agenda Foundation, Sept. 1980.

54. Lillian Breslow Rubin, *Worlds of Pain: Life in the Working Class Family* (New York: Basic Books, 1976), p. 174.

55. U.S. Department of Labor, Employment and Training Administration, Manpower Research Monograph No. 21, *Dual Careers,* (1970) Vol. 1, p. 77.

56. Miller, *Happiness Is Homemaking* (Harrisonburg, Va.: Choice Books, 1974), pp. 11, 20.

57. Ibid., pp. 87–92.

58. Marabel Morgan, *Total Woman* (New York: Pocket Books, 1975), pp. 79, 76, 142.

12. THE BREAKDOWN OF THE SEX-TYPING OF JOBS

1. These numbers refer to the total rural plus urban labor force. 1900: U.S. Department of Commerce, Bureau of the Census, *Special Reports: Occupations at the Twelfth Census,* Table 1 (for persons 10 years and older). 1960: Idem, *U.S. Census of Population 1960: Occupational Characteristics,* Table 21 (for persons 14 years and older).

2. U.S. Department of Labor, Women's Bureau *1975 Handbook on Women Workers,* p. 11.

3. "Estimates of the duration of women's worklives in the future would seem to indicate at least twenty-five years of market work after childrearing, with an overall worklife that averages only about a decade less than that of men." Juanita M. Kreps and R. John Leaper, "Home Work, Market Work, and the Allocation of Time," *Women and the American Economy: A Look to the 1980s* (Englewood Cliffs, N.J.: Prentice-Hall, Inc., 1976), p. 68. Note, however, that the age-participation profiles shown in Table 12-1 do not follow one age cohort through the life cycle, but rather represent a picture taken at one point in time of women in different stages of the life cycle.

4. U.S. Department of Labor, Bureau of Labor Statistics, *Employment and Earnings* (Jan. 1981), p. 191. These statistics only apply to employment in nonagricultural industries.

5. In 1900 (for women 10 years and older), U.S. Department of Commerce, Bureau of the Census, *Occupational Trends in the United States: 1900–1950* (1958), *Working Paper* 5, p. 6; in 1960 (for women 14 years and older), idem, Bureau of the Census, *Historical Statistics, from Colonial Times to 1970,* p. 140.

6. Table 12-2 shows the position of women in labor force or exclusively in the home *at one point in time:* the percentage of women who have ever been in the labor force is much higher. As we noted in Chapter 11, in 1980, only 8% of women over sixteen had never been in the labor force.

7. Valerie Kincade Oppenheimer emphasizes the pull of this increased demand in her excellent book, *The Female Labor Force in the United States: Demographic and Economic Factors Governing Its Growth and Changing Composition,* Population Monograph Series No. 5 (Berkeley: University of California, 1970).

8. Calculated from U.S. Department of Commerce, Bureau of the Census, *Special Reports: Occupations at the Twelfth Census.* 1904, Table 1, and idem, U.S. Census of Population: 1960, Subject Reports, *Occupational Characteristics,* Table 2.

9. U.S. Department of Commerce, Bureau of the Census, *Occupations: 1900*, Table 1, and *Occupational Characteristics 1960*, Table 2.

10. Quoted in Eleanor Flexner, *Century of Struggle* (New York: Atheneum, 1974), p. 115.

11. For a detailed study of the entrance of women into the masculine professions, see Barbara J. Harris, *Beyond Her Sphere: Women and the Professions in American History* (Westport, Conn.: Greenwood Press, 1978). For medicine in particular, see Mary Roth Walsh, *"Doctors Wanted: No Women Need Apply"* (New Haven: Yale University Press, 1977). Walsh notes that the spelling out of formal requirements for the practice of medicine probably aided women's entrance into it (pp. 14–15).

12. U.S. Department of Labor, *Nontraditional Occupations for Women of the Hemisphere—The U.S. Experience, 1974*, pp. 21–23.

13. Mary Wollstonecraft, *A Vindication of the Rights of Women; with Strictures on Political and Moral Subjects* (London: Printed for J. Johnson, 1792); Charlotte Perkins Gilman, *Women and Economics: A Study of the Economic Relationship between Men and Women as a Factor in Social Evolution* (Boston: Small, Maynard & Company, 1898).

14. These changes have been overlooked by many social scientists who have studied overall indices of occupational segregation. These indices show little or no change in the overall degree of sex-typing, since the entrance of women into masculine jobs has been counterbalanced by the entrance of large numbers of other women into clearly feminine clerical jobs. See Edward Gross, "Plus Ça Change . . . the Sexual Structure of Occupations Over Time," *Social Problems*, Fall 1968, 16, pp. 198–208, and F. Blau and W. Hendricks, "Occupational Segregation by Sex: Trends and Prospects," *Journal of Human Resources*, Spring 1979, 14, pp. 197–210.

15. For a more detailed analysis, see Michelle Patterson and Laurie Engleberg, "Women in Male-Dominated Professions," in Ann H. Stromberg and Shirley Harkness, eds., *Women Working: Theories and Facts in Perspective* (Palo Alto, Calif.: Mayfield Publishing Co., 1978).

16. Statistics compiled from the U.S. Department of Commerce, Bureau of the Census, *Census of Population: 1960: Occupational Characteristics*, pp. 11–20 (for persons 14 years and older), and U.S. Department of Labor, Bureau of Labor Statistics, *Employment and Earnings* (Jan. 1980), pp. 174–75.

17. U.S. Department of Labor, Employment and Training Administration, R8D Monograph 24, *Years for Decision*, Vol. 4, A Longitudinal Study of the Educational and Labor Market Experience of Young Women, pp. 115, 136–37.

18. Ibid.

19. There is a growing literature on this subject. Cynthia Fuch Epstein's *Woman's Place: Options and Limits in Professional Careers* (Berkeley: University of California Press, 1970) was one of the first, and remains an excellent examination of the problems women face in masculine professions. Margaret Hennig and Ann Jardim's *The Managerial Woman* (Garden City, N.Y.: Anchor Press, 1977) investigates the problems of women in managerial jobs. Rosabeth Moss Kanter's *Men and Women of the Corporation* (New York: Basic Books, 1977) provides an insightful analysis of the same issues.

20. Epstein, *Woman's Place;* Hennig and Jardim, *Managerial Woman;* Kanter, *Men and Women;* Michael Korda, *Male Chauvinism: What It is and How It Works* (New York: Ballantine, 1979); and U.S. Department of Labor, *Women in Traditionally Male Jobs: The Experiences of Ten Utility Companies*, 1978.

21. See Kantor, *Men and Women*, pp. 226–27.

22. Kantor, *Men and Women*, pp. 232–37. Kantor has also written cogently of the difficulties of being a token—being in the limelight, "boundary heightening" of the differences between majority and minority groups, being stereotyped—difficulties which apply equally to blacks, hispanics, and women. See *Men and Women*, Chap. 8.

23. *Women in Traditionally Male Jobs*, p. 101.

24. Ibid.

25. Ibid., p. 20.

26. See Hennig and Jardim, *Managerial Woman*, Part I, for an excellent discussion of the way in which feminine socialization hinders women's success in management.

27. See Catherine MacKinnon, *The Sexual Harassment of Working Women* (New Haven: Yale University Press, 1979).

28. There was extensive media coverage of this incident, including the cover story in *Fortune*, Nov. 3, 1980.

29. Hennig and Jardim, *Managerial Woman*, pp. 42–43.

30. Carole Hoffman and John Shelton Reed, "Sex Discrimination?—the XYZ Affair," *The Public Interest*, No. 62 (Winter 1981), pp. 25–27.

31. Neo-classical economists have developed this useful concept. For an explication, as well as a brief overview of the neo-classical analysis of discrimination see Annette M. LaMond, "Economic Theories of Employment Discrimination," in Phyllis A. Wallace and LaMond, eds., *Women, Minorities, and Employment Discrimination* (Lexington, Mass.: Lexington Books, 1977).

13. THE BREAKDOWN OF THE SEXUAL DIVISION OF LABOR IN MARRIAGE

1. U.S. Bureau of Labor Statistics, "Marital and Family Characteristics of the Labor Force." Special Labor Force Report 237 (January 1981), p. 49.

2. This comes across forcefully in studies of working-class marriages. See Mirra Komarovsky's *Blue-Collar Marriage* (New York: Vintage Books, 1967), Lillian Breslow Rubin's *Worlds of Pain: Life in the Working Class Family* (New York: Basic Books, Inc., 1976), and Nancy Seifer's *Absent from the Majority: Working Class Women in America* (New York: National Project of Ethnic America, 1973).

3. "He won't hear of my taking this restaurant job," said one wife in her husband's presence. Her husband then said to the interviewer, "The men get fresh with waitresses. I see it myself all the time." Komarovsky, *Blue-Collar*, p. 72.

4. See Lois Hoffman and F. Ivan Nye, *Working Mothers* (San Francisco: Jossey-Bass Publishers, 1974), and Mary Jo Bane, *Here to Stay* (New York: Basic Books, 1976). Also Ronald J. Burke and Tamara Weir, "Relationship of Wives' Employment Status to Husband, Wife, and Pair Satisfaction and Performance," *Journal of Marriage and the Family*, 38 (May 1976), pp. 278–87.

5. John Scanzoni calls these marriage types "complements" and "equal partners," and adds "junior partners." "Contemporary Marriage Types: A Research Note," *Journal of Family Issues*, 1 (March 1980), pp. 125–40.

6. U.S. Department of Labor, Women's Bureau, *1975 Handbook on Women Workers*, p. 29.

7. For examples of this, see Komarovsky, *Blue-Collar*, p. 68.

8. John Scanzoni and Greer Litton Fox, "Sex Roles, Family and Society: The

Seventies and Beyond," *Journal of Marriage and the Family*, 42 (Nov. 1980), p. 751. This article is an excellent review of research on the family in the 1970s. See also Claire Vickery's insightful article, "Women's Economic Contribution to the Family," in *Subtle Revolution: Women at Work*, edited by Ralph E. Smith (Washington, D.C.: The Urban Institute, 1979).

9. Kathryn E. Walker and Margaret E. Woods, *Time Use: A Measure of Household Production of Family Goods and Services*, American Home Economics Association, 1976, Table 3.5.

10. Vickery, "Women's Contribution," p. 195; Joseph Pleck and Michael Rustad, "Husbands' and Wives' Time in Family Work and Paid Work in the 1975–76 Study of Time Use" Working Paper, 1980, Wellesley College Center for Research on Women. As Pleck points out in "Men's Family Work: Three Perspectives and Some New Data," *The Family Coordinator* (Oct. 1979), while the absolute quantity of household work done by the husbands did not change, the proportion did, since the wife's household work decreased.

11. Walker and Woods, *Time Use*, 1976.

12. In surveys in 1965 and 1973, Robinson found that only 30% of employed women wished that their husbands helped more with the household chores. College educated women, black women, and women with one or two children were more likely to wish for more help. John P. Robinson, Janet Yerby, Margaret Fieweger, and Nancy Somerick, "Sex-Role Differences in Time Use," *Sex Roles: A Journal of Research*, 3:5 (Oct. 1977), p. 455. Joann Vanek's analysis of national survey data in 1965–66 found that only 30% of employed wives wanted additional help from their husbands, even though they reported receiving only two or three hours of assistance. "Housework, Wage Work, and Sexual Equality," Sarah F. Berk, ed., *Women and Household Labor* (Beverly Hills: Sage, 1980) p. 284.

13. M. Poloma and T. Garland, "On the Social Construction of Reality: Reported Husband–Wife Differences," *Sociological Focus*, 1971, 5, pp. 40–54.

14. Karen Mason and L. Bumpass, "U.S. Women's Sex Role Ideology, 1970," *American Journal of Sociology*, 80 (1975) cited in Vickery, p. 115.

15. J. Robinson, *Change in Americans' Use of Time: 1965–1975* (Cleveland: Communications Research Center, Cleveland State University, 1977), cited in Pleck and Rustad.

16. Vickery, "Women's Contribution," p. 197.

17. Rubin, *Pain*, pp. 176–77.

18. U.S. Department of Commerce, Bureau of the Census, Current Population Reports, "American Families and Living Arrangements" (Series P-23, No. 104), p. 9.

19. Mirra Komarovsky, *Dilemmas of Masculinity: A Study of College Youth* (New York: W. W. Norton & Company, 1976), pp. 35–36. Komarovsky found many men unwilling to marry women who seemed equal or superior to them in intelligence.

20. Scanzoni and Fox, "Sex Roles, Family and Society," p. 75

21. Komarovsky, *Dilemmas*, p. 251.

22. Ibid.

23. Ibid., p. 37.

24. Of course, there are other reasons for marital conflict; furthermore, the one-earner family is not without contradictions.

25. U. S. Department of Commerce, Bureau of the Census, Current Population Reports, "Divorce, Child Custody, and Child Support" (Series P-23, No. 84), p. 2;

"Some Recent Changes in American Families," idem, Current Population Reports (Series P-23, No. 52), p. 10. Isabel V. Sawhill and Heather L. Ross's, *Time of Transition: The Growth of Families Headed by Women* (Washington D.C.: Urban Institute, 1975), has a detailed analysis of this phenomenon, as well as one of its results—the rise of the female-headed family. See also Hoffman and Homes, "Husbands, Wives, and Divorce," in Greg J. Duncan and James N. Morgan, eds., *Five Thousand American Families—Patterns of Economic Progress* (Ann Arbor, Mich.: Institute For Social Research, The University of Michigan, 1976), Vol. 4; Hoffman and Nye, *Working Mothers*; and Bane, *Here to Stay*. Sandra Hofferth and Kristin A. Moore, in "Women's Employment and Marriage," in *The Subtle Revolution: Women at Work*, edited by Ralph E. Smith (Washington, D.C.: The Urban Institute, 1979), pp. 108–10, discuss the empirical literature on divorce and the two-earner family, which seems to reach no clear conclusions.

26. Mary Jo Bane, *Here to Stay*, p. 136.

27. The female-headed household has risen even more rapidly than the divorce rate because divorced women, now more independent minded, live with their relatives less often than previously. U.S. Department of Commerce, Bureau of the Census, Current Population Reports, "Families Maintained by Female Householders 1970–79" (Series P-23, No. 107), p. 1. Female-headed households constituted 15% of the total number of families in 1979, up from 11% in 1970; they represent 12% of white families, 41% of black families, and 20% of Spanish-origin families (p. 5).

28. Glick "Some Recent Changes," p. 13.

29. Ibid., p. 5.

30. The number of household heads who were reported as living apart from relatives while sharing their living quarters with an unrelated adult of the opposite sex increased eight-fold between 1960 and 1975. Ibid., p. 13.

31. U.S. Department of Commerce, Bureau of the Census, Current Population Reports, "American Families and Living Arrangements" (Series P-23, No. 104), p. 10.

32. As Herb Goldberg writes in *The New Male* (New York: William Morrow & Company, 1979), p. 286:

The nature of the traditional male–female relationship is such that women's passive-submissive posture results in the development of unconscious anger and rage toward the man she inevitably comes to resent being controlled and used by. All traditionally conditioned women are therefore potential or latent "man haters."

Likewise the pressure on the traditionally conditioned man to:

1) Constantly prove himself;

2) Repress his needs and emotions;

3) Take responsibility which results in feeling guilty;

4) Be granted sex on a limited and controlled basis subject to his "good behavior";

5) Thwart his own impulses to be playful, spontaneous and expressive in order to live up to the image of the mature husband and father;

6) Be unable to express and deal directly with his resistance, boredom, conflict, resentment and so on in the relationship;

8) Put himself second,

all build up underlying currents of anger and resentment. All traditionally conditioned men are therefore potential or latent "woman haters."

33. Many studies have noted the frustrations of blue-collar workers; indeed, they

have become a major corporate concern, due to their effects of increasing absenteeism and reducing product quality. See, for example, "Work in America," Report of a Special Task Force to the Secretary of Health, Education and Welfare (United States Department of Health, Education and Welfare, Dec. 1972).

34. See Marc Feigen Fasteau, *The Male Machine* (New York: McGraw-Hill, 1974), Chap. 10, and Karl Bednarik, *The Male in Crisis,* translated by Helen Sebba (New York: Alfred A. Knopf, 1970), Chap. 3.

35. Joe E. Dubbert's *A Man's Place: Masculinity in Transition* (Englewoods Cliffs, N.J.: Prentice-Hall, 1979) has an excellent discussion of the place of sport and war in the development of nineteenth-century masculinity; Bednarik notes the increasing passivity of men's sports involvement in *The Male in Crisis,* pp. 19–20.

36. Some analysts of contemporary manhood convincingly argue that, while women's liberation is often interpreted as an attack on men's position, it in fact promises to liberate men. See Warren Farrell, *The Liberated Man* (New York: Random House, 1974), Chap. 10; Herb Goldberg *The New Male* (William Morrow & Company, 1979), Chap. 15; Andrew Tolson, *The Limits of Masculinity* (London: Tavistock Publications, 1977).

37. This is stressed by Goldberg in *The New Male*.

38. Arland Thornton and Deborah Freedman, "Changes in the Sex Role Attitudes of Women, 1962–1977: Evidence from a Panel Study," *American Sociological Review,* 44 (Oct. 1979), p. 833.

39. K. Mason, J. Cazijka, and S. Arber, "Change in U.S. Women's Sex-role Attitudes, 1964–1974," *American Sociological Review,* 41, cited in Vanek "Housework, Wage Work," p. 285.

40. Some social scientists have described the twentieth century change in the family as the rise of the companionate marriage, the marriage where spouses are companions. I prefer to conceive of this development as the rise of the symmetrical marriage so as to stress the breakdown in the former complementarity of the sexes; it is true that as husband and wife begin to participate in similar activities, it is easier for companionship to develop between them. The adjective "symmetrical" was first used to describe such marriages by Michael Young and Peter Willmott in their book, *The Symmetrical Family* (New York: Pantheon Books, 1973).

41. Deborah Durfee Barron and Daniel Yankelovich, Public Agenda Foundation, "Today's American Woman: How the Public Sees Her," prepared for The President's Advisory Committee for Women, September, 1980, p. 80.

42. See, for example, Nancy Adair and Casey Adair, *Word Is Out: Stories of Some of Our Lives* (New York: New Glide Publications and Dell Publishing Company, 1978). Since most gays are still "closeted" due to the virulence of discrimination, it is difficult to estimate the prevalence of this trend.

43. U.S. Department of Labor, Bureau of Labor Statistics, *Handbook of Labor Statistics 1979,* Table 57, p. 114, and *Monthly Labor Review* (April 1980) "Special Labor Reports: Summaries."

44. U.S. Department of Labor, Bureau of Labor Statistics, *Perspectives on Working Women: A Databook,* Bulletin 2080 (Oct. 1980), p. 83.

45. Joseph H. Pleck and Michael Rustad, "Husbands' and Wives' Time in Family Work and Paid Work in the 1975–76 Study of Time Use," Working Paper, 1980, Wellesley College Center for Research on Women, p. 12.

46. M. Hunt, "Today's Man: Redbook's Exclusive Gallup Survey on the Emerging Male." *Redbook* (Oct. 1976), cited in Vanek, "Housework, Wage Work."

47. James A. Levine, *Who Will Raise the Children?* (New York: J.B. Lippincott Company, 1976), p. 160.

48. Ibid., p. 47.

49. The following analysis is my interpretation of the reproduction of the social differentiation of the sexes in the family. It is based in the feminist analysis of personality development presented by Nancy Chodorow, *The Reproduction of Mothering: Psychoanalysis and the Sociology of Gender* (Berkeley: University of California Press, 1978) and Dorothy Dinerstein, *The Mermaid and the Minotaur: Sexual Arrangements and Human Malaise* (New York: Harper & Row, 1976).

50. The problems in masculine development caused by the absence of the father from the home have been analyzed by the Frankfurt School as well as Parsonian sociologists. See, for example, "The Family" in the Frankfurt Institute for Social Research, *Aspects of Sociology* (Boston: Beacon Press, 1972) and Talcott Parsons and Robert F. Bales, *Family, Socialization and Interaction Process* (New York: Free Press, 1955). The psychoanalytic research on masculinity is summarized and critiqued in Joseph H. Pleck, *The Myth of Masculinity* (Cambridge, Mass.: The MIT Press, 1981), especially Chap. 7.

51. Chodorow and Dinerstein urge parenting by both sexes as a means to achieving equality and improved relations between the sexes; however, they fail to connect this development with the elimination of the social differentiation of the sexes.

CONCLUSION: THE BREAKDOWN OF THE SEXUAL DIVISION OF LABOR

1. Much of feminist analysis expresses this conception: men are accused of restricting women to low paid jobs, both to allow men to monopolize the good jobs and to force women into dependence upon and unpaid service of men in the home. This book has presented a different interpretation.

2. Christopher Lasch analyzes the rise of such narrow self-seeking in twentieth-century America in *The Culture of Narcissism: American Life in an Age of Diminishing Expectations* (New York: W.W. Norton, 1979).

3. A pair of new surveys of 374 major corporations by New York's Catalyst Career and Family Center found that 76% were concerned about two-career family problems because they affect recruiting, employee morale, productivity, and profits; 83% said that men were increasingly feeling the need to share more in parenting; 67% of the companies noted growing resistance to transfers. "Women at Work: Employers Have New Attitudes," *Detroit Free Press*, August 28, 1981, p. 7A.

4. See Frederick C. Thayer, *An End to Hierarchy and Competition: Administration in the Post-Affluent World* (New York: New Viewpoints, 1981), for an excellent beginning of a discourse on the necessity for and promises of this transformation which, oddly, totally ignores the sexual division of labor. Socialism and socialist countries have long had the goal of replacing the class inequality of the market with egalitarian, cooperative planning. One of the mistakes of traditional socialist analysis has been its ignorance of the centrality of hierarchy *between workers* to masculinity. As a result, most socialists have not built into their vision the rejection of the sexual division of labor and of masculinity; without this, however, their efforts to eliminate inequality and hierarchy are doomed to failure.

Index